The BRAINWASHED

*From Consumer Zombies
to Islamism and Jihad*

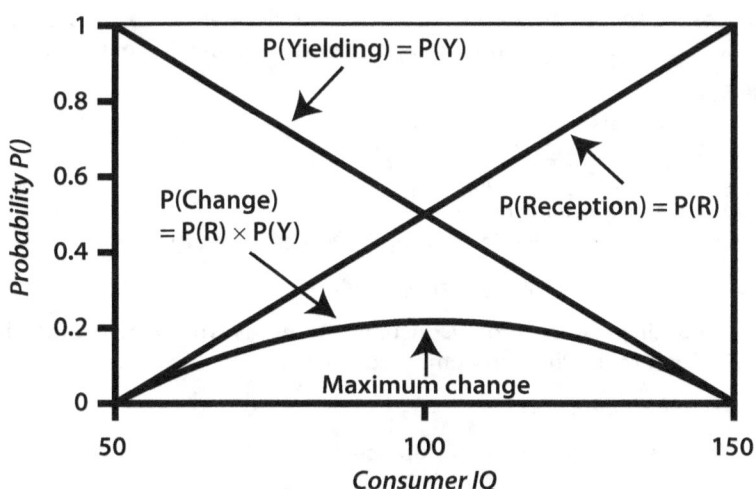

**G. A. Mohr, PhD
Edwin Fear**

Copyright © 2016 G. A. Mohr & Edwin Fear

All rights reserved worldwide.

No part of this publication may be reproduced, stored in a retrieval system, or transmitted in any form or by any means, electronic, mechanical, photocopying, recording, or otherwise, without the prior written permission of the publisher.

Publisher:
Inspiring Publishers
PO. Box 159 Calwell ACT Australia 2905
Email: publishaspg@gmail.com
http://www.inspiringpublishers.com
National Library of Australia Cataloguing-in-Publication entry.

Author: Mohr, G. A. (Geoffrey Arnold), 1946

Title: **The Brainwashed : From Consumer Zombies, To Islamism and Jihad**/
  Dr Geoff Mohr PhD.; co-author, Edwin Fear.

ISBN: 9781925346459 (pbk)

Notes: Includes bibliographical references.

Subjects: Persuasion (Psychology)
  Social pressure.
  Propaganda.
  Persuasion (Psychology)
  Consumer behavior—Psychological aspects.
  Civil society—21st century.

Other Creators/Contributors: Fear, Edwin, author.

The BRAINWASHED

G. A. Mohr, PhD
Edwin Fear

Also by G. A. Mohr

A Microcomputer Introduction to the Finite Element Method

A Treatise on the Finite Element Method

Finite Elements for Solids, Fluids, and Optimization

The MBS: A Course in Management Science

Finite Elements & Optimization for Modern Management

Natural Finite Elements using Basis Transformation

The Pretentious Persuaders,
A Brief History & Science of Mass Persuasion

Curing Cancer & Heart Disease,
Proven Ways to Combat Aging, Atherosclerosis & Cancer

The Variant Virus, Introducing Secret Agent Simon Sinclair

The Doomsday Calculation, The End Of The Human Race

The War of the Sexes, Women Are Getting On Top

Heart Disease, Cancer, & Aging:
Proven Neutraceutical & Lifestyle Solutions

2045: A Remote Town Survives Global Holocaust

The History & Psychology of Human Conflict

Elementary Thinking for The 21st Century

The 8-Week+ Program to Reverse Cardiovascular Disease

Also by Edwin Fear

The Evolving Universe:
Relativity, Redshift and Life from Space
(with G. A. Mohr & Richard Sinclair)

World Religions: The History, Psychology, Issues & Truth
(with G. A. Mohr)

World War 3: When and How Will it End?
(with G.A. Mohr & Richard Sinclair)

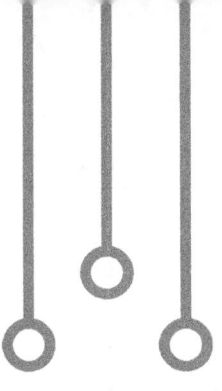

TABLE OF CONTENTS

Preface 9

Chapter 1: Like Zombies 17

Chapter 2: Language and Learning 35

Chapter 3: Conditioning, Memory & Brainwashing 52

Chapter 4: Attitude Formation and Measurement 73

Chapter 5: Religion 90

Chapter 6: War and Terrorism 109

Chapter 7: The Arts 131

Chapter 8: The Sciences 146

Chapter 9: The Industrial Revolution 164

Chapter 10: Education 180

Chapter 11: Politics 200

Chapter 12: Big Business 218

Chapter 13: The Mass Media 238

Chapter 14: Advertising 251

Chapter 15: Econobabble 271

Chapter 16: So, Have You Been Brainwashed? 289

Chapter 17: Global Disaster 302

Chapter 18: Islamism and Jihad 318

Chapter 19: The Biochemical Threat 351

Chapter 20: World War 3 356

Chapter 21: Reverse Evolution 409

Chapter 22: Some Solutions 442

Bibliography 464

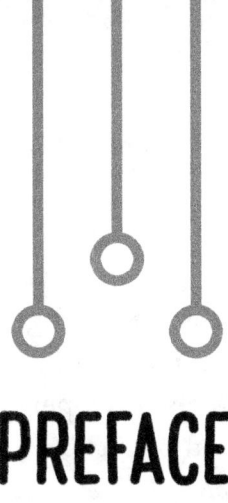

PREFACE

The foundation stone for this book is the contention that modern man has, since he first developed it, used the great skill of advanced language that sets him apart from other animals to *persuade* his fellow man to adopt his views on religion, to labour endlessly to build temples to nonexistent Gods, and to go war with other groups of men.

The Agricultural Revolution saw men live in larger groups within which they took on an increasingly wide variety of specialist roles, paving the way for the modern *consumer society*.

Since the industrial revolution man has become a master at selling all manner of new contrivances to his fellow man, regardless of whether he really needs them or not and, indeed, irrespective of whether they may do the 'sucker' who buys them more harm than good on top, of course, of the initial insult of taking his usually hard earned money.

The ninth edition of the Concise Oxford Dictionary has a reasonably flexible definition of brainwashing:

> **brainwash** (v.tr): *subject (a person) to a prolonged process by which ideas other than and at variance with those already held are implanted in the mind.*

The classical Roget's Thesaurus lists brainwashing under *teaching* and *misteaching*. Various other thesauruses suggest synonyms such as condition, convert, convince, evangelize, indoctrinate, instill unduly influence, program, reprogram, persuade, predispose, propagandize, proselytize, soften up, stipulate, tyrannize, work on

Sometimes referred to in psychology as *thought reform*, 'BW' is an extreme form of *social influence* aimed at changing a person's views without their consent and often against their will, and is discussed further in Chapter 3.

In modern society attempts to persuade us to 'buy' some 'product' emanate from many sources such as:

➢ Often self-appointed and self-serving religious gurus.
➢ Leaders persuading us to engage in ethnic conflict.
➢ Writers and artists trying to influence us.
➢ Scientists pushing their often hair-brained ideas and gadgets.
➢ Industrialists urging us all to buy their new and usually unnecessary, if not downright wasteful, products.
➢ Educators who expect more and more of us to spend longer and longer listening to them regurgitate from one or two books which they themselves hardly understand.
➢ Religious leaders selling their 'brand' of religious BS.
➢ Politicians lying to us to get our vote, for example Western 'pollies' mumbling about so-called democracy when, in fact, we have *oligarchy*.
➢ Big business trying to urge us to become lifelong consumers of products such as junk food, cigarettes, beer, wine, insurance, cable TV, their Internet servers, mobile phone services etcetera.
➢ The big-business-run media selling their pro-capitalist spin on things day and night.

➢ Advertising companies, some of whom employed psychologists a hundred years ago (Eagly and Chaiken, 1993).
➢ Economists mumbling 'econobabble'. No matter which way the economic winds blow they will say all is well.

Each of these areas is discussed in this book. Taking on this range of topics inevitably makes the book something of a history of modern man so that the first chapter briefly discusses man's evolution and, in particular, the unscrupulous leaders who have brainwashed us into following their usually misguided bullshit.

Aspects of the science of persuasion are discussed at various points throughout the book, particularly in Chapters 2 and 3 which discuss how we developed language, the skill that sets us apart from other creatures, memory, conditioning, and brainwashing, and also in Chapters 4 and 14, which discuss attitude formation and measurement, and advertising.

Most other chapters then briefly discuss some of the key history in the areas listed above, occasionally pointing out examples of how leaders in these areas try to persuade or 'brainwash' us into doing as they please.

Along the way we see that human history is really a catalogue of disaster that continues unabated. This cannot go on indefinitely as, to take just one example, we have almost exhausted reserves of that very finite 'black gold' oil. Having built our megacities and their massive freeway systems around the car we are faced with having to reverse this trend quite suddenly and soon.

Consider also the AIDS epidemic in Africa and the continuing turmoil in the Iraq, Syria, Afghanistan, Libya and much of Northern Africa where dozens of Islamic terrorist groups control large areas, resulting in continuing and bitter conflict and mass migrations greater than those of World War 2.

The largest industries in the world are those of arms and drugs, an unacceptable situation. Millions starve in some poor countries while children in the more affluent West are being turned into brainwashed zombies carrying a drink bottle in one hand and a mobile phone in the other while dressed in increasingly ridiculous and impractical clothes and behaving as badly as their screen and pop music idols.

In his interesting book *Paper Money* Adam Smith bemoans the million dollar house prices in California in the early 1970s (Smith, 1981). That situation has spread to most of the major cities of the Western world so that in Australia the "Great Australian dream" of owning one's house is now beyond most of today's young people.

If this is so-called democracy then it is not good enough. At least socialism, usually referred to by the more emotive and incorrect term communism, might give your children a roof over their heads and some certainty of being able to have a sensible career.

They might also hope to have a lasting marriage and bearable standard of living in which they are not addicted to Coke, junk food, drugs, booze, cigarettes, mobile phones, the 'gee whiz' but largely useless Internet, ridiculous clothes, gambling, etcetera, all symptoms of a sick amoral society in terminal decline as Rome was nearly two millennia ago.

God is not the answer but an invention that has had few positive results but many bad ones such as interminable wars. At best, religion is a waste of time, at worst it is preached by paedophiles and used as an excuse by politicians and terrorists for war.

The answers lie within ourselves. Human beings are only animals, but we were clever enough to invent antiseptics, anaesthetics, antibiotics and nuclear power. At least a *few* of us were.

Then there are the unscrupulous arms dealers, pharmaceutical industries that peddle such addictive things as tranquilizers and antidepressants, the medical industry which puts you on blood pressure medication for years rather than treat the root cause (atherosclerosis) and then carves you up to put in heart bypasses which prolong life no more than careful diet and exercise (Cooke and Zimmer, 2002).

The education business has grown out of all proportion. Twelve years at school is too long, let alone a few more in day care centres, and then countless years can be wasted studying such ludicrous courses as postgraduate diplomas in Sexology and Puppetry.

Over 50 years ago it was found that average IQ in the UK had decreased and continuing decline was predicted. Recent studies confirm that this *reverse evolution* is actually happening globally.

The picture is bleak to say the least and World War 3, thanks to widespread Islamic terrorism, is happening on a grand scale right now (Mohr, Fear & Sinclair, 2015).

If Islamic State (IS) get hold of biochemical weapons, or nuclear material for 'dirty bombs', as they have been trying to do for some time, then Nevil Shute's book *On The Beach* may come true, except that the present author in his book *2045* predicts small isolated towns like Cooktown in far northeast Queensland are the most likely survivors of the global nuclear and biochemical holocaust that might occur (Mohr, 2014).

The book includes a chapter on Islamists and Jihad because such people are amongst the most heavily brainwashed in history and they are now a global threat.

Myself, I have had nothing but bad experiences with Muslims, beginning with Horrible Publishing Group, effectively a one-man publishing business in Sydney that I paid an extortionate $17,000 to print four of my books. The so-called "editor", Fayez Horrible, "terminated" my fourth contract when I complained about him having done nothing for almost 18 months. When, at further expense, I went to court, this Muslim man told lie after lie and the matter was dismissed to be heard in his home state, something I could not afford to do. This crook then removed the first 3 books from sale and had me charged with harassment, thereby cheating me of yet more money and causing me immense worry and trouble.

This nasty man is besotted with the Arab world and at a public book launch he raved that the USA had killed more people in Europe than the Nazis in WW2, and that the USA had "orchestrated" the Pearl Harbour and 9/11 attacks. He even raved that the Port Arthur massacre in Tasmania in the 1990s had been "orchestrated", presumably he meant also by the USA.

Indeed, the real reason this nutter went mad at me is that I made a joke about Muslim preachers being none to clever, another about my father's name being Courtney Balthazar Oppenheim Mohr and my thus being 'JC2' who would condemn all Muslims to hell, and then, frustrated by seemingly interminable delays, using the phrase "Islamic incompetence". Typical of Islamic extremists, he went nuts over one or two of these three harmless jokes/statements.

A similar example reported in the Herald Sun on 22/7/2016 was a former Palestinian refugee unsuccessfully suing the paper for religious vilification, earlier having complained about discrimination for being an "Arab" by RMIT because he and 2 other students and a teacher had been accused of cheating on an exam. This 'sensitivity' of Muslims is one of many factors that make them difficult to deal with, and at present non-Muslims are tiring of them to the point of more and more of us coming to the view that Muslim immigration should be banned, or at least disallowed from countries where groups such as IS are active.

As for 'orchestration', just a few days before the aforementioned court case my home was invaded by 'hit men' one night at 3 AM and I was nearly killed. At first I thought that they might have been after a recent Muslim neighbour who had used my address for his and one of his two wives' driving licences, so that I received their traffic infringement notices. Then, because this invasion occurred just a few days before the court case, I decided that the most likely 'organizer' of this invasion might well have been Fayez Horrible.

Fayez Horrible's public anti-US ravings, his books about Muslim matters and predicting Western decline, along with his declared interest in "the Arab world" are worrying when now more people have been displaced by Islamic terror groups than were displaced in WW2, this being WW3, of course. Indeed, I found a LIKE from an "Islamist" for his largely one-man company on FACEBOOK, and I feel that this man and his terrorist-inspired ravings are dangerous and he should be locked up somewhere like Guantanamo Bay.

I was also displeased when I used a Muslim real estate agent to sell a house, helping him do so after the first 'OFI'. I then gave him 5 free copies of my recent books but he was too mean to ever give me one cent for them, though I did ask for a small, polite 'donation' more than once.

On three occasions I found Muslims overly sensitive, on two of these security guards at public venues assaulting me verbally when I merely joked that I did not think them necessary as an ISIS attack was not likely, one of them repeating the Islamist mantra that the US had "staged" the 9/11 attacks.

On the third occasion, when I remarked outside a restaurant called the 'Taj Mahal' that this was a Muslim temple, one of three swarthy, dark-haired men outside replied: *So, do you want to make something of it?* No doubt these thugs had been influenced by the public ravings of such ISIS propaganda pushers as Fayez Horrible of Horrible Publishing Group.

The present book concludes with suggestions that might help save the human race from what seems like a disastrous future of resource depletion, war, famine and disease of Biblical proportions and, in turn, a *reverse evolution* of mankind.

Finally, I should note that, despite being related to Anne Boleyn, whose husband founded the Church of England, and being brought up in the C of E both at school, and as a choir boy in Christ Church, St Kilda, where my father had also suffered the same fate, I quickly lost interest in religion as a teenager. For example, myself and a couple of school friends used to arrive at school circa half an hour late twice a week on the days when we were supposed to be attending a service in Melbourne Grammar School's senior school chapel.

Similarly, in his column in Melbourne's *Herald Sun* newspaper on 27/7/2016, former Victorian Premier Jeff Kennett wrote: *I remember attending church and Bible studies in my youth. Eventually I had to decide in my late teens whether to continue with church functions on Sundays or go yachting. I chose yachting.*

I am grateful to those with whom I have been able to discuss my work from time to time, including, of course, the co-author Edwin Fear, and also Richard Sinclair, co-author of other books. Special thanks also to the publishers, who have once again done an excellent job.

Geoff Mohr
Melbourne, MMXVI.

Chapter 1
LIKE ZOMBIES

zombie 1. Orig., the snake-deity of voodoo cults in W. Africa, Haiti and the southern U.S.; hence, a supernatural power that may reanimate dead bodies or a body so reanimnated.

2. *colloq.* A person resembling a revived corpse; a dull or slow-witted, or apathetic person 1941.
The Shorter Oxford Dictionary, 3rd edn, Oxford University Press 1973.

A LONG HISTORY

Men have used pretentious bullshit of one kind or another throughout history to persuade, if not brainwash, others into doing as they want, for example:

- Witch doctors or *shamans* claiming mystical powers over illness.
- Religious leaders claiming knowledge of some god or other.

- Throughout history the building of religious and other monuments has enslaved millions.
- Throughout history leaders have led us like lemmings into disastrous wars for little or no reason using religio-political rhetoric.
- Political leaders periodically try and persuade us to vote for them.
- Economists spout 'econobabble' to constantly assure us that, no matter which way the economic wind blows, its direction is favourable.
- Since the industrial revolution, especially, we have been persuaded to rush en masse to buy the latest model of every type of contrivance.
- Advertising companies, some of whom employed psychologists a hundred years ago (Eagly and Chaiken, 1993), are often able to ensure that their marketing campaigns target consumers of all ages to the point at which they end up spending most of their lives and all their money buying products they can't really afford, don't really need, and which in many cases are downright harmful one way or another.

The sorry truth is that mankind has been inveigled into 'buying' all manner of 'products' almost at the will of the 'seller' throughout its history.

Thus we have, as often as not, been led like lemmings from one disaster to another, these tending to grow in magnitude like our now excessive population:

lemming n. 1 any small vole-like Arctic rodent of the genus Lemmus and related genera, including L. lemmus

of Norway which is noted for mass migrations during which it attempts to cross large bodies of water.
2 a person who unthinkingly joins a mass movement, esp. a headlong rush to destruction.

The Concise Oxford Dictionary, 9th edn, Oxford University Press 1997.

CONSUMER ZOMBIES

The result is that our consumer societies have evolved to the point at which we have been reduced to brainwashed zombies shuffling along with a mobile phone in one hand, a drink bottle or cigarette in the other, and wearing jeans once intended for farm workers but which we have been led by the nose for nearly 50 years to believe are 'trendy.'

In more affluent countries we drive tank-like four wheel drives down the freeway just to go shopping and live in or aspire to live in a 'McMansion' with a heated swimming pool and sauna.

Regardless of the climate or weather houses and offices are open plan and air conditioned, requiring massive energy usage. Our gas-guzzling cars are also air conditioned, increasing the rate at which we use up the fast vanishing oil reserves on the planet.

Worse still, nothing is built to last, most products have built-in obsolescence, and many others are 'disposable' after first use.

Belatedly we are becoming aware that this is a recipe for disaster and that we are fast exhausting some of the planet's most precious resources and polluting it terribly in the process.

What led to us becoming such gullible consumer zombies who, like the planet, have also been exploited?

To understand what then led us to this sorry state we should, of course, begin at the beginning.

EVOLUTION OF TRIBAL MAN

Chimpanzees, with which we share 96% of the same genes, are quite sociable animals and live in groups of 20 to 60, forming into subgroups of adults (male and female), all-male groups and groups of mothers and offspring. African gorillas also live in bisexual groups of between 2 to 30 but which do not comprise smaller subgroups.

The best known studies of chimpanzees were conducted by Jane Goodall and associates in the Gombe National Park on the edge of Lake Tanganyika in Tanzania (van-Lawick Goodall, 1971).

Ultimately, Goodall was quite disillusioned to find that *tribes* of chimps were led by an alpha male and would occasionally have small wars with neighbouring tribes, these resuming at intervals over periods of many years. She concluded that they were all too much like humans!

Comparisons of blood proteins and the DNA of the African great apes with that of humans indicates that the line leading to modern people did not split off from that of chimpanzees and gorillas until comparatively late in evolution, perhaps 6 million to 8 million years ago.

Fossils of the first *hominines*, the *australopithecines*, have been discovered dating to 5 million years ago. This genus seems to have become extinct about 1.5 million years ago, but before doing so one of seven species of australopithecines, *Australopithecus africanus*, evolved into the genus *Homo* between 1.5 and 2 million years ago.

The earliest evidence of stone tools comes from sites in Africa dated to about 2.5 million years ago. These tools have not been found in association with a particular hominine species.

Around 1.7 to 1.9 million years ago two new species of large brained, small-toothed hominines emerged, *Homo ergaster* in Africa and *Homo erectus* in Asia. Later *H. erectus* skulls possess brain sizes in the range of 1100 to 1300 cc (67.1 to 79.3 cu in), within the size variation of *Homo sapiens*.

A number of archaeological sites dating from the time of *Homo erectus* reveal a greater sophistication in toolmaking than was found at the earlier sites. Evidence found at the cave site of "Peking Man" in northern China, suggests that *H. erectus* used fire.

The remains of the foundations of an oval structure built by a *Homo erectus* group were found at the Terra-Amata site in France, and within this structure there was a fireplace (Weiss and Mann, 1978).

The *Homo* species spread widely and by 350,000 years ago planned hunting, fire making, wearing of clothes, and probably burial rituals, were well established.

Between 200,000 and 300,000 years ago, *Homo sapiens* evolved.

The Neanderthals or *Homo sapiens neanderthalensis* had similar DNA to modern man and occupied parts of Europe and the Middle East as early as 120,000 years ago. They lived only in family groups, the men being hunter-gatherers to feed the family.

The Neanderthals left cave paintings which were an important evolutionary advance. These often depicted a simple activity, perhaps a precursor to the highly pictorial hieroglyphic script of the ancient Egyptians (Egerton Eastwick, 1896).

Though Neanderthals had 10% larger brains than modern man, there is some evidence that the part of the cerebral cortex devoted to language and thinking in modern man was underdeveloped in Neanderthal man, casting some doubt on whether Neanderthal man was capable of modern spoken language. Thought by some to be a different evolutionary branch, the Neanderthals disappeared from the fossil record about 30,000 years ago.

Differing in appearance, modern humans or *Homo sapiens sapiens* evolved in southern Africa or the Middle East perhaps 90,000 to 200,000 years ago and 70,000 years ago began to spread to all parts of the world, reaching Europe about 40,000 years ago, soon outnumbering, perhaps interbreeding with, and finally supplanting the local, earlier *Homo sapiens* populations.

Like chimpanzees, homo sapiens sapiens formed tribes and there is evidence of religion, recorded events and art dating from 30,000 to 40,000 years ago implying the advanced language and ethics required for the ordering of social groups.

EVOLUTION OF RELIGION AND THE 'BRAINWASHERS'

Around the same time homo sapiens developed cave art, about 100,000 years ago, he would have developed language and, eventually some form of 'pictorial' communication which eventually evolved into hieroglyphic script, then cuneiform script, and finally the symbolic writing we now use.

Typically each tribe had a leader, a religion, and a common language and culture.

The first forms of religion involved such beliefs and practices as

(a) *Animism*, a belief that plants, inanimate objects and natural phenomena had souls or spirits.
(b) *Polytheism*, a belief in multiple Gods, sometimes attributing certain acts of nature to each.
(c) *Ancestor Worship* teaching that a tribe's people were descended from a common ancestor.
(d) *Immortality* or belief that the dead live on as spirits.

Eventually these religions evolved into the *monotheism* that dominates the world today. At the outset, however, it was the tribal elders who passed on tribal beliefs from one generation to another. Along the way *shamans* or 'witch doctors' claiming some special connection with the spirits appeared, along with religious rites and ceremonies.

In groups of hunter-gatherers, as with many other species of animals, the 'dominant' males were, of course, responsible for protection of the group from external threats which, just as with chimpanzees, often took the form of other 'tribes' or groups.

At the same time, however, the supposedly wiser elders still indoctrinated the young into religion and had considerable influence, if not control, over the 'dominant males.' Their weapons for control ranged from rhetoric to dire threats of a vengeful spirit or God.

Thus from the ancient Greeks through to the middle ages a study of *rhetoric* was considered important because of its use to bullshit people into doing as political and religious leaders wished. Francis Bacon (1561 - 1626), for example, studied Elizabethan logic and rhetoric at Cambridge University for two years, leaving at the age of 14, a point we return to in Chapter 10.

The agricultural revolution and the consumer society

About 12,000 years ago the agricultural revolution, in part enabled by development of primitive forms of permanent housing, led to the growth of human societies from small tribes to those of settlements of hundreds and eventually, as farming became more productive, thousands of people.

More efficient farming allowed more specialization, for example millers, bakers and weavers. Such people were *producers* of a particular product so that the rest of the society became *consumers*.

The agricultural revolution, then, was the beginning of the *consumer society*. In these growing societies religion became increasingly important as a means of imparting ethics and standards.

These larger societies now had houses and farms to defend, however, so that the need for stronger males for territorial defence grew and with it the influence that military leaders had upon society. This may have led to the appearance of leaders of towns or regions involving a few nearby towns and, eventually, monarchs.

In some societies, however, priest kings emerged, but generally 'church' and 'state' have remained separate entities to this day, both doing their utmost to control their societies.

These growing societies and the organizations within them, especially the army and the church, took on hierarchical forms and the main weapons of control ranged from verbal *persuasion* to threats throughout a chain of command to see that the rest of the population towed the line.

Unfortunately, however, the ambitious/aggressive/assertive people who literally fight their way to leadership positions through impatience, stupidity and deceit have done far more harm than good and our unending history of war, practically useless temples and other monuments to stupidity attests to this, a point revisited in following chapters, particularly Chapter 17.

These wasteful leaders were *consumers* of, in particular, the *good*s provided by builders and the *services* of large numbers of domestic slaves and large armies of soldiers.

In the rest of society the mercantile infrastructure of the consumer society that we have today began to evolve with open air markets largely giving way to shops and barter systems giving way to currency.

THE MODERN CONSUMER SOCIETY

Our highly structured modern consumer societies do not have the problem of one all-powerful leader but countless little Hitlers:

The Brainwashed | 25

Capitalism tends to produce a multiplicity of petty dictators each in command of his own little business kingdom. State Socialism tends to produce a single, centralized totalitarian dictatorship, wielding absolute authority ... through a hierarchy of bureaucratic agents.
Aldous Huxley, Ends and Means (1937).

These psychopathic little Hitlers make life miserable in every area of human activity, for example:

- Hypocritical religious leaders whose choir boys have all too often been asked to do much more than sing.
- Military officers, particularly NCOs, who bully troops to the point at which death is preferable to marching out of step.
- Artists who often earn indecent amounts of money inflicting atrocious art, movies and music on us.
- Scientists whose every invention is marketed to the point at which everyone has to have one.
- Industrialists whose factory slaves resemble automatons and zombies forced to work harder than animals would be allowed to.
- Educators who imprison children in school far longer than necessary to simply brainwash them into routine until they are more than old enough to join the work force.
- Politicians who lie through their teeth during each election campaign to try and win enough votes and then, if elected, continue to assure us that their mistakes are not mistakes and that they are actually improving things when, quite obviously, the human race is racing towards catastrophe.

- Business leaders whose gigantic salaries dwarf those of their employees and whose gullible shareholders accept usually minuscule returns on their investments.
- Electronic and print media executives who ensure that we are fed trivia and follow the official line that glosses over the increasingly wide cracks in our corrupt and decaying society.
- Economists who constantly bleat about the exchange rate, inflation, unemployment and other numbers in much the same way as do news readers reporting on the weather. No matter what new disaster occurs they always assure us that all is well when often the country may be virtually bankrupt.
- Advertising gurus who are so good at brainwashing us that, for example, many people are turned into zombies wearing uncomfortable jeans and baseball hats and carrying a mobile phone in one hand and a drink bottle in the other.

So it is, therefore, that in modern society we have leaders in all walks of life ranging from religious, educational, business and political leaders, to those in the arts and sciences, who spend a good deal of effort in brainwashing us with repetitive bullshit so we will 'buy' their product which may be anything from fast food to one side or other of a political fence.

HOW WE ARE PERSUADED

Effective persuasion of people en masse involves several key factors including:

- Simple messages are more effective that complex ones and these should target the appropriate *segment* of the population.

- From early in our evolution we *homo sapiens sapiens* have been talked down to by tribal and religious leaders that pitch to us from 'on high.' Today, however, the pulpit has been largely replaced by the TV screen but it is still important to remember that effective ads take the high ground by having an air of authority and confidence.
- Messages should be structured to ensure (Robertson, 1970):
    (1) C*ognitive response* to the message involving
        (a) *Awareness* of the product's existence.
        (b) *Knowledge* of the product's features.
    (2) Positive a*ttitudinal response* to the message, that is
        (a) *Liking* of the product.
        (b) *Preference* for the product.
    (3) The desired *behavioural response* to the message, that is
        (a) *Conviction* that the product is worth buying.
        (b) *Purchase* of the product.
- This *cognitive/attitudinal/behavioural* or 'CAB' approach to advertising is *conditioning*, where now an advertisement is a *stimulus*, and conditioning is discussed in some detail in Chapter 3.
- The proportion of the target population that remembers a message increases with the number of repetitions and thus follows a *learning curve*. The learning curve for populations is quite likely to take a hyperbolic form and the Mohr Plot of Fig. 10.1 can be used to establish the asymptote of such hyperbolae.
- Frequency of messages should be limited to avoid *advertising wearout*. The *three-hit theory* is that only 3 ads are needed to make consumers aware of a product, make them perceive its relevance to their needs, and inform them of its benefits,

but it needs to be realized that more like a dozen ads will be needed to ensure that a substantial proportion of the population will see the ad (Schiffman et al., 2001).
- Consumer memory follows the *forgetting curves* of Fig. 14.3 so that advertising campaigns must be periodically renewed.
- Appealing to people's secondary *psychological needs* such as achievement and beauty, rather than their primary and regular 'anything will do' *physical needs* such as hunger and thirst.
- Pitching messages at those with a relatively low 'consumer IQ' because high 'CIQ' increases likelihood of messages being understood but reduces likelihood of being influenced by them. This *reception-yielding* situation is illustrated in Figure 14.2 and the 'get em young' notion that this suggests is well illustrated by the quotation that opens Chapter 14.
- Taking advantage of the fact that for brainwashed modern man his car and the brand of soft drink or beer he drinks is an important part of his *identity*. Similarly, for a woman the way she does her hair and makeup, and the way she dresses are part of her identity. In other words, just as we describe different species of animals by their appearance and habits, we view other people in the same way.
- We humans are suckers for anything new and effective advertising need not appeal to our higher instincts or the advancement of mankind. For example, supposedly civilized societies happily copied people their explorers thought 'savages' by taking up tobacco en masse. That our love of novelty has 'regressed' us is discussed in Chapter 21.
- We are not simply persuaded as individuals, however, but also en masse or sociologically. The key to this is *imitative*

and *social learning* so that just one or two of a particular group of people need to be persuaded to a buy product and then, one by one, others in the group will follow their lead.
- We often *imprint* upon a particular type or group of people and adopt their behaviours and imprinting, imitative learning, and modeling are discussed further in Chapter 2.
- Finally, it is important to realize that, as discussed in some detail in Chapter 2, our memories are 'hard wired.' That is, unless neurons are damaged physically, memories that have been stored in long-term memory are permanent. This is why it is we remember some of our earliest childhood experiences and why we find it so hard to give up some of our habits.

PERSUASION OR BRAINWASHING?

Today advertising is so repetitive and effective in reducing us to consumer zombies that the results are comparable to those of conditioning of laboratory animals described in Chapter 3. In other words, it goes a little, if not a long way beyond just *persuasion*.

Colloquially, at least, most would agree that it would be fair to use the term *brainwashing* but, strictly speaking, this originated in connection with 'conversion' of American prisoners by the Communists during the Korean War in the early 1950s.[1]

Sometimes referred to in psychology as *thought reform*, 'BW' is an extreme form of *social influence* aimed at changing a person's views without their consent and often against their will.

To this end BW combines three approaches:

(a) The **coercive** or 'just do it' approach which is concerned only with *compliance* and not with your attitudes and beliefs.

---

[1] The Three D's Method used in this context is described at the close of Chapter 3.

(b) The ***persuasion*** or 'do it because it will make you feel good, happy, healthy or successful' approach.
(c) The group-based ***education*** or 'do it because it's right' approach which is much used for *propaganda* campaigns.

The 1999 Encyclopedia Brittannica describes BW as **coercive persuasion,** noting its origins as a means of political or religious indoctrination. It also notes that it is a *"colloquial term"* usually *"applied to any technique designed to manipulate human thought or action —."*

The third edition of the American Heritage Dictionary of the English Language gives two definitions of brainwashing:

1. Intensive, forcible indoctrination, usually political or religious, aimed at destroying a person's basic convictions and attitudes and replacing them with an alternative set of fixed beliefs.
2. The application of a concentrated means of persuasion, such as an advertising campaign or repeated suggestion, in order to develop a specific belief or motivation.

WordWeb 6 defines the adjective 'brainwashed' as:
1. *Subjected to intensive forced indoctrination resulting in the rejection of old beliefs and acceptance of new ones* "brainwashed prisoners of war"; "captive audiences for TV commercials can become brainwashed consumers"

Indeed, most of us now associate brainwashing with persuasive advertising, political campaigns, mass media, and perhaps education. In fact BW is perceived to be so widespread that it is a major concern for many people and a search for 'brainwashing' on the Internet gives over 2 million results for *media brainwashing*.

Just three examples are:

[1] A 1995 report that "hard-up" schools in the UK used free educational packs provided by McDonald's which were littered with references to McDonald's and its products. (www.mcspotlight.org/media/press/brainwashing.html)
[2] Claims that, because it supposedly misled the public over the 9/11 attacks, the American news media *"is the largest, most expensive, mass-brainwashing machine ever assembled in human history. It is a machine that so completely brainwashes the nearly 300 millions Americans, that the Nazis' infamous Propaganda Minister Josef Goebbels would be envious"* (Wolfe, 2001).
[3] Claims that after WW1 psychological warfare research at the Tavistock Centre in London resulted in *"a theory of mass brainwashing, involving group experience, that could be used to alter the values of individuals, and through that induce, over time, changes in the axiomatic assumptions that govern society"* and that this work found application in both the UK and the US media (Wolfe, 1997).

US journalist Walter Lippmann was involved in Britain's WW1 'psywar' effort and was first to translate Sigmund Freud's work into English. In his 1922 book *Public Opinion* he wrote of the brainwashed masses:

". . the mass of absolutely illiterate, of feeble minded grossly neurotic, undernourished and frustrated individuals is very considerable, much

more considerable, there is reason to think, than we generally suppose. Thus a wide popular appeal is circulated among persons who are mentally children or barbarians, whose lives are a morass of entanglements, people whose vitality is exhausted, shut-in people, and people whose experience has comprehended no factor in the problem under discussion."

Some of this is a bit 'over the top' but, if we consider that advertising has reduced most of us to brainwashed zombies wearing uncomfortable if not ridiculous jeans and carrying a mobile phone in one hand and a drink bottle or cigarette in the other, then 'brainwashing' is a serious issue.

And make no mistake, it must certainly be fair to call today's high pressure TV and radio advertising brainwashing. After all, in line with the original brainwashing of POWs, the victims are seated in a room and screamed at for hours each day with up to 10 ads blaring at them in each of all too frequent ad breaks (make that up to 50 ads per ad break in Brazil, according to Cateora (1996)).

After all, 50+ years ago advertising managed to make about half the adult population take up smoking, a downright unpleasant practice in reality. If advertising can do that then it can make us do just about anything short of eating shit.

For this reason, therefore, the term *brainwashing* is used frequently in this book because no other single word exists to convey just what religious mantras and rituals have done for millennia and what increasingly ubiquitous, repetitive and persuasive advertising does today.

CONCLUSION

The extent to which man has been brainwashed, one way or another, to adopt countless religions, periodically fight wars over them, and in modern times become mindless consumer zombies is regrettable.

We should all hope that we will never be subjected to *coercive persuasion* or *brainwashing* in its 'original' form but few of us would disagree that we are perhaps now subjected en masse to something far more subtle, far more effective and sometimes, at least, far more sinister and detrimental to both ourselves and, in turn, the world we live in.

After a discussion of the related topics of language, learning, memory, conditioning, and attitudes in Chapters 2, 3, and 4, following chapters discuss the various areas in our societies in which we are may be subject to some form of 'persistent persuasion' or 'brainwashing'.

Then Chapter 17 discusses the disastrous consequences of our excessive population and consumption such as resource depletion, pollution, desertification, and global warming.

Chapter 18 discusses Islamism and Jihad, Islamic terrorism being so rife around the world that some believe that we are now, in fact, in the midst of World War 3 (Mohr et al. 2015).

WordWeb 6 defines Islamism as:
1. The monotheistic religious system of Muslims founded in Arabia in the 7th century and based on the teachings of Muhammad as laid down in the Koran "Islamism is a complete way of life, not a Sunday religion."
2. A fundamentalist Islamic revivalist movement generally characterized by moral conservatism and the literal interpretation of the Koran and the attempt to implement Islamic values in all aspects of life.

It then defines 'fundamentalist' as: *The interpretation of every word in the sacred texts as literal truth.*

It is the latter point that is key here, Islamic terrorists often citing some of the many texts in the Koran advocating jihad.

Chapter 19 discusses the threat of biochemical war, noting that the Islamic State (IS) terrorist group has recruited scientists to develop biochemical weapons.

Chapter 20 discusses 'World War 3', i.e. the ongoing rash of Islamic terrorism currently afflicting the world that has its roots in the jihad commanded in the Qu'ran, using such events as the creation of the state of Israel in 1948 as an excuse.

Chapter 21 proposes another consequence of excessive and careless breeding of which there has been evidence for almost 100 years, that of *reverse evolution,* namely a deterioration of mankind both physically and in terms of intelligence.

The final chapter, Chapter 22, then suggests some solutions to these problems.

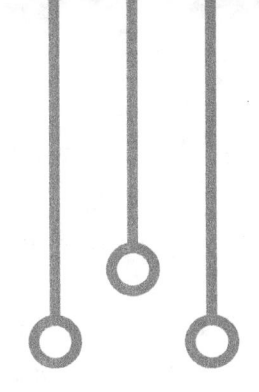

Chapter 2
LANGUAGE AND LEARNING

Some people have argued that language is what makes the human species different from other species.
Roger Bell and Ralph Hall,
Impacts: Contemporary Issues & Global Problems,
The Jacaranda Press, Milton QLD (1991).

THE DEVELOPMENT OF LANGUAGE

As noted in Chapter One, there is some doubt whether Neanderthal man had developed language. Doubtless the roots of language lie in the 30 different vocal sounds made by vervet monkeys (Insight, 1982), no doubt related to *lallation* or meaningless mumbling in infants. Given some encouragement they are then ready to learn such 'baby talk' as

da da, ma ma, wee wee
gee gee, puff puff, bow wow

The messages in any language are built up from a relatively small catalogue of elementary speech sounds. These sounds are combined to form a finite number of words from which sentences are built up.

Generally, these words are *arbitrary* and do not sound like or have any other relationship with the things they represent but there are a few exceptions such as some of the words for animal noises (a phenomenon called *onomatopoeia*).

Language involves a *duality of patterning* (Foss and Hakes, 1978) in which it relates two different forms of representation: an external *phonological system* for sound and an internal *semantic system* for meaning. These two systems are related by a language's *syntactic system*.

We understand a sentence spoken to us because our brain stores it temporarily in our short-term-memory (STM) and compares it to the word and language rules stored as *semantic memory* in our long-term-memory (LTM). If we *rehearse* the message in STM it may be stored in LTM.

THE MEMORY SYSTEM

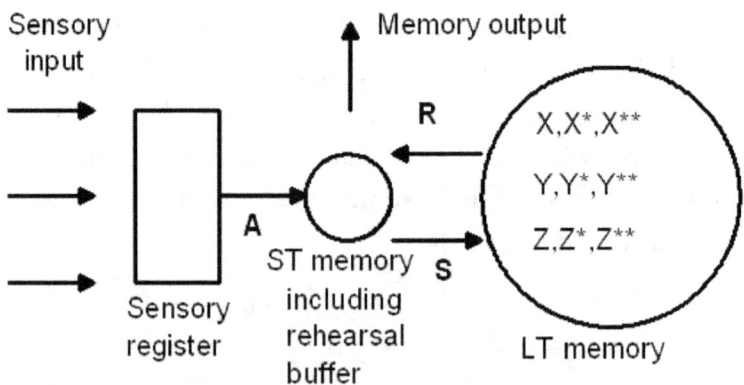

Figure 2.1. Information processing model of memory.

Figure 2.1 shows a simple information processing model of memory (Atkinson and Shiffrin, 1968). In this, the *sensory register*, located in a part of the brain called the thalamus, processes information from sensory channels associated with vision, hearing and other senses.

The visual sensory register can hold 10 - 20 bits of information for only about 1 second, whereas the auditory sensory register can hold information for up to 4 or 5 seconds.

Of the up to 20 bits of information that our visual registers can accommodate with a brief glance, for example an array of letters of the alphabet, we can only remember four or five of them, this number being called the *span of apprehension*.

As a consequence most information in the sensory registers is lost but that to which sufficient attention is paid is transferred to the *short-term-memory* (STM), located in a part of the brain called the hippocampus. Here it is held for about 20 - 30 seconds and some of it is processed by being rehearsed in the *rehearsal buffer*, the rest being lost.

This model fits everyday life fairly well. For example, when somebody tells you a phone number and you are interrupted while dialing it you are likely to forget it because it will be lost from STM. This is because the STM holds only about 5 - 9 items and, under certain conditions, as few as two or three.

Sternberg (1966) conducted an experiment that illustrates how memory, in this case STM, works. He showed a group of people sets of from 1 to 6 digits and seconds later asked them if the set contained a particular digit. Response times were closely proportional to the number of digits shown, demonstrating that the coding of the set in STM was searched serially or one digit at a time.

In the rehearsal buffer such processes as repetition of the information link it to information already stored in memory and then pass it to *long-term-memory* (LTM) where it remains for periods of days up to a lifetime. In LTM information is *consolidated*, a process that may take from half an hour up to months. If consolidation is somehow interrupted some memory loss occurs.

Most LTM information is stored in the cerebral cortex, the 'thinking' part of the brain which is much more developed in humans than in other species.

Simple passive repetition of information, or *maintenance rehearsal,* is not sufficient to ensure that items are passed to LTM. The active process of e*laborative rehearsal,* involving reorganization of the material and attaching meaning to it is more likely to pass information to LTM.

There are four types of LTM:

[1] *Procedural memory* or implicit memory is 'knowing how' to perform some skill, often learnt by procedural or implicit learning. Procedural learning is discussed later in this chapter.
[2] *Declarative memory* is 'knowing that' or memory of data or facts and events.
[3] *Episodic memory* of prior life experiences is a type of declarative memory.
[4] *Semantic memory* such as words and language rules is another type of declarative memory which involves more 'preprocessing' in STM than episodic memory.

In such processing even inherently organized material is *subjectively organized* by the learner into categories. Up to a point, it is found that the more categories used the better the material can be recalled.

Semantic memory uses *constructive processes* to store information in an organized manner, often into a hierarchical structure of categories and sub-categories.

Recall of the information then occurs by *reconstructive processes*. With these speed of recall depends upon the hierarchical level at which information is recalled, more general 'heading' information being recalled more rapidly than specific information.

Thus, when we have difficulty remembering a person's name, for example, we often can only remember one or more names similar in some respect such as their first letter and then finally remember the required name anything from seconds to days later.

Memory processing also makes much use of images and *concrete* images are easily formed for words like 'cat' whilst *abstract* images for words like 'mercy' are more difficult to form.

Australian aborigine elders, for example, remember centuries of tribal history by associating important events with environmental features and recall and pass on this history by 'walking through' these places.

Information stored in LTM is easier to recall if it is stored with *retrieval cues* which are associated with 'blocks' of information. Individual items within these blocks are then stored with 'tags'.

How easily information is recalled later depends much upon how well it has been associated with images, categorized and provided with cues.

An example of how images affect information recall from LTM occurs if witnesses who saw a speeding car crash are asked:

"*How fast do you think the car was going when it* _____*?*" with the final verb having such variations as *contacted, hit,* and *crashed*.

Speed estimates will increase in the order of these three verbs by as much as 25% because the new information in the wording of the question conflicts or *interferes* with the memory and associated images of the event in LTM.

Information that has been stored in a well-organized fashion can sometimes be recalled by *redintegration*, the process by which some event such as a 'leading question' unlocks a rapid sequence of memories that may be connected by a chain of associations.

This is the ideal situation when we read an exam question. One or more words in the question quickly trigger recall of a stream of relevant information. If the exam is the usual written answer one we tend to forget part of the answer before we can write it down.

HOW WE UNDERSTAND LANGUAGE

The way in which text is remembered provides an insight into why key words are important in the memory process. It is believed that text is not stored in memory literally but as a number of *propositions*, each of which has a *relational term* for which there are *arguments* (using the latter word in the same way it is used in connection with mathematical functions, especially when they are used in computer programs).

The sentence "Tom hit Jack", for example, is remembered as

(HIT, TOM, JACK)

If later "Tom apologized for hitting Jack" this is stored as

((APOLOGIZE, TOM), (HIT, TOM, JACK))

with the simple proposition of the original memory embedded in a complex one. Here the 'strong' word HIT acts as a key word and it is linked directly to the word TOM in long-term memory.

There is no doubt that a deer can remember events such as, "Lion killed deer" as a visual memory stored in *episodic memory*. As a result the *declarative memory* 'danger' would be added to the neuron in LTM storing the image of a lion, or perhaps to a newly formed adjacent neuron.

Some clue to how humans developed language is found by observing that howler monkeys have massively developed larynxes and hyoid bones (the bone that supports the tongue) so that their spectacular howls can be heard for miles.

Somehow, somewhere, humans gradually evolved with the physical attributes required to produce a variety of sounds and began to associate these with objects, passing this knowledge on to following generations.

As noted in Chapter 21, Krech's remarkable environmental enrichment experiments with rats demonstrated vividly that the gradually growth in the development of human language was undoubtedly largely responsible for the evolution of the large cerebral cortex that distinguishes modern man from other species.

THE SPREAD OF LANGUAGE

Somehow language spread with the migration of early humans, perhaps during the Agricultural Revolution, so that some languages have similar words, for example for father

pater (Latin), *padre* (Italian), *pere* (French)
vater (German), *father* (English)

Just as European languages are rooted in Greek and Latin, oriental languages have roots in ancient Chinese and languages in the Middle East have roots in the ancient Babylonian and Egyptian languages.

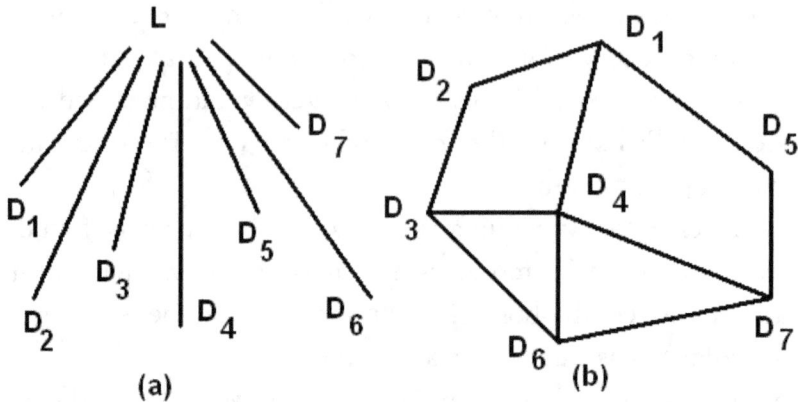

Figure 2.2. Language and dialects: (a) according to the notion of pure language; (b) a more accurate representation.

There are now, of course, many languages and many more dialects. As a rule of thumb, two people speak the same language if they are mutually intelligible. Two exceptions are the Chinese dialects Mandarin and Cantonese which are not mutually intelligible. Another is that Norwegians can usually be understood by Swedes.

Language, however, is not a 'pure' thing such that any variation from it is impure or substandard, as depicted in Fig. 2.2(a). From the point of view of modern linguistics Fig. 2.2(b) is the more nearly correct picture and it avoids linguistic chauvinism, a notion that has often led to one group of people trying to impose their language on another. This view also corresponds to way in which language spread globally.

LANGUAGE DEVELOPMENT IN INFANTS

At birth the human brain is relatively large compared to the body. Almost all the neural cells that will ever be available are present but only a basic network of the *axons* and *dendrites* that connect *neurons* together exists. At the outset these connections develop as the infant learns basic perception and motor skills, the long *axons* that extend from the brain cells then receiving signals from *receptor cells*, such as the small hair cells in the inner ear, or sending signals to *effector cells* in the muscles.

This development in the bulk of the brain parallels that in all animal species and is that necessary for basic functioning and survival.

What sets humans apart, however, is the considerable development of the *cerebral cortex*, the envelope of brain cells that covers the brain. This is where our thinking and storage of abstract memory information such as language occurs.

Development of the articulatory mechanisms required for controlled speech and the cortical mechanisms that control them is a slow maturational process that occurs in *Broca's area* of the frontal

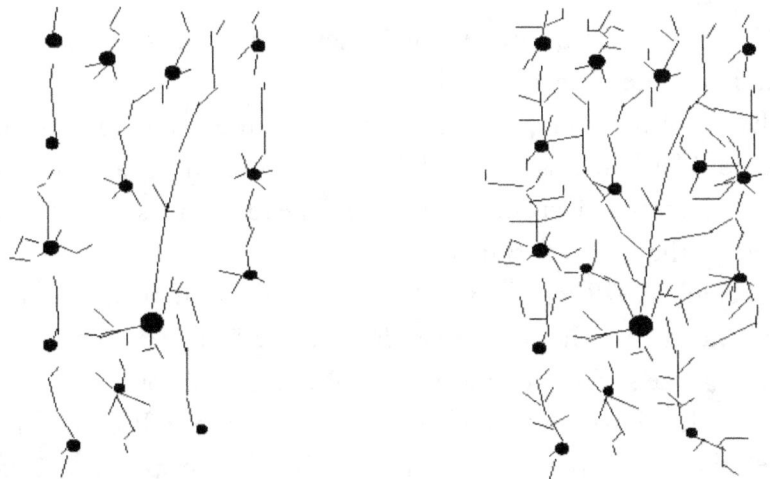

Figure 2.3. Postnatal development of the human cerebral cortex around Broca's Area (language related): (a) newborn; (b) 1 month.

cortex. It has been suggested that babbling, however, is a sub cortical process.

Semantic memory of language is stored in *Wernicke's area* of the temporal lobe of the cerebral cortex.

Figure 2.3(a) shows a small part of the cerebral cortex of a newborn child in which long *axons* extend from the neurons and form branches. Fine *terminal arbors* at the end of these branches connect at *synapses* to the short *dendrites* surrounding other neurons. Figure 2.3(b) shows considerably more dendrites and branching of the axons at the age of one month (Foss & Hakes, 1978). At the age of 24 months the neural network is a good deal denser.

The network continues to develop in following years and the neurons, while not increasing in number, do increase in size.

In addition, the motor nerve pathways that control such activities as speech production must gradually develop sheaths of the protein *myelin* that prevent 'short-circuiting' of impulses between nerve tracts.

As a result of this gradual brain development each human characteristic is developed at a different rate.

Eye coordination, for example, develops much more rapidly than speech. Nevertheless, for the first few months the infant may smile at any moving object such as a dummy head whereas later it may be upset by the faces of strangers.

Packard (1978) cites a vivid example of the importance of timing. In this two Harvard researchers studied the way kittens learnt to recognize shapes and patterns, a physiological ability that develops in the fourth week. If the kittens were blindfolded for this week they effectively became blind for life. There appear, therefore, to be periods when the infant's brain is extraordinarily receptive to behavioural and personality development so that it is easiest to change a child's intelligence for better or worse before the age of four.

IMPRINTING

Imprinting is an important part of the early learning process in higher animals that plays a significant part in brain development.

Konrad Lorentz, an Austrian ethologist, demonstrated this by being the first moving object seen by ducklings after hatching. He waddled in a squatting position and quacked and soon the ducklings assumed him to be their mother and followed him about and flew to him when he quacked.

In other famous experiments baby monkeys have been persuaded to accept a foam-rubber dummy monkey complete with feeding bottle as their mother and kittens have been imprinted to accept as fellow kittens rats placed in their cage.

It has been suggested that the most critical period for imprinting in humans is from six weeks to six months and in this period the human infant develops attachments, particularly to its mother.

As the experiment of blindfolding four week-old kittens demonstrated, neural links in the brain close at certain ages for every function. Similarly, it is difficult to become a top musician if you start late.

Imprinting occurs, at least to some extent, in the learning of languages, so that becoming truly bilingual gets more difficult as one gets older. When older it is well nigh impossible to master a second language with the same ease, fluency and accent as the first.

Much of our language learning is stored as *semantic memory*, one of four basic long-term-memory types discussed earlier in this chapter. Semantic memory is very stable so that the meanings of words or the rules for their use may never be forgotten.

Some experiments have shown that semantic memory stores information in logical hierarchies which go from general categories to specific ones, so that clusters of words with related meanings are stored in the same location in the brain.

Much of this stable memory base for language and other knowledge is founded by imprinting at a very early age and it is important to take advantage of this in educating young children.

MODELING

According to some experts the critical period in a child's intellectual, social and emotional development is between eight and eighteen months.

During this period, in particular, much of a child's learning is by *modeling* or *imitative learning*, also referred to as *learning by observation*.

It is desirable, therefore, for parents and others to use controlled modeling with infants in order to give them a head start in learning language and other skills.

After only four weeks babies begin to mimic the mother's mouth movements in speech and babbling begins at about two months, followed by laughter at about three months.

At six months *lallation* begins, that is, the baby utters repeated sounds such as ma ma ma or ba ba ba. At 10 months the baby begins to try to copy sounds made by the parents and by the end of the first year it may have learnt one or two real words.

In the first years much of the effort in training children is directed at development of survival skills such as eating, learning to walk and potty training. Modeling plays an important part in this, for example in the process of learning to walk, where the infant has had plenty of opportunity to watch the actions of adults.

Learning in a child's first year could be much advanced, therefore, by conscious and careful use of modeling, that is, demonstration of skills to be developed such as development of effective and clear speech.

In these early efforts use could be made of pictures and objects with which to associate the baby's first word efforts, for example the mother pointing to herself when vocalizing ma-ma.

Much of the time we also instinctively use *conditioning*, that is, repetitive presentation of items associated with simple skills to be learnt, often followed by praise when satisfactory progress is made.

At this early stage the cot can become the infant's first learning centre and objects that might be helpful to its learning can be placed within the infant's field of view, for example a picture of a dog in order to teach the word 'bow-wow'.

Here advantage might usefully be made of a TV set to play tapes or DVDs of simple movies, for example involving objects the words for which are to be learnt, perhaps including the numbers 1 to 4.

Demonstrating the possibilities for abstract learning at an early age, chimpanzees have been found better able to recognize the symbols for the numbers 1 to 4 than groups of objects up to four in number.

The important point, however, is that a good deal of patience is needed in the education process, particularly at the outset. Time is taken for memories to develop and fix and it is perhaps best to be a month or two ahead of the child's expected capabilities in trying to inculcate knowledge and skills for, as we all know, in later life it can be years after getting a certain idea that we actually get around to acting on it.

What is certain, however, that the sooner a mother begins to talk to her baby the better and, to a lesser extent perhaps, the same no doubt applies to many other areas of early learning.

GROUP MODELING

At around the third month the baby recognizes the mother and smiles at her. Before this point it will be amused by many objects, including strangers, but now attachments have been formed by imprinting and it may be upset by strangers.

Within the first year, therefore, it would make good sense to involve the infant in *play groups* involving small groups of mothers and infants. In these early efforts at group activities can be attempted and the child can begin its social development.

Packard (1978) raised the interesting possibility of the use of professional people to teach by modeling.

These people would be trained to know the periods during which learning of various areas of knowledge areas can best be commenced and in how best to use modeling techniques to initiate that learning. Such people would then visit the home or attend play group sessions.

Packard noted that an experiment with a form of group modeling was undertaken at New York Medical College. This began with twenty pairs of mothers and babies when the babies were only four weeks old and lasted three years at the end of which the children were compared with those of a control group. The children in the experimental group were a good deal more advanced in language and other skills than the control group.

Indeed, some experts doubt the competence of the modern family for child rearing and believe that more professional efforts are essential to help develop emotional stability and intellectual development in infants.

VOCABULARY GROWTH IN EARLY CHILDHOOD

When children reach the age of one the pace at which learning can take place greatly increases.

Much of what has already been learnt will have been learnt by modeling, for example the ability for form words. Other skills like that of standing upright and then walking will have been learnt in part by conditioning and the associated reinforcement of praise as progress towards the objective is made.

Now learning can be accomplished with a host of aids such as pictures, simple books and educational toys.

In addition, more formal processes such at those of rote learning of words can be used. At the outset the words to be learnt should carefully chosen, for example objects within the child's everyday

Table 2.1. Words learnt with age.

Age (years)	Words learnt
1	3-5
1.25	15
1.5	25
1.75	100
2	250
2.5	450
3	900
4	1550
4.5	1900
5	2100
5.5	2300
6	2550

environment to allow associative processes to help fix the words in long term semantic memory.

By this formative age the child has been out and about a good deal and optimistic attempts have been made to teach it many words of which it will have learnt only a few.

As shown in Table 2.1, however, word learning occurs at a quite rapid rate from here on, to the point at which a basic command of language has been obtained at age five.

Whilst the first year is instrumental in learning to begin to talk, in the second year a comparatively massive growth in vocabulary occurs. Thereafter the rate of increase is approximately linear but slows down as the child comes to grip with a widening range of subjects at school.

By the time they have learnt to read a little, however, children are able to learn things by *cognitive* learning which *processes* and stores *abstract* information.

Latent learning occurs when subjects are exposed to a body of information, rather than in small parts, and they then apply that information later on, perhaps in a test.

A laboratory example of this is that an experimental group of rats allowed to roam a maze will then do better in learning to get through it for a reward than a control group with no prior experience of the maze.

At school children are taught by presenting them with visual and verbal information to learn subjects in discrete 'blocks'. Here cognitive and latent learning occur and revision exercises and tests are used to reinforce and correct their knowledge.

CONDITIONING

Much early learning occurs by

(a) Imprinting, that is selection of a person to imitate.
(b) Imitative learning, that is, imitation of others.

Parents and teachers also use a good deal of *conditioning*, that is, repetitive presentation of information to be learnt, accompanied by occasional doses of positive and negative reinforcement. Conditioning, therefore, is discussed in more detail in the next chapter.

Imitative learning and modeling are important until middle age, if not beyond. Advertisers can rely on it to allow *social learning* to occur in groups of children so that only a few of them may be directly influenced by an advertisement but some of their friends and classmates are then likely to copy them resulting in a pyramid effect.

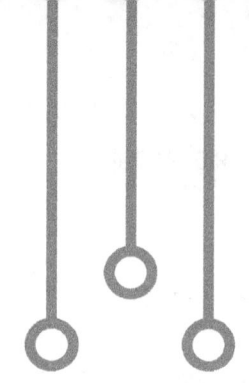

Chapter 3
CONDITIONING, MEMORY AND BRAINWASHING

The real persuaders are our appetites, our fears and above all our vanity. The skillful propagandist stirs and coaches these internal persuaders.
Eric Hoffer, *The Passionate State of Mind* (1955).

"For your own good" is a persuasive argument that will eventually make a man agree to his own destruction.
Janet Frame, *Faces in the Water* (1961).

INTRODUCTION

The preceding chapter dealt briefly with modeling which plays a crucial part in the early learning of infants. Mention was also made of how we also instinctively use *conditioning*, for example repetitive presentation of items associated with simple skills to be learnt, often followed by praise when satisfactory progress is made.

Conditioning is a fundamental learning process but it also has applications in psychotherapy, for example behaviour modification using *aversion therapy*, and thence more sinister ones in 'brainwashing' prisoners of war or crime suspects to obtain information from them or to make them 'switch sides'.

In the modern era, however, it is more relevant to everyday life than ever as conditioning is used to some extent in advertising to repetitively expose people to a brand name. They quickly develop recognition of the brand and, before long, some degree of acceptance, if not approval.

Much of the excessively long and drawn out education process is also conditioning for obedience and routine. Military training, of course, is one of the more extreme examples of conditioning. Some understanding of the mechanics of conditioning is therefore well worthwhile in an age when we are confronted with it almost at every turn.

CLASSICAL CONDITIONING

Classical conditioning, or learning by association, was first demonstrated by Ivan Pavlov's celebrated experiments with dogs in the 1890s.

In these he noted that a caged dog's mouth salivated when it saw food on a pan swung within its reach. Here the food is the *uncontrolled stimulus* (US) and salivation is the dog's *uncontrolled reaction* (UR)

Next, a bell was rung shortly before presentation of the food and the dog's saliva collected in a cup to measure the amount. Here the bell is the *controlled stimulus* (CS).

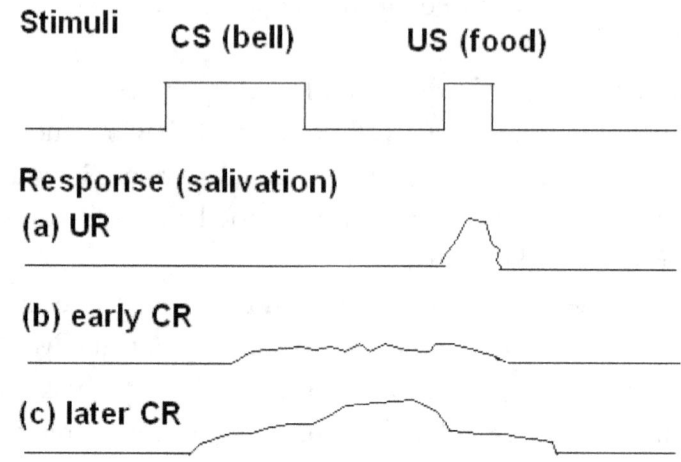

Figure 3.1. Pavlov's classical conditioning experiment:

It was found that the after a few repetitions of the paired stimuli of bell and food the dog would begin to salivate with the ringing of the bell alone, this being the *controlled reaction* (CR).

(a) Bell precedes food presentation.
(b) Bell the only stimulus.
(c) US resumed temporarily - then only CS giving result shown.

Similar results can be obtained with almost any stimulus that consistently evokes a reflex response such as electrical shock. A dog or a human given a mild shock to a leg will quickly withdraw the leg.

If the electrode giving the shocks is attached to the leg, on the other hand, flexion of the leg will occur in response to shock, the US. Then when a prior conditioned or 'neutral' stimulus is given as warning conditioned response is developed and remains after the US is removed.

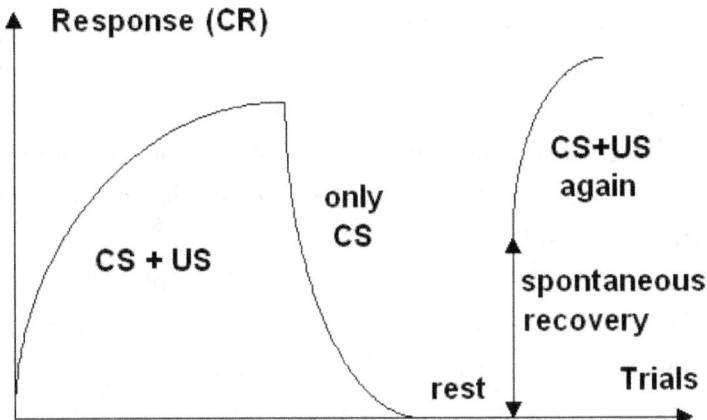

Figure 3.2. Conditioning, extinction and recovery.

After many trials the results can be graphed as a *learning curve*. Typically this takes the form shown in Figure 3.2 where the curve gradually flattens as the number of trials increases.

Here the US and CS remain paired. If the US is removed, however, *extinction* occurs and the response (the CR) decreases. Then, if the US is again added after the CS, the response recovers, the initial amount of response being called the *spontaneous recovery*.

Advertising often uses classical conditioning by repeatedly associating a product with positive ideas and images, thereby encouraging people to have positive feelings towards the product itself.

OPERANT CONDITIONING

Operant conditioning, or learning by consequences, is characterized by the use of *reinforcement* which encourages a response in which the subject *operates* in some way, rather than just exhibiting a passive reflex response as in classical conditioning.

The classical experiments in operant conditioning were conducted in the 1940s by Skinner, a Harvard psychologist. In these he placed a rat in a box in which there was a lever that delivered food to it when pressed.

Initially the lever was operated from outside and soon the rat learnt the association between seeing the lever move and the appearance of food.

After a while it operated the lever itself to obtain food and continued to do so with increasing frequency as it became more familiar with the routine, as shown in Figure 3.3.

In the result of Figure 3.3 the rat in the 'Skinner Box', as it came to be called, took 15 minutes to successfully operate the feed lever. Four more intervals of about 15 minutes occurred before following

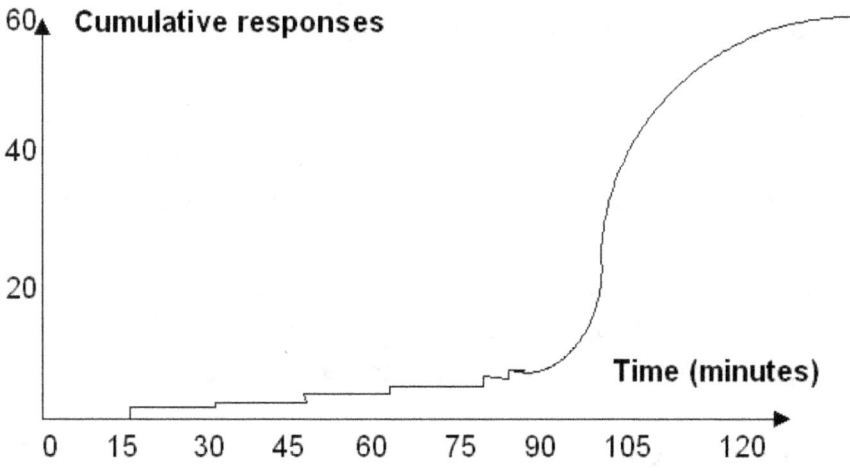

Figure 3.3. Operant conditioning responses by rat in Skinner Box. First response at 15 minutes, second at 30, third at 45, but after 75 minutes the rate of response becomes high.

operations when, the rat having fully learnt the procedure, the rate of operation accelerated markedly.

We instinctively use operant conditioning in bringing up children, the reinforcement to encourage desired actions being smiles and vocal approval.

Note that the timing of reinforcement is important. In a Skinner box, for example, the greater the time delay between the rat pressing the lever and the delivery of the food the longer it will take the rat to associate the two events and thus learn the feeding operation.

As with classical conditioning, *extinction* occurs when reinforcement ceases. This 'unlearning' process may be stronger still when *negative reinforcement*, typically some form of punishment in the educational context, is used.

Conditioned physical responses may be accompanied by emotional feelings or responses and many of our feelings are developed by conditioning.

In the case of classical conditioning *conditioned emotional responses* (CERs) may develop. Indeed, our feelings about many people and other things in our lives develop in this kind of way.

Advertising is also a case in point where an ad reminds us of a familiar product, evoking feelings of recognition and approval whilst the implications for education are all too obvious.

Generalization and discrimination

When alternative conditioned or 'signal' stimuli are used in classical conditioning the subject may learn to *discriminate* between them and respond more strongly to one than the other.

In Pavlov's classical experiments, for example, he found that dogs also responded to a buzzer as a CS instead of a bell, but less strongly.

This is called *generalization* and the more similar the alternative CS the better the response. Sometimes, however, the conditioned responses occur when a new but similar CS is used that has never been paired with the US previously.

In this way a child can develop a fear of dogs after being bitten by a black dog. It may then generalize that fear into a phobia about other harmless black objects.

When two stimuli are used but pairing of the US or 'reward' is not maintained with the second stimulus the subject develops *discrimination* and begins to learn to ignore the second stimulus.

BEHAVIOUR SHAPING

In operant conditioning *shaping* can be used to speed up the process. In Skinner's rat experiment, for example, shaping might begin by remote operation of the 'food lever' only when the rat gets close to it, gradually decreasing the distance of the rat from the lever before the lever is operated.

Then the lever is only operated when the rat touches the lever. Next the lever is only operated when the rat attempts to depress it.

Thus behaviour shaping involves reinforcing *successive approximations* to the desired behaviour pattern.

In this way conditioning can be accelerated and quite complex patterns of behaviour can be taught, a familiar example being circus bears that have been taught to ride bicycles in this way (Lindzey, Hall, Thompson, 1978).

Packard (1978) reported that up to 20% of teachers in the eastern USA were systematically using behaviour modification techniques that involved systematic use of rewards and punishments in their classrooms.

Two teachers in Montana went too far by extending the 'Skinner box' idea to a four-foot high box for miscreant students. It had no lighting and no ventilation other than two small holes for observation. The relatives of a retarded child that had been locked in this box complained and the teachers were sacked.

A better example of a method of behaviour improvement was employed by a team of behaviour shapers from the University of Kansas. They had the teacher play a 'game' in which the class was divided into two teams and the team which incurred fewer violations of several rules for class behaviour was given various rewards. The investigators reported good results.

Objections to such applications of behaviour shaping are that they focused on restricting behaviours such as talking in class whereas advocates of 'open' classrooms encourage a freer learning environment.

The advent of the PC in schools, however, has brought a highly mechanized learning process, some aspects of which progressive educators are pleased with.

With the use of appropriate teaching software, PCs become a 'teaching machine' with which students can learn at their own pace and receive instant reinforcement for correct answers.

REINFORCEMENT SCHEDULES

To this point we have assumed reinforcement, when used, was applied on a continuous basis, that is, after each response.

In operant conditioning reinforcement can also be made according to some fixed schedule. Examples include:

[1] The *fixed-ratio schedule* gives reinforcement after a certain number of responses.

[2] The *fixed-interval schedule* where reinforcement is given after a fixed interval of time, regardless of how many responses are made.
[3] In *variable-ratio* schedules reinforcement might come, for example, after three, then six responses, then three again. Similarly *variable-interval schedules* vary the time intervals between reinforcement.

Another obvious alternative is *random interval reinforcement*, that is, choosing an average interval and multiplying it by a random number between 0 and 1 produced by successive applications of a random number generator such as the RND( ) function of BASIC and other computer programming languages.

As might be expected, extinction is slower after cessation of scheduled reinforcements. This is the situation in human life where, for example, parents can only occasionally reward or punish a child's behaviour.

The result is that we may continue doing things we were shaped to do early in life long after reinforcement has ceased.

PRIMARY AND SECONDARY REINFORCEMENT

A primary reinforcer, or unconditioned reinforcer, is effective for an untrained subject, for example food as a positive reinforcer or electric shock as a negative reinforcer.

A secondary reinforcer, or conditioned reinforcer, must be learnt by being paired with a primary reinforcer.

In a Skinner box, for example, a gong could be sounded every time the primary reinforcement of food was obtained. As in classical conditioning, the subject would associate the gong with the food and soon it would become an effective secondary reinforcer.

A better example occurs in child rearing where parents typically reward children for good behaviour with food treats or presents as primary reinforcers, accompanied by praise as secondary reinforcement. Ultimately the secondary reinforcement of praise may become the most frequently used and important form of reinforcement.

Contiguity of reinforcement, that is the time interval, is also important. The smaller the interval in time between the two reinforcements to be associated, the sooner the secondary reinforcement is learnt.

UNDERSTANDING THE WORKINGS OF THE BRAIN
The role of chemicals

An example of the power of conditioning is cited by Packard (1978).

This came about from experiments with flatworms whose brains have only about 400 cells. The worms were conditioned to "scrunch up" when seeing a light go on when this was followed by electrical shocks. It was found that when the worms were cut in half, or even several pieces, the pieces regenerated brains that remembered the conditioning.

Similar results were then obtained with various species of vertebrates.

Even more startling was the 'memory transferability' achieved by making soup of the brains of rats conditioned to shun darkness and feeding it to hamsters. The injected hamsters soon began to shun darkness!

This led before too long to the suggestion that students should eat their professors!

Later Georges Ungar and coworkers detected a peptide compound ¶ in the brain of a conditioned rat that caused it to avoid darkness.

[¶ Peptides link chains of up to thousands of amino acid molecules to form *polypeptides*. Proteins are naturally occurring polypeptides].

They pooled the brains of 4000 rats to obtain a sample of this compound large enough for analysis and synthesis of the compound (Ungar et al., 1972).

Subsequently Ungar's group reported discovering several other brain peptides that seemed to transfer learning from one animal to another (Jonas, 1974).

The role of electricity

That electrical stimuli in the brain play an important part, however, was demonstrated graphically by Jose Delgado by rigging a bull for radio-triggered mild electrical stimulation of a part of its brain (Delgado, 1971). He then stood in front of the animal. When it charged the tiny electrode in its brain was triggered and the bull stopped. After triggering the stimulation several times the bull was so pacified that it allowed witnesses of the experiment into the ring without charging them.

In humans electrodes implanted in the brain have been found to cause recall of long forgotten memories.

It has been found that the speed of conduction of impulses or *action potentials* in nerves is approximately proportional to the square root of the fibre diameter, a result familiar in cable theory (Schmidt-Nielsen, 1979). In myelin coated axons, however, the conduction speed is approximately proportional to the fibre diameter.

The 'strength' of memories

Memory storage is sometimes so effective and indelible that sometimes we can't forget things we would like to such as bad habits.

Sometimes *motivated forgetting* suppresses memories of traumatic experiences but this generally occurs subconsciously and we are not able to control the repression process at will.

One clue is that when we do consciously forget certain things we quickly dismiss them from our thoughts as soon as they enter them. When happier thoughts cross our minds, on the other hand, they may linger a little longer and almost involve a euphoria comparable to that which might be induced by small doses of tranquilizers like alcohol.

In other words we use processes like elaborative rehearsal to 'tag' memories with appropriate emphasis as important, good, bad and so on.

It is also clear that we have different 'layers' of memory so that past memories are in 'background memory' and take from seconds to days to recall.

Presumably items in foreground memory are chemically tagged and, over time, the pathways and neurons that store them become depleted in these markers.

Supporting this view, research in Sweden found changes in RNA in rat's brains compared to those of a control group after they had been given a learning task.

Such work clearly demonstrates that, just as DNA stores genetic coding, macromolecules of RNA play an important role in memory processes.

Effect of experience

The environment enrichment experiments with rats of Krech's group at Berkeley are mentioned in Chapter 21. These were perhaps the first physical evidence that the brain is modified by experience.

MEMORY STRUCTURE

Figure 3.4 shows a proposed structure in which the brain stores information about animals as categories and sub-categories with properties attached to each 'node' in the structure (Collins et al., 1969).

Some experimental results do not fit this model, for example Ripps et al. (1973) found that people were quicker to agree to the truth of the statement: *A cat is an animal* than they were to the truth

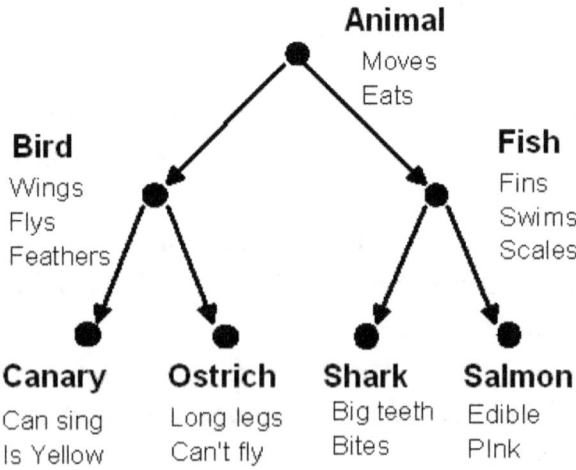

Figure 3.4. Hierarchical organization of the mental lexicon.

of the statement: *A cat is a mammal.* They argued that MAMMAL should be closer to CAT than ANIMAL in the hierarchy.

More important, however, is that the word ANIMAL is much more frequently used than the word MAMMAL and frequency of reference to a memory certainly does enhance the speed of recall.

The present author would also argue that the brain almost certainly must store memories in a *precedence network* based on the order in which learning occurs.

In such a network a memory search that succeeds in finding a 'connection' or *common* property shared by a 'new' item in short term memory and an item in long-term memory might then store the data on the new item in the same physical area.

Then, for example, the first live animals that most children encounter might well be cats or dogs so that they will begin forming the memory structure shown in Figure 3.5.

Here four memories have the *common property* 'animal' and cat is the first animal encountered by an infant and thence the first

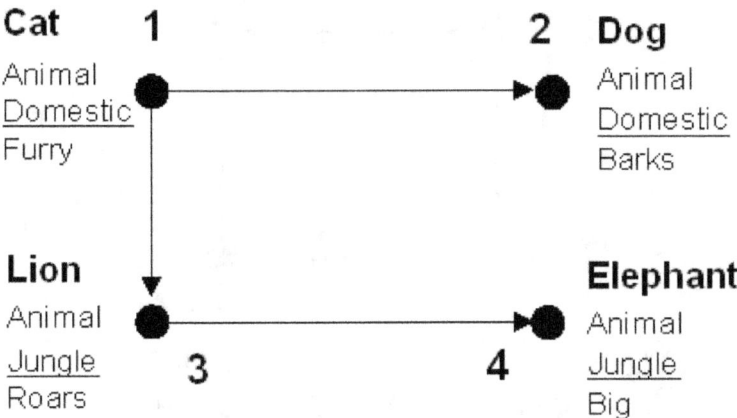

Figure 3.5. Precedence memory network.

memory stored (at node 1, perhaps one or more brain cells). The second memory is dog, the third lion, and so on. Then cat and dog are associated by the property *domestic* (in the child's language perhaps 'house' or 'nearby') whilst lion and elephant are associated by the common property *jungle*.

Such memories have a considerable visual 'content' and the ease of recall of a memory will depend its 'strength' which will depend on such factors as the degree of elaboration with which it was committed to long-term memory and the frequency and recency with which the memory has been revisited.

NETWORK MODELS OF THE BRAIN

As noted in Chapter 2, long axons extend from neurons and their terminals connect to the short dendrites of other neurons in the brain.

Such networks can be modeled using the *Finite Element Method* (FEM). As a very simple example Figure 3.6 shows a direct current

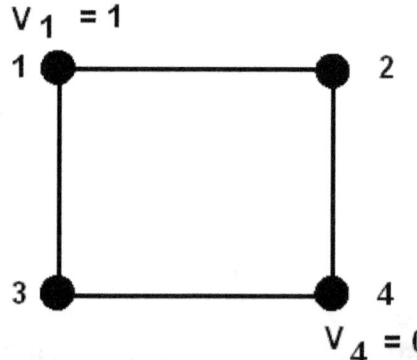

Figure 3.6. FEM model of simple DC network
Resistances 12, 13, 24, 34 all = 1.
Potential at node 1 is 1 and at node 4 it is 0.

(DC) network with four resistance *elements* connecting four *nodes* (corresponding to a group of neurons storing a memory item) and this corresponds to the simple *precedence memory model* of Figure 3.5.

The numerical FEM model for this 'structure' is obtained by summing matrices for each element formed by using Ohm's Law to write the current flow in each element ij as

$$Q_{ij} = (V_i - V_j)/R_{ij}$$

where V_i and V_j are the voltages at nodes i and j at each end, and R_{ij} is the *resistance* of the element.

$$\begin{Bmatrix} Q_{ij} \\ -Q_{ij} \end{Bmatrix} = (1/R_{ij}) \begin{bmatrix} 1 & -1 \\ -1 & 1 \end{bmatrix} \begin{Bmatrix} V_i \\ V_j \end{Bmatrix}$$

Then writing the two equations for current flow at each end of the element as a matrix we obtain

Doing this for each element and writing the entries from their *element matrices* in a *system matrix* in positions corresponding to the node numbers for each element we obtain the system equations:

$$\{Q\} = \begin{Bmatrix} Q_1 \\ Q_2 \\ Q_3 \\ Q_4 \end{Bmatrix} = \begin{bmatrix} G_{12}+G_{13} & -G_{12} & -G_{13} & 0 \\ -G_{12} & G_{12}+G_{24} & 0 & -G_{24} \\ -G_{13} & 0 & G_{13}+G_{34} & -G_{34} \\ 0 & -G_{24} & -G_{34} & G_{24}+G_{34} \end{bmatrix} \begin{Bmatrix} V_1 \\ V_2 \\ V_3 \\ V_4 \end{Bmatrix}$$

where $G_{12} = 1/R_{12}$ is the reciprocal of the resistance or *conductance* of element 12.

This *assembly* process for the system matrix is easily done by a computer program and the matrix problem can be solved using a short matrix solution routine (Mohr, 1992).

First, either input or output currents must be specified at some nodes to 'force' current flows. Alternatively, voltages are specified for at least two nodes, one of these being a 'datum' potential which is often zero.

This is done in the present example, in the program calculating equivalent current 'loads' by multiplying the columns in the system matrix for 'specified voltage nodes' by the voltage specified at them and adding the result to the load matrix { Q } or array V( ) in the program.

Then the problem is solved to determine the nodal voltages or potentials and the element currents are calculated using

$$Q_{ij} = (V_i - V_j)/R_{ij}$$

A short QBASIC[1] program that assembles and solves this problem is given below. Here key notation is

NN(,)	matrix storing the element node numbers
R( )	matrix storing the element resistances
C(,)	the system matrix
V( )	the nodal voltages
NP	number of nodes
NE	number of elements
NS	number of nodes with specified voltage
a$, b$	format specifier strings
X, S	temporary numbers

---

[1] QBASIC was included with DOS 5 and has been used in recent books on PCs. With a first line 'Show' added the same code lines can be used in VB if attached to a form but now a separate (text) file is needed to read the data.

The program reads the data in lines 3, 5 and 9, 'deploying' the element matrices into the system matrix in lines 6 and 7 and modifying the RHS 'load' vector V( ) for the specified voltages in line 11.

Then only lines 14 to 20 are required to solve the problem using Gauss-Jordan reduction, a standard method of inverting matrices, also applying this to the load vector V( ) to obtain the solution directly (Przemieniecki, 1968).

Here X is first used to store the *pivot* for 'row division' operations (line 14) and then used to store the 'row multiplier' (line 17) for the row subtraction operations (line 19) and doing these on the RHS vector V( ) (line 17) as well yields the solution.

Note that the RHS line numbers are not part of the program.

```
DIM NN(20, 2), R(20), C(20, 20), V(20)                      1
a$ = "###": b$ = "#######.###"                              2
READ NP, NE, NS                                             3
FOR K = 1 TO NE                                             4
READ I, J, R: NN(K, 1) = I: NN(K, 2) = J: R(K) = R          5
C(I, I) = C(I, I) + 1 / R: C(I, J) = C(I, J) - 1 / R        6
C(J, I) = C(J, I) - 1 / R: C(J, J) = C(J, J) + 1 / R        7
NEXT                                                        8
FOR K = 1 TO NS: READ N, S                                  9
FOR I = 1 TO NP                                            10
C(N, I) = 0: V(I) = V(I) - S * C(I, N)                     11
C(I, N) = 0: NEXT I                                        12
V(N) = S: C(N, N) = 1: NEXT                                13
FOR I = 1 TO NP: X = C(I, I): V(I) = V(I) / X              14
FOR J = I + 1 TO NP: C(I, J) = C(I, J) / X: NEXT           15
FOR K = 1 TO NP: IF K = I THEN GOTO NEXK                   16
X = C(K, I): V(K) = V(K) - X * V(I)                        17
```

```
FOR J = I + 1 TO NP                                          18
C(K, J) = C(K, J) - X * C(I, J): NEXT J                      19
NEXK: NEXT K: NEXT I                                         20
PRINT " Node Voltage"                                        21
FOR I = 1 TO NP                                              22
PRINT USING a$; I; : PRINT USING b$; V(I): NEXT I            23
PRINT " Element Current"                                     24
FOR K = 1 TO NE: I = NN(K, 1): J = NN(K, 2)                  25
Q = -(V(J) - V(I)) / R                                       26
PRINT USING a$; I; J; : PRINT USING b$; Q: NEXT              27
DATA 4,4,2                                                   28
DATA 1,2,1, 1,3,1, 2,4,1, 3,4,1                              29
DATA 1,1, 4,0                                                30
```

The data appended to the program (lines 28 - 30) is for the problem of Figure 3.6 for which the solution is $V_2 = V_3 = 0.5$ and currents = 0.5 for each element.

The foregoing program also proves very useful for modeling hierarchical networks in Chapter 22.

FEM network models lend themselves to 'structural' models of memory such as that of Figures 3.4 and 3.5.

That the resulting numerical model is a matrix suggests that some form of database model might also be used to model memory storage in the brain, not a particularly startling idea!

Another possibility is to combine the two model types so that each node in Figure 3.6 is a database of some category like those in Figure 3.4 and the links between the nodes are the *joins* between common *fields* in these databases.

As there are about 10^{12} neurons in the human brain, however, we can only hope to model its memory processes on a small scale.

LONG-TERM POTENTIATION

The resistance of each element in Figure 3.6 can be compared to the *frequency* of use of a path in the brain's network and the voltage at each node can be compared to the *strength* of a memory 'image' or information 'bundle' stored in a neuron.

In practice a signal between two neurons is an electrical impulse passed along the axon of the first to the dendrites of the second via a synaptic junction. At this junction neurotransmitter chemicals pass the signal across a 'synaptic gap.' Evidently these chemicals react with RNA or peptide macromolecules in the neurons that play a role in memory *coding*.

In the case of classical conditioning, therefore, with frequent 'dosing' in this way the storage of a memory is made more permanent, an effect called *long-term potentiation* (Vander et al., 1994). Therefore, a more realistic FEM model of a neural network might include a capacitance property for nodes so that the charge stored at these could model the strength and/or recency of a memory.

BRAINWASHING

The term 'brainwashing' derives from a Chinese word and BW was first used by the Chinese military on Americans captured in the Korean War in trying to convert them to communist ideology using 'The Three D's' method:

[1] *Debilitation*: 'Softening up' by sleep and food deprivation.
[2] *Dread*: Rough treatment and threats of torture or death.
[3] *Dependency*: The subject realizes that they are dependent upon the brainwashers for survival and is treated as converted and allowed to mix with other converts who complete the persuasion process.

The American Heritage Dictionary of English defines brainwashing as:

> **1.** *Intensive, forcible indoctrination, usually political or religious, aimed at destroying a person's basic convictions and attitudes and replacing them with an alternative set of fixed beliefs.*
> **2.** *The application of a concentrated means of persuasion, such as an advertising campaign or repeated suggestion, in order to develop a specific belief or motivation.*

In line with the second definition, most people now believe that a great deal of brainwashing is done via the mass media. In the present work, therefore, the term *brainwashing* is generalized to include implanting ideas where none existed before, not just changing a person's ideas. This is important in view of the predilection of advertisers to target children of all ages when they are open-minded, if not naive, and thus willing to try new things.

In this context advertising needs only to succeed in a small percentage of the target age group and *social learning*, a form of imitative learning, will occur and ensure that other members of the target group follow the lead of those first persuaded by the advertising.

The results are nothing short of spectacular, of course, as young children are persuaded en masse what to wear, how to act, and to smoke, drink Coke, buy mobile phones, etc.

This, indeed, is *conditioning* on a grand scale.

As well as in advertising, conditioning techniques are used in the many stages and areas of life mentioned in Chapter One.

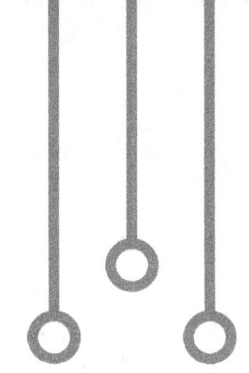

Chapter 4
ATTITUDE FORMATION AND MEASUREMENT

The body of science described in this book could only have been developed in democratic societies, where attitudinal influence is the form of control that is most often relied upon.
Alice H. Eagly and Shelly Chaiken,
The Psychology of Attitudes (1993).

INTRODUCTION

The preceding chapter discussed conditioning which has important application in education where forcing pupils to sit out each day conditions them for productive life. Some aspects of conditioning are also involved, of course, in advertising and other forms of persuasion.

In the present chapter a brief introduction to the mechanics of attitude and belief formation is given. Of particular importance in advertising, *mere exposure research* and attitude measurement are also discussed.

Forbes' *contact hypothesis* regarding interactions between ethnic communities is briefly considered, this being of considerable importance in relation to religious persuasion, and, therefore, also having some relevance to advertising.

THE FORMATIVE YEARS

The period from age 12 to 30 has been termed the *critical period* for formation of attitudes and it can be divided into two parts (Morgan et al., 1979):

(a) Adolescence, during which parental, educational, peer group, advertising and sociological influences are largely responsible for development of most of the attitudes a person will form through life.
(b) Young adulthood, a time when commitments such as choosing a vocation and marriage occur, and one in which attitudes tend to *crystallize* or 'freeze' for life.

In part this crystallization may involve attempts at *cognitive consistency* in which we tend to make our attitudes relatively consistent with one another and thus avoid *cognitive dissonance* or conflicting attitudes.

An example of this might be that a person who goes to considerable effort to maintain good health, for example by exercising regularly and maintaining a healthy diet, is less likely to smoke or condone doing so.

Heider's *balance theory* is of the cognitive consistency type and assumes that we try to maintain consistent and balanced or harmonious relationships with other people and our environment. According to this theory we would not marry a person with whom we disagreed on major issues about which we felt strongly, such as abortion (Morgan et al., 1979).

That attitudes do indeed crystallize or 'firm up' in young adulthood was confirmed by a US survey of women college students in the 1930s which, when followed-up 20 years later, found that for most issues on the 'conservative-liberal' dimension the women's attitudes, except for a slight "conservative drift" typical of older people, remained the same as they had been in their twenties (Newcomb, 1963).

That attitudes tend to firm up in adolescence and young adulthood has, of course, important implication for marketing along the lines of 'get-em young and get-em for life,' an aim exemplified very well by the quotation that opens Chapter 14.

EXPECTANCY-VALUE MODELS OF ATTITUDE AND BELIEF FORMATION

The most popular models of attitude formation towards an object, action, or event, are the expectancy-value models of attitude formation which are expressed as a summation of evaluations of each of several attributes of the object of the form:

$$\text{Attitude, } A = {}_{i=1}S^n \, e_i \, v_i \qquad (4.1)$$

where e_i is the *expectancy* about the object for attribute i, that is its score on a simple scale as to the subjective probability or extent to which the object has this attribute, v_i is the *value* or 'evaluation' of the attribute on a similar scale, and n is the number of attributes considered (Eagly & Chaiken, 1993).

For example, a person is reasonably sure that a new soft drink Choke a Dope has nice taste and is trendy but considers that it is too expensive. Using scales of 0 to 10 for e_i and -10 to 10 for v_i he might thus rate the soft drink as follows:

Attribute 1 (taste): e_1 = 5/10, v_1 = 7/10
Attribute 2 (trendy): e_2 = 6/10, v_2 = 5/10
Attribute 3 (price): e_3 = 10/10, v_3 = -5/10

giving an attitude score

$$A = (5 \times 7 + 6 \times 5 + 10 \times -5)/100 = 15/100 = 0.15$$

whereas a 'moderately good' score in which 5/10 is given for each expectancy and value would yield A = 0.75, whilst a 'middling' score of zero for each rating v_i would, of course, yield A = 0.

In practice there might, of course, be many more attributes and, perhaps, we might average the score as $A = {}_{i=1}S^n\, e_i\, v_i\,/n$, giving 0.05 in the foregoing example, and such scores have been found to correlate well with attitudes assessed by evaluative semantic differential items (Eagly and Chaiken, 1993).

INFORMATION INTEGRATION MODELS OF ATTITUDE FORMATION

The information integration theory of attitude formation calculates the response to a series of stimuli i as

$$R = w_0\, s_0 + {}_{i=1}S^n\, w_i\, s_i \qquad (4.2)$$

where w_i and s_i are respectively the weight and scale of a person's attitude to a set of n items of information, and w_0 and s_0 are the weight and scale value of the person's initial attitude (Eagly & Chaiken, 1993).

Here the scale value of information is its location on the evaluative dimension and the weight is its *importance* or psychological impact in relation to the individual's judgment.

Simple summation models such as that of Eqn 4.2 emphasize the importance of using multiple 'selling points' in advertising.

If the sum of the weights is required to be one then the model becomes an averaging model, but averaging models are more generally expressed as

$$R = (w_0 s_0 + \sum_{i=1}^{n} w_i s_i)/(w_0 + \sum_{i=1}^{n} w_i) \qquad (4.3)$$

The initial attitude parameters w_0 and s_0 may in some instances, that of religion being perhaps the best example, represent 'intergenerational' attitudes acquired from a very early age from family and society at large.

Such initial attitudes, of course, may involve *prejudice*, for example ethnocentricity or racism, and, as history shows, such prejudices are often firmly rooted and perhaps could only be modeled by assigning them an exceptionally large weight.

More important in the modern consumer society, however, is social or imitative learning and in this context w_0 and s_0 represent initial attitude acquired by social learning from a peer or social group.

For example, a person believes that Christianity provides good moral codes (attribute 1) and that Christ did exist and provide a good exemplar of how we should live (attribute 2), but doubts that God really exists (attribute 3). Even if God did exist, however, in view of man's disastrous history he has a low evaluation of this last attribute, so that, using scales 0 to 10 for both w_i and s_i, he might thus rate Christianity as follows:

Attribute 0 (initial attitude): $w_0 = 5$, $s_0 = 5/10$ (i.e. 'halfway' values)
Attribute 1 (morality): $w_1 = 8/10$, $s_1 = 8/10$
Attribute 2 (good life model): $w_2 = 8/10$, $s_2 = 8/10$
Attribute 3 (God): $w_3 = 2/10$, $s_3 = 1/10$

giving a response score

$$R = [(5 \times 5 + 8 \times 8 + 8 \times 8 + 2 \times 1)/100]/[(5 + 8 + 8 + 2)/10]$$
$$= [155/100]/[25/10] = 1.55/2.3 = 0.674$$

whereas a 'middling evaluation score' with 5/10 for both the weights and scale values for attributes 0-3 would give $1/2 = 0.5$.

In contrast to simple summation models such as Eqn 4.2, averaging models emphasize the need to have a limited number of effective selling points in advertising.

Set size effect can be demonstrated by assuming all weights = 1 and an initial attitude score of 50 on a scale of 0 to 100. Then if all further pieces of information have a score of 100 the resulting weighted average score for k additional attributes is

$$R = (50 + 100k)/(1 + k) \tag{4.4}$$

giving the values 50, 75, 83.3, 87.5, . . . for 0, 1, 2, 3, . . . pieces of information, resulting in the hyperbola converging towards the asymptote $R = 100$ shown in Fig. 4.1.

As might be expected, this hyperbolic result takes the same general shape as a learning curve, emphasizing that there is a diminishing return for each additional piece of information about a given

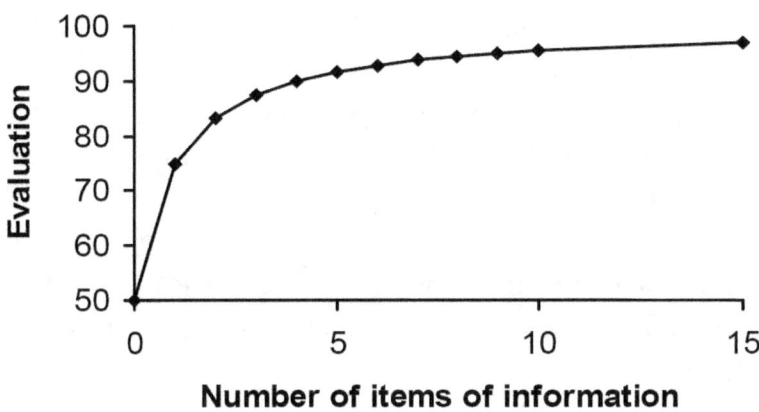

Figure 4.1. Theoretical set-size effect.

subject, albeit with the unrealistic assumption that every piece of information has the same weight (w_i).

The *three hit theory* of advertising mentioned in Chapter One (i.e. that three ads are needed to make people aware of a product, its relevance, and its benefits) would give (with $k = 3$) $R = 87.5$ (on a scale 0 to 100) in Eqn 4.4, or $R = 75$ if there is no initial attitude, i.e. $s_0 = 0$ so that the number 50 in the numerator is omitted.

This is a reasonably good result and, indeed, of some relevance, the present author often finds that it takes three goes to remember items of information, presumably because they were not retained in the short term memory register (see Fig. 2.1) long enough in the first instance.

THREE-VALUE MODEL

A more general 'three-value' model is obtained by combining the expectancy-value and information integration models to obtain

$$R = b_0 \, w_0 \, s_0 + {}_{i=1}S^n \, b_i \, w_i \, s_i \qquad (4.5)$$

so that three ratings are associated with each attribute (Mohr, 2009):

(1) A *belief* b_i or subjective probability or extent to which the object has the attribute (=e_i in Eqn 4.1).
(2) A *weight* or importance rating w_i (=w_i in Eqn 4.2).
(3) An evaluation or *scale value* s_i (=v_i in Eqn 4.1 and s_i in Eqn 4.2).

For example, a woman considers a dress that she has tried on in a ladies fashion shop is 'trendy' and her scores for this attribute might be

(1) b_i = 7/10 (she is fairly sure that it possesses this attribute).
(2) w_i = 8/10 (trendiness is quite important for a new dress).
(3) s_i = 9/10 (she rates it as very trendy).

Whilst a good deal more difficult to use in practice, this model does emphasize that it is sometimes desirable to consider both *belief* and *importance* considerations in assessing attitudes.

LOGICAL FORMATION OF ATTITUDES

McGuire (1960) proposed that people maintain beliefs that are connected by the rules of formal logic. Whilst most of our early attitude formation is via parents, education, peer groups, advertising, etc., it is at least sometimes true that we take 'time out' to think about things and may reassess an attitude, trying to do so in a logical way.

As a simple example consider a confectionery product with the three attributes T = tastes OK, N = looks nice, and P = price is OK, and a positive attitude to the product is denoted as A.

Using a little symbolic logic in which $\rightarrow$ mean 'implies', $\wedge$ means 'and', $\sim$ means 'not', and denoting A = attitude to the product is OK, we can write

$$\sim P \rightarrow \sim A$$

i.e. if the price is not OK then nor is attitude to it.

If ∨ means 'or' we might also write

$$(T \wedge P) \vee (N \wedge P) \rightarrow A$$

i.e. if taste and price are OK, or if the product looks nice and the price is OK, then attitude is OK.

The example is a little trivial, however, but no doubt we do indeed sometimes reevaluate an attitude and use a little logic in doing so, but, generally, our attitudes are formed by the educational, imitative and information integration processes.

There is, however, scope for educators, religions, and advertisers to try and win us over with a little simple logic along the lines, for example, of: "You like to be comfortable so why not try - - -", an approach compatible with the cognitive consistency theory of attitude formation.

THE CONTACT HYPOTHESIS

Forbes (1977) proposed that ethnocentricity of different ethnic groups tended to be increased by cultural differences and (presumed negative) contact between them, expressing the ethnocentrism within two groups A and B as

$$E_a = a_1 C_t D_t \tag{4.6a}$$
$$E_b = b_1 C_t D_t \tag{4.6b}$$

where a_1 and b_1 are assumed to be positive, and are measures of the latent tendency of each group to respond ethnocentrically to each other, C_t is the amount of contact between the two groups at time

t and D_t is the magnitude of the cultural differences between the two groups at time t.

He further proposed that the amount of contact and the cultural differences between the groups depended upon their proximity, incentives for contact such as trade, and upon the ethnocentrism of the groups, expressing this as

$$C_{t+1} = C_t (1 + g)/(1 + a_2 E_a + b_2 E_b) \quad (4.7)$$
$$D_{t+1} = D_t (1 + a_3 E_a + b_3 E_b)/(1 + hC_t) \quad (4.8)$$

where g is a factor that represents all the factors that determine growth or decline in contact other than the repulsive ethnocentrism and cultural differences of the two groups.

In equations 4.7 and 4.8 ethnocentricity decreases contact and increases cultural differences, as might be expected.

The denominator of the last equation ensures that cultural differences are reduced by contact so long as h is positive (the normal situation).

Contact theory has obvious application in marketing, PR and other activities involving persuasion, for example,

[1] It emphasizes that attitude changes with contact or, in general, information transfer, as we have already seen in Fig 4.1, for example.

If contact is 'positive', however, rather than negative as has generally been the case throughout man's sorry history, then equations 4.6 could be modified to reflect this by writing them in the form

$$E_{a,t+1} = E_{a,t} - a_1 C_t + a_4 D_t$$

where a_1 and a_4 are positive. Indeed, it might be hoped that the latter situation might be more likely in today's age of electronic communication and high speed travel. Moreover, it is in this situation that such equations might be applicable to advertising with E = 'resistance.'

[2] It reminds us that ethnic or 'local' considerations are important in international marketing of a product.

[3] It reminds us of the importance of targeting advertising towards an appropriate demographic for a product, and that cultural differences exist between teenagers and their parents and, more so, their grandparents.

MERE EXPOSURE RESEARCH

Persuasion studies on message repetition usually focus on the effects of repeated exposure to *information* about attitude objects.

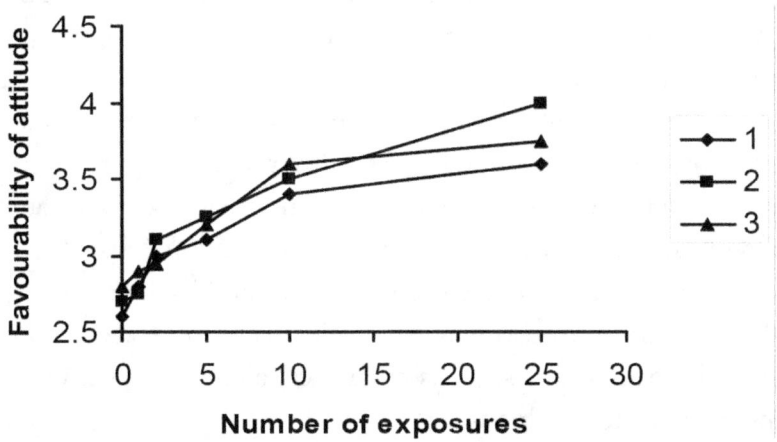

Figure 4.2. Increase in attitude favourability with increasing number of exposures to:
1. Turkish nonsense words.   **2.** Chinese-like characters.
3. Photographs.

In a classic monograph Zajonc (Zajonc RB, 1968) dealt merely with the objects themselves. Fig 4.2 illustrates the increase in attitude favourability with repeated exposure to three types of stimuli, showing a somewhat asymptotic behaviour similar to that of learning curves.

This result is comparable to the size effect seen in Fig. 4.1 insofar as increasing response is seen with increasing amounts of information, albeit repetition of the same information in the case of mere exposure.

Contact hypothesis, however, should be remembered here because it reminds us that oft repeated attempts at persuasion can also be irritating and result in negative attitudes, and some especially loud, haranguing radio and TV advertisements are good examples of this.

Implications of mere exposure in education are obvious, principally that students grow accustomed to new and perhaps difficult at first subjects, if not blasé about them, given time and repeated classroom exposure to them.

The latter observations might remind us that with repeated exposure we become accustomed to, if not hardened to, 'bad things' in life. For example, this is how children endure an excessive number of hours and years in classes and how adults endure jobs which may be, in reality, exceedingly tedious, arduous and boring.

It is also how, unfortunately, individuals become accustomed to essentially bad things such as cigarettes, alcohol, and drugs, perhaps in that order. This is, of course, good news for purveyors of such products.

MEASUREMENT OF ATTITUDES

One of the earliest methods of psychophysical scaling was Thurston's *method of equal-appearing intervals*. In this a panel of judges rates each of a set of attributes of an object (for example a new product) according to an ascending scale such as 0 - 10. Then the mean value of the ratings of all judges is the scale value of the attribute on the attitude dimension. For example, Table 4.1 shows the scale values that might be established for a new soft drink Choke a Dope.

Then for surveys, the mean of the scale values of the attributes selected by respondents is their assessment of an object. To obtain more reliable results attributes that are rated inconsistently by the judging panel are not used for surveys.

Likert's *method of summated ratings* was designed to be much easier to use than the method of equal-appearing intervals but to be at least as reliable. In this approach a large pool of items which are chosen intuitively for their relevance to the attitude object is used.

These items usually consist of statements of belief but statements about behaviours or affective reactions can also be used.

Table 4.1. Example scale values for new soft drink Choke a Dope.

Attribute	Value on scale 0 - 10
I don't like it.	0
It makes me feel ill.	1
It is very sweet and must have lots of sugar.	2
It has a nice colour.	3
The bottle looks nice.	4
My friends like it.	5
It is trendy.	6
The price is good.	7
It tastes nice.	8

Typically each item is presented to respondents in a multiple-choice format such as:

1. Strongly disagree.
2. Disagree.
3. Undecided.
4. Agree.
5. Strongly agree.

Then, for example, a survey on attitudes towards women might contain questions like:

(a) Swearing is more objectionable from a woman.
(b) Intoxication in women is worse than in men.

With scores from 1 - 5 given to each of perhaps a dozen or so such questions the total score is then obtained for each respondent.

Desirably an initial pool of items should be pilot tested on a group of people to eliminate ambiguous and nondiscriminating items which tend to result in neutral responses. This can be done by examining the *item-total score correlations*, each of which correlates the respondents' scores on an item with their scores summed over all the items. Then a good item will have a positive correlation and better items have higher correlations.

Likert Scaling is widely used, for example to assess the response to political advertising campaigns, and a simple example of it is given in Chapter 16.

GUTTMAN SCALING

This approach gives stimulus-person scaling simultaneously and results in a matrix of data called the *Guttman scalogram*. For example, suppose we have five rods of from 5 to 7 feet in length

Table 4.2. Guttman scalogram.

Persons	Stimuli (rods)				
	C	E	B	D	A
2	1	1	1	1	0
4	0	1	0	1	0
3	1	1	0	1	0
6	0	0	0	0	0
5	0	1	0	0	0
1	1	1	1	1	1

*e.g. person 2 is taller than C, E, B, D but not A

(the exact lengths are not known) and ask each respondent to place a one in the Guttman scalogram matrix shown in Table 4.2 when they are taller than a particular rod. This raw data is then reorganized to give the result in Table 4.3.

Table 4.3 is obtained by placing the column with least ones at the left, the column with the most ones at the right, and so on.

Table 4.3. Reordered Guttman scalogram.

Persons	Stimuli (rods)					Score
	A	B	C	D	E	
1	1	1	1	1	1	5
2	0	1	1	1	1	4
3	0	0	1	1	1	3
4	0	0	0	1	1	2
5	0	0	0	0	1	1
6	0	0	0	0	0	0

Then the row with the maximum number of ones is placed at the top (this is for person '1' in our example and hence this is the tallest person) and that with the least ones is placed at the bottom.

The result is an upper diagonal matrix, as shown in Table 4.3, resulting in a score for each person shown on the right side in Table 4.3, this giving the ordinal ranking for each person.

The preceding example of Guttman scaling was for physical stimuli, when a perfect upper triangular matrix resulted. Generally, however, this is not the case when attitudinal stimuli are considered.

An example is Bogardus' social stimulus scale, illustrated in Table 4.4, in which respondents are asked to judge how closely they would relate to people of various nationalities or races.

Such attitudinal stimuli do not yield a perfect upper triangular matrix but it has been suggested that when about 90% of the non-zero entries do appear on or above the diagonal that this *coefficient of reproducibility* value is acceptable.

The Guttman scalogram has the advantage that the degree to which the reordered response matrix is 'triangularized' gives an immediate indication of the reliability of a survey. More complex to use, it is generally only usable for relatively small surveys, such

Table 4.4. Bogardus' social stimulus scale.

	Acceptance level					
	Would marry	As a friend	Would give a job	Allow as citizen	OK as visitor	No contact
Armenians						
Bulgarians						
Canadians						
etc.						

as in-house surveys of consumer groups in advertising offices where it is an ideal tool.

CONCLUSION

Effective persuasion is all about changing attitude (where this, indeed, is necessary) so that some understanding of theories of attitude formation as cumulative or integrative processes is most important.

The later chapter on advertising (Chapter 14) discusses the important trio of cognitive, attitudinal, and behavioural responses and also McGuire's Reception-Yielding model of attitude formation, one that is particularly applicable in such contexts as advertising and religion.

Very relevant to attitude also is the vexatious question of ethnic conflict and, indeed, the equations of Forbes' contact hypothesis do emphasize that, over time, attitudes change. Moreover, models like that of contact hypothesis could be applied to the effects of advertising.

The results of mere exposure research compellingly indicate how attitudes to new stimuli tend to improve given repeated exposure to them, the bottom line being that it is by such means that we are reduced to consumer zombies from cradle to grave.

Finally, measurement of attitudes is, of course, especially important in many areas such as consumer and political campaign surveys. Though perhaps only applicable to relatively small surveys, the Guttman scalogram is useful because the degree of triangularization of the reordered response matrix gives an immediate indication of the accuracy of a survey.

Chapter 5
RELIGION

Where questions of religion are concerned, people are guilty of every possible sort of dishonesty and intellectual misdemeanor.

Sigmund Freud,
The Future of an Illusion (1927), ch. 6.

Religion has always been the wound, not the bandage.

Dennis Potter (1935 – 1994),
British playwright, *Observer*, London,
April 10, 1994: 'Sayings of the Week.'

INTRODUCTION

To begin with let us quickly gather some logical thinking apparatus:

[1] The algebra of sets in which, for example, if the set of integer numbers is denoted as N, then the number 3 is a member of N which we denote $3 \in N$. Then, if we call the set of prime numbers P, this is a *subset* of N which we denote as $P \subset N$.

[2] Propositional calculus is one in which simple statements or propositions are either true (T) or false (F) and these simple statements are connected by:
(a) The *conjunction* 'and', denoted as $\wedge$.
(b) The *disjunction* 'or', denoted as $\vee$.
(c) The *conditional* 'if ... then ... ', denoted $\rightarrow$.
(d) The *biconditional* 'if and only if', denoted $\leftrightarrow$.

$\rightarrow$ is sometimes called *implication* and $\leftrightarrow$ is sometimes called *mutual implication*. Negation is denoted as $\sim$ so that, if a proposition p = T then $\sim p$ = F.

Now we are ready to tackle the question of the existence of God with a little logical thinking.

THE INVENTION OF GOD

Some of us belong to the set of Christians C, others are Buddhists B, others Muslims M, another lot are Hindus H, others might still subscribe to the polytheist ideas of the Greeks and Romans, and some of us are atheists A who might believe in another ridiculous idea - that the Universe U began with the Big Bang BB.

For the author GM we can say $GM \in A$, except when having his weekly nervous breakdown, when he believes that it was all started by somebody or something (he's not sure which so you'd better place an each way bet rather than go to war over it) called *Number One*.

This is proved as follows (not in order):

If God existed (G) then he created the Universe (U): $G \rightarrow U$
If the Big Bang occurred then it created the Universe: $BB \rightarrow U$
On day one U existed: $U \rightarrow (\sim G \wedge \sim BB)$

If nothing existed on day one (*N*): $N \rightarrow \sim GM$
I do exist: $GM = T$

There you have it already! Note that, as in FEM analysis of a simple network in Chapter Three we need a *datum* or 'break in point' in the foregoing list of propositional calculus statements. Here it is GM is true and then we can work backwards to see that ~ N, so U and thus ~ G and ~ BB from the third last statement.

Rather pointlessly, we can also add the exclusive disjunction

$$(U \vee N) \wedge \sim (U \wedge N)$$

That is, U or N but not both.

So who invented the *idea* of God?

Godlike properties were an early 'tribal' *polytheistic* belief used to explain phenomena that early man could not understand such as lightning, the stars and so forth.

Early on some desperate witch doctor hit on the *monotheistic* idea of praying to an ethereal God to cure some sick person, perhaps the chief. That puts the witch doctor in a position of some power and influence. If, by chance, the chief gets well then no doubt the 'WD' would make a great song and dance of it. I'm sure he did just that.

One of the worst results is that a large proportion of the world's population wastes its time praying to some nonsensical God rather than talking to each other. If that time were spent being friendly to other people then, perhaps, there would be far less conflict in the world.

All over the globe we are still slogging it out over this religion crap like children fighting over whose doll is nicest but childish would be too kind a word for it. *Criminal* is the word that should be used and the priests and politicians who provoke wars in the name of God, or so-called democracy for that matter, should be shot and that would save a lot of lives in the long run.

MOTIVATION

Aristotle was first to assert that our goal was to become more nearly what we were intended to be. Psychologists refer to this is as *self-actualization* and Maslow viewed this as striving to reach our potential (Robertson, 1970; Lindzey at all, 1978). He defined two kinds of needs:

(a) *Basic needs* such as hunger, thirst, sex and security.
(b) *Metaneeds* such as achievement, beauty, goodness, justice, order and unity.

Maslow defines achievement as a basic need but the present author prefers to classify it as a 'higher' or more human metaneed.

First, we must meet our basic or 'animal' needs. That done, we can turn our attention to the higher 'human' metaneeds and thence self-actualization as a human being. These needs provide *primary goals* that may motivate us towards *secondary goals* such as money in order to achieve them.

Most of our basic needs are *intrinsic motivations*. Of these, *competence motivation* is perhaps the most basic and is learnt by infants challenged by goals such as standing up in their cot or walking.

Most of our metaneeds are *learned goals*. Achievement motivation, for example, can be inculcated by parents or teachers. *Social motivations* such as justice are also acquired in this way.

The authors conclude from this that we are, basically, *animals*. Nothing demonstrates this more than the incredible success which advertising, with the help of the 'pyramid effect' provided by social and imitative learning, has had in reducing millions of people into zombies wearing jeans and carrying a drink bottle in one hand and a mobile phone in the other.

Like conditioned rats they are in a great hurry going nowhere down a tunnel of despair in search of rubbish that they have been brainwashed into believing to be desirable, trendy and having the appropriate image. The transnational companies are giving us the Anglo-American decreasing IQ problem discussed in Chapter 21.

The same could be said throughout history of the countless armies of brainwashed young men fighting for their God, king and country.

The extent to which we are human we might be the degree to which we have self-actualized in terms of meeting the more aesthetic and social metaneeds compared to the extent to which we have succumbed to advertising and some of the more animal or basic needs such as greed for money.

We might define this as the *net social achievement* or NSA. This we can evaluate using Mohr's 10th Law which is that we should judge things out of 10 and not as black or white and right or wrong. Thus we could judge a person's humanity by their value of this NSA, but not now limiting the range of possible values.

Then, for example, we might rate Jesus Christ very highly in terms of his NSA because he did great good though he was poor.

A filthy rich capitalist who gave but a tiny fraction of his great wealth to a charity, on the other hand, we might rate poorly. In fact we might give them a negative rating because their great greed must have deprived countless needy people of desperately needed money whereas their comparatively small benefactions would do comparatively little good. In other words, on balance, their net social achievement would be a large negative number.

Such robber barons we might describe, therefore, as 'not long out of the tree', an expression that reminds us of our animal origins, a consequence of which is that we still are animals, though some of us more so than others!

What then is the motivation involved in religion? Clearly it is a metaneed and ideally it would provide us with the social motivation to do the right thing by our fellow man.

Usually, however, church and state go hand in hand, especially when wars are begun when priests are always happy to condone the slaughter because they have God on their side. So does the enemy, of course, so what the hell are they really fighting for?

POMP AND CIRCUMSTANCE

The propagation of religion is firmly based on the usual tools of brainwashing, that is pitching the message repetitively and strongly from on high and 'getting them young'.

As shown in Figure 5.1, with greater 'arousal' or motivation, performance improves and there is an optimal level of performance. Certainly, the rites, rituals and bible bashing of all religions are

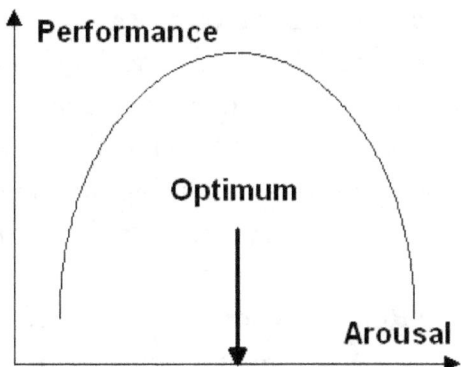

Figure 5.1. Performance variation with level of arousal.

designed to put the fear of hellfire into you and, should the national leader desire it, make you march off to war.

In peacetime, however, religion is, as Karl Marx observed, *"the opium of the people"* so that, as Napoleon Bonaparte put it:

> *Religion is what stops the poor from killing the rich.*

This statement reminds us that religions always impart some morality to their followers, for example the Ten Commandments of the Christian Bible. The sixth of these says quite clearly that we should not kill one another yet Christians have been crusaders and imperialists on a grand scale for several hundred years, something that Muslims around the world are now beginning to revolt against using the usual weapon of the revolutionary, terrorism, that is, small random attacks rather than large scale war which their limited resources do not permit.

As for the other Christian commandments, Western society is now so decadent that one cannot help but wonder if Armageddon is indeed due.

RELIGION AND EDUCATION

In Western Civilization our recorded history of education centres around the Greek and Roman civilizations, in which monastic education had a parallel with Buddhist training.

From those early times until today there remains for the teacher a social obligation to search for 'pure' knowledge and to impart practical knowledge and skills needed for specific roles in society.

Both Greek and Roman higher education placed much emphasis on equipping young men for roles as soldier-citizens able to play a part in and protect the state. Much of our modern philosophy and science, however, we owe to the teachers of those periods.

The final stages in classical Roman education were the Trivium (grammar, rhetoric, logic) and Quadrivium (music, astronomy, geometry, arithmetic) and these were the basis of the medieval arts course in Europe centuries later.

Elsewhere in Europe, before the medieval period academic pursuits were largely limited to clerical education in monasteries.

By the twelfth century, however, a few *cathedral schools* had been established and these began to place more emphasis on lay education by studying law, albeit mainly clerical law.

Gradually small schools were established in most towns where basic education in reading and writing was given for a few years. Few families could afford to pay for such education, however, and much of the population was semiliterate at best.

The thirteenth century saw the development of the first Universities, in Paris and Oxford, and the fourteenth and fifteenth centuries saw many new Universities established in Europe, increasingly with a more localized emphasis. In these training was based on the three stages of membership of the craft-guilds: apprenticeship, journeymanship and mastership.

The ancient Trivium and Quadrivium, however, were still the framework of the arts course that all had to take before moving on to the higher courses of Theology, Medicine and Law.

To this day, therefore, such landmarks as King's College Chapel in Cambridge remind us of the key role religion played in education.

Thanks to the role of religion in education at countless schools, and still in some Universities, countless millions are still brainwashed almost daily for much of their lives.

RELIGIOUS IMPERIALISM

"The oldest and most repeated justification for imperial activity was the Christian mission to go into the world and preach the Gospel, bringing salvation to the 'heathen'. Early imperialist activities by the Spanish and Portuguese carried the pope's blessing for this endeavour." Cowie et al. (1994).

Rudyard Kipling extolled the virtues of such imperialism as being a responsibility:

> *Take up the White Man's burden -*
> *Send forth the best ye breed -*
> *Go, bind your sons to exile*
> *To serve your captive's need;*
> *To wait in heavy harness,*
> *On fluttered fold and wild -*
> *Your new-caught, sullen peoples,*
> *Half-devil and half-child.*
> R. Kipling, *Rudyard Kiplings Verse*, Inclusive edn. Hodder & Stoughton, London (1949) pp 371-372.

So it was that England, France, Germany, Portugal and Spain sailed the high seas and colonized much of the world. In the process they usually decimated the heathen natives, in some cases such as in Tasmania, extinguishing them altogether.

These Christian imperialists also plundered the countries they colonized, at first of gold and silver and later of oil. They were also able to farm these countries, for example the British tea and cotton plantations in India and North America. To top it all off, of course, they had slave labour to work the plantations.

In addition, the imperialists were able to create new assured markets for their industrial products in their colonies. To keep the slaves in the colonies in line, of course, they were brainwashed with religious propaganda.

MARKETING RELIGION

In the USA Christianity has been so heavily marketed that it has been desacralized, for example by:

- Religious symbols such as stylized crosses in the jewelry business.
- Religious holidays, particularly Christmas, have become materialistic occasions devoid of the original meaning.
- Christian sects increasingly market their message on TV to insomniacs.
- The Catholic Church hired a prominent public relations firm to promote its anti-abortion campaign (Solomon, 1992).
- The Mormons spent $US12M on a campaign in *Readers Digest* and *Newsweek* called *On Campus* to recruit college students as clergy (Solomon, 1992).

Perhaps more than most advertising religious advertising is fairly blatant brainwashing seeking to modify beliefs.

ETHNIC CONFLICT

To try to understand ethnic conflict, consider only two ethnic or linguistic groups A and B separated by a boundary. The amount of contact or 'social exchange' between them is obviously the same for both groups.

Now define the term *ethnocentrism* (Forbes, 1997) to represent the segregation, discrimination and prejudice that so often exists between ethnic groups.

The level of ethnocentrism in each of the two groups will depend upon its situation, traditions, and institutions, and upon its level of contact with outsiders.

Forbes postulates that the ethnocentrism in the groups is increased by contact. His *contact hypothesis* was presented in Chapter 4 and is the opposite to the expectations of most people because it is assumed that the contacts are 'negative' in nature, ranging from dress and behaviour differences construed as impolite or 'foreign' to acts of violence or even terrorism.

Conversely, ethnocentrism in the groups will diminish during the intervals between contacts.

Theories of ethnic conflict, therefore, borrow a little from those of learning and advertising where attitudes and forgetting curves are important, and these are discussed in Chapter 14.

For the present, however, one cannot help but think of the tribal conflicts that Jane Goodall witnessed amongst chimpanzees and wonder whether the contact hypothesis might apply equally well to our evolutionary cousins!

The chimpanzee groups, however, have only different physical location and their conflicts may be largely acts of territorial defence, albeit one suspects, with some measure of 'foreigness' or ethnocentrism involved as well.

With humans, however, we have different races, religions and political creeds to fight over before we even get down to business, another area of considerable competition and, sometimes, conflict.

Through much of our catastrophic history it is the *brainwashing* that we are subjected to by religious and political leaders that has been largely responsible for the endless imperialism and war that has ravaged mankind so greatly.

GLOBAL TERRORISM

One of the best examples of conflict between religious sects is that of Northern Ireland where Catholics and Protestants have been at loggerheads for almost a century with thousands of innocent people being maimed or killed (Holland, 1999).

The release of deadly sarin nerve gas in the Tokyo subway by the religious cult Aum Shinrikyo was, from the point of view of world publicity, a relatively isolated event.

This small group isolated its converts and brainwashed them for long periods and had ambitious plans which included obtaining nuclear weapons (Lifton, 1999).

Osama Bin Laden, of course, had been on the side of the Americans in helping the Taliban fight the occupying Russian forces in Afghanistan in the 1980s (Nojumi, 2002).

In the 1990s he and his associates in Al Qa'ida turned their attention to the Americans with the bombing of several US embassies in the Middle East and Africa, culminating in the spectacular plane attacks of September 11, 2001.

Besides the Taliban and Al Qa'ida there are numerous other Muslim organizations around the world such as Islamic State (IS), Jemaah Islamiah (JI), Hamas, Hezbollah, and other fundamentalist Islamist groups in Libya, Chechnya, Indonesia, Pakistan and the Philippines.

The famous economist Keynes said that war was like digging a hole and pouring money into it, a phenomenon we like to call the *Keynes hole*.

Trying to run the world is an expensive business and people used to joke not long ago that England was still paying off the Napoleonic wars. The US is now in that sort of position with its debts still mounting to the point that the World Bank is considering taking action. Worse still the US economy is in great trouble. The Enron disaster and Chinese takeover of IBMs PC business may have been early warnings, but the GFC saw major banks collapse and major bailouts being required for others and for both GM and Chrysler (the latter has now been taken over by Fiat).

The US already has bases all over the world and a massive peacetime defence budget. In addition, for about a decade Al Qa'ida and other groups have had over 100,000 US troops tied down in Iraq and then Afghanistan and elsewhere in the Middle East.

There have been countless military intelligence blunders in modern times (Hughes-Wilson, 1999) and Iraq was yet another. Removal of Sadam Hussein is exactly what Bin Laden, and perhaps the Saudis, who now own much of the USA as well as the UK, would have wanted.

An article in *The Australian* newspaper on 3 November 2004 reported that Bin Laden had vowed in one of his regularly released videotapes to send the US broke. He claimed that every dollar spent by Al Qa'ida on terrorist strikes had cost the US $1 million in economic damage. He estimated the US deficit at more than $US 1 trillion.

In reality the US deficit for that year was just under $0.4 trillion but the US national debt was close to the $US 7.4 trillion statutory limit. In 2011, after a tense holdup in Congress, it was increased to $US 15 trillion.

Elsewhere terrorism has continued, for example the bombings in Bali, England and Spain in recent years.

In the Western world we were brainwashed with constant pictures of Sadam Hussein holding a rifle and misguided innuendo about weapons of mass destruction (WMD) long before the most recent US-led invasion. We ourselves began to feel that we would scream if we heard the term WMD once more. It was an orchestrated litany of lies, of course, as usual in the case of drumming up support for a war, or almost any other cause for that matter.

Islamic terrorists, however, willingly go to the extreme of suicide bombers, statistically a very effective weapon because their own losses are a small proportion of those of their opponents.

As in most military training, doubtless the training used by terrorists to turn people into suicide bombers involves a good deal of brainwashing and does away with the pointless parade ground drills of traditional armies.

THE SHAM OF RELIGION

Using religion as a pretext for war is old hat. Bin Laden and associates, for example, are fighting to get Americans out of the Middle East where they have had most of the oil leases since the 1930s.

Back then there was no Israel, just the quite large country called British Palestine. With oil already of great strategic importance Jack Philby went to Saudi Arabia. Jack had been in MI6, then called the SIS, and (supposedly) been discharged from it.

Jack was the father of the famous counterspy Kim Philby who was recruited around the same time by the KGB in Cambridge, along with Guy Burgess, Anthony Blunt and Donald MacLean.

It is said that Jack Philby helped found the kingdom of Saudi Arabia and then, disgruntled with England, set about giving most of the oil exploration leases to American companies, a reason why Bin Laden and associates belatedly want the US out of that country.

For Syria, whose oil reserves have been exhausted by foreign companies, it is too late, but this is one of a number of countries that will long harbour a grudge against such economic imperialists as the UK and US.

Another sham is that of Christmas where the image of the jolly Santa Claus is used to promote consumer mayhem during what was once a religious festival. The image dates back to a 1881 cartoon by Thomas Nast in which the jolly figure is a caricature of a man who has accumulated a wealth of worldly possessions (Solomon, 1992):

> *"- our contemporary image of Santa Claus was shaped by the famous nineteenth century cartoonist Thomas Nast, whose rendering of Santa was related to other drawings related to 'fat cats' like Boss Tweed and the Robber Barons, greedy capitalists who exploited the poor and lived in useless luxury. Santa stands in opposition to Christ as a God of materialism. Perhaps it is no coincidence, then, that he appears in stores and shopping malls - secular temples of consumption.*

Christianity is based on the absurd belief that Jesus Christ rose from the dead. This is definitively impossible: *when you are dead you are dead*. The Romans crucified thousands of people, however, and it was not uncommon for some of them to hang around alive for days. In fact, JC was drugged but still alive when taken down from his cross by disciples, his later appearances confirming this (Mohr & Fear, 2015).

That there were few such appearances then suggests that he left the region, no doubt to escape capture by the Roman authorities.

As Mohr and Fear (2015) show, all religions are, of course, BS invented to gain influence, status, power and money.

What seems certain is that we are the result of evolution occurring on a tiny planet in an incredibly large Universe (Mohr, Sinclair & Fear, 2014). Just one elliptical galaxy named NGC 4261 is 100 million light years away. It contains the mass of 100,000 suns spiraling towards a black hole 1.2 billion times heavier than the Sun (Goodwin, 1996).

The galaxy cluster known as Abell 2218 is located in the constellation Draco and is 1 to 2 billion light years from Earth. Its total mass is 50,000 billion times that of the Sun.

Countless stars are millions of times brighter than the Sun and have surface temperatures several times greater than that of the Sun (which is approximately 6,000 °C).

These sorts of numbers make talk of God creating the Universe and then having some special interest in us quite absurd. No ethereal spirit with the psychological characteristics of a person could create anything, let alone something so mind bogglingly huge as the Universe.

As an exercise in the Peter Principle,[1] the authors wrote the book *World Religions* (Mohr & Fear, 2015). This proposes the new religion Mohronism which has 10 laws, the ninth being that God's prophet is the famous *Murphy* of the renowned Murphy's Law[2] which explains human history so well.

---

[1] In a hierarchy every employee rises to his own level of incompetence. A corollary is: In time every post tends to be occupied by an employee who is incompetent to carry out his duties.
[2] Everything that can go wrong will go wrong.

Another Irishman Jonathan Swift gets it halfway right with:

*We have just enough religion to make us hate,
but not enough to make us love one another.*

Thoughts on Various Subjects (1711).

The authors consider the first half of that statement right but believes that, as all the evidence in the world today suggests, people brainwashed with higher doses of religion or religious fundamentalism seem to develop even stronger prejudice and hatred for others.

Finally, perhaps the greatest sham is the blatant hypocrisy of religion, the most disturbing example in modern times being the many Christian priests in many countries found guilty of paedophilia and pederasty. Similar sins have been found to be committed by Muslim clerics.

The sheer hypocrisy of these dirty old men beggars belief, as do such silly stories of people doing the definitively impossible and rising from the dead. If you really do believe in zombies, i.e. the living dead, then perhaps you have been brainwashed to the point of being one yourself!

ISLAM IS A SATANIC RELIGION

Many now believe that Islam is a harmful, evil religion, Theodore Shoebat saying:

Islam is a form of Satanism. - - - Islam being a religion that was founded to deliberately to destroy the Church, is a religion of Satan, and is thus Satanism. Both Muslims and Satanists have burned down churches, and that is because they are both enslaved by the dark power of demons.

(www.shoebat.com/2014/18/24)

In another article entitled *Why Islam, And Every Satanic Religion, Must Be Banned*, he reports:

> *A Muslim man named Ibrahim in New Jersey beheaded and dismembered two Coptic Christians and buried their bodies in a backyard.*
> *A British man who converted to Islam beheaded an 82 year old woman with a machete.*
> (www.shoebat.com/2014/09/08).

Another article posted on the internet says:

> *Islam, as a religious system, is entirely of Satanic origin. The Devil is behind every aspect of it. It is a "monotheistic" form of the ancient moon worship that Abraham left in Iraq 2000 BC, but his descendants through Ishmael have continued. When Muslims circle the Kabah on mass, the Devil is the true object of their worship.*
> (www.bible.ca/islam/islam-encyclopedia-
westerners-need-to-know-list.htm).

Another internet article headed *The Qur'an's Deception Passages* says:

> *the Islamic god is called "The Greatest Deceiver" (Qur'an 3:54).*
> *Unfortunately because there are over 1.6 BILLION Muslims on the planet, even a SMALL fraction of this number can equate to 70 Million People who are in support of Islam's radical ideology!*
> (www.deonvsearth.com/who-is-allah-evidence-discovered)

Yet another internet article says:

> ***I am an ex-muslim*** *and one time staunch defender of Muhammad and Islam. It is my sincere hope to save as many Muslims as I can from the curse of Islam. It is an evil and barbaric ideology which has no place in 21st century civilized world. I will prove here without any doubt that*

Islam is a bogus religion and Muhammad and Quran have nothing to do with any god

(www.falseislam.org).

The Hindu philosopher Vivekananda said of Islam:

Now, the Muslims are the crudest in this respect, and the most sectarian. Their watch-word is: there is one God (Allah), and Mohammed is His Prophet. Everything beyond that not only is bad, but must be destroyed forthwith, at a moment's notice, every man or woman who does not exactly believe in that must be killed; everything that does not belong to this worship must be immediately broken; every book that teaches anything else must be burnt. From the Pacific to the Atlantic, for five hundred years blood ran all over the world. That is Mohammedanism.

CONCLUSION

A study by social scientist Gregory Paul published in the *Journal of Religion and Society* in 2005 used data from international surveys and research organizations to find much evidence that religious beliefs can, on balance, do society more harm than good:

"In general, higher rates of belief in and worship of a creator correlate with higher rates of homicide, juvenile and early adult mortality, STD infection rates, teen pregnancy and abortion in the prosperous democracies."

He found the US the most "dysfunctional of the developing democracies, sometimes spectacularly so," with rates of gonorrhea in adolescents up to 300 times those in less devout democracies.

The authors, in the current light of endless global terrorism and conflicts in the Middle East and elsewhere, find a good many people are disillusioned with religion, believing it has done more harm than good.

Chapter 6
WAR AND TERRORISM

The broad mass of a nation . . . will more easily fall victim to a big lie than a small one.
         Adolph Hitler, Mein Kampf (1933), ch. 10.

All wars are planned by old men in council rooms apart.
         Grantland Rice, Two Sides of War (1955).

WARMONGERS

When Adolph Hitler came to power in Germany in 1933, the book *Why War?* by Albert Einstein and Sigmund Freud, the world's two most famous living Jews, was thrown on the Berlin book bonfire along with Einstein's. Four of Freud's five sisters were to die in the death camps by the end of World War II (Cornwell, 2003).

In Germany they came first for the Communists, and I didn't speak up because I wasn't a Communist. Then they came for the Jews, and I didn't speak up because I wasn't a Jew. Then they came for the trade unionists, and I didn't speak up because I wasn't a trade unionist. Then they came for the Catholics, and I didn't speak up because I was a Protestant. Then they came for me and by that time no one was left to speak up.

Martin Niemoeller, attributed.

That Hitler was a bit cranky was witnessed on one occasion by the famous pioneer of thoracic surgery Ferdinand Saerbruch. He had been summoned by Hitler so that he could be sent to attend to the Turkish Minister for Foreign Affairs who was seriously ill (Sauerbruch, 1953).

Having earlier been warned about Hitler's temper, Sauerbruch was taken to a large room to wait for Hitler who arrived preceded by an enormous dog which bounded towards Sauerbruch.

Used to dogs, Sauerbruch stood stock still and spoke soothingly to the dog. Hitler threw a colossal tantrum on account of the dog's lack of aggression which lasted several minutes and threatened to have Sauerbruch arrested but Sauerbruch, as he had done with the dog, managed to calm Hitler down.

There are those, admittedly few, who viewed Winston Spencer Churchill too as something of a warmonger. Educated for the military at Sandhurst, there is no doubt that Churchill enjoyed a fight whether in the army or in parliament (Churchill, 1959).

A consummate writer, Churchill could easily craft a speech to persuade a nation at the worst of times:

The sufferings of a people or class may be intolerable, but before they will take up arms and risk their lives some unselfish and impersonal spirit must animate them.

> *In countries where there is education and mental activity or refinement, this high motive is found in the pride of glorious traditions or in a keen sympathy with surrounding misery.*
> Churchill WS, *Churchill In His Own Words*, Capricorn Books, New York (1966)

The latter part of this statement, however, is in accord with the verse by Kipling given in Chapter Five and referring to the 'White Man's burden' to colonize heathen nations and lift them to civilized standards. As we noted there, this was also good for business and the European colonizers also plundered the nations they took over (Cowie at al., 1994).

Perhaps the key words in this statement are *glorious traditions* for indeed there can be no nation in history with a longer and bloodier history of war, one which they may have inherited from the occupying Romans almost two thousand years ago, and also the Normans nearly a thousand years ago.

MILITARY TRAINING

Nowhere is brainwashing used more extensively than in military training. The constant marching to the screaming of sergeants is conditioning the troops for total obedience so that, when the time comes, they will unhesitatingly leap into action without thinking of the risks to themselves.

Perhaps the most extreme example of brainwashing, however, is that of children selected and brainwashed by the CIA to act as agents (Hersha, C, Hersha L, Griffis D, 2001). Electric shock and drugs were used to condition them to carry out orders. In one training drill a small group of children were strapped to wired chairs and subjected to electric shocks which they could avoid if they pressed a button that would administer shocks to the other members of the group instead.

Though only in their early teens, the girls were trained to use sex as a weapon. The tactic they were taught was to go to bed with a man and slip some poison into his drink during the evening.

MILITARY INTELLIGENCE

Nations have had military spies and information or intelligence gatherers since Roman times, if not before. The 'spook' business is not as glamorous as in the movies and can be sordid and messy (Doyle, 2000).

A case in point would be the 'Cambridge four' of Philby, Blunt, Maclean and Burgess recruited by the KGB in the early 1930s. No doubt they helped Stalin win World War II hands down (Philby R et al., 2000).[1]

Stalin was also helped by a group of Soviet Jews code named MAX which fed the Germans the lie that, around the time of the battle of Stalingrad, the Russians were weakening. Nothing could be further from the truth and the Russians dropped powdered Tularemia bacillus on the unsuspecting Panzer divisions in Stalingrad, an act that may have been the decisive turning point in the war (Alibek, 1999).

One of the greatest intelligence blunders of all time was the FBI in the USA ignoring several intercepted signals during 1941 that suggested the Japanese might attack Pearl Harbour (Hughes-Wilson, 1999).

---

[1] Philby's information emboldened Stalin prior to the crucial Yalta conference. He also helped thwart a number of covert CIA-SIS Cold War operations against the USSR, for example that in Albania in 1949.

Still recovering from the Great Depression which nearly destroyed the Union, the USA had no 'overseas' intelligence organization at that time.

In more recent times the Weapons of Mass destruction fiasco leading up to the Iraq invasion of 2003 was, perhaps, not so much an error but an excellent example of brainwashing the public into accepting the necessity for yet another war. This was done with repetitive showing in the media of a picture of Sadam Hussein holding a rifle.

The same sort of negative imagery is used in the TV documentaries and print articles about Hitler that still appear every week or so. 'War begets war' it is said and the author's are of the view that such propaganda is brainwashing to keep us willing to accept the possibility of war against anyone our government chooses to declare an enemy and denigrate heavily prior to war. We, the brainwashed public, will associate the new villain shown with Hitler and agree that he must be dealt with.

On military intelligence, however, there is no doubt that the allies were well aware of Hitler's treatment of the Jews both before and early in WWII. Much more could have been done to liberate people from the death camps but it would have been sound military policy to let Hitler continue to devote resources to decimating his own population.

THE BRUTAL REALITIES OF WAR

War has always been a brutal affair. The Romans crucified captured enemy soldiers in droves. Mass graves have been discovered after many wars and the Nazi Holocaust of WWII was the most spectacular instance of genocide in human history, though Stalin's purges may have killed just as many people, if not more.

During the religious based conflict in the former Yugoslavia a journalist visited a death camp in Bosnia and wrote (Silber & Little, 1996):

*The men are at various stages of human decay and affliction, the bones of their elbows and wrists protrude like pieces of jagged stone from the pencil thin stalks to which their arms have been reduced ...
There is nothing quite like the sight of the prisoner desperate to talk and to convey some terrible truth that is so near yet so far, but who dares not. Their stares burn, they speak only with their terrified silence and eyes inflamed with the articulation of stark, undiluted, desolate fear-without-hope.*

In 1987 the first author had the misfortune to meet Shaun Carew at the 'Espy', a famous hotel in Melbourne's St Kilda suburb. Proudly Celtic, he served in the British Army's campaign against the red peril in Malaysia circa 1951, remembering 2 sentries on guard duty having to sit backs to either side of a tree in fear of communist guerrillas. He had a terrible temper easily ignited by anyone saying the wrong thing and some attributed this to a steel plate in his head, a result of war service. In one bad mood, for example, he tried to rebreak a kneecap the first author had broken tripping and then cart-wheeling 20+ feet down a two-story flight of airport stairs and landing heavily on one knee.

WAR AND BIG BUSINESS

War is an essential part of capitalism and can only be abolished by changing the present social system. This is the task which history has assigned to all those who suffer most by war.
George Padmore, Africa and World Peace (1937).

War and big business go hand in hand. The arms trade is the world's largest (Sampson, 1977; Pringle and Spigelman, 1981) and, as a result, large tracts of land in several parts of the world remain littered with land mines which continue to maim innocent people.

The arms race of the cold war was certainly one of the best examples of Keynes' view that war was like digging a hole and

Table 6.1. US & Soviet Nuclear Armaments (Bethe, 1991).

	US	USSR
Delivery vehicles		
ICBMs (intercontinental ballistic missiles)	1,050	1,400
SLBMs (submarine launched missiles)	630	950
Bombers	350	140
Total	**2,030**	**2,490**
Warheads		
ICBMS	2,150-2,250	5,500-6,400
SLBMs	4,750	1,750-1,900
Bombers	2,500-3,500	280-550
Total	**9,400-10,500**	**7,530-8,850**
Equivalent megatons		
ICBMs	1,300	5,900
SLBMs	800	1,200
Bombers	3,500	900
Total	**5,600**	**8,000**

pouring money into it. The staggering number of nuclear missiles (see Table 6.1) accumulated by the USSR and USA, along with of large stockpiles of biological weapons, was one of the greatest acts of insanity in history.

Note that, in table 6.1, 2 megatons = 1.59 equivalent megatons. The latter is the best measure of the area that can be destroyed, whereas megaton is the best measure of fallout.

Had that money been spent helping educate and thence control population growth in the poorest parts of the world the outlook for the human race would not be as bleak as it is.

That humans devote so much time to accumulating weapons of war is great insanity and those responsible should be brought to justice and, of course, we need to make nuclear and biochemical weapons illegal.

For the companies that manufacture arms, naturally, war is good for business, including modern cold war or 'rocket rattling'.

The punched card system of recording data was invented in Germany by Herman Hollerith in the late 19th century. By the 1930s, however, IBM controlled about 90% of the world's market in punch cards and sorters.

At that time the CEO of IBM was the unscrupulous Thomas Watson who happily agreed to take on the task of accumulating data on all the Jews in Germany (Black, 2001). For the purpose he gathered together a number of IBM subsidiaries in Germany under the name Dehomag and in 1933 one-half million census takers went door to door gathering information to fill out questionnaires on each household in the country. The information included the religion of the head of the household and whether the person was in a mixed marriage.

IBM continued to work for Hitler throughout WWII, as did a few other US companies such as Du Pont who provided chemicals used to gas Jews.

TERRORISM

The term global terrorism is the catch cry of many leaders around the world to the point that it is becoming very boring. Terrorism is the weapon of the revolutionary, of course, whereby small groups of people can disrupt governments with far larger armies at their disposal.

Religious based terrorism was discussed in the preceding chapter and this is ethnic conflict, more often than not between sects within the same country or region thereof.

The purpose of terrorism with a religious pretext is not always clear. The grievance of the Palestinians at having lost most of the land that was called British Palestine in the 1930s is readily understandable.

In Northern Ireland the situation is much less clear. The media make only the obvious clear, as always, in this instance that the conflict is between the Protestants and Catholics. They do not reveal the reason, namely that the originally Catholic north of Ireland was annexed by the British about two centuries ago. The Catholics, therefore, simply wanted removal of British control of the country which was, until relatively recently, administered from London. The Protestants, some of whom had migrated to Northern Ireland as part of the British occupation, were naturally seen as the enemy and therefore made a target of ongoing terrorism (Hollingsworth and Fielding, 1999).

The French revolution disposed of the monarchy and had a socialist basis. So did the 1917 Russian revolution. The revolutions in China in 1947 and Cuba in 1959 also had a socialist aim.

As Fidel Castro put it:

*Revolution is not a bed of roses,
it is a struggle to death between the future and the past.*

Castro was of such concern to the US that no less than 30 attempts were made on his life during the 1960s.

The Russian Revolution, on the other hand, had the powers that be in the UK and US even more concerned and the British secret service provided considerable covert support to the White Russian army resisting the revolution. When that failed they began counter terrorist activities against the new Russia, for example Lieutenant Agar's sinking of the Red Fleet cruiser Oleg in Kronstadt Harbour in 1919 (Brook-Shepherd, 1998).

It seems certain, therefore, that Hitler's socialist Nazi party would also have been a matter of concern to the UK and US governments. One cannot help wonder, therefore, whether England found Hitler's invasion of Poland an excellent excuse to go to war with them. After all, much more time could have been allowed to try and seek a diplomatic solution.

It is true, however, that Hitler had publicly declared considerable territorial ambitions years earlier and, perhaps, the anti-socialist motive was just a part of England's willingness to war with Germany.

As with the question of why the allies did nothing about the concentration camps, we may never know the answer. As the US politician and reformer Hiram Johnson put it in a speech to the US Senate in 1917:

The first casualty of war is the truth.

This is especially true of terrorism where just one or two malcontents can form a small but growing group and foment in them hatred and prejudice. Whether they claim to be fighting for a Christian or Muslim cause, for example, or for a political ideal such as socialism, one cannot always be sure that their real motive is not simply power, to which end they inveigle others to do their dirty work for them.

BIOLOGICAL WARFARE

Biological warfare dates back to Roman times when dead soldiers were thrown into the water supplies of cities under attack.

In modern times the Russians dropped tularemia on the unsuspecting German Panzer divisions freezing on the outskirts of Stalingrad during WWII, bringing them to a virtual standstill for some time (Alibek, 2000).

Before that the Japanese used biological weapons on the Chinese during the 1930s. During air raids they dropped porcelain canisters of fleas infected with plague and other primitive biological weapons and killed thousands of Chinese in rural areas of Manchuria (Alibek, 2000).

Iraq had a modest BW research program and in the late 1980s Sadam Hussein used primitive BW material such as mustard gas on the Kurds in Northern Iraq. In the Middle East, Israel and other Arab counties such as Syria are also thought to have engaged in BW weapons research.

In 1995 the religious cult Aum Shinrikyo released sarin nerve gas in the Tokyo subway (Lifton, 1999), killing 12 people and injuring 5,500.

The USSR had an enormous BW research program with many research centres and storage facilities (see Table 6.2).

Table 6.2. Soviet BW facilities (Alibek, 2000).

Location	Nature of facility
Almaty	BW research [reserve for times of war]
Aralsk	testing grounds
Berdsk	BW research and production [reserve]
Golitsino	BW research
Irkutsk	BW research
Kirisi	unspecified
Kirov	BW research and production
Koltsovo	BW research
Kubinka	unspecified
Kurgan	[reserve]
Leningrad	BW research
Lyubuchany	BW research
Minsk	BW research
Moscow	10 BW research, 5 unspecified
Nukus	testing grounds
Obolensk	BW research
Omutninsk	BW research and production [reserve]
Otar	BW research, testing grounds
Panza	war mobilization
Pokrov	BW production [reserve]
Rebirth Island	testing grounds
Reutov	storage
Saratov	unspecified
Sergiyeb Posad	BW research and production

Location	Nature of facility
Shikhany	testing grounds
Stalingrad	BW research
Stepnogorsk	BW production [reserve]
Stritzhi	BW research and production
Sverdlovsk	BW research and production
Tashkent	BW research
Vilnius	unspecified
Vladimir	BW research
Vladivostok	BW research
Yoshkar-Ola	unspecified
Zima	storage

Table 6.3. Soviet & US peak BW agent production levels in metric tons per year (Miller et al., 2001).

Agent	USA	Soviet U
staphylococcal enterotoxin B	1.9	0
tularemia	1.6	1,500
Q fever	1.1	0
anthrax	0.9	4,500
Venezuelan equine encephalitis	0.8	150
botulinum	0.2	0
bubonic plague	0	1,500
smallpox	0	100
glanders	0	2,000
Marburg	0	250

Table 6.4. ther BW agents studied in Russia (Alibek, 2000).

>Argentinian haemorraghic fever (Jinin)
>Bolivian haemorraghic fever (Machupo)
>brucellosis
>dengue fever
>Ebola virus
>epidemic typhus
>Lassa fever
>Russian spring-summer encephalitis

After WWII the US also implemented a large BW research program, though not nearly as extensive as that of the USSR (see Tables 6.3 and 6.4). This US program was based mainly at one facility, Fort Detrick in Maryland.

In this frightening arsenal the haemorraghic filoviruses Ebola and Marburg are amongst the most frightening because they are highly contagious and turn all the body's organs to liquid.

At the main Russian BW research facility Vektor a scientist named Ustinov accidentally infected himself with Marburg virus. In the 15 days it took him to die a new more virulent strain developed in his bloodstream. The Russians called it Marburg Variant U and weaponized it for delivery by SS16 and SS17 rockets.

On the 6th of April 2005 *The Australian Newspaper* reported that a new outbreak of Marburg virus in Luanda, the capital of Angola, had killed 169 people. A day or two later the toll had risen to over 200 dead.

To date, however, there have been no large scale BW attacks but in December 1943 news arrived in London that Germany intended to use a pilotless plane or rocket called the V-1 to deliver biological weapons. US intelligence learnt that they intended to use botulinum and the US had already developed an antidote to botulinum. By the summer of 1944 they had manufactured 4,000 gallons of this antidote, enough to immunize 700,000 troops (Regis, 1999).

In the spring of 1944 a worried Winston Churchill asked the US to provide him with 500,000 anthrax bombs. Churchill wrote in a memorandum, *"We should regard it as a first installment."*

The Americans set up for production, aiming to produce a further 500,000 anthrax bombs for their own use. Fortunately, the task was never completed owing to the first successful atomic bomb test in July 1945 and then its use on Hiroshima in August, ending the war a month later.

That Germany, the US and UK were preparing for massive BW warfare towards the end of WWII, therefore, suggests that there is a serious risk of future BW warfare on a large scale.

The Clinton government in the US received numerous intelligence reports during the 1990s that it was "highly likely" that a terrorist group would threaten or launch a BW attack on the US within "the next few years" (Miller et al., 2001).

Well into the future, therefore, nuclear *and* biochemical warfare (NBC) will remain a threat.

INFRASTRUCTURE WARFARE

Information warfare (IW) is another threat to which the US is particularly vulnerable and it seems likely that some of the most sophisticated 'viruses' that have been let loose on the Internet might have been produced by terrorist organizations such as Al Qa'ida who have vowed to bankrupt the US.

If such organizations can disrupt the banking systems or the stock exchanges of their major opponents such as the US and UK then serious damage could be done (Adams, 1998; Alexander, 1999).

IW is, of course, only a particular form of *infrastructure warfare* and poisoning water supplies, disrupting power and oil supplies, destroying bridges and hijacking aircraft are just a few of the many alternatives open to terrorists.

September 11, of course, was a spectacular example of such warfare. That numerous anthrax letters were posted around the country, resulting in the closure for long periods of public buildings, was perhaps another. Here there was no great aim to cause loss of life but, more important perhaps, to cause panic and disruption.

Another example of 'media spin', akin to brainwashing over time, the anthrax attacks were written off as having originated locally and being of little consequence. That seems unlikely indeed and it is only a matter of time before further attacks of this kind occur.

THE USA

As long as there are sovereign nations possessing great power, war is inevitable.
Albert Einstein, 'Einstein on the Atomic Bomb', *Atlantic Monthly*, Nov. 1945.

Nowadays the USA is often referred to as the world's only superpower. Since 1917 it has stood alongside the British in resisting socialism and protecting capitalism.

That fight began with their failed counter revolutionary activities against Russia in 1917 and continued against Hitler's socialist Nazi party in WWII. It resumed in Korea and Malaya in the early 1950s and continued in Vietnam.

Over the last 50 years covert activities have overturned numerous governments deemed undesirable in the name of democracy.

Most recently Sadam Hussein, sometimes referred to as a Marxist and a fan of Stalin, has been overthrown.

In all this the propaganda about democracy is churned out ad nauseam almost daily:

> *It is politics which begets war. Politics represents the intelligence, war merely its instrument, not the other way around. The only possible course in war is to subordinate the military viewpoint to the political.*
> Karl Marie von Clausewitz, *The War* (1883).

As we shall discuss in Chapter 11, we have only Westminster style parliamentary democracy in much of the West, not true democracy as Aristotle defined it. In the US, which is now almost a shrine to capitalism, the Republican party is run by a group of rich families including the Kennedys, Rockefellers and Bushs. Both they and the Democrats, on the other hand, rely so much on funding from big business that they can hardly be called impartial or representative of the common people.

Increasingly, thanks to a global marketplace increasingly dominated by transnational companies, this is the case in other so-called democracies as politicians are persuaded, if not bribed, to sell public assets and utilities which private operators are not prepared to invest in to expand them to meet growing demands. On the contrary, they are more interested in pruning their costs to increase their bottom line.

At present the US economy is in dire straits, in part because the greed of companies like Nike in using cheap Chinese labour in situ has seeded the growth of what looks likely to become the world's largest economy in a decade or two.

Yet China still has a socialist government, India is somewhat that way inclined, and Russia is still run in a somewhat totalitarian way. In this environment it looks likely that the US will have increasing difficulty selling its democracy message, let alone enforcing it. As Kissinger put it (1999):

> *Blessed by history and a benign environment, we are tempted to view our power as a dispensation and to use it to impose our preferences. Such an attitude runs the risk of being viewed as hegemonic by the rest of the world and will gradually be opposed by it. Excessive reliance on power and excessive insistence on our virtue may wind up corroding the very values in the name of which our policy is being conducted.*

Like many other species, man is a territorial animal. It is only thanks to the agricultural revolution that we began to live in larger groups. Indeed, until relatively recently in history Australian aborigines and Bushmen of southern Africa were hunter-gatherers and their diet was not much dissimilar to that of chimpanzees (Weiss and Mann, 1978).

Stalin won WWII and took as much territory as Hitler had coveted. The Korean War has been called an unfinished one. The Vietnam War was comprehensively lost by the Americans. China has said it will be patient about Taiwan but expects to reclaim it eventually (Kissinger, 1999).

THE ENEMY WITHIN

We must in one voice, cry out that we will not tolerate their stinking, murdering, lying, corrupt government.

Louis Beam, speech at the 'Rocky Mountain Rendezvous' (1992), a meeting of several far-right groups. *I suspect Americans will begin engaging in terrorism on a scale the world has never known.*
William Pearce, author of *The Turner Diaries* (1978) and leader of the National Alliance, a US neo-Nazi group.

Another problem that might face the US in the future are several sectarian and religious militia groups such as the Klu Klux Klan, Aryan Nation, Posse Comitatus, The Order, The Texas Militia and many others (Dees, 1996; Jones and Israel, 1998; Snow, 1999).

The 1995 Oklahoma City bombing, in which 168 people were killed, was the most spectacular act of terrorism on US soil before the September 11 attacks. The FBI charged Timothy McVeigh and Terry Nichols with the bombing but only McVeigh was convicted. McVeigh's chief defence counselor, however, found that McVeigh and Nichols had had contacts with Aryan Nation, other people with neo-Nazi sympathies and, most interesting of all, Nicholls had been to the Philippines several times were he had been in contact with a Ramzi Yousef who in turn had had contact with Al Qa'ida and Osama Bin Laden (Jones and Israel, 1998).

Not only must the US expect further attacks from external organizations like Al Qa'ida, there is also the very real possibility of further attacks organized by one or more of its many militia groups. If these attacks were made with even small nuclear weapons or, worse still, halfway sophisticated BW agents, then yet more cracks will appear in a country already morally and economically bankrupt.

The bottom line, perhaps, is that if the West once feared and painted the USSR as some frightening kind of monster (doubtless they thought likewise of the US), then the US as the 'world's only superpower' will be seen as an enemy by many other countries and creeds who will over time wear the US down, just as the USSR was worn down not long ago.

It seems likely that the disenchanted groups within the US will play a part in that process. In addition, corrupt executives on excessive salaries will play their part in that process of decay. It would be going too far to predict a revolution in the US, but not to foresee that its days as the pre-eminent world power that it once was are numbered.

Indeed, with the US in serious economic trouble yet again, in mid 2011 it was suggested that the American dollar should be replaced as the major global currency by a basket of currencies such as the US dollar, the Yuan, the Deutschmark and the Yen.

TWO PERSONAL EXPERIENCES

The first author, despite a number of attempts, could not get the CIA to release their file on him and has himself been the victim of an act of terrorism committed by MI5 or MI6 and/or the CIA (bedfellows anyway).

This was in 1992 when he posted a largish box containing the one-off OUP 600 pp typescript of a book back to Oxford, having added his corrections from a final proofreading to the copious typesetting notes already added by a copy editor at OUP.

One fifth of the package was stolen at London airport and a none too subtle leaflet headed 'understanding private industry' left inside.

He assumed, therefore, that the spooks responsible presumed that he had been tarred with the same socialist brush as my father, a long-time member and one-time President of the Australia-Soviet Friendship society. Now that, old boy, is an act terrorism! One which caused both the first author and OUP lost time and money.

One episode when 'GAM' was 9 was classic spooks stuff. His father, a well-known socialist, physicist on Rutherford's atom-splitting team, and member of the Australia-Soviet Friendship society, took a 6 month sabbatical in 1956 to visit and tour (with a personal guide) the USSR.

During that time the first author, along with a brother, witnessed through a slightly open blind a newly appeared man supposedly living next door (not for long, however) having intercourse with my mother in the afternoon on her bed in her bedroom. Classic stuff, that is, how to screw with your enemy and screw up their lives.

CONCLUSION

An article in the August 20-21, 2011, edition of *The Weekend Australia* sums it up quite well:

"The number of worldwide terrorism attacks rose to 11,604 last year [2010], up by more than 5 per cent from the 10,969 in 2009" and "terrorism last year claimed 49,901 victims, who were killed, injured or kidnapped."

"In Afghanistan, terrorist attacks rose by 55.6 per cent last year to 3307, compared with 2125 in 2009. In Iraq, attacks rose to 2688 from 2458 the report said."

"Counter-terrorist and defence officials said al-Qa'ida remains an increasing threat to Western interests.

Notably, the *same edition* of that newspaper reports on an economic war game conducted with dozens of people working in the financial sector at the Warfare Analysis Laboratory in Maryland USA in 2009.

The China team won and the article points out how and why China is a "huge threat." China is the biggest holder of US debt so that: "If China were to dump this debt it would totally screw with the [US] economy."

Enough said, except to ask how would the US respond?

At present, however, much of the world is afflicted by Islamic terrorism, countries throughout the Middle East and much of Africa being terrorized by dozens of mostly Islamic terrorist organizations. Some of these, for example Islamic State (IS), now control large areas of several countries, resulting in mass migrations on a hitherto unprecedented scale. Indeed, some writers, including the present author, now refer to this situation as *World War 3* (Mohr, Fear & Sinclair, 2015).

In this book it is suggested that the creation of the state of Israel in the UN-mandated British Protectorate of 'Palestine' in 1948 was one of the key 'seeds' of WW3. The 'seed' for the creation of that new state came with the Balfour Declaration of the 2nd of November, 1917. According to Chambers Dictionary of World History (1993) this was:

A short communication from the British Foreign Secretary, A.J. Balfour, to Lord Rothschild, expressing the British government's disposition towards a Jewish national home in Palestine. The central portion reads: "His Majesty's Government views with favour the establishment in Palestine of a national home for the Jewish people ... it being clearly understood that nothing shall be done which may prejudice the civil and religious rights of existing non-Jewish communities. Britain having received the Mandate for Palestine in 1920, the vagueness of the Balfour Declaration was clarified in 1923; Jewish immigration was to be encouraged; an appropriate Jewish body formed to that end; the rights of non-Jews were to be protected; and English, Hebrew and Arabic were to be given equal status. However, the ensuing two decades showed Britain to be either unwilling or unable to deliver its promise to the Jews, especially in view of increasing Arab hostility to Jewish immigration.

Chapter 7
THE ARTS

*Art has increasingly become the concern of
the artist and the bafflement of the public.*
Henry Geldzahler, US curator, art critic.
"The Art Audience and the Critic,"
in *Hudson Review*, New York, Spring 1965.

*Pop artists deal with the lowly trivia of possessions
and equipment that the present generation is
lugging along with it on its safari into the future.*
J. G. Ballard (b. 1930), British author,
Interview in *Books and Bookmen*, London, April 1971.

THE EVOLUTION OF THE ARTS

Cave painting by primitive man was perhaps the beginning of man's artistic efforts. Much of man's early art depicted activities such as hunting and it was not until circa 5000 BC that the technology of painting had evolved to the point at which crude portraits of people could be made.

Circa 5000 BC the Babylonians had quite sophisticated artwork on their pottery, as did the Egyptians circa 3000 BC.

Circa 500 BC the Greeks took architecture to heights we still admire today and the Romans continued this style. Both cultures built impressive venues for political, theatrical and sporting events, the distinction between the two having become somewhat blurred in recent times.

The French word *papier* comes from the Latin word *papyrus*. Several hundred years BC the Chinese developed papyrus from the inner bark of the mulberry tree (Eastwick, 1896).

Around the 11th century AD the Arabs made paper from raw cotton, a practice which found its way to Europe where parchment, that is dried animal skin, was still used for writing.

Paper-making appeared first in Spain and Germany in the 14th century and the first evidence of the use of paper being made in England is in a work printed by Caxton about 1490.

It was not until the 18th century, however, that papermaking in England developed to the point that it was competitive with the best products from Europe.

Over the next 400 years various alternative materials were used for papermaking and numerous patents were taken out in England during the 19th century for the use of wood to make paper. With the use of wood pulp the massive publishing industry of the 20th century developed, a consequence being the loss of most of the world's forests.

During the Renaissance such artists as da Vinci and Michelangelo took painting to a new level with several innovations in technique.

In the 19th century modern styles of art emerged. In Picasso's painting, for example, people were only caricatures and objects were vague or 'abstract.'

In the 20th century photography and then movies and television were developed, leading to the massive entertainment arts industries of today.

THE HISTORICAL ROLE OF ART

Most of us usually think of art in terms of simple portraiture but early cave painting showed animals and men hunting them. Around the beginning of recorded history circa 5000 B.C. events such as wars were depicted on pottery and buildings. In India, on the other hand, Hindu temples showed carvings of people dancing and even involved in sexual acts.

From early times art also depicted religious events, symbols and gods and this sort of symbolism remains a cornerstone of religious practice.

Such symbolism is also used ad nauseam in politics to promote nationalism and in advertising to encourage brand loyalty.

Nowhere more than here is *brainwashing* more blatant and more effective. The keys to its ongoing success are exactly those same elements using in conditioning experiments with animals, that is:

(a) A special environment or backdrop is used in presentations.
(b) In these the uncontrolled stimuli (US) are the presentations and the controlled stimuli (CS) are special symbols, for example the cross for Christians or the swastika for Nazis.
(c) The uncontrolled reactions (UR) are emotions evoked by the US. The controlled reactions (CR) are similar emotions evoked by just the symbols (the CS), for example the word *Coke*.

As discussed in Chapter 14, the purpose is to promote a positive *attitude* to the product, whether this be religious, political or material.

ARCHITECTURE

The classical architecture of the Greeks and Romans is still evident in the columns at the front of public buildings in cities around the Western world today.

These buildings were built a hundred or more years ago and for over 50 years architects have adopted simpler more functional lines.

This is especially evident in the high-rise buildings that dominate the central business districts of most major cities of the Western world today. These are largely an engineering exercise, however, and the architect's role is limited to such decisions as whether to use tinted glazing and what sort of finish to use on the exterior cladding.

In the special case of sporting venues, however, some of these are increasingly reminiscent of Rome's Coliseum, whilst in other public buildings angular lines which seem influenced by modern art styles such as cubism are sometimes used (Carter, 2004).

ARCHITECTURAL FOLLY

A Scottish union leader remarked that the high rise public housing buildings of Glasgow seemed to him an *"architectural representation of a filing cabinet,"* a view that would no doubt be readily agreed to by most of the inhabitants of such buildings.

The same sentiments would seem even more applicable to high rise office buildings which might then be described as 'filing cabinets for people and files' in which people are busy building up great piles of largely useless files.

It is all too typical of human stupidity that we build these grotesque high-rise buildings as a modern fashion. Many high reinforced concrete buildings have had a short life of only 30 or 40 years as a result of so-called 'concrete cancer', an expression adopted as a result of extreme ignorance. The cause is corrosion of the steel reinforcement embedded in the concrete columns and beams. Corrosion occurs because concrete is far from impermeable to moisture and is particularly prevalent in areas fairly close to the sea, as indeed most major cities are, because the sodium chloride in sea water accelerates corrosion considerably.

An example of a fetish for building tower structures was to be had in William Beckford (Nicholas, 1982). In 1795 he set a small army of 500 labourers to work to build the tower of Fonthill Abbey at his family estate in Wiltshire. The tower was 300 feet high and built in indecent haste in timber and cement. It took six years to complete but crashed to the ground at the first decent gust of wind.

Undeterred Beckford began again to rebuild the tower, adding stone to strengthen it. The task of reconstruction took seven years. A few years later a slump in his business forced him to sell. Shortly after this the rebuilt tower collapsed again!

Meanwhile, Beckford had moved to Bath where he built another tower, but now only 130 feet high. It still stands today, more than will be able to be said for most of today's high rise buildings in the not very distant future.

LITERATURE

A useful sample of ancient literature has survived, most notably the writings of such Greek and Roman philosophers as Aristotle, Socrates and Pliny the Elder.

What purpose and audience such writings had is not clear but, presumably, such works were read in forums of scholars and teachers, perhaps as an educational exercise.

Much early Chinese writing also survives, as does much writing from India, for example the *Kama Sutra*, a Sanskrit treatise on the art of erotic love.

The most influential early writings were those on religion, notable examples being the Christian Bible, written by several prophets and disciples, and the Koran, the Islamic sacred book believed to be the word of God as dictated to Muhammad and written down in Arabic.

Religion, perhaps regrettably in view of its use as a pretext for prejudice and ethnic conflict, still plays a major role in the world today and the problems in Northern Ireland, the Middle East, Chechnya and elsewhere are unfortunate evidence of this.

In the USA sects such as *Christian Identity* use religion to justify their extremist racist and antigovernment views (Dees, 1997). Such extremist groups often write their own 'bibles', for example William Pearce's *The Turner Diaries*, a fictional account of an Aryan revolt that begins with the bombing of a government building and culminates in the mass annihilation of Jews and blacks.

Throughout history much writing has also been on politics, ranging from Aristotle's *Politics* (circa 335 B.C.) to Karl Marx's *Capital* (1867). Marx and his small family lived a miserable life plagued by poverty and ill health and he was kept afloat financially largely by Friedrich Engels who came from a fairly well-off family (Wheen, 1999).

Nevertheless, Marx's writings were clearly influential and his arguments persuasive, so much so that they played a part in inspiring the 1917 Russian revolution.

Writing was also an important means of preserving and propagating the knowledge gained by scientists throughout recorded history and today there are hundreds of scientific periodicals for this purpose.

This brings us to the important role of writing in education where books have been the foundation of teaching and learning in modern times. As a notable example, Harvard University was founded by John Harvard, in part with the bequest of only a few hundred books.

Literature has also played an important part in helping modern man occupy his leisure time. Here stage and screenplays also play an important part in entertaining us.

Finally, countless magazines and newspapers combine the roles of information dissemination and entertainment. A few of these promulgate religious and political views and serve as propaganda or, in other words, their purpose is brainwashing.

MUSIC

The ancient Egyptians had families which devoted themselves to music and the Hebrews probably acquired their knowledge of music from them. The Jews had both wind and string instruments and the ancient Greeks had the lyre, flute, trumpet and pan pipes as their main instruments (Egerton Eastwick, 1896).

The early hymns of the Christian Church, for example the Gregorian chants named for Pope Gregory, stemmed from Hebrew and Pagan origins and form the basis of our modern music.

In the 9th century harmonies were introduced and the idea of representing musical notes on horizontal lines was conceived by the Benedictine monk Guido of Arezzo in 1022. The science of counterpoint developed in Holland in the 14th and 15th centuries and in the 16th century madrigals became popular in England.

In the 17th century Albinoni, Vivaldi, Scarlatti and others took music to new heights in Italy. In the 18th century Bach was followed by the 'German line' of Handel, Hadyn, Mozart, Beethoven, and Wagner, that influenced Austrians such as, Bruckner, a Wagner fan, and Georg Tintner, a Bruckner fan (Buchdahl Tintner, 2011).

Such composers as Vivaldi and Bach wrote a great deal of Church music and the role such music plays in promulgating religion is perhaps exemplified by the use of young choir boys to sing it.

Different styles of music and dance are also important characteristics of different cultures.

Indeed, a little snobbery goes into European classical music, sponsored as it often was by the Church or State, as evidenced by the audiences being dressed formally and clapping almost any standard of performance rapturously and at length.

Nowhere was this made more obvious than in the USSR where classical composers were dissuaded from 'more modern' music and Western popular music branded as decadent.

Even in the USA the iconic Elvis Presley was at first considered likely to be a bad influence on the young. Later, however, such singers came to be seen as symbolic of the 'free West' and Presley may have been used as a political role model by drafting him for military service.

Indeed, during the 1960s and 1970s in particular, pop music such as that of *The Beatles* was smuggled into the USSR. During that same period protest music and concerts are thought to have played a part in bringing about withdrawal of the US army from Vietnam.

Elvis Presley once spoke of 'rock and roll' music as having its roots in Negro spiritual music. Indeed, in the 21st century pop music seems to have come full circle and become quite base and primitive.

This is just one example of the 'reverse evolution' or *devolution* taking place in the West as the young are brainwashed into clone-like modes of dress and behaviour and to carry a mobile phone in one hand and a bottle of soft drink in the other.

Their parents are brainwashed almost as much, for example into buying four wheel drives with massive engines to drive only short distances to huge shopping complexes.

The advertisements for such products rely in part on music to accompany their oft-repeated messages.

Finally, a good example of the use of music in the brainwashing process is the word jingo:

> *jingo, n. (pl. -oes): a supporter of policy favouring war; a blustering patriot. [17th c.: originally a conjuror's word: political sense from use of by jingo in a popular song, first applied to those supporting the sending of a British fleet into Turkish waters to resist Russia in 1878]*
> The Concise Oxford Dictionary, 9th edn, (1995)

MOVIES AND TV

Stage plays such as those of Shakespeare date back to Greek and Roman times but have been rendered almost obsolete by the advent of the movie. Movies are based on a 'screen play' but these, in turn, are often based on books but often involve extravagant sets and shooting in several locations.

The photographic basis of the movie led to the cartoon movies of Walt Disney and others and these must be acknowledged as being a form of modern art.

Many movies involve the use of computer graphics and this, one supposes, must also be accepted as a modern art form.

Nowhere is brainwashing used to greater effect than in the movies where for decades American heroes have dominated the screens of movie theatres and TV sets around the world.

Such movies have always glorified war and, indeed, Adolph Hitler was one of the first to realize the full power of movies as a propaganda weapon. Thus, even when only fragments of German divisions were retreating from Russia during WWII, theatres in Germany were showing film of happy German soldiers in the process of conquering Russia.

Perhaps the best recent example of the propaganda use of TV was the frequent use of pictures Sadam Hussein holding a rifle in the year or two leading up to the second Gulf War in 2003. At the same time unjustified claims that an already pulverized Iraq had weapons of mass destruction were made almost daily.

Here we wish to restrict attention to 'the Arts' and thus movies, or 'screen plays' performed by actors and cartoon or graphic characters, and we shall continue discussion of the electronic media in Chapter 13 where the brainwashing role of the news media will be briefly discussed.

TV campaigns of news and documentary films that give a government encouraged slant on a current situation in international affairs are often augmented by appropriately selected movies.

Indeed, at a time when Arab resistance organizations often refer to the West as *"the crusaders"* it is interesting to see a new movie about the many failed crusades of the 11th, 12th and 13th centuries in which Europeans sought to vindicate the right of Christian pilgrimage to Jerusalem (Egerton Eastwick, 1896). No doubt this movie will somehow paint defeat as glorious victory.

More than music, movies reflect our cultures. In the West, regrettably, the overall picture is of a society in a state of decay.

An example of this are the increasingly graphic scenes of violence and sex in Western movies.

The result is young men acting more and more like animals and cities with walls covered with graffiti all too reminiscent of cave painting but a good deal more senseless.

Young girls dress more and more like tribal maidens and have sex with at least several boys at an early age. By the time women have reached thirty they have often had two or more long-term relationships and are ready to be left like damaged goods on the shelf. Those able to stay in a relationship long enough to have children have a high probability of that relationship breaking up while children are still young.

That Hollywood actors pioneered the practice of divorce and perhaps several marriages is here worth note. Not only are some of our modern art forms a mirror of our culture, they are also the means by which that culture is being debased.

Nowhere is this more obvious than in the sex industry which churns out increasing numbers of horrendous movies freely available in all large cities in sex shops which also sell a wide variety of magazines and other 'sex-based' products.

Thanks to media marketing that is akin to brainwashing because it will influence you or someone near to you ere long, we are witnessing *The Descent of Man*, to borrow a book title from Charles Darwin.

Increasingly we are more and more like rats being conditioned in a Skinner box (see Chapter Three). We are not being taught to press a lever to obtain a reward such as food, however, we are being taught to be careless with respect to violence and sex by the greedy CEOs of the movie industry.

In their multimillion dollar mansions and on their million dollar yachts and airplanes they doubtless feel better than the rest of us. These people are Orwell's pigs as he so clearly meant us to see them.

CENSORSHIP

Censorship has almost always existed in the arts and also the sciences. No better examples could there be than those of Aristotle, condemned to death for neglecting the established divinities and corrupting students with notions of others, or Galileo who was forced by a Papal inquisition to abjure his belief in the Copernican system of the sun surrounded by the earth and other planets, only escaping torture thanks to the interposition of an influential friend (Egerton Eastwick, 1896).

These were examples of ideological censorship. An example of covert political censorship occurred in India in the 1960s when the CIA closed down two book-publishing companies which had been encouraged by the Russians to print books about Russian heroes.

Against this, we now have anal American movies being pumped out which encourage young men to behave violently and destructively and young girls to copy the current fashion of being thin, to bare their midriffs and wear tight pants to show off the bottoms.

Until relatively recently in history, even the mildest descriptions of sexual acts were prohibited in literature and the movies. In the

1950s, for example, Hollywood movies were not allowed to show a married couple in a double bed and only in two adjacent single beds instead.

In a Western society cracking at the seams almost anything now seems possible and censorship laws permit extreme violence and explicit sex scenes and nudity to be shown to children in their early teens.

Worse still, young children have access to child pornography and other smut on the Internet, homosexuality is paraded in the street and marriage has become almost untenable.

Mindless US TV series show macho policemen struggling to control an increasingly decadent and immoral society. Likewise, staff in offices and hospitals are depicted as stressed as the result of the preaching of such people as F. W. Taylor nearly 100 years ago. Taylor, an engineering graduate, wrote a pioneering book on operations management which, for example, suggested that piece rates were the best means of achieving greater productivity (Taylor, 1911).

That same principle has been put into great use in Nike and other factories in China to employ thousands of young girls to work ridiculously hard to increase profits and thence the ludicrously large salaries and bonuses of executives of US companies. The last laugh, however, will one day be upon the USA as they have helped kick start the now rampant Chinese economy that bids fair to put the already morally and economically bankrupt USA in the shade.

A de facto form of censorship also comes about in relation to the arts. Few people can afford tickets, let alone the clothes required to avoid looking out of place, to attend symphony concerts. In Australia, therefore, the young go to all night raves where drugs are taken freely.

Worse still, on Friday and Saturday nights the Australian ABC TV shows a decadent music video clips program called RAVE from around midnight until 7 AM to encourage the 'rave' mentality. Rather than censorship we seem to have government approved and provided programs setting our children the worst possible example. In other words they are being brainwashed into becoming Americanized zombies.

As for painting, all over the world young men have caught the habit of using spray cans to paint city walls with graffiti. Only the rich, on the other hand, can afford to buy paintings.

In Australia, the US, UK and several other countries we seem to live with a great deal of political censorship and brainwashing to accept, for example, government policies supportive of war and against trade unions. Yet at the same time there is a distinct lack of censorship in cultural areas that would seem to suggest that we are supposed to become violent, sexually permissive, perhaps homosexual, slaves. This lack of censorship is because 'anything goes' for business for whom taxes have been almost halved in recent decades.

In other words we are in the midst of a sociological reversal of evolution on a grand, if not biblical, scale and are being brainwashed more than ever before to accept the situation in order that a few unscrupulous people can increase their already enormous wealth.

A SAD MUSIC STORY

The first author knew the second (of three) widows of the late Georg Tintner, an Austrian composer/conductor and recently his third wife had his sad story published (Buchdahl Tintner, 2011).

Tintner always conducted without a score and is best remembered for his interpretations of Bruckner's works. He was a truly eccentric vegetarian and teetotaler who could not watch TV or kill anything living. He could not afford a car usually, thanks to child support payments to his first two wives, so rode his bicycle great distances fully dressed up to conduct. As a result he suffered sun damage to his skin and later lesions in his mouth. Eventually cancer spread to his brain and a man who would not kill even a fly plunged suicidally to his death at age 82 from the 12th floor of a building in Canada.

Chapter 8
THE SCIENCES

*The physicists have known sin, and this is
a knowledge they cannot lose.*
J. Robert Oppenheimer, MIT lecture, Nov. 25, 1947.

INTRODUCTION

Having discussed the arts briefly in the last chapter it should now be noted that science, strictly speaking, is study with a view to acquiring new knowledge whereas art is the business of applying that knowledge. Very often the two overlap, of course, but it would surprise most of us to realize that a carpenter, for example, is an *artisan* and, therefore, practices an art! So too is an engineer or applied scientist unless he or she deliberately engage in theoretical research.

In the following chapter we shall mostly discuss 'pure sciences' such as mathematics, physics and chemistry, and 'applied sciences' such as mechanical, electrical, electronic and computer engineering are discussed elsewhere in this book.

MATHEMATICS

Amongst the earliest known mathematicians were Euclid and Pythagoras and some rate Euclid as one of the three greatest mathematicians in history, along with Isaac Newton and Carl Friedrich Gauss (Kirk, 1972).

Euclid founded modern geometry with a large collection of theorems and their corollaries. Pythagoras is remembered for his algebraic theorem which calculates the square of the length of the hypotenuse of a right-angled triangle as the sum of the squares of the lengths of the two other sides.

Newton, along with Liebnitz, is remembered for being a pioneer of the *calculus of variations* and for much else such as his celebrated three laws of motion and his laws of optics and cooling.

The Normal Distribution curve of statistics is sometimes called the Gaussian distribution because it was developed by Gauss. Gauss also developed methods for solving simultaneous algebraic equations, for numerical integration and much else. These latter techniques are of considerable importance in one of the newest and most important areas of mathematics, *numerical methods* (Mohr, 1992).

Numerical methods became important with the introduction of digital computers. Among these the *Finite Difference Method* was of particular importance as it allowed approximate modeling of *continua* with arbitrary shapes and boundary conditions for the first time (Southwell, 1946).

In the mid 1940s aeronautical engineers in Germany developed *matrix structural analysis* to analyze the stresses in aircraft structures (Argyris, 1960). This was the precursor to the powerful *Finite Element Method* (FEM), the first paper on which was presented at a conference in 1954 (Turner et al., 1956). The finite element method has been applied to the analysis and optimization of problems in the mechanics of solid and fluid continua (Mohr, 1992) and also to a range of problems in such areas as operations research (Mohr, 2004, 2005).

Similar matrix methods of analysis have been used in theoretical physics to model the structure of atoms (Alder et al., 1963).

FEM, therefore, is perhaps the most important development in the history of mathematics because (Mohr, 1992):

(a) It involves geometry, calculus and continuum mechanics.
(b) It can be applied to a wide range of problems in engineering, applied science, applied mathematics, and theoretical physics.
(c) It can be applied to nonlinear problems and can include statistical considerations.
(d) It can be used to optimize the systems analyzed.

The downside of the aeronautical industry, for which FEM was invented, has been massive production of airplanes and rockets as part of such insanity as the arms race between the USSR and USA which occurred at the expense of far more important global problems.

THEORETICAL PHYSICS

Perhaps the earliest law of physics still used today is Archimedes Principle (Yuan, 1967). This states that the buoyancy force acting on a submerged body is equal to the weight of the displaced liquid.

Newton, however, was undoubtedly the most outstanding physicist in history and he is credited as being the founder of *Natural Philosophy* which we now call physics.

Newton made many contributions to mathematics such as the Binomial theorem, methods named after him for finding square roots of numbers and the roots of polynomial equations and, most of important of all, calculus which he called 'fluxions.'

He discovered the refraction of light and proposed laws of cooling and gravitation. It is thought that an accident in 1692 in which he lost the records of 20 years of his work affected him greatly (Egerton Eastwick, 1896) and perhaps contributed to him being remembered as somewhat eccentric:

> *He lived the life of a solitary, and like all men who are occupied with profound meditation, he acted strangely. Sometimes in getting out of bed, an idea would come to him, and he would sit on the edge of the bed, half dressed, for hours at a time.*
> Louis Figuier, *Vies de Savants* (tr. B.H. Clark, 1897)

Today Albert Einstein is perhaps more famous but his celebrated equation $E = mc^2$ is really rather self-evident. That is, for a particle in a state of perpetual motion its kinetic energy is not the usual $mv^2/2$ but double it simply because it has not had to accelerate from rest.

His special theory of relativity really borrows from the already experimentally observed Lorentz-Fitzgerald contraction and is a sweeping generalization of this which is proved as follows (Eddington, 1924):

In 4-D space we allow a point (x_1, x_2, x_3, x_4) to move to $(x_1 + dx_1, x_2 + dx_2, x_3 + dx_3, x_4 + dx_4)$ and write the square of the distance moved in the quadratic form:

$$ds^2 = g_{11}dx_1^2 + g_{22}dx_2^2 + g_{33}dx_3^2 + g_{44}dx_4^2 + 2g_{12}dx_1dx_2 \quad (8.1)$$

where the coefficients g_{11} etc. are functions of x_1, x_2, x_3, x_4 and there are six 'cross' or g_{ij} terms.

Using rectangular coordinates the 'cross' terms in Eqn 8.1 vanish (equivalent to taking a vector dot product) and the coefficients g_{11} etc. reduce to unity so that we have

$$ds^2 = dx^2 + dy^2 + dz^2 + dy_4^2$$

Let $dy_4 = icdt$, assuming now that c is real (recall $i = \sqrt{-1}$), giving

$$ds^2 = dx^2 + dy^2 + dz^2 - c^2dt \qquad (8.2)$$

Now consider a clock moving (slowly) from $(x_1,0,0)$ to $(x_2,0,0)$. The reading of the clock will be proportional to $\int ds$ where

$$-ds^2 = c^2dt^2 - dx^2 = c^2dt^2(1 - (dx/dt)^2/c^2) \qquad (8.3)$$

so that, denoting the speed $dx/dt = u$, the clock reading will be proportional to

$$\int_1^2 (1 - u^2/v^2)^{1/2} dt = (t_2 - t_1)\sqrt{1 - u^2/c^2} = (\delta t)\beta \qquad (8.4)$$

where β is the *Lorentz transformation*.

Hence if the clock travels with *finite* speed u it moves slowly (compared to conventional [ours] measurement), a phenomenon called *time dilation*.

As a consequence it also follows that length and mass alter in this moving (relative to us) system:

$$L^A = L(1 - u^2/c^2)^{1/2}$$
$$M^A = M(1 - u^2/c^2)^{1/2}$$

and the contraction in length observed is called the *Lorentz-Fitzgerald contraction*.

Einstein's general theory of relativity included the effect of gravity on the foregoing equations and occupied many of his later years of work (Einstein, 1922). Like the special theory it does not have great practical applications and its main relevance is to astronomy and astrophysics.

Much political capital is made of names like Newton and Einstein. Newton's name is one of those which continue to bolster a declining England's reputation and Einstein was offered the presidency of Israel but declined it.

EXPERIMENTAL PHYSICS

Perhaps the most momentous achievements in experimental physics were those of Ernest Rutherford who achieved the first artificial transmutation of atoms in 1919 using alpha particles from radium to transform Nitrogen atoms into Oxygen atoms (Gaines, 1970):

$$^{14}_{7}N + ^{4}_{2}He \rightarrow ^{1}_{1}H + ^{17}_{8}O$$

The atom was first split by Cockroft and Walton at the Cavendish Laboratory (Cambridge, England) in 1931 by using artificially accelerated particles (protons) for the first time to split a Lithium isotope into two alpha particles (i.e., Helium nuclei):

$$^{7}_{3}Li + ^{1}_{1}H \rightarrow ^{4}_{2}He + ^{4}_{2}He$$

Rutherford was in charge of the Cavendish labs at the time and his work led to the development of the atomic bomb, a development that some hoped would lead to an end to war (Oppenheimer, 1954).

The discovery of nuclear fission also led to the development of nuclear power which may play an important part in coping with the imminent shortfall in world energy supplies that will result from increasingly rapid depletion of finite coal and oil deposits.

Much propaganda was involved in one of the greatest acts of insanity in human history, the nuclear arms race between the USSR and the USA after WWII. Had the enormous amounts of money this wasted been directed at educating and thence controlling populations in the poorest parts of the world it would not be facing the immense problems it is today.

There is much propaganda and misinformation too about nuclear power. According to the Club of Rome's report on man's environmental and resource depletion problems, projected annual release of nuclear wastes from the cooling towers of nuclear power plants in the US in 2000 was a massive 30 million Curies (Meadows et al., 1974). A Curie is the radioactive equivalent of one gram of radium and is such a large amount that environmental concentrations are usually measured in microcuries.

In other words, the long-term safety of nuclear power is very doubtful.

CHEMISTRY

Perhaps the most important advance in chemistry occurred in 1869 and was the development by the Russian chemist Dimitri Mendeleyev of a periodic table of elements based on their atomic weights (Carey, 1995).

Finding three gaps in his table Mendeleyev boldly predicted the discovery of three new elements, even predicting their atomic weights, and was thought by some to be a charlatan. In the next few years, however, the three elements he had predicted were discovered and named *gallium, germanium* and *scandium.*

One of the most momentous discoveries in chemistry was that of gunpowder. Gunpowder is referred to in early Arabic manuscripts, however, and it is thought that gunpowder may have been discovered in India and used for deflagration centuries before it was known in Europe.

Gunpowder was first used for firearms in Europe around the end of the 13th century and Roger Bacon, who died in 1292, gives the composition for gunpowder in one of his treatises (Egerton Eastwick, 1896).

The unfortunate role that gunpowder has played in human history needs little elaboration here. It does provide yet another telling example of the vicious role played by the unscrupulous arms industry which markets its products effectively to governments around the world.

BIOLOGY

Study of the biology of earth's many life forms has gone on for several hundred years. Perhaps the greatest breakthrough in biology was the discovery and modeling of DNA (deoxyribonucleic acid), a large biochemical that had first been isolated in 1871.

The Canadian physician Oswald Avery proved in 1944 that DNA affects hereditary traits. Previously the general consensus was that proteins carried the hereditary information that cells need to split off from others and grow.

In February 1951 Linus Pauling, the most famous chemist of his time, published a paper in which he demonstrated the helical structure of proteins and proposed that this might be common to many large and complex molecules in nature.

In 1953 American biochemist James Watson and British biophysicist Francis Crick proposed the double helix structure of DNA. Both were typically brilliant, arrogant and eccentric scientists who had been wisely teamed together by the head of Cambridge's Cavendish laboratories, Sir Laurence Bragg (White, 2002).

This great step in biology was important in the understanding of human heredity and disease. It is also particularly helpful in the difficult task of unraveling the complexities of cancer, a process involving cells with mutations 'outgrowing' ordinary cells.

In such pure science there is less likelihood of misapplication here but mention of cancer here might remind us of the fact that the tobacco industry knew full well the addictive nature of smoking and its very strong statistical association with lung cancer victims but had no qualms in continuing to advertise their product to young and old.

MEDICINE

The Romans are known to have practiced surgery around the time of Christ. Leonardo da Vinci conducted autopsies in order to study anatomy and drew accurate drawings of human heart valves. His report of two autopsies on an old man of 100 who had died quietly and a young child is credited with being the first description of *arteriosclerosis* (Carey, 1995):

> I carried out the autopsy to determine the cause of such a calm death and discovered that it was the result of weakness produced by insufficiency of blood and of the artery supplying the heart and other lower members, which I found to be all withered,

> shrunken and desiccated. The other postmortem was on a child of two years, and here I discovered the case to be exactly the opposite of the old man.

One of the ten most important advances in the history of medicine occurred in 1629 when British physician William Harvey developed an experimental model of the circulatory system which demonstrated contraction of the heart and consequent blood flow (Famighetti 1998).

Another occurred in the late 19th century when French microbiologist Louis Pasteur and German physician Robert Koch proved the germ theory of disease, an idea dating back at least as far as 100 BC, Pasteur calling the responsible organisms bacteria.

Around the same time British physician Joseph Lister found that carbolic acid killed germs and thence pioneered antiseptic surgery before which nearly all patients died after operations requiring perforation of the peritoneum.

The first antibiotics were penicillin, discovered in 1928 by British bacteriologist Alexander Fleming, and sulfa drugs, discovered in 1932 by German chemist Gerhard Domagk.

Remarkably, British physician Edward Jenner discovered that vaccination was a successful defence against the smallpox virus much earlier (1796).

There have been many wonderful and highly beneficial advances in medicine in the last few hundred years. There have also been many negative developments, for example the excessive use of certain types of operations, for example unnecessary use of Caesarean sections and hysterectomies.

More recently angioplasty and heart bypass operations have become commonplace though they often do nothing to prolong life whilst involving a short term risk of complications. Often careful diet and exercise regimens over a period of years will slow or even reverse atherosclerosis and this alternative should be considered before the drastic step of open-heart surgery is undertaken (Cooke and Zimmer, 2002).

Cosmetic surgery, of course, hardly needs mention in the context of unnecessary operations.

Here marketing new procedures before they have had sufficient long-term testing occurs and cosmetic surgery often does more harm than good, an example being the breast implants given to countless women around the world which later leaked and had to be removed.

Unnecessary prescriptions are another unfortunate modern practice, an example being long-term prescription of medications for high blood pressure. This is often done without trying to treat the root cause of the problem, atherosclerosis, which by clogging small capillaries causes an increase in pressure in the rest of the circulatory system.

As large blood vessels also become clogged the problem worsens and the most important thing in treating cardiovascular disease is to implement, as far as possible, a strict diet and exercise regime to at least minimize further damage. In the short term only, BP medications might also be justified if there is thought to be imminent risk of heart attack or stroke.

Part of the problem here is the power of the few multinational pharmaceutical companies that market their products persuasively to the medical profession and sometimes to consumers as well. Nowhere has this been more blatant than in the field of psychiatry.

MODERN DIET

Over a century ago homeopathic medicine used to encourage such absurd practices as taking minuscule dosages of arsenic to improve one's health.

This is comparable to the media blurb we hear today advising that a glass or two of red wine a day is good for you because it contains antioxidants. Little matter that all manner of fruit and vegetables do, or that alcohol is a poison.

Little more than a decade ago some doctors still said publicly that less than 10 cigarettes a day might be acceptable in view of the fact that tobacco smoke is a brain stimulant and might therefore make one operate better.

Fortunately, that message is no longer heard. Instead a glass or two of red wine is recommended as beneficial, a suggestion which people are unlikely to restrict themselves to when they open a bottle of wine.

Until relatively recently the medical profession has been scandalously negligent in speaking out against the stupidity of addicting young children to sugar, allowing them things full of fat such as milk, chocolate, junk food and snack foods fried in oil.

Yet another example of successful brainwashing, advertising of junk food, confectionery and soft drinks goes on more urgently than ever with such dietetically dangerous products stationed at supermarket checkouts so that young children accompanying a parent while shopping can demand them.

PSYCHIATRY

Sigmund Freud (1865 - 1939) developed psychoanalysis which some regard as the first method of examining the human mind. He also proposed the division of the psyche into ego (our outer self), super-ego (our conscience) and id (our inner self).

Modern psychiatry now assesses a wide range of personality problems such as anxiety, obsessive behaviour, depression, hysteria, schizophrenia and paranoia. It also assesses problems of psychopathic behaviour such as delinquency, abnormal sexual behaviour and drug addiction (Davies, 1971).

The term hysteria comes from the Greek work *hustericos* meaning 'of the womb' because ancient Greeks associated a certain type of neurotic behaviour with childless women. This indicates that man has long had an interest in trying to understand human psychology and behaviour.

The field of psychiatry, however, has a disgraceful history. As late as 1815 the Bethlehem madhouse in England exhibited lunatics every Sunday and made a considerable amount of money in the process (Youngson and Schott, 1996).[1]

At the Bicêtre hospital in France attendants used whips to make the mad perform dances to provide traditional entertainment. At the Charenton asylum the infamous Marquis de Sade presided over theatrical performances by the inmates!

In the USSR dissidents were often confided to asylums for the insane, a policy no doubt practiced elsewhere.

The practice of lobotomy was particularly scandalous.

It can be traced back to Dr Gottlieb Burckhardt, the superintendent of a psychiatric hospital in Switzerland, who in 1890 drilled holes in the head of six severely agitated patients, thereby altering their behaviour with varying degrees of success.

His work may have been remembered when in 1935 John Fulton at Yale University removed the frontal lobes from two chimpanzees, changing their behaviour greatly. Dr Walter Freeman, an American neurologist, was recovering from a nervous breakdown when in July 1935 he attended a seminar given by Fulton.

Egas Moniz, a celebrated Portuguese neurosurgeon also attended the seminar and two months later in Portugal he

---

[1] The word Bedlam is a corruption of "Bethlehem."

performed the first *leucotomy* by drilling a small hole in the skull and injecting alcohol into it to destroy the fibres in the frontal lobes of the patient.

The operation succeeded in making the patient less agitated and overtly paranoid but made her rather more apathetic and dull than Moniz had hoped. Nevertheless, further operations were performed and the procedure was refined by drilling six holes in the skull.

When he published he gave no hint of the downside of his procedure and Walter Freeman was bursting with enthusiasm to try it and he enlisted the aid of a neurosurgeon James Watts to carry out his first leucotomy on 14 September 1936.

A week later the patient became incoherent and could not even recite the days of the week and when asked to write could only scribble nonsense. Her speech improved in following days and they operated on another five patients.

In November 1936 Freeman and Watts published a report in which they wrote:

> *In all our patients there was a ... common denominator of worry, apprehension, anxiety, insomnia and nervous tension, and in all of them these symptoms have been relieved to a greater or lesser extent.*

Freeman and Watts renamed the procedure *lobotomy* and made it more drastic by drilling only two holes in the side of the head and using a canula, the tubing from a six inch heavy-gauge hypodermic needle, to pave the way for a cutting tool to destroy targeted brain tissue.

Watts became so proficient that he could thread the canula through the brain from the small hole on one side of the head to that on the other.

Though not qualified to do so, Freeman began to perform lobotomies on his own and became a celebrity in the process. He also simplified the procedure by using electroshock to subdue the patient and then plunging an ice pick into their head, usually producing a person at least halfway towards a zombie.

Often the procedure was repeated a second and third time and Freeman, a neurotic with severe depressive symptoms who needed 3 Nembutal to sleep at night, enthusiastically continued his crude procedure years after it had been discredited.

Such surgery had been performed on more than 40,000 people in the USA alone by 1955. Fortunately, lobotomy has fallen out of favour though it is probably still practiced occasionally.

The misinformation that allowed this brutal procedure to be performed for some 30 years, however, is all too typical of a world in which we are fed misinformation and brainwashed into accepting any new procedure or product no matter how dangerous.

Another scandal in psychiatry, in the authors' view, is the way in such drugs as valium are prescribed over the long term to people. Such drugs are bound to be addictive and when patients forget to take their daily dose there will inevitably be withdrawal symptoms.

Such drugs, like the brain stimulant tobacco or the depressant and tranquilizer alcohol, alter pulse rate and blood pressure. Smoking two or three strong cigarettes in an hour, for example, will increase pulse rate significantly. The sudden change when the next 'dose' of the drug is missed is what we know of as withdrawal symptoms, in the case of alcohol an increase in blood pressure and pulse rate.

Unless absolutely necessary, therefore, it seems madness to addict people to such drugs when they might only be briefly affected by some stressful event in their lives.

Still more reprehensible, however, is the virtual invention of such 'diseases' as Attention Deficit Hyperactivity Disorder

(ADHD) as a poor explanation why young children are not doing well at school. They are then put on drugs for the long-term and may well be left feeling that they will suffer this really nonexistent disease for life.

All this is good for the medical profession as they can provide parents and teachers with an answer for why children are not doing well scholastically. They can also much increase the size of the practice with the many visits the child will have to make for further prescriptions.

It is also good for the pharmaceutical profession which sometimes in the past has rewarded doctors financially or with holidays and other perks to encourage them to prescribe their drugs.

In the case of ADHD we firmly believe that, except in the case of mental retardation, the problem will usually be one of poor study habits and motivation, often exacerbated by lack of a home environment that encourages good study habits and a much too long and drawn out education system.

Krech's experiments with rats are noted in Chapter 21. These tellingly demonstrated the positive effects of enriched environments on the brain development of rats.

Maria Montessori provided clear evidence that an enriched environment accelerates learning ability by taking poor children in Rome and placing them in stimulating classrooms with many interesting puzzles and objects to work with. The children were reading enthusiastically by three or four and were well into geometry by five or six.

Not only are most children brainwashed into semi-zombies by their mid-teens, if not before, by the media and advertising, they are often drugged to ensure they are almost brain dead!

This is called freedom in morally and often bankrupt Western societies.

ALTERNATIVE MEDICINE

Today many alternative medicine practitioners abound, for example *naturopaths* who advocate such ludicrous practices as *aromatherapy* and *reflexology*, and practitioners in Chinese medicine who advocate the sometimes dangerous practice of acupuncture.

To suggest that such practices might be helpful with such common ailments as influenza is absurd.

Added to this there are organizations that specialize in weight loss programs, health centres incorporating gyms and swimming pools that provide fitness programs, companies that have cures for baldness and countless other business keen to take money from gullible people.

Another example of brainwashing are the long-winded infomercials shown on TV in the early hours to persuade us to buy often ridiculous beauty treatments and fitness equipment and programs.

What is needed most, perhaps, is an alternative medicine approach to the increasing pressures placed upon the worker-slaves by rampant capitalism. In this regard such activities as Pilates might be useful. The trouble is that these will simply consume more money!

CONCLUSION

In recent centuries in particular, science has advanced dramatically in a wide range of areas. As always in human history, however, many new scientific developments have tended to do more harm than good, the arms industry being a prime example.

Another is the growing practice of over-prescription of drugs for the long term for problems ranging from high blood pressure and prostate enlargement to depression and ADHD.

In Australia, for example, an incredible 250,000 prescriptions for ADHD were being made per year in 2006. It seems that something far worse than Orwell's 1984 is at hand when we now medicate and/or incarcerate those with any deviation from psychological and behavioural perfection.

More disturbing, in 2010 an Australian Federal Court judge found that the arthritis drug Vioxx doubled risk of heart attack, an example of how many drugs have dangerous side-effects.

An amusing example of how scientists are prone to mislead us, if not themselves sometimes, is given in an essay by Michael Gardner (Carey, 1995). In this a German geology professor Johann Beringer who, like many American fundamentalists, did not believe that fossils were relics from millions of years ago, held that most fossils were carved by God himself when experimenting with his creations of life.

He was therefore delighted when his helpers began to unearth stones with images of strange insects, birds and fishes never seen before. Then stones with Hebrew letters appeared and in 1726 Beringer published a huge Latin treatise on these findings. Colleagues suggested that he had been the victim of a hoax but Beringer refused to believe them.

Eventually, it was said, a stone turned up with the professor's name on it. His reputation was ruined but he was immortalized by his folly, a new edition his misguided treatise being published 27 years after his death, a translation of it being published in the USA in 1963.

The bottom line: In 2005 a Greek epidemiologist concluded from a study of 49 medical research articles that about half of published science turns out to be wrong.

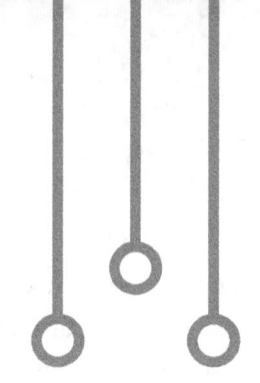

Chapter 9
THE INDUSTRIAL REVOLUTION

It is brought home to you ... that only because miners sweat their guts out that superior persons can remain superior.
George Orwell, The Road to Wigan Pier (1937).

INTRODUCTION

Some of the pure sciences such as mathematics, physics and chemistry were discussed in the last chapter, including medicine because it was perhaps the first science that occupied man's attention.

Here the innovations of mechanical and electrical engineering that led to the industrial revolution are discussed, this in turn leading to advances in the building and arms industries.

The agricultural revolution led to man living in small communities and towns (Cipolla, 1974). As far back as the ancient Egyptians, however, priests and military men held the highest positions in the country and the king was always from one of these two backgrounds (Egerton Eastwick, 1896). Ruled by monarchy supported by a host of priests and military men, the common man through much of history since that time has been condemned to serfdom.

With the advent of the industrial revolution these peasants moved to the cities to work as little more than slaves in factories, a process that has been taking place in modern China in recent years.

MACHINES FOR AGRICULTURE

Bulls were tamed by castration around 4500 BC in Western Asia and horses were tamed in India around 2500 BC (Cipolla, 1974). In Europe the steppe horse was tamed somewhere between 2000 BC and 1500 BC in the Lower Volga and Hungarian regions of Europe.

These horses and oxen were harnessed for plowing, originally using the throat-and-girth harness and later the modern collar harness.

Wheeled vehicles were used in Sumeria and in the Indus Valley circa 3000 BC and their use spread into Egypt, and possibly China, before 1500 BC. The earliest wooden cartwheel found in Europe was estimated as dating back to 1900 BC and was found in a Neolithic roadway in the Netherlands.

The horseshoe is thought to have been invented by Celtic inhabitants of the Alps circa 400 BC and prolonged the working life of horses and oxen considerably.

Jethro Tull made the first seed-drill about 1701 and used it on his own land despite much opposition from his labourers (Odle, 1966). He did not patent it until 1733.

WATER AND WIND POWER

Sailing boats are depicted on Egyptian vases dating 3500 BC and were plying the Eastern Mediterranean by 3000 BC (Cipolla, 1974).

Water-mills appeared at around the same time, in the first century BC, in Europe and China (Cipolla, 1974). In China they were first used to blow metallurgical bellows whereas in Europe they were used to grind grain and press olives. In medieval times their use was extended to producing cloth, paper and iron.

Windmills date back to Persia in the 7th century AD and appeared in Europe and China in the 12th and 13th centuries respectively.

Until the industrial revolution, however, man's use of water and wind power was limited.

POWER FOR TEXTILES

James Hargreaves, who had worked as a carpenter and hand-loom weaver in Blackburn, Lancashire, was asked by his employer to make an improved machine for carding wool (untangling the fibres) in their raw state. Observing an ordinary spinning wheel he hit upon the idea of a spinning jenny which could spin several threads at once. His first spinning jenny was made in 1764 (Odle, 1966).

In 1768 a mob of angry cotton labourers gutted Hargreaves' house and destroyed his machinery. He moved to Nottingham and, with a partner, took out a patent for his machine in 1770.

In 1769 Richard Arkwright took out a patent for a horse-powered spinning-frame. In 1775 he patented a carding machine and made other machines for drawing and roving cotton, reducing it to thinner strands for feeding to the spinning-machine.

In 1789 a mob smashed up his mill but he continued his work regardless and in 1790 he applied steam power to his spinning frames. In that same year he heard that a mob was preparing to march on his Derbyshire mills and he organized a battery of guns and issued 1500 small arms and 500 spears to all able-bodied men in his employ. The would-be attackers dispersed before reaching any of his mills.

STEAM POWER FOR INDUSTRY

Thomas Savery patented one of the first steam engines in the late 17th century. His device worked by pouring cold water into a steam filled vessel to create a vacuum which then drew up water from mines (Odle, 1966).

IN 1712 Thomas Newcomen invented a steam engine for the same purpose using the same 'condensation-vacuum' principle but which used a piston working within a cylinder that could be linked to other equipment, the greatest single advance in the history of steam power.

In 1769 James Watt patented a design which dramatically improved the efficiency of the steam engine by using a stop cock to pass the steam from the cylinder into a separate condenser.

Watt's engines used steam at a pressure of only 5 lb per square inch (5 psi) but by 1812 Richard Trevithick was making much more efficient steam engines with pressures of 40 psi, sometimes extending this to an unheard-of 150 psi.

In 1840 James Nasmyth built a steam hammer to press steel plates for ship building. His design was adopted in Europe for various metal forming processes and steam power and the industrial revolution had begun in earnest.

STEAM POWER FOR TRANSPORT

In 1788 Scottish engineer William Symington built the first steam boat, a small pleasure craft. By then he had already build steam road locomotives and fourteen years later he built a steamboat which towed two 70-ton barges (Odle, 1966).

In 1801 Richard Trevithick built a steam road locomotive and in 1804 he built the first steam locomotive to draw a load on rails, carrying 10 tons of iron and 70 men in 5 wagons at 5 miles per hour.

In 1825 a locomotive designed by George Stephenson pulled 12 wagons of coal and 21 wagons of passengers for ten miles at speeds of up to 12 miles per hour, taking 65 minutes for the journey. This success led to the construction and opening of the Liverpool-Manchester Railway in 1830.

In 1837 Isambard Kingdom Brunel built the 1340 ton steamship *Great Western*, the first true Atlantic steamship. It had 750 horse power (HP) but his third and last great ship, *Great Eastern*, had a massive 8300 hp.

Later the Parsons steam turbine was adapted for use in ships. It did not prove economical for low-speed ships but was used successfully for naval vessels which it drove to speeds of up to 35 knots.

ELECTRIC POWER AND LIGHT

In 1819 Danish scientist Oersted discovered electro-magnetism. In England only two years later Michael Faraday showed that electric current could be turned into continuous mechanical motion, the principle behind the electric motor. Ten years later Faraday made the first experimental dynamo which turned mechanical energy into electrical energy (Odle, 1966).

In 1884 Charles Parsons built his first steam turbine. It span at 18,000 RPM to produce 75 amperes of current at a potential of 100 volts. This was the forerunner of the massive hydroelectric and coal-fired power-stations of today.

William Murdock piped gas into his cottage in Cornwall in 1792 to illuminate it. Prior to that time oil lamps had been used for artificial lighting.

In 1798 he began work on providing lighting for the Soho works of Boulton & Watt which manufactured steam engines for dewatering mines. By 1804 the firm was ready to start selling Murdock's primitive lighting equipment.

Early in the 18th century Humphry Davy invented the electric arc-lamp which was used in mines but was too hot and costly for use in houses. In these two sticks of carbon almost touched and the arc closed the circuit.

Joseph Swan began experiments to develop incandescent electric lights in 1848. By 1860 he had developed carbon filaments with the strength and flexibility of metal. These he placed in glass bottles from which the air had been exhausted but he was not able to develop a good enough vacuum to prevent the filaments simply burning up.

Five years later an air pump that created much better vacuums was developed in Germany by Sprenger. It was a further ten years later, however, before Swan met Charles Stearn, a bank clerk familiar with the Sprenger pumps. They repeated Swan's 1860 efforts using a Sprenger pump with better results and, after further work, Swan's lamp was demonstrated in public in 1878. In 1881 he formed a company to make and install lamps and in that year his lamps were installed in the Savoy theatre, on a passenger ship and in the House of Commons.

In 1879, working along similar lines to Swan, Thomas Edison made a successful electric light bulb and patented it in Britain, Swan having patented his procedure for evacuating his bulbs a few months earlier. Fortunately, dispute was avoided by forming a joint company.

THE ELECTRIC TELEGRAPH

The electric telegraph was developed by Charles Wheatstone and William Fothergill Cooke and first used in 1837 between the Euston and Camden Town railway stations, some two miles apart (Odle, 1996).

In 1839 their telegraph was installed between Paddington and West Drayton railway stations, a distance of 13 miles apart. By 1868 over 16,000 miles of telegraph line had been installed in England.

In 1851, after a first unsuccessful attempt in 1850, the Brett brothers laid and successfully tested an undersea cable between Dover and Calais.

The service was immediately opened to the public and was the forerunner of the intercontinental cables spanning the oceans that we have today.

In 1867 Alexander Graham Bell patented the telephone which became the massive global telecommunications industry of today.

Indeed, with the advent of the mobile phone brainwashing of people into zombies seems to have reached an unsurpassable level!

NEW MATERIALS

The Romans used cement-lime blended with silica to produce the first really weather-resistant cement but it was not until the 18th century that inventors began trying to produce artificial cements (Odle, 1966).

It was Joseph Aspdin, a Leeds bricklayer, who in 1824 patented Portland cement, naming it after the stone which he thought it resembled. His cement was made by mixing finely ground chalk and clay and burning it at high temperature to produce clinker which, when finely ground, produced cement far superior to any before.

In 1839 John Bennet Lawes, after three years of experiments, found that calcium phosphate was an effective crop fertilizer. He had produced 'superphosphate' by using acids to decompose bones and mineral phosphate. He soon found it cheaper to use mineral calcium phosphate, large deposits of which had been found abroad, and thus the fertilizer industry was begun.

In 1856 Henry Bessemer developed the steel-making process named after him. Before that time, steel-making was slow, inefficient and expensive. In the Bessemer converter fine jets of air are forced through the crude iron. This oxidizes impurities such as carbon, phosphorus, silicon and sulphur, in turn creating intense heat well above the 1500 °C melting point of steel.

The result was that in the next 40 years the production of steel in Britain went up 30 times and the cost of steel was reduced by 80%. Everywhere cast iron was replaced by steel and in 1883 the first steel ship was launched.

Polythene was discovered in 1933 at ICI. It is made by compressing the gas ethylene and extruding the resulting solid. In 1938 the first ton of polythene was made by a commercially viable plant.

Highly flexible and waterproof polythene is used in a wide variety of ways, for example for packaging consumer goods. More important, it was the first of many man-made plastics.

The synthetic fibre Terylene was discovered by J.R. Whinfield and J.T. Dickson in the laboratories of the Calico Printers' Association in Lancashire in 1941. Subsequently it was developed commercially in collaboration with ICI and widely used for clothing.

THE MOTOR CAR

In the 1850s, James Young, a Scottish chemist established the basis for oil refining. In 1851 E.L. Drake drilled 70 feet through bedrock in Pennsylvania and began the development of the American oil industry (Cipolla, 1974).

In 1860 a French engineer J.E. Lenoir patented a gas engine. In 1884 Dr N.A. Otto made a gas engine with a four-stroke cycle. A year later Daimler-Benz cars took to the road successfully using petrol engines and the Otto cycle.

The rest is history, as they say, and reciprocating engines were used in the first aircraft engines until the first jet airplane was designed by Frank Whittle and flown successfully in 1941.

Vance Packard entitled a chapter of a book *America's Toughest Car - and Thirty Models Later* (Packard, 1960). For a similar reason Ralph Nader rose to prominence in the USA during the 1960s with his book *Unsafe at Any Speed*, the point of which was that cars are more of a fashion statement than anything else and, therefore, just another example of the almost universal practice of *planned obsolescence.*

With the current fad for four-wheel drive cars with massive engines which are driven on sealed roads in perfect condition to go shopping we encounter another of the finest examples of brainwashing.

MEGACITIES

Worse still, our major cities have become bloated by building them around the car. The result is city centres filled with unsightly high rise office buildings which resemble massive filing cabinets in which multinational companies make their offices.

Workers in these miserable offices often commute absurd distances back and forth each day along choked freeways while, all the while, the planet's finite oil reserves are rapidly running out.

It suits the transnational companies, of course, to have their offices and factories in a limited number of such megacities around the world. That is the way of globalization.

It cannot be more economic, however, to ship cars from one side of the world to the other. The high cost of this must inevitably be borne by the consumers.

It cannot be best to develop a nation around one or two megacities and at the whims of transnational companies and this has long been realized by many people who are often called 'left-wing', the usual propaganda of big business.

An underdeveloped nation, and Australia could be deemed an example because of its comparatively low population density, is surely better developed by building larger numbers of cities with no more than a million people in each.

Austin, the capital of Texas, one of the richest states in the USA, for example has a population of around half a million. In the same state Dallas and San Antonio have populations around a million, Forth Worth about half a million and Houston approaching two million, presumably because it is on the coast.

In Australia we have more than 40% of the total population crammed into Sydney and Melbourne, an insane situation no doubt brought about in part, at least, by transnational companies usually basing themselves in these two cities.

RADIO AND TV

In 1896 the Italian physicist Guglielmo Marconi patented the first wireless telegraph. In 1901 he successfully sent signals between Newfoundland and Cornwall and in 1914 he began experiments which led to the 'beam' system of directed long distance transmission.

In 1889 the English photographer William Friese-Greene, after much experiment, patented sensitized celluloid for fixing photographic images and the same year successfully took his first moving pictures on it.

In 1925 John Logie Baird was first to transmit pictures from one room to another. He showed his system to the Press and a scientific society and a company was formed to develop it. Eleven years later, the BBC began regular transmissions using his system but eventually chose to use the Russian-American Zworykin's system because it was able to obtain better definition by using more lines (Ogle, 1966).

Both radio and TV have had a great effect on our lives, providing and endless source of free entertainment and communication to people all over the world. The downside of this is the endless brainwashing new programs and advertisements subject us to and we shall discuss these subjects further in Chapters 13 and 14.

THE PC

The digital computer was an important invention but early devices were large and very expensive and affordable only to large companies, government organizations and Universities.

In the 1970s 'minicomputers' were developed which were about the size of a refrigerator and these were typically able to handle a dozen or more computer terminals. These terminals began in the mid 1970s to switch from teletypewriters to 'video display units' (VDUs) which are now called monitors.

Minicomputers usually used BASIC, a simplified version of the powerful but unwieldy FORTRAN computer language which had been designed for use with punch cards. BASIC was developed by Kemeny and Kurtz at Dartmouth College (New Hampshire) in the early 1960s and early versions required only 16 kb of RAM.

In 1975 the first microcomputer was sold, a clumsy box + switches affair with storage of only 256 bytes. In the same year Tiny BASIC, consisting of just 20 pages of code, was written and many versions of this quickly appeared and, also in 1975, Gates and Allen launched Microsoft Corporation with their version, this being marketed with the Altair microcomputer.

A flood of microcomputers with as little as 16 kb of RAM then appeared, the Sinclair ZX80, the Apple, the Commodore 64, the Spectravideo, the HP85 and many others, all having their own version of BASIC.

In the early 1980s IBM quit their near monopoly of the electric 'golf ball' typewriter market, switching to production of *PCs* with about a MB of RAM. Now there was a flood of PCs, Apple, IBM, ICL, NEC, Olivetti etc., as well as many IBM 'clones.'

With the advent of a MB of RAM or more Chris Cochran and American Planning Corp's MegaBasic appeared to make full use of it. Then came Visual Basic (VB) which was used to produce the Windows operating system.

The downside of this was the great amount of *value adding* that occurred in developing PC software. Originally the DOS operating system and its predecessors were given free with every PC, along with a version of BASIC.

The latest versions of Windows, however, have become increasingly expensive. So too have the latest versions of VB and Microsoft Office. As a result, if you now want VB to learn BASIC as well as a word processor, a DB program, and a spreadsheet program, then you will have to pay a lot more than the price of a perfectly good PC!

This is a somewhat radical change from buying a computer with startup software free in the early days of the PC business and it is not surprising that many people regard Bill Gates as something of a robber baron.

CONCLUSIONS

So what has all this to do with brainwashing and consumer zombies? A brief history of the industrial revolution allows a brief look at examples of people inventing new things. The point is, perhaps, that overnight somebody might invent a new, useless and possibly harmful type of drink, say Choke a Cola. Are you going to feel impelled to buy it?

In the same vein here is a list of examples, most of them relating in some way to the inventions discussed in this chapter, of how the advertising industry might make a sucker of you:

[1] Inventions for agriculture were fine, but how about more recent inventions in the food business such as:
   (a) Coke: why on earth won't people support the local brand?
   (b) Junk food: 50 million people eat junk food every day, a very sad commentary on just how brainwashed we are.
   (c) Kellogg's: ditto (even we can add sultanas to cereal).
   (d) Confectionary: addicting young children to sugar is criminal.

[2] Wind power? That reminds us a little of the countless unnecessary and often ridiculous sports, including sailing.

[3] Clothes? They used to say fashion goes in cycles. Now the girls try to look and act like boys and the boys try to look and act like apes. We therefore think we are in a cycle with a much larger 'time diameter', namely reverse evolution.

[4] Trains and ships? The travel industry is certainly one of the most wasteful and pointless. Generally people spend a lot of money to spend their time in foreign bars and restaurants. My father used to call tourists rubber necks which is appropriate.

[5] Electrical goods? When the first author was young simple yo-yo's where a craze. More recently portable CD players and Ipods are the craze.

[6] How ubiquitous the mobile phone has become as a result of marketing and the pyramid effect of social and imitative learning is hard to believe.

[7] New fabrics? Yes, the first author is old enough to remember buying clothes in new fabrics such as Dacron and Terylene because they were new.

[8] Cars? As said earlier, another fine example of how gullible we are and how corrupt big business is. As discussed in Chapter 12, Clive Sinclair built a halfway credible electric car for about 25% of the petrol car price in the mid 1970s.

[9] Megcities? When big biz expects people to work longer hours and some of them have to commute for 2+ hours a day they might be tempted to buy an inner city apartment and live in a filing cabinet for people as well as work in one. They might as well have a brain transplant with a dog as donor to complete the happy picture.

[10] Radio and TV? Try counting (in Australia) the number of ads in a bracket sometimes, and then note how many of them are for foreign products. Why should we worry about the commies when these crooks have taken over the country already?

[11] The PC? The way we were pushed into using the Internet is one of the finest examples of treating people like rats in a Skinner box that we have seen.

The bottom line is that workers of the industrial revolution in England in the 19th century rented a house in a row of look-alike houses and worked in a factory at the end of this depressing street. On Saturday nights they could scarcely afford a couple of pints of lousy beer from the pub at the end of the street, all of which was no doubt owned by the man who owned the factory. Thus this lifestyle was comparable to that of slaves in Rome who lived in the bowels of a very large house.

Today workers live in a somewhat comparable way, housing being increasingly unaffordable and there is no security in marriage, employment or anything else.

In Australia company taxes have roughly halved in the last 20 years which means that the workers are footing most of the tax burden. In any case even the smallest companies can write off assets and use such artifices to escape tax all together.

In like fashion executives with exorbitant salaries, bonuses and share options are able to minimize tax.

The workers are not. If they beat the odds and manage to pay off a house the increasingly privatized health care business will take it away from them if they live to any great age.

The reality is that in a capitalist society you have to be born rich. Many of the greatest inventors during the industrial revolution were examples of that, often having to work in poverty to develop their ideas and then sell them for a pittance to large companies.

So, if you can't beat them, join them and make/import and/or sell some simple product(s). It's easier than making them and a hell of a lot easier than inventing them! The problem is you might need some startup capital which we can't help you with, and that brings us back to the problem of capitalism really stifling human life far more than providing anything like freedom for most people.

The bottom line is that most people in the world are now condemned to being little more than slaves, if they can even get a job that is, and they are thus *deprived by the depraved* executives who make up to $1,000 a minute for making sure businesses are more profitable, a result being that ordinary people stand longer in queues like brainwashed sheep waiting to be fleeced.

Chapter 10
EDUCATION

Whereas a rattle is a suitable occupation for infant children, education serves as a rattle for young people when older.
Aristotle, Politics bk 8 (1340 BC).

Indeed one of the ultimate advantages of an education is simply coming to an end of it.
B.F. Skinner, The Technology of Teaching (1968).

A BRIEF HISTORY OF EDUCATION

In Western Civilization our recorded history of education centres on the Greek and Roman civilizations. In the last stages of the classical Roman education system the Trivium (grammar, rhetoric, logic) and Quadrivium (music, astronomy, geometry, arithmetic) evolved and these were the basis of the medieval arts course in Europe centuries later (Niblett, 1969).

Elsewhere, before the medieval period academic pursuits were largely limited to clerical education in monasteries.

By the 12th century, however, a few cathedral schools were well established and these began to study law, albeit mainly clerical law.

Gradually small schools were established in most towns where basic education in reading and writing was given for a few years. Few families could afford to pay for such education, however, and much of the population was semiliterate at best.

The thirteenth century saw the development of the first Universities, in Paris and Oxford, and the 14th and 15th centuries saw many new Universities established in Europe. In these training was based on the three stages of membership of the craft-guilds: apprenticeship, journeymanship and mastership.

The ancient Trivium and Quadrivium, however, were still the framework of the arts course that all had to take before moving on to the higher courses of Theology, Medicine and Law.

A preliminary examination was required for entry to the first apprenticeship stage, one of study, at the end of which the student was examined for the bachelorship. The bachelor was then still under instruction but assigned certain courses of lectures. Then finally he was examined for his mastership, a licence to teach.

In the 14th century the Inns of Court were established in England to meet a growing demand for teaching common law

In 1368 the master-surgeons formed a guild and in 1540 the Company of Barber-Surgeons was set up with a monopoly of practice and teaching.

In both law and medicine, therefore, professions were raised in status and competence by initiatives of their members that were more responsive to the needs of society than academic institutions.

During the renaissance, as in biblical times, apprenticeship remained the main method of training.

The 17th century saw interest in science increase and new colleges began training in technologies such as mineralogy and glassblowing. By the end of the century most scientific work in England took place in laboratories in London, not in Cambridge and Oxford.

The 18th century saw many new academies established which spread higher education to a middle class of trade and industry.

In the 19th and 20th centuries the school curriculum grew to place more emphasis on science to educate students for an increasingly technological world.

Today, however, students in most Western countries spend at least 12 years at school and this is excessive. The early years of school are, as much as anything, simply conditioning for the routine for working life.

To add insult to this injury tertiary education courses have been introduced for a myriad of areas for which they were not required in the past.

Worse still, countless absurd postgraduate courses such as Sexology and Puppetry have been introduced, reducing the education system to long drawn out farce.

PRESCHOOL EDUCATION

Early brain development was discussed in Chapter Two. It is very important to take advantage of this capacity for early learning to provide infants with a stimulating environment which should include a 'personal learning centre' (PLC) that includes educational pictures and toys.

By the second year they should be involved in small learning groups supervised by a specialist teacher so that they can begin real learning (Packard, 1978). In the third year they should begin kindergarten for at least a couple of days a week and these learning efforts should continue. By now they have a modest vocabulary and are capable of *cognitive learning* which processes and stores *abstract* information.

At this stage deliberate effort should be made at 'IQ building', noting that IQ tests include questions testing verbal, spatial and numerical ability. If a child has a problem with numbers, for example, early detection and correction of this will prevent far greater problems later.

Then, given a head start,[1] they should commence school at age four, rather than the usual five in most countries.

LEARNING CURVES

Suppose the degree to which a person or group has learnt something or been conditioned is given by the probability $p = 0$ to 1, and p depends on n, the number of repetitions of the learning process.

If we assume that the learning process is hyperbolic so that the degree of learning gradually increases towards 100% or the asymptote $p = a$ with $a = 1$, then this is represented by the hyperbola of Figure 10.1(a), the equation for which is $p = an/(b + n)$

This equation can easily be rearranged to give

$$n/p = (b + n)/a$$

so that if we plot n/p against n the straight line of Figure 10.1(b) is obtained and the magnitude of the intercept with the n axis $= b$ whilst, of more interest, the inverse slope of the line equals the horizontal asymptote a of the hyperbola.

---

[1] 'It's never too early to start teaching our kids', The Weekend Australian, Aug. 13-14, 2011.

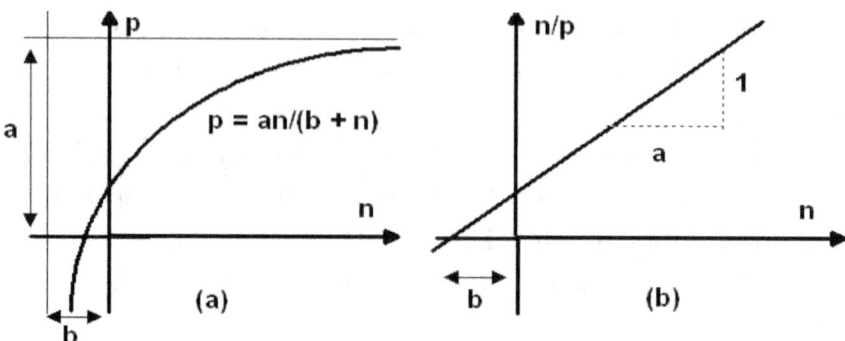

Figure 10.1. Mohr Plot for learning.

In experimental situations this plot is useful in testing whether results are indeed hyperbolic and, if so, estimating the 'ceiling' value towards which some variable is converging.

Applied to the memory of a single person we set $a = 1$ and a typical result might be $b = 3$, $n = 3$, giving $p = 0.5$, or 50% memory retention after three repetitions. Here p is either:

(a) How well an item is learnt. People's names might be a good example of this. Ourselves, we often think one needs about three repetitions of such things to remember them.
(b) How much of a 'block' of information is learnt. An example might be a list of names where, because of *interference*, words at the beginning (the *primacy effect*) and end (the *recency effect*) are remembered best.

For a slower learner, on the other hand, b might double to 6 so we need $n = 6$ to get $p = 0.5$ or 50% learning.

Applied to conditioning of the populace by advertising, p is the proportion of the population affected and larger values of the asymptote b which flatten the curve might occur when there are two or more competing advertisers in the market. In politics this highlights the advantage of dictatorship.

In education it perhaps highlights the importance of avoiding conflicting messages so that it is often best to learn one subject at a time.

THINKING

In education the four elements of thinking should be used carefully:

[1] **Images.** We often use *visual imagery* in thinking. For example, we often find it easier to describe the shape of something by sketching it or a physical operation by demonstrating it.
[2] **Symbols.** Language involves the spoken and written use of symbols. These symbols can be words, mathematical formulae, pictures (including diagrams, maps and graphs) or gestures that represent either *objects, operations, relationships* and *qualities*.
[3] **Concepts.** Concepts can be defined as categories that represent a class of objects, events or qualities wherein each item has a number of common features. A simple example are birds which 'mentally' are a concept and these have common properties such as two legs, wings and the ability to fly and lay eggs.

   Such categorization is important for both efficient learning and memory storage and efficient recall and thence thinking.

   Learning of concepts is made easier by *transfer* when they are similar to already familiar concepts.

   When driving, for example, when you see a set of traffic lights (a concept) you note which colour is 'on' and quickly decide (a thinking process) what action to take.

[4] **Rules.** Rules involve connections between features of a concept and between different concepts.

In the example of traffic lights we should know the rules and have only to choose 'yes' or 'no' as to whether we follow the appropriate rule.

The rule for traffic lights might be represented as

(green = go) OR (amber = slow down) OR (red = stop)

and the rule for driving might be written

(accelerator = go) OR (no accelerator = slow) OR (brake = stop)

so to stop at a red light we have to connect the two rules, a process probably carried out in short term memory.

CREATIVE THINKING

Creative thinking to obtain new ideas often involves *divergent thinking* (Morgan et al., 1979) and typically occurs in three stages:

(a) **Preparation:** define the problem and resources needed.
(b) **Incubation:** acquire information and think or dwell on the problem.
(c) **Assembly:** combine information to form the solution.

In a much too drawn out education system endless classes with a lecture format should occasionally be replaced by sessions with a seminar format. Sometimes these could involve *brainstorming* to solve a problem, for example devising an effective advertising campaign for a product.

Group brainstorming has been found effective because:

[1] People tend to have twice as many ideas in the group situation because of the more stimulating environment, 'cross fertilization' of ideas and arousal of competitive spirit.
[2] Alternation of individual and group thinking improves results.
[3] As more ideas are produced they tend to improve.
[4] Second sessions a few days later improve results because of the 'incubation' process so important in creative thinking.
[5] The group uses *critical thinking* to evaluate the ideas.

SHORTENING THE SCHOOL PROGRAM

No better example of *Parkinson's Law* exists than in education. Parkinson's Law is simply (Parkinson, 1980):

Work expands so as to fill the time available for its completion.

Leonardo da Vinci and Michelangelo were apprenticed at age 14 and Francis Bacon went to Cambridge University at age 12 and left at age 14.

The development of modern science from the 16th and 17th centuries is, perhaps, one of the reasons for the considerable growth in the number of years required at school.

Nevertheless, our system of 12 years at school is far too drawn out and should be reduced to 10 years for the 'average' student, this involving six years at primary school and four at secondary school.

Here the curriculum for the last four secondary years could remain much as now so that reduction to 10 years would be achieved by condensation of the first eight years of the 12 year system to six.

This might simply involve

(a) Making preschool education compulsory and thus removing the need for at least the first year at school.
(b) Acceleration of the learning of the three R's in the first few years and elimination of most unnecessary material.

The result should be better educated and brighter children who will be better prepared for life and the faster pace of tertiary courses.

LESS FRAGMENTATION

Classes at both school and University are usually scheduled in a somewhat haphazard fashion so that hours of subjects A, B and C appear as A, B, C, A, B, C and so on. This results in a 'parade of clowns' effect that does more to confuse students than anything else.

The present author has always found it better to, for example, give two lectures consecutively, rather than at almost random times in the week a day or more apart.

This has the advantages of:

[1] It saves students and/or staff a considerable amount of inconvenience.
[2] It results in better learning because more *proactive interference* and less *retroactive interference* occurs (Morgan et al., 1979).
[3] A break of about 10 or 15 minutes is allowed in the middle and this provides a good opportunity for questions and discussion.
[4] The result is a more mature and friendly seminar approach and more motivated, inquiring and effective students.

Similarly, in the first years of school it might be better to tackle the 12 times tables, for example, by devoting a few weeks to it, rather than spreading it over years.

Then if the learning task is returned to a week or two later it should be found that *latent learning* has occurred and good progress has been made.

Indeed, it might be a good idea in later school years to fit classes into four days to allow students a fifth week day to do homework. If unnecessary activities were removed as far as possible then, for example, just half an hour more of formal classes per day might allow all the required class work to be fitted into four days.

Application of this less fragmentary approach is possible at University when students might have four or five subjects with one day of the week dedicated to each, rather than having them randomly spread throughout the week in bits and pieces.

UNIVERSITY COURSES

There has been excessive proliferation in new University courses. My father, also an academic, used to joke about there being degrees in bee keeping in the USA. At the more reputable Universities there this may not, in fact, be the case. In Australia, however, this has come to pass with degrees where none were needed before, examples being journalism, marketing, nursing and viticulture.

There has also been a plethora of new postgraduate certificates and diplomas and Masters Degrees. Some of these, such as courses in Sexology, Puppetry or Citizenship studies are either lightweight, absurd or both.

Material that is really essential should have been included in undergraduate courses.

Some so-called postgraduate courses, on the other hand, introduce an entirely new vocational area. If these are all that is really required in these areas then these courses should be offered as relatively short undergraduate certificate or diploma courses.

That we have masters "courses" at all is questionable. Mastership in Universities took its meaning from the Master status conferred by the craft-guilds of 500 or more years ago and was given after a relatively short period of teaching experience. Consequently, Cambridge and Oxford award Masters Degrees on completion of undergraduate courses.

Why then do 'latter day' Universities enslave their students for a couple of further years in usually redundant, if not frivolous Masters Degrees?

The answer undoubtedly comes in two parts:

(a) The education bureaucrats are ignorant.
(b) Simply money. The longer the education process, the more "products" and the more money to be made.

Research degrees may also be questionable. As just noted, Masters degrees as separate and additional courses are redundant. As for PhDs, historically these were awarded for further self-study, usually by academics. This has no connotation of teaching so that it is absurd that graduates are now able to be enrolled as "students" and then used as slave labour at the whim of supervisors for often impractical, if not useless, research topics.

TAFE

TAFE, an acronym for Technical and Further Education that originated in the UK, is an important alternative to University for school leavers. Here students are trained for the *real* occupations in the basic industries essential to human life, that is, food, clothing and shelter.

In contrast, and increasingly so, University courses are, strictly speaking, unnecessary. In other words we can usually live without a doctor or lawyer, house builders can usually do without an architect or engineer if need be. People used to run businesses without business degrees and we certainly don't need degrees in Sexology and Puppetry.

Many TAFE courses are part-time ones for apprentices. Unfortunately, many apprenticeships are unreasonably long and bordering on exploitation of a cheap labour source. An example are hairdressing apprenticeships which we believe take up to 6 years in Australia, certainly too long when most us would think a couple of weeks training would suffice.

Another looming problem is the slow introduction of diploma and degree courses in business to TAFE institutes when absurd numbers of people already do these in the Universities. Even MBA courses, let alone undergraduate business courses, are lightweight material that could and should be taught at school.

PROBLEMS IN EDUCATION

There are many problems in the education sector today, including:

[1] Children being incarcerated in long-day-care centres which, cruelly, do little more than expensive babysitting almost from birth. This is an inhuman practice that reduces children to toys that amuse parents after work, a sick situation that must do more harm than good.
[2] As the discussion of brain development in infants in Chapter Two points out, the early years are a critical time that should

not be lost. Weiss and Mann (1978), for example, refer to a project in Milwaukee that found that children given more attention by the mother or a specially trained teacher, showed markedly higher IQ.

This is no doubt the reason that only children tend to have higher IQ and that, in families with more than one child, the eldest child has a slightly higher IQ on average (Vernon, 1960).

The youngest child in larger families, on the other hand, does not do too badly compared to those 'sandwiched' in the middle and perhaps most deprived of attention.

[3] As noted earlier, 12 years at school is too long and 10 years would be a more sensible norm.

[4] There is far too much rote learning at school.

[5] Poor teacher training. Sykes (1995) reports widespread disillusionment with modern teacher training, much of which is a hotchpotch of psychology, sociology and history that cannot develop real expertise in any of these areas.

He cites several examples of recent doctorates in education being granted for dissertations with such titles as:

"The use of goal setting and positive self-modeling to enhance self-efficiency and performance for the basketball free-throw shot" for a PhD at the University of Maryland.

After such largely useless studies, Sykes laments, 'educrats' move into educational administration and oversee a decline in standards over the whole spectrum of education comparable to that evidenced by their largely irrelevant doctoral studies.

[6] Declining academic standards. A survey of 24,000 students in twelve countries by the Educational Testing Service in Princeton found that, compared to 40% of US students scoring at the 500 level in a standard test, the results were 78% for Korea, 73% for Quebec and 69% for British Columbia (Sykes, 1995). A similar decline in standards has occurred in Australia.

[7] In the USA outcome based education (OBE) has gone a long way towards disallowing fail grades, instead allowing students to retake tests until they pass. The idea of this is to avoid attaching negative labels to students, and much effort is also made to avoid attaching positive labels to the brightest students as well.

[8] Similarly, OBE eschews 'tracking' to permit accelerated learning for gifted students, despite conclusive evidence of its positive results, in this way ensuring that the overall standard of education is lowered further.

[9] In the USA new 'soft' approaches to teaching and grading reading and maths have led to a dramatic decline in literacy and numeracy skills.

[10] Drugs for school-age children. The overlong school education system should bore anyone with half a brain. To make matters worse increasing numbers of 'unruly' children are diagnosed with such doubtful disorders as Attention Deficit Hyperactivity Disorder (ADHD) and prescribed drugs such as Ritalin to sedate them.

In the USA and Australia in turn, increasingly large numbers of children suffer this fate. Reports of up to 15% or more children in some areas being on such drugs have not brought action to curb this disturbing trend as yet, but visions of a future society in which both parents and children have to be drugged to cope are unacceptable.

[11] Overgrown educational bureaucracy. In the US in 1960 one third of education employees were not classroom teachers. By 1991 46.7% were non-teaching staff and the teaching staff's share of the total payroll had shrunk from 54% to 41%. Much the same has occurred in England and Australia both in school and tertiary education.

[12] Growing up faster. Today's young, thanks to better nutrition grow faster than in the past. Da Vinci observed that children were half their ultimate height at age three. Now that figure is about 55%. Along with that, in part because of the ubiquitous media today, in many ways they mature faster than ever before. Many children by their mid-teens, therefore, are becoming bored with school and drop out. Robertson (1981), for example, reported that 100,000 assaults against teachers occur in US schools each year. Doubtless this is one of several factors that contribute to the increasing discipline problem in schools.

[13] There are far too many assignments, tests etc. at school and University. When the first author was an undergraduate and teaching in Universities in Australasia there were 8 subjects in second year engineering, yet in Engineering Maths students were given sheets full of problems each week. It should be all about showing *how* to do things and giving *answers*, not asking endless questions. At Auckland University these maths problem sheets often involved 2 or 3 different areas lectured by different people, an absurd situation. Including the secretary who typed them, up to four morons helped fill their week redoing these sheets each year, a fine example of Parkinson's Law for both the staff and students.

Needless to say:

(a) The staff were simply a pathetic, mindless bunch of no-hopers who had never, and never will, achieve anything.

(b) The students were somewhat demoralized. Eight Uni. subjects in a year is too much, let alone being asked to spend up to several hours on the worse than useless homework for just one of them.

[14] Many University courses overlap with school. At Auckland University, for example, top school leavers were exempted from the first year of the course. Q: Why on earth, therefore, was that year needed at all? A: To employ a few more dumb academics.

Excessive growth in tertiary courses.

[15] The ridiculous University courses like those in sexology were mentioned earlier in the chapter. MBAs etc. are not much better and are now so common that with an MBA one might now only be able to gain employment as a salesperson, if that.

[16] Once upon a time correspondence courses were poorly regarded. We are such slaves to fashion, and thence brainwashing, that the morons in Universities are happy to run courses by *distance education* over the Internet.

[17] There is insufficient emphasis on developing inquiring minds capable of finding answers to their own questions, rather than zombies so used to endless rote learning and tests that they have become too tired and bored to care about anything but going through the motions of life as perpetual consumers and slaves to big businesses that produce and sell mass marketed consumer products.

PERSONAL EXPERIENCES

Perhaps an example of the decline of Western Empires, particularly England post WWII, it was the first author's 'Cambridge connections' that, in part at least, destroyed his arguably brilliant academic career. His first quick, but satisfactory at least, 300 page book effort on the Finite Element Method (FEM) in 1979 was sent to CUP at his father's unwise suggestion (avoid the devil you know).

Two reviews followed via an editor who is said to have knocked back Hawking's first book, one sensible, the other ridiculously imploring "a treatise of two volumes" (ridiculous because if in doubt err on the side of caution).

Forced to follow the latter, the project became a nightmare so that, new to Auckland University in 1980, at the end of the year he nearly killed himself condensing it to 330 pages. Subsequently the 'tome', as he came to call it, slowly expanded again.

By the time it got to 500 pages again he was demoralized by a pathetic new Cambridge PhD (in maths). He held that "Civil Engineers (such as he) are stupid". He asked his old HOD in Melbourne to help on it. Three's a crowd they say, and ultimately the HOD bullied him into 'walking the plank' at the end of 1984, virtual suicide for an academic pushing 40.

He endured many witless interviews by morons for top jobs from 1985 through to 2008, the last being to head up a new Australian secret service research organization, a farcical situation as he had had the Cambridge VC, who his vague nocturnal [and perhaps subliminally desperate] phone calls annoyed, have him tailed around the streets of Melbourne's St Kilda day and night by 'spooks,' their interest perhaps related to the fact that the CIA will not release their file on him.

Another example of Western decline was the fact that, picked up on a point at the viva voce for his (Cambridge) PhD by the external examiner (an older and computer illiterate Cambridge man, of course), the first author proved that he and/or his Indian research student, had faked their results.

Better still was the night watchman [ex British army] in the computer centre where he worked alone each night possible till dawn. When he first met him he piped up with: "What this country needs is another war to get it going again."

After resigning under extreme pressure in Auckland he remained on the dole (or nothing at times) but continued his work in poverty (as usual), publishing the aforementioned 'tome' with OUP in 1992 after 13 years of effort. For a couple of those he minded two half-dead parents, during which his father did, indeed, die. Meanwhile, not uncommon many people agree, 'big brother' sold their house and spent half the proceeds doing a cheap renovation on a cheap replacement house.

Work also continued on his 'name' field of FEM, a cruel irony being finding in 1998 that, in his one paper on FEM, the ex-HOD he had tried to joint his long-running 'tome' with had faked his results. To do the right thing he had put his name on a shorter book that he managed to get published fairly quickly in Melbourne (1986) and London (1987). The ex-HOD rewarded him by saying at one point in 1985: *"If you fuck this up I'll make sure you never get a job in Australia."*

He succeeded: the first author never felt able to use him as referee, whilst the Auckland HOD, hindsight made clear, was back-stabbing him, the bottom line being that, in a world full of corruption, there is no truer cliché than 'power corrupts' and, therefore, it you have 2 bad bosses in a row, as 'GAM' did, you are in trouble if left without friends in the right places, as he was.

Indeed, having suffered all too many interviews by panels of 'done nothing, never will' morons around Australia and overseas, sometimes over a couple of days and organized by numbskulls in redundant HRM departments (a fine example of Parkinson's Law), the first author is in no doubt that recruitment procedures need change. For example, why not introduce a little real intelligence into the procedures, for example giving candidates copies of the referee reports and a list of questions 'on notice' (in writing) well before interview? That would make things far more open and honest.

The first author in the mid-1990s wrote an entire MBA course involving 14 subjects ranging from business finance, economics, maths and OR, IT and numerical methods, to the more lightweight areas of BP (business policy), business law, HRM and advertising.

The concise lecture notes came to about 400 somewhat cramped pages and he tried to publish this course without luck, but was pleased that an editor at Heinemann agreed with his proposition that, a lucrative Harvard invention, MBA courses could now be found *"on every street corner,"* yet another example of how the USA has debased the education system.

CONCLUSIONS

IQ in the UK diminished by 1.5% between 1920 and 1950 (Vernon, 1960) and two decades ago it was claimed that the average American IQ was diminishing (Fancer, 1985), some claiming that it is now dropping by about 1 point per generation. Judging by the international survey results quoted earlier this has, indeed, happened and the country is deep into reverse evolution.

Australia is probably the most Americanized country in the world and our education system, particularly in the Universities, has certainly become farcical. There it is no longer a matter of education but one of highly paid 'educrats' who have never done anything significant overseeing invention of increasingly ludicrous courses to advertise to increase the size of the University.

From birth to death it is all corporate stuff at the day care centre, school and University and, increasingly, those being brainwashed pay for the privilege.

With the invention of more silly courses and nearly everyone having an MBA students are expected to study longer and longer.

During the first author's undergraduate student days a lecturer explained that, owing to the *time value of money*, we would not in our lifetimes make as much money as a plumber who had started work at 15, even if we were paid substantially more. Plumbers make far more money now than they did way back then!

If your parents spent a lot of money on a private school education the comparison is even worse. Unless they were rich they should have spent just a little of that money to give you the edge at a government school. The rest they should have invested at a good interest rate to buy you a shop in which to start up a lucrative business.

Then you might not need to go to University to study Accountancy, Architecture, Engineering, Dentistry, Law, or Medicine, businesses in which it really is best if you start up your own practice and that may be in a shop front office anyway!

As for postgraduate study, this is a form of slave labour. The first author recalls a physicist saying "You're past your best at 26." True of nearly all bludging academics who regurgitate from some text book they don't understand and sit on their backsides while graduate students do their research for them.

Chapter 11
POLITICS

A democracy exits whenever those who are free and are not well-off, being in the majority, are in sovereign control of government, an oligarchy when control lies with the rich and better born.
　　　　　　　　　　　　Aristotle, *The Politics* (343 BC)

Just as Darwin discovered the law of evolution of organic matter, so Marx discovered the law of evolution of human history.
　　　　　　　　　　　　Friedrich Engels, said at the funeral of Karl Marx (1883).

INTRODUCTION

　　Man's first leaders were tribal elders who passed on learning and wisdom to the young. It is probable that most practical learning came from their parents, however, and that leaders simply brainwashed tribes with religious and other bullshit, as they still do today.

In many parts of the world tribes were polytheistic and often believed in *animism*, that natural objects possess a soul (Bell and Hall, 1991).

With the coming of the Agricultural Revolution small communities and towns were built up and *pantheism*, the belief that God and the universe are the same, become widespread in Asia. A little later monotheism emerged in the Middle East.

Some of the preachers of these religions eventually became 'priest-kings' with secular as well as religious authority. This in turn led to the form of monarchy that prevailed throughout much of the world from the time of the ancient Egyptian civilization circa 3000 BC.

IMPERIALISM

Man's imperialism first assumed grand proportions in the Egyptian Empire. Alexander the great is so-called because he founded the great Greek Empire. The most impressive of the ancient empires was the *Pax Romana* which dominated Europe from circa 30 BC until 476 AD (Cowie et al., 1994).

In the seventh century the Islamic empire began to develop and early in the eighth century it had spread to Spain and threatened France.

From this Islamic zeal sprang the Turkish Ottoman Empire which established control over Asia Minor, captured Constantinople in 1453, and over the next 200 years conquered the whole of the Balkan Peninsula and Hungary. The Ottoman Empire survived until 1919.

In the Renaissance of the 14th and 15 centuries came Portuguese exploration of much of the world, and this was followed by exploration and colonization of much of the world by several European nations.

This imperialism had a strong economic motive because it provided new sources of raw materials needed for the industrial revolution and created new markets for industrial products.

As noted in Chapter Five, however, European imperialism had the religious pretext of 'civilizing' heathen natives. The truth is that it was monarchs who encouraged exploration and colonization for nationalistic and economic reasons.

DEMOCRACY

Aristotle's remark about oligarchy which opens this chapter is an important reminder that, as then, we do not have *real* democracy today.

The populations of the Greek city-states of his time rarely exceeded 10,000 people, all the 'citizens' of which voted with black and white stones on the questions of the day in open forum.

Aristotle's complaint was that it was only the men and not women or slaves who were allowed this privilege and slavery, of course, can hardly be equated with democracy.

In most of the world today we do not have anything like real democracy. We have, in fact, Westminster type *parliamentary democracy*, a very brief history of which is (Mackenzie, 1950):

Pre 1066 (Saxon times). The barons and King met each year at Easter, Whitsun and Christmas.
1258 (in the reign of Henry III). A meeting of the barons of England at Oxford was the origin of the *House of Lords*.
1264. Simon de Montfort, on the King's behalf, organized a meeting of two knights from each county.
1265. Two citizens from each county were included in the latter meeting, constituting the origin of the *House of Commons*.

In the reign of Elizabeth I the puritans became the first party and were the opposition to the crown.
In the reign of Charles I the cavaliers and roundheads emerged as two opposing political forces.
1681. The origin of the names *Whig* and *Tory*.

This system has evolved in England, Australia and New Zealand into the two main parties being a conservative party, which supports the capitalist ruling class, and a Labour Party which traditionally supported the workers or modern-day slaves.

The Conservative Party is said to be *right wing* and the Labour Party *left wing*, a fine example of the power of emotive language.

Now, however, big business has considerable influence on both parties and the policies of the Labour Party are often more conservative than those of its opposition conservative party.

The result is a revolving door parody of democracy in which stooges become our leaders for relatively brief periods but their policies are greatly influenced by the business sector and the economic imperialism of traditional allies in war, in Australia these being the US and UK.

In this parody the 'fat cats' of the public service wield more influence in policy-making than do average members of parliament (Self, 1977).

CAPITALISM

While so-called democracy prevails in most of the world, the reality is that, with the world's markets becoming increasingly global, transnational companies and thence unrestrained capitalism provides the power and influence that runs the politics of most countries.

In the 1930s John Maynard Keynes proposed that a multiplier effect existed such that small increases in government spending in the community have a much greater effect upon the productivity of the nation. This is the *fiscal* approach and was widely adopted by many countries in the West for about 50 years.

Milton Friedman and other economists favour the free market or *monetarist* economic philosophy. This stems from the 17th century and is based on the equation (Wonnacott and Wonnacott, 1979)

$$MV \text{ (aggregate demand)} = PQ \text{ (aggregate supply)} \quad (11.1)$$

where
　M = the amount of money in circulation (per year)
　V is its velocity of circulation (in transactions per year)
　P = the price of goods in circulation
　Q = the quantity of goods in circulation (per year)

Here V is the only relatively stable quantity and is based on the fact that, when you buy a product, the money you pay for it might be passed on quite soon as wages for somebody in the company you bought the product from. Then that person spends their wages on food and other necessities, and so on. Typically V takes a value of around 4 in modern economies.

This little or no government monetarist approach has led to more rampant capitalism than ever before. As a result an 'establishment' that effectively rules capitalist countries is formed (Blondel, 1963).

This establishment deplores the mildest hint of socialism and thence government ownership of industry, or even influence over industry. *They* tell government to reduce company taxes further and to cut back on government spending to do it and governments continue to heed them.

Effectively running military-industrial countries like the UK and US as they do, the barons of capitalism have ensured that their governments fight the evil threat of socialism, for example leading to the British secret service providing considerable covert support to the White Russian army resisting the 1917 revolution. When that failed they began counter terrorist activities against the new Russia such as Lieutenant Agar's sinking of the Red Fleet cruiser Oleg in Kronstadt Harbour in 1919 (Brook-Shepherd, 1998).

Some evidence of such policies was given by the first president of the National Civic Federation in the USA when he wrote in 1909: "Our enemies are the socialists and other labor people and the anarchists among the capitalists."

In the 1970s David Rockefeller funded the Trilateral Commission which in 1975 funded a meeting of multinational corporate executives to consider the "excess of democracy" afflicting advanced capitalist countries and to "rationalize the US economy through capitalist dominated planning and in conjunction with other leading capitalist nations to reassert US authority on a world scale" (Crough et al., 1980).

MODERN NEO-COLONIALISM

Former colonies of rich nations remain heavily linked to the First World in dependent relationship often termed 'neo-colonialism' (Bell and Hall, 1991). Reasons for this dependency include:

> ➢ International trade and investment policies usually favour the rich nations which, for example, often set tariffs to protect their own agricultural industries.

- Multinational companies are sometimes more powerful than Third World countries and establish factories using cheap labour, using the threat of withdrawal from the country to keep wages very low.
- The practice of lending large sums of money to poor countries has left them with unpayable debt burdens which have undermined their economic growth.
- Western investment policies, educational programs and aid usually benefit the elite and modern sectors of Third World economies, distorting development patterns and reducing economic diversity.
- Western advertising of products such as tobacco and bottle milk formula has distorted consumption patterns in some poor countries and also caused long-term health problems.
- The high cost of Western arms cripples strife-torn countries in such places as Africa.
- The high cost of Western pharmaceutical products, for example for treating AIDS, adds another crippling burden to the fragile economies of poor countries in Africa.

Not surprisingly the former USSR was actively trying to encourage socialist governments in some poor countries in northern Africa in the 1970s and 1980s. The political situation in some of these countries remains unstable at the present time.

SOCIALISM

It is important at the outset to note that *socialism* refers to the 'means of production' being owned by the state whereas *communism* refers to the means of production being owned by the people. The two terms are often confused but in a complex and highly technological modern society it is doubtful that communism is practical. It is doubtful, for example, that the very large companies required in some industries, many of these now transnational ones, can be owned and run by the 'people', taking people to mean those in a particular community.

What is clear, however, is that the 1848 Marx-Engels manifesto was anti-capitalist and this was the real spirit of the 1917 Russian revolution, a spirit which many believed would eventually spread globally. This revolution created a socialist state with a long term view towards forming a communist society.

Marxists argue that the capitalist *class* accumulates increasingly more capital or a 'surplus value' in fact created by the workers. The working class, therefore, are left to accumulate misery or, as Marx put it:

In proportion as capital accumulates, the lot of the labourer be his payment high or low, must grow worse.

Critics of this view will point out that in practice state ownership leads to totalitarian government which makes the people worse off, rather than better.

Marxists will also argue that in capitalism monopolies or oligopolies must eventually develop, in turn influencing the political system so that something akin to totalitarianism can result.

In defence against this view critics of Marxism will argue that it is better to reform the capitalist system, not replace it, for example by introducing antimonopoly laws.

Theoretical arguments aside, revolutions have always occurred when there are high levels of unemployment and poverty.

Capitalism, however, relies upon a substantial pool of unemployed to keep the price of labour down (Sweezy, 1946). As a result, some studies found little reduction in poverty in the USA in the years 1947 - 1960 (Townsend, 1970) whereas socialism has reduced poverty and famine in China dramatically (Maxwell et al., 1977).

THE USSR SYSTEM

Though the USSR has been more or less dismantled, some aspects of its system remain whilst socialist systems operate elsewhere in the world. Moreover, the communist party in Russia, for example, still has a good deal of support. Hence some discussion of the USSR system as it was is still worthwhile, principal features of that system being:

In the USSR policy was based on five year plans. Critics would argue that this was too inflexible and did not allow for adjustments. But business plans might typically be five year ones and allow for adjustments, so this argument is invalid.

Without a free market coordination was difficult. Supposing we wished to increase steel production, for example, then we needed extra plant to make it and in turn extra steel to make the plant, but where could we get if from? In other words it is difficult to be self sufficient as a single entity despite a perhaps massive size.

Again the argument is invalid, there being nothing to stop a country like Russia from having two steel organizations, typical of the common duopoly situations in the USA.

Circa 1970 investment in the USSR ran at about 30% of GNP (about the same figure as Japan at the time and twice that for the USA), this funded by a 30% general sales tax (GST). This high level of investment was aimed at building industry but resulted in excessive restrictions in consumption and chronic shortages in goods.

Such a rate of expansion, however, was never going to be permanent and therefore must have been a positive developmental stage, a period of shortages for the general public being far less of a problem than the sacrifices involved in war, economic or otherwise.

In the USSR system there was effectively no such thing as unemployment as everyone could be given a job, however unproductive.

Russia has now established a free market economy but still has an authoritarian government whose style is reminiscent of that of the USSR and which has much more control over the economy and business than in the West.

WHAT OF THE FUTURE?

Not long ago some economics texts asked the question about socialism and capitalism: "Are the systems converging?"

About the USSR, at least, it is now safe to say that its system has changed and some aspects of socialism, such as centralization of power, have been much reduced. Before the USSR was dismantled, however, there had long been changes such as a greater tendency to pay highly skilled workers more, less interventionist government and slow opening up to outside (and hence not state) capital.

About the future in the USSR, or China, for example, it therefore seems safe to say that there has been a move in the direction of capitalism (and democracy, but this is not necessarily synonymous with any particular economic system).

What can we say about the USA and like countries? Clearly there is some disenchantment with the two party system that may begin to crystallize somewhere. In Australia, for example, three independents and the Greens party currently (2011) hold the balance of power in both the legislative lower house of representatives and the upper house or senate which is required to approve legislation from the lower house.

In the USA, on the other hand, it is not impossible to imagine a (rich, if not very rich!) independent being elected president.

Some mention should now be made of the Arab and other Muslim countries that have attracted much attention of late. These, taken collectively, may have an increasing voice and influence in world affairs.

Finally, what can we say about China? What influence will such a potentially powerful country have in the future? Presumably it will increasingly join the global economy and consequently move a little to the right politically.

PROPOSALS FOR CHANGE

Some authors suggest that inequality in capitalist societies should be reduced by reducing the inheritability of wealth, in other words by increasing death duties (Broom et al., 1980).

This is an unpopular proposal to both the rich and the middle class. As a result the Australian state of Queensland abolished death duties many years ago and other states only apply them to large fortunes.

Others have suggested a policy of equalizing outcomes, an approach that might penalize effort as well as inheritance (Jencks et al., 1975).

A more original and interesting proposal was made by Peter Jay (1981), a former economics editor of *The Times*:

> *- - that the enterprises which create the wealth, the firms, the corporations, should belong to, be owned by, should have their directors exclusively appointed by and their*

The Brainwashed | 211

net assets and their residual earnings should belong to, and exclusively to, the people who work at them.

Jay suggested that it is an accident of history, not a law of economics, that the entrepreneur has tended to be the person who supplied the risk capital. He proposed that in modern economies worker-owned companies should be able to raise debt finance from banks and equity finance from shareholders in the usual way.

Capitalists are happy to have their workers become shareholders, of course, because shareholders do not have to be paid dividends in bad times whereas banks always require interest to be paid on loans.

Jay's proposal goes a lot further and might eliminate the absurd salaries, share and rights bonuses, and retirement packages we see today. Indeed, it would only seem fair that *all* workers for a corporation should receive share issues as a nontaxable part of their income.

A criterion that the modern welfare economist employs in deciding whether a given change is 'efficient' was developed by Vilfredo Pareto (Buchanan and Tullock, 1962). This relies on the ethical postulate that the 'welfare' of a group of individuals is said to be increased if

[1] Every individual in the group is better off, or if
[2] At least one member of the group is better off, without any member of the group being made worse off.

This is illustrated for the case of just two individuals X and Y in Figure 11.1 where the axes measure 'welfare' or 'utility' of the individuals and any point on the line $X_m Y_m$ is a Pareto-optimal state.

Any movement from such a point to another point on or outside the curve must reduce the utility of one of the individuals.

If we assume some initial position A, then moving to any point on the curve between B and C is clearly Pareto-efficient because both parties are better off. Moving to point D, on the other hand, is not Pareto-efficient because *Y* will be worse off.

Here it should be noted that a person is deemed better off when they move from one position to another freely of their own choice, that is, 'better off' is subjectively evaluated. A common example might be people who reduce their working hours and salary in order to improve their overall quality of life.

There are clearly many changes that can be made to either of the capitalist and socialist extremes that might result in a compromise that might improve the overall position of people. That monarchies no longer play an active role in government in the world is an example that significant change is indeed possible.

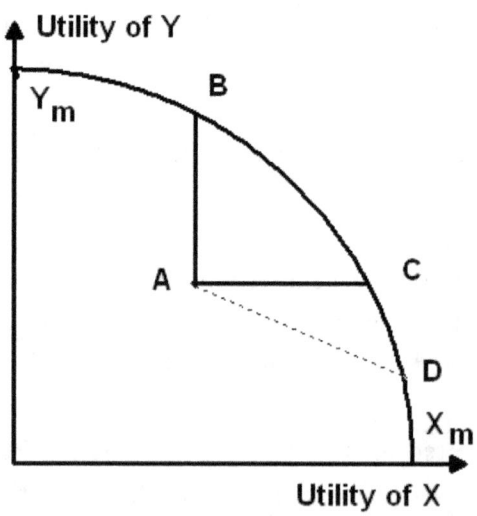

Figure 11.1. Illustration of Pareto-optimal states.

THE FIRST AUTHOR'S FATHER

The first author's father, 'CBO' as students called him, worked in Rutherford's team in Cambridge University's Cavendish Laboratories when they split the atom in 1931 (see Chapter 8). Subsequently, having got wind of such developments, the KGB ran meetings at Cambridge and Oxford which, ostensibly on the basis of decrying the prospects of war with Germany, influenced students and staff like Kim Philby, Donald MacLean, Guy Burgess and Anthony Blunt to become lifelong socialists and double agents for Russia within the British secret service.[1]

CBO too was a socialist, being a long-time member and one-time president of the Australia-Soviet Friendship Society, an organization kept under close scrutiny by ASIO and its allies.

On consumerism he held that something was not a bargain at any price if you didn't need it, and also that the more gadgets you owned the more trouble and expense you will have maintaining them. He never smoked and drank very little, at one time introducing the family to the range of Baitz liquers after Friday dinners, the company having been started by a Russian immigrant.

A brilliant student, he had been dux of his school and also Melbourne University before going to Cambridge. An 80 year old maths teacher at MGS taught both he and the first author and remembered CBO well, once saying to the first author: *I hope you will be as good at mathematics as your father.*

CBO Mohr often took his family to Chinese restaurants and deplored advertising which he thought unnecessary and found very irritating, especially on radio and TV. Now China's still booming

---

[1] In fact, Philby later said that he had been recruited first and had recommended the other 3 of the 'Cambridge Four' (Knightly, 1988).

economy is much based on cheaper products, not only because of cheaper labour which unscrupulously greedy capitalists are happy to exploit, but also because the Chinese spend comparatively little or nothing on advertising.

Ourselves, we believe in *real democracy*, more of a middle ground between socialism and capitalism such as occurs in China, economically at least, with spectacular success.

This would involve governments still owning at least some of the banks and most, if not all, of the essential utilities because, undoubtedly much of the current economic malaise in many of the Western economies today is because Governments have sold off these cash cows to avoid growing debt and help pay for often bad and expensive election promises.

Now they have nothing left to sell. As it is, in Australia, at least, bank and mining company profits are obscenely great whereas Government ownership of some of the banks and resources gives more competition and control in the sector. In contrast, China is able to exert far more control over its interest and exchange rates and thence its economy, and the results speak for themselves.

PERSONAL EXPERIENCES

While in Auckland the first author lived close to the city in the suburb of Mount Albert. Going to vote one day in 1984 he noticed an Auckland University colleague handing out how to vote cards. This made him think about politics a little. After all, he had been to Churchill College Cambridge and he was reminded of that polling day by seeing a few years later that the Labor member for Mount Albert, a female senior lecturer from Auckland University did, indeed, become Prime Minister.

Notable too on that day, his perpetually backstabbing wife agreed the night before to vote National like him so that their votes didn't just cancel out. In fact, her vote opposed his, a typical act of lying and deceit. With wives like that you don't need further enemies to increase the already hopeless odds against you but, of course, that deceitful woman turned just about everybody possible against him.

Back in Melbourne, in 1987 'GAM' did join the St Kilda West branch of the Liberal Party, attending meetings with his Thatcheresque English lady friend. At the outset he was offered presidency of the branch which he foolishly declined. Ultimately he tried for pre-selection in the state seat of Melbourne Ports in 1988 and the federal seat of Aston in 1989.

A minor technical objection to his modest campaign was revealed in 1988 so that didn't help, though the man who won back the pre-selection was hopeless and never had a chance.

In 1989 the seat in question was miles away from where GAM lived and he was a complete outsider who only appeared in the area for just the one day of pre-selection.

Still you never know, perhaps he might yet resurrect one day as a politician. After all, Winston, as Margaret Thatcher always referred to him, became PM again at age 76.

CONCLUSION

In Westminster the Tories vs. Whigs farce has changed to Tories vs New Labour, with the Liberals on the fringe somewhat.

A former Australian finance minister wrote in his 2011 book *Dumbing Down Democracy* that politicians now consider appearances far more important than outcomes, lamenting that the resulting "sideshow syndrome" was eroding informed democracy as the basis of decision-making.

Thus we conclude that the politico-economic systems of both the 'east' and the 'west' will doubtless continue to change slowly. Whilst current trends are towards freer capitalist markets it is certain that this trend may be slightly reversed at some point.

The communist party in Russia might currently have less than 50% of the vote but that might not last. Thus Russia could be counted as roughly 8 on the 'commie scale' at present, as could China, with India perhaps about 6.

Some countries in South America and much of Africa, on the other hand, are in a state of economic collapse, as usual, and God only knows what 'colour' their politics is. In some cases not simply 'red' to whatever extent, but often the politics of chaos one supposes.

China, currently in the middle stages of a 1960s style Japanese economic build up, will play an increasing role in the world economy. So too will Russia and India.

Indeed, Russia and China, of course, have a common socialist past and retain cooperation in some areas. For example, in July 2016 it was announced that they would hold joint naval exercises in the South China Sea in September, this at a time of international tensions over China's disputed territorial claims in the area.

China, of course, is not immune from corruption. Some claim, for example, that corruption by government officials is rife, some having siphoned off large amounts of money to remote banks, eventually investing the laundered money in the US and elsewhere.

One of the Chinese companies involved in this activity, Longtop Financial had Deloitte as their auditor for six years but, after recent forensic investigations, Deloitte felt forced to quit.

As noted in Chapter 6, however, China is now the biggest holder of US debt, so that the aforementioned corruption (according to Deloitte) may, in fact, be part of how that came about, perhaps with some degree of official encouragement from the Chinese government at large.

Regardless of the politics of a country, however, politicians will always mislead the brainwashed public. Edward Suchman gave useful definitions of some of the tactics used to cover-up failures in policy (Davis, 1974):

[1] *Eye-wash:* deliberately selecting for evaluation only those aspects that 'look good' on the surface.
[2] *White-wash:* avoid any objective evaluation.
[3] *Submarine:* 'torpedo' the program.
[4] *Posture:* use evaluation as a 'gesture' only.
[5] *Postponement:* delay needed action by pretending to seek the 'facts'.

So what can you do about it? Most of us realize just how cynical the so-called democratic process in the world today is and we don't care.

One thing you can do, however, is become a member of the local branch of the political party of your preference. At the meetings of this you will be able to express an opinion that will be heard by at least one politician, as well as the other members of the branch.

Perhaps you might even end up starting your own party, or at least thinking about running for election yourself!

Then it might pay to remember a tactic for getting on with people mentioned in John Dean's book *Blind Ambition*. Dean was President Nixon's Attorney General and the youngest ever to occupy that post. He wrote that in the White House at that time they used the term *stroking* to describe how one can 'butter up' (with perhaps artificial compliments, praise, niceness etcetera) a person who one wanted to persuade in some way. Worth considering!

Chapter 12
BIG BUSINESS

*A society in which consumption has to be artificially
stimulated in order to keep production going
is a society founded on trash and waste, and
such a society is a house built upon sand.*
    Dorothy Sayers, British writer (1893-1957)

*The public has become pretty cynical about big
business and for good reason. Sometimes our cars were
so bad, they felt we built them that way on purpose.*
    Lee Iacocca (referring to the Chrysler Corporation)
    Iacocca: An Autobiography (co-written
    with William Novak, 1985) ch. 15.

MOHR'S LAW OF MONEY

The fundamental principle of capitalism is the exponential growth law (equation 12.1):

$$d(\$)/d(t) = \text{const.} \times a \; (= \text{activity}) \qquad \text{where } a = \text{const.} \times \$$$

Here the rate at which money is made is proportional to the rate of business activity, this in turn proportional to the amount of money available to fund this activity.

Combining the two constants above as $k = c_1 c_2$ we have equation 12.2:

$$d(\$)/d(t) = k\$ \text{ where } k \text{ is the } \textit{growth factor.}$$

This is *separable* which means that it can be integrated in the form

$$\int d(\$)/\$ = \int k \, d(t) \qquad (12.3)$$

giving, with the inclusion of the initial values, the exponential growth law (equation 12.4)

$$\log_e \$ - \log_e \$_0 = k(t - t_0), \quad \text{or} \quad \$/\$_0 = exp[k(t - t_0)]$$

If, for example, the growth rate is 10% per year, that is $k = 0.1$, then over 10 years we obtain the growth ratio $\$/\$_0 = 2.7$, so that we have nearly *tripled* our money. Not bad at all!

The same law governs population growth (using a symbol such as x for population in place of $\$$), for example if every 25 years 0.5 more children are born than people die we have $k = 0.02$, and this will give a 22% increase in population every 10 years, or 2.7 times in 50 years.

Noting that old adage about suckers

There's one born every minute.

this population growth could also be factored into the calculation of Equation (12.4), further increasing the profits.

Finally, note that the foregoing calculation considers business *growth*, not interest rates. In most cases the business is financed by both debt (bank loans) and equity (share issues) and interest and dividend payments need to be subtracted from the growth ratio result. If the cost of capital, that is the weighted average of the interest rate and the dividend rate is 10%, the same as the growth rate, then we will have had to pay out this 10% ten times so the profit = (growth ratio - 1) = (2.7 - 1) = 1.7. Still quite good as we have here borrowed *all* the money for the business and repaid none of it. If we now repay all the debt we are still left with a tidy 0.7 profit.

THE FINANCE AND INSURANCE INDUSTRIES

The crux of how the banking system works is as follows. The reserve bank holds the *statutory reserve deposits* (SRDs) of the trading banks, a set ratio called the *reserve ratio* (R) of their total deposits.

Suppose, for example, $R = 0.2$ and \$M1 is deposited by a customer in a bank. The bank can now lend \$M0.8 to a customer who passes this (by cheque) as payment for property etc. to a customer of another bank who deposits the cheque. This second bank can now lend 80% of this amount and so on, so that a series of demand deposits results:

$$\delta D = \text{original deposit} + 80\% \text{ of latter} + 80\% \text{ of latter} - - - -$$
$$= 1 + (1 - R) + (1 - R)^2 + - - - - = 1/[1 - (1 - R)] = 5 \quad (12.5)$$

so that \$M5 of demand deposits are created as a result of the original \$M1 deposit, an effect called the *multiplier effect*.

If you are the only bank in town, of course, then all the business flowing from this one deposit is yours! In other words, the banking business is easy money compared to real work.

Indeed, around 1200 AD the church reviled people who charged interest on money and by the 17th century the Jews were despised by some people in Europe because of their association with banking and money lending. Indeed, this may have been Hitler's gripe with them. Another theory is that he had caught syphilis from a Jewish prostitute but that seems less likely.

The insurance industry is another nice one to be in. Again something like a multiplier effect occurs so that you need only have enough funds to cover a small fraction of the number of insurance policies you issue.

On a smaller scale, of course, is the pawnshop, a pretty ruthless and sad business if there ever was one, and interest rates of the order of 10% per month are the norm.

Some say that second hand shops, and thus pawnshops, thrive in times of depression (Batra, 1988). Like all too many other businesses the pawn business has gone multinational with companies like Cash Converters. This is obviously because now rampant capitalism has created a large underclass in most of the world. In England, for example, the lower class have a life expectancy 11 years less than the well-off, a figure that would be causing riots if it applied to a racial group.

VERY BIG BUSINESS: ARMS AND DRUGS

The arms race is the world's biggest business (Sampson, 1977; Pringle and Spigelman, 1981) and a ruthless one too, resulting in huge areas of the world being littered in land mines that kill and main innocent people years after they were laid.

Ancient man, presumably, made spears for hunting and then started using them in tribal warfare, perhaps a bit like using the kitchen knife as a weapon today.

A poster published in *New Internationalist* many years ago pointed out that world expenditure on arms every two weeks was then sufficient to provide "adequate food, water, education, health and housing for everyone in the world" (Bell and Hall, 1991).

Perhaps the figure 'two weeks' no longer applies but even if it were now four weeks that is still scandalous.

At a wild guess, the world's population is at least twice what is sustainable in the long term with a reasonable standard of living for all, 'reasonable' implying a fairly substantial use of resources by everyone.

Had the immense amounts of money wasted on the cold war between the USSR and the US and its allies been plowed into educating and thence reducing population growth in the poorest countries on earth then the outlook for the human race might not be so bleak as it undoubtedly is at present.

Worse still, continuing massive arms sales around the world can only lead to further conflict on a global scale. Good for business if you are in the arms business! Bad perhaps if you are not.

This is a situation that must be addressed, for example by immediately banning both the use *and* possession of nuclear and biochemical weapons.

Obviously land mines should be banned as well.

Perhaps a little optimistic, one might as well go a little further and ban any kind of bombs, cannons, and perhaps even guns as well.

That the arms industry is so massive is a symptom of sick societies infecting a sick world. Another is the huge illegal drugs industry which is often said by the news media to be the world's second biggest industry.

In this evil business the wholesale markup is 500 or even 1000 percent, the huge profits being laundered, a process involving 3 stages:

1. Immersing: replacing cash with bank accounts, traveler's cheques and other negotiable instruments or valuable objects.
2. Layering or 'heavy soaping': creating a 'paper trail' often involving foreign banks, for example Banco Ambrosini which had branches in the Bahamas, Luxembourg, and Nicaragua but not in London or Wall St.
3. Repatriation and integration or 'spin drying' (Robinson, 1998).

If we included alcohol then certainly the drug business would be the world's biggest. If one then included the businesses that involve alcohol such as hotels, and thence the tourist industry, hotels, pubs, clubs, brothels and restaurants, and heaven knows what else, then it is easy to see that Western economies would collapse if booze were banned. Just loosing the excise on booze would put a pretty big hole in national budgets.

The tobacco business, of course, used to be one of the greatest users of advertising and the booze business still is. Here the pyramid effect of social learning also plays a major role in getting children hooked for life and, of course, the best businesses are those which persuade and brainwash us into becoming lifelong consumers of their products.

JUNK FOOD

The junk food business is now, of course, a massive international one and every day staggering numbers of people around the world eat junk.

Then there are almost countless other junk food businesses such as KFC, Wendy's (= Hungry Jack's in Australia), Subway, Pizza Hut and countless Chinese take-away and old-fashioned fish and chips shops.

These all seem to involve the psychology of eating something unhealthy every day, as well as 'proper' healthy food.

To add insult to injury, fat-laden hamburgers, pizzas and chips are washed down with Coke and other sugary soft drinks.

Of course, junk food is marketed heavily to brainwash children with the general concept, not just the particular brand, and there is always a junk food shop around the corner to tempt children on their way to and from school.

To this unhealthy consumption we can add heavy-in-fat chocolates, sugar loaded sweets, and several types of salty snacks fried in unhealthy oil. These products too are marketed heavily to brainwash children directly or through the pyramid effect of social learning.

We can also add countless other unhealthy items in the supermarkets such as frozen pizzas and pies, high-in-fat biscuits, and soft drinks.

ENTERTAINMENT, BOOZE, SPORTS, GAMBLING AND SEX

The movie business is still big and TV, videotape and DVD perhaps make it bigger than ever. Similarly, the music business remains big thanks to the CD and, latterly, MP3 players.

Nowhere more than in these businesses are children brainwashed into acting like characters they identify with, in order words acting stupidly, aggressively and irresponsibly.

At 'rave' parties for young people primeval music seems to go hand-in-hand with drugs and booze. All good for business!

Sport, of course, has become big business too. The once tribal affair of young men occasionally playing games with stones and spears has turned into a global business in which an almost endless variety of sports and games are played.

Not long ago the various types of football were played between local teams on Saturday afternoons. Now they are played on two or three days a week both in the afternoons and evenings and televised to millions.

Motor car racing is a big business well supported by motor manufacturing companies in most countries and the Formula 1 championship series is a billion dollar business event contested in almost 20 countries and televised globally. Motorcycle racing is also a big business.

Golf and tennis are now massive sports with their main championships also televised globally.

The world soccer championships vie with the Olympic games for the title of the biggest sporting event in the world, both involving massive amounts of money.

Not only are many sports big business, they are also associated with massive amounts of advertising and the most highly paid sports stars, who already earn millions, earn even more from appearing in advertisements.

In addition, the sports equipment industry is also massive.

Gambling is now one of the world's biggest businesses. Gambling associated with horse racing is fairly big business but the casino and poker machine industries are truly massive international businesses.

As Skinner boxes do to rats, poker machines seem to hypnotize some people, with the result that they become problem gamblers some of whom ruin their lives by getting into debt way beyond their means.

Remarkably too, it is often more women than men, and often older people, that we see playing the pokies morning, noon or night. Presumably younger men are more interested in booze, watching sport on the TV or playing pool, darts etc.

The sex industry is now big business with legalized up-market brothels being a far cry from the seedy back street affairs of the past.

Sex shops abound in major cities, selling pornographic magazines and videos, and strange sexual equipment.

Ads for phone-talk or dating with sexy ladies and men appear on TV and newspapers and many of these are doubtless simply fronts for prostitution.

Many of these are for homosexuals who in our permissive, decadent and decaying society might eventually outnumber heterosexuals in some cities such as San Francisco.

Closely associated with entertainment, booze, and sex, the tourism industry is also massive. This literally props up many industries such as the airlines, as well as the economies of several countries.

Technology based industry

With the industrial revolution came the need to sell products such as:

[1] Transport: cars, boats and airplanes.
[2] Clothing: new fabrics, some with such features as 'permanent press.'
[3] Food: tinned and frozen food and countless new food products created in laboratories such as packet soups.
[4] White goods: refrigerators and washing machines.
[5] Home appliances such as motor mowers, vacuum cleaners, toasters, blenders etc.

[6] Radio and TV.
[7] Recorded music and movies.
[8] PCs, computer software and computer games.
[9] The burgeoning phone industry, including the Internet.
[10] The wine cask has helped expand the wine industry and the 'widget' (a small plastic ball) has helped give beers like Guinness their traditional head when poured from a can.

Perhaps there was no better product innovator in the 20th century than Clive Sinclair. He began making miniature amplifiers in the 1960s, then radio kits, then a 2 inch flat screen TV. In the early 1970s Sinclair's company made pocket calculators with many functions. These were small and much cheaper than competing models and a further development was the Wrist Calculator, a technical disaster but modest commercial success.

Then Sinclair moved into the fledgling microcomputer market and in 1978 produced the MK14, a computer kit with only 256 bytes of RAM that sold for around £40 only but needed a £34 VDU (video display unit) to interface with UHF TV sets and a £10 tape unit to store programs.

This was followed in 1980 by the ZX80. This was based on the MK14 but had 1 kb of RAM, came assembled for £100 and used a truncated version of ANSI Minimal BASIC. Additional 1 kb memory chips cost £16 each, however, so that to compete with its nearest competitor the Acorn Atom the total cost ran to around £300 (Adamson and Kennedy, 1986).

In 1981 Sinclair's company followed with the ZX81 which had 4 kb of ROM to store the operating system and some BASIC. With a 16 kb RAM pack included it sold for £120. The ZX81 was a great success and was one of the first microcomputers to spread the market beyond hobbyists to children and schools. Sales were 500,000 worldwide in 1982.

The ZX Spectrum followed in 1982, a colour computer amenable to simple computer games which played a key role in the massive expansion of the microcomputer market. It was followed by the Sinclair QL or 'Quantum Leap' microcomputer in 1984.

By the mid 1980s, however, IBM, ICL, Olivetti, Hitachi and many other competitors had moved into the PC market with machines with at least 640 kb RAM. Sinclair's QL microcomputer cost £400 but with monitor and printer included this rose to almost £1,000. Originally designed to have 32 kb ROM another 16 kb had to be 'tacked on' to hold the QDOS operating system and the QL's SuperBASIC.

The QL was beset with hardware and software bugs from the outset and was outsold by its cheaper predecessor the Spectrum. This was in part because the QL had failed to meet the requirements of business users whereas the Spectrum retained a games market amongst children.

At the same time Sinclair was losing money on his electric tricycle, the C5. All too typically of the impatient Clive Sinclair, this was a hastily conceived affair with a polypropylene body which measured about 6 feet long by 2.5 feet high and wide and was driven by a modified washing machine motor made in Italy. The worst bungle was that it had only lead-acid batteries to keep the price low but longer lasting nickel-cadmium batteries should have been used to give the C5 longer range.

The ugly C5 was priced at only £400 whereas one of its only competitors, the Dutch Whisper cost around £4,000 but at least looked like a conventional car. Seen by many as more of a toy than a practical vehicle the C5 was a commercial disaster.

At the start of the 20th century 35% of the vehicles sold were electric and at the time of the launch of the C5 in 1985 there were 30,000 electric vehicles in commercial use in the UK, 90% of these 'milk floats'.

As with most of his inventions Sinclair had aimed 'too small' and too cheap and he ran into financial difficulties. He was bailed out in 1985 by the publishing magnate Robert Maxwell but in 1986 was forced to sell his PC business to Amstrad. Nevertheless, he had played a major part in the PC revolution.

VALUE-ADDING

One thing that Bill Gates could have taught Clive Sinclair is value-adding. Originally the operating system and some form of BASIC came free with your PC. Bill Gates changed all that!

Now you can buy a perfectly good new PC for around $A800 if you look around and, if you are lucky, that might include a basic 'home' version of the Windows OS. But if you want latest full versions of Windows and Visual Basic that will set you back around $A2000. If you want a business version than runs on several PCs Microsoft Office will set you back circa $A1000.

This has been achieved by an immense amount of value-adding, bells and whistles covering the skeleton of a basic product that would otherwise cost a great deal less. One of these is MS Internet Explorer which, despite complaint and litigation from opposing software companies, is pushed at you to make you more likely to use MS as an Internet provider, yet another example of how big business tries to lead us by the nose and very often succeeds.

The modern motor car is a superb example of value-adding, the bells and whistles including four-wheel drive, CD players, electric windows, TV, and heaven knows what else. Very few have dual circuit braking systems, standard on Volvos long ago, which should be mandatory!

For subliminal stupidity, though, you can't go past including TVs on the front of huge stainless steel refrigerators that cost thousands. Never mind that you'll throw this expensive hulk out when the motor, which is probably worth about $20, packs up! You really have to be brainwashed to buy one of these, even if you do have too much money.

PLANNED OBSOLESCENCE

In a mid 1950s article in the *Journal of Retailing* marketing consultant Victor Lebow suggested that (Packard, 1963):

> *Our enormously productive economy ... demands that we make consumption our way of life, that we convert the buying and use of goods into rituals, that we seek our spiritual satisfaction, our ego satisfactions, in consumption ... We need things consumed, burned up, worn out, replaced, and discarded at an ever increasing rate.*

It seems that, as always, the government agreed with big business because in mid-1960 reports from the US administration advocated that faster tax write-offs of business equipment should be permitted to allow for business equipment becoming obsolete earlier (Packard, 1963).

As the second quotation introducing the present chapter suggests, the car industry is perhaps the classic example of planned obsolescence. Cars could be made to last you for life but that would not be good for business.

Tyres are an example of this. A 1959 article in the *Journal of the Society of Automotive Engineers* (USA) stated that Consumer Union had found that over a three-year period the tread-wear life of a range of tyres had declined by 18% (Packard, 1963).

More recently the plastic lids on many washing machines or the plastic doors on the freezer compartments of many refrigerators were a fine example of planned obsolescence.

Another occurs in the cheaper brands of sound equipment put out by multinational companies. In these you will find that some important feature such as the controls for such things as the tape drives will change every year or so. With this experimentation comes a virtual guarantee of something going wrong before 'too long'.

PRIVATIZATION AND GLOBALIZATION

An ongoing process in the West has been privatization of government run public utilities such as public transport and electricity, gas and water supply. Along with this the practice of outsourcing road building, recruitment and other activities has long been on the increase. These businesses are a licence to print money because they are essential services so that they *can't* go out of business. When the private company gets into trouble they are invariably bailed out by the government.

The multinational companies that persuade countries to sell off their assets invariably sack a good proportion of the work force as soon as possible so that the government has to foot the bill for yet more people on the dole.

The negative effects of globalization are felt nowhere more than in the clothes industry were brands such as Nike set up factories in Mexico, China and other poorer regions of the world to make use of their cheap labour that will work under conditions that would not be tolerated elsewhere.

Indeed, everywhere you look privatization and globalization are having negative effects and taking us back to Dickensian conditions and lifestyles.

In Australia one government organization once controlled all our phones and our mail. The now massive phone industry is now entirely privatized, resulting in decreased government revenue so that new taxes such as a GST were needed.

As things stand there is little left for the government to sell except its soul, if it has one that is, which much, if not most, of the public doubts.

Such sales have retired a good deal of government debt but, with almost no tariff protection remaining for local industry, foreign debt has begun to climb yet again. But in the future there will be nothing left to sell and we shall regress amongst the nations to what might be termed a 'second world' status, if we have not reached that point already that is.

No matter how bad things really get, however, don't hold your breath waiting for the government to admit it rather than brainwash you with the usual 'econobabble' and empty lies.

THE WORKERS

In the wake of the Industrial Revolution there came an increase in capitalism and thence globalization of many industries.

The results have included a massive increase in white collar workers at the expense manual workers (Blondel, 1963), including farm workers. This has decimated rural communities which, arguably, constituted man's natural way of life.

It cannot be deemed natural, on the other hand, for man to live or work in what a Scottish Union leader termed "an architectural representation of a filing cabinet."

In these tall buildings workers for 'heartless' multinational companies or ever greedier national ones work longer and longer hours in ever worsening conditions (Packard, 1961):

> *Even the layout of the large office is coming more and more to resemble that of the factory, with straight-line flow of work and in some cases assembly belts for moving paper work from one point to another. Each worker does a fragment of the complex operations.*

Increasing use is made of casual labour without holiday or any other halfway humane entitlements. In Australia the age at which women can get the old-age pension has increased from 60 to 65 and the pension age will increase to 67 for everybody in a few years.

These days even women with very young children are expected to work when once they didn't yet the liars in government or the purblind economists will assure you that we never had it so good. Nothing could be further from the truth with house prices absurd in capital cities, ever worse working conditions, children sent to long-day-care almost from birth, and ever decreasing standards in schools and everywhere else in the community.

In the USA things are so bad that one in six children live in poverty. In the UK, as noted earlier in this chapter, the poor have an average life expectancy 11 years less than the rich, a shocking figure that would cause riots and revolution in countries where people are less heavily brainwashed.

WHITE COLLAR CRIME

White collar crime has always been rife. In recent years we have only seen the tip of a great iceberg come to light in the media.

Routinely companies:

[1] Sack workers and refuse to pay them pension and other entitlements.
[2] Lie about their profitability and trade when insolvent.
[3] Fiddle their taxes using such artifices as massive and premature asset write-offs.
[4] Pay executives increasingly inflated salaries and bonuses as well as giving them huge stock parcels and options annually and upon retirement after only a few years. In contrast, shareholders are often struggling retirees make minimal return on their investment after inflation is taken into account.

On the latter point it might be noted that Plato felt that the top people in a society should be paid no more than five times as much as those earning least. Several decades ago some people felt that ratio should not exceed 20. Now ratios of about 500 are almost commonplace.

Everyday examples of white collar crime include bank employees embezzling money, lawyers absconding with trust accounts and doctors fiddling their books with entries for treatments never carried out, for example one doctor who would issue government 'patient service' forms to friends at parties to fill out (Hall, 1979).

Examples of jailed corporate crooks in Australia in recent times include (*The Weekend Australian*, April 16-17, 2005):

> The CEO of a real estate company who bribed a politician.
> The leader of a women's group stole $A4 million from it.

- A merchant bank CEO who obstructed investigation into its failure.
- The CEO of an investment company who committed fraud.
- The CEO of a retail chain misappropriated company funds.
- The CEO of a corporate empire "stripped" it of $A1.2 billion.
- A leading stockbroker convicted for insider trading.

The part IBM played in recording the details of Jews later sent to the Nazi death camps was noted in Chapter Six. In 1998 a consortium of Swiss banks settled out of court to the tune of $US1.25 billion for transferring the accounts of thousands of Holocaust survivors to the Nazis around the beginning of WWII.

THE FUTURE

Recently, the first author heard some fool who is global head of a leading US advertising agency talking about a book *Lovemarks* he had just had published. He advocated marketing products so that people would come to identify with and 'love' them and had lectured such rubbish in Cambridge, Stanford and like-minded Universities.

At the moment the USA, much of it already having been bought up by petrodollars since the 1970s oil price hikes by OPEC (Smith, 1981), and since then by Japan, China etc., is gain on the verge of financial crisis and has had to yet again increase its limit on foreign debt. This is exactly what Osama Bin Laden pledged that he would help bring about.

A few years ago the Chinese hi-tech company Lonovo took over IBM's PC business and China's second largest TV set maker has just merged with a French company to form the world's largest TV maker of TV sets.

The South Korean white goods company LG makes one in every three microwave ovens in the world and now has almost half of the US market for small refrigerators.

This is selling sand to the Arabs stuff which bodes ill for the already troubled US economy. It forebodes an even greater role for Asia in the world market.

The Chinese, however, ignored pleas to take over the bankrupt MG-Rover car business in the UK, seemingly good business tactics!

No doubt parts of Africa will follow the Chinese lead and industrialize using cheap labour to get an early edge in the global marketplace. By the time that happens resource depletion in an already grossly overpopulated world will become even more frightening.

Do they brainwash the citizens of China? Surely the situation cannot be as bad as in the "force-fed society" of the USA (Packard, 1963). Surely not as many as one in six children in China live in poverty, as in the supposedly richest country in the world, the USA. Surely the average life expectancy of the poor is not 11 years less than that of the well-off, as it is in the UK.

Surely too the Chinese are unlikely to become as decadent as the West any time soon and, one hopes, they do not have the appetite for war that has punctuated the history of England and later its now staunch ally the US.

Still, given time, no doubt the Chinese will become as corrupt and incompetent as we are in the West.

For example, obsession with growth has led to the building of whole cities of empty high-rise apartment blocks that few can afford, suggesting China's growth will slow and plateau ere long, in part because wages will gradually increase, reducing its competitive advantage in manufacturing.

As for Australia, as far back as 2007, Tim Colebatch, economics editor for the Melbourne 'Age' newspaper said that the average household could no longer afford the average home, suggesting that tax breaks such as 'negative gearing' which helped subsidize property investors be phased out.

This then, is another example of how things are stacked in favour of big biz so that the rich get richer and the poor get poorer, a process on the verge of having gone too far for the community at large to tolerate in some countries such as the USA and, to a lesser extent, Australia.

Australian author David Williamson summed up the behaviour of highly overpaid CEOs nicely with:

> *"Once you're on top the last thing on your mind is the long-term survival of your firm and the care of its employees. The thing to do is slash and burn and get the share price up temporarily by cost-cutting measures made at considerable human cost, then getting the resulting bonuses you've built into your already huge package, before the firm you've gutted falls to pieces. By that time you'll have a golden handshake and be off to another corporate trough."*

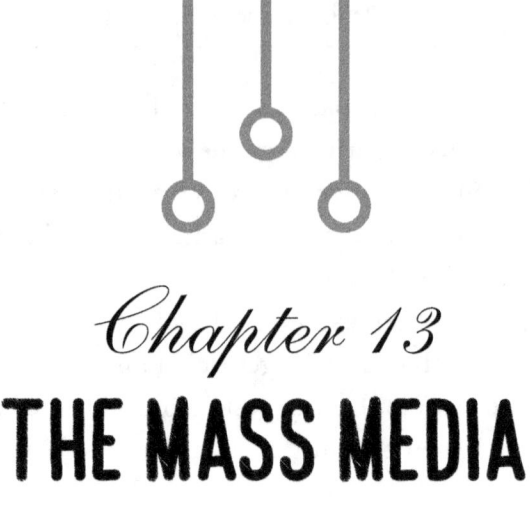

Chapter 13
THE MASS MEDIA

The idea that the media is there to educate us, or to inform us, is ridiculous because that's about tenth or eleventh on their list. The first purpose of the media is to sell us shit.
Abbie Hoffman, speech at U South Carolina
(September 16, 1987)

The whole world is becoming humanoid - creatures that look human but aren't. - - The whole world's people are becoming mass produced, programmed, numbered and . . .
Peter Finch as Howard Beale
in the movie *Network* (MGM, 1976)

THE PRINT MEDIA

The *Acta Diurna* of the Romans contained daily official reports, and the Chinese claim to have had a similar journal of much greater antiquity (Egerton Eastwick, 1896).

The earliest regular newspaper is thought to have been the *Notizie Scritte* published in Venice around the middle of the 16th century. The paper could be seen at various places in the city for the price of a small coin, the *gazeta*, from which came the term Gazette.

Around the end of the 16th century casual publications of various professions, parties and other special interest groups had limited circulation in England. In 1622 the one-page *Certaine News of the Present Week* was first printed and followed by many other one-page weeklies.

Later, two-page newspapers circulated twice a week appeared, eventually being printed daily. In 1785 a newspaper renamed *The Times* three years later was established and by 1829 it was eight pages. During the Crimean war the first war-correspondent letters appeared and the circulation rose to over 50,000. The era of the modern newspaper had begun.

Today's major newspapers are larger than ever and many have large weekend supplements devoted to such things as additional news commentary and the arts.

Articles in major newspapers tend to become a routine mix of such topics as major local and international events, local and international politics and crime, traffic other accidents, business news and sporting news

In most of these areas outcomes or results will be reported, along with editorial comment and discussion of coming events.

The many local and regional newspapers naturally focus more on events in their area so that, for example, plans for alterations to a local park might be a main article.

There are also many magazines which focus on news in special interest areas such as business, cars and computers.

For all newspapers and magazines advertisements are a major source of revenue. There are also a few newspapers and magazines devoted to advertising second hand goods for sale or to advertising products such as cars and computers.

As ever, editorial comment in the major newspapers is usually very guarded so that a rare hint of dissent with government policy is barely noticeable.

Ways in which editorial policy can influence politics, however, include:

> By simply giving less coverage to one party than another.
> By giving heavy coverage to a mistake or embarrassing incident involving a member of one party.

Over time, therefore, newspapers can have a considerable political effect and always have, so much so that they have often been subjected to government censorship.

Newspapers also play a cultural role, most obviously in discussing local arts and sporting events. The quotation that commences the next chapter is an excellent example of this role and the way in which advertisers can use newspapers to brainwash the young into becoming lifelong consumers of their products.

RADIO

Radio has been one of the great advances in human life. It allows international communication of news, embraces the people of most cities and towns, and plays an important role in ambulance, police and other essential services.

Radio has evolved from a novelty in its early days to a habit of modern life. The first author recalls the first 24 hour broadcasting by a radio station in Melbourne taking place in the early 1960s. Since then radio has evolved in major cities to provide a wide variety of 24 hour AM and FM stations such as:

- 24 hour news.
- Classical music.
- Popular music.
- 'Old time' music.
- Talk-back.
- Sports.
- 'Traditional' radio: a mix of news, sport, music etc.

Most of these are supported by a good deal of advertising and it is often claimed that many people spend more time listening to radio than they do watching TV and that, therefore, radio ads are more effective.

Radio stations have much smaller audiences than prime time TV, however, though in Australia the government owned ABC radio sometimes has a good sized audience. No doubt, therefore, it will eventually be privatized!

Some of the talk-back stations cater for the sick, deranged, drunk and lonely in the later evening and throughout the early hours of the morning.

Whether radio has much effect politically is doubtful, TV playing a much greater role in this area.

Culturally, however, radio has great influence. The latest styles of pop music are played to the young and this has always had an effect on their behaviour.

Before the 1950s popular recording artists sang in a semi-classical style or were 'crooners' like Bing Crosby who only older people could identify with.

In the mid 1950s the young Elvis Presley was viewed as a potentially bad influence on the young. He was endorsed by such well-known TV personalities as Ed Sullivan, however, and that seemed to overcome early prejudice from the older generation, or at least guarantee the approval of the younger generation.

There is no doubt, however, that rock and roll music has had a bad effect on the young as its performers were often doubtful characters afflicted with all the vices. Inevitably a whole generation was influenced by such behaviour and began themselves to behave less politely and become a little more immoral. If the lyrics of a popular song talked about 'having it off' in the back seat of a car, then young people of that generation would do just that.

Currently we still have stylized singers who 'croon' a song and dress according to some current fashion. We also have bee-bop and other pop music styles that have become more and more 'in your face'. These sorts of songs are accompanied by music clips with scenes of dark and desolate alleys in the poor parts of major cities that project an image of loutish behaviour and crime that seems to rub off on young males in particular.

Popular music has occasionally had positive effects, for example through songs protesting war, and there are those that claim that the 'hippie' and 'flower power' movement in the USA of the late 1960s and early 1970s had through a few large pop concerts played an important role in galvanizing public opinion against the Vietnam war and bringing it to an end.

Evidence of the power of pop music is seen in the emergence of radio stations run by religious organizations that play 'nice' pop music for the young with only occasional interviews or ads concerning religious opinions and events.

Finally, some evidence of the power of radio is exemplified by Radio Vatican in Rome which can be heard globally on the Internet. This, no doubt, plays an integral part in the Vatican's ongoing task of propagating Catholic propaganda.

The 'brainwashing' role of radio, however, became relatively limited with the advent of TV because this became a far more potent medium for political and other propaganda.

TELEVISION

TV has an enormous impact on modern life and people typically watch TV for at least 3 or 4 hours on most days.

The wide variety of shows on TV includes news, current affairs, interviews, panel discussions, documentaries, movies, sitcoms, children's programs, live sport, sporting panels, quizzes, cooking, home renovation and reality shows.

Most of these types of shows play a cultural role and in Australia they are a mixture of US, British and local products, exactly in line with our traditional alliances.

Many documentary shows, particularly those about past wars and other events in history, tend to reinforce those alliances. A notable example are the almost weekly documentary shows concerning Adolph Hitler which seem designed to keep us 'conditioned' for the concept of justified war and the next 'villain' around the corner that our allies the US or UK want to denigrate as a lead-up to yet another war.

As with newspapers, TV news has editorial controls rarely allowing much criticism of the status quo. The many interviews on current affairs shows allow politicians and others to express a view, but only in short 'grabs' which have little impact.

Occasional panel discussion shows allow groups to express their views but again only in short grabs, a sequence of views contradicting each other having little influence on an audience.

As with any media, however, by judicious choice of material shown the public can be brainwashed most effectively.

In Australia, for example, recent Prime Ministers seem to have had a media team that even Hitler might have envied, one that has them seen on TV almost every day saying a few mindless words on some topic or engaged in some public event to identify themselves with the public. As a result, a typically unlikely politician becomes highly successful.

Children's shows on TV play a positive role. Early morning and afternoon shows help keep very young children occupied and entertained and also have some educational content. In the later afternoon shows which sometimes include quizzes help entertain older children and sometimes have significant educational content.

An example of TV brainwashing of the public

A fine example of TV brainwashing of the public in Western nations occurred before the 2003 invasion of Iraq when for months pictures of Sadam Hussein holding a rifle were shown almost daily, accompanied by misguided speculation on whether he possessed Weapons of Mass Destruction (WMDs).

This charade was so persistent as to make many viewers want to scream the next time they heard the term WMD. The purpose of this orchestrated litany of lies and deceit was clearly to 'condition' people into acceptance of the forthcoming military invasion of Iraq by the US and the few of its allies willing to assist it.

In fact, Iraq had been so severely weakened by the 1991 invasion and subsequent sanctions and continuous bombing in the broad 'no-fly' zone placed through it that is was incapable of anything but minimal resistance.

The whole shabby and gutless affair was possibly at the behest of the Saudis, with whom the Bush family had strong connections, perhaps still regarding Sadam as a long-term irritation in the region.

Just as Osama Bin Laden wanted, however, the Iraq invasion has damaged an already sick American economy even further and removed Sadam from power, opening the way for eventual fundamentalist Islamic control of the country. Indeed, another possibility is that Al Qa'ida themselves may have fed the long-incompetent CIA misinformation about Iraq possessing WMDs to suck them into invasion.

RELIGION AND MORALITY ON TV

Religious shows on TV mainly appear in the early hours of Sunday morning. These are bible bashing US shows which cannot be watched and taken seriously by many.

In Australia, however, there is an interview show that concerns itself with religion around midnight during the middle of the week and the government run ABC runs a program on Sunday evenings which shows documentaries on religious topics.

These few shows with a religious basis, however, cannot have much influence on an increasingly immoral society. In fact many of the banal sitcoms and movies now involve high levels of foul language, violence and sex which should not be seen by anyone, let alone children.

Panel shows also involve plenty of poor language, somewhat stupid and loutish behaviour and too much joking about sexual matters.

Some of the ridiculous and voyeuristic reality shows are also completely tasteless. *Big Brother* was filled with bad language, silly behaviour and obscene talk on such absurd topics as farts. *Survivor* seems bent on reducing groups of people to a more nearly primeval state, exactly mirroring the reverse evolution taking place in our society which is so much encouraged by ever lower moral standards in TV.

To top it all off there are those ads shortly after midnight for sex shops and 'sex' chat lines for 'straight' and homosexual people which are a sad reflection on a sick society.

Worse still, however, is the increasing level of violence on TV and at the movies. Inevitably the result is 'copy cat' behaviour in the society made audience to these movies (Cipolla, 1974):

> *It is disturbing to see that still today, even in the most advanced countries, in large sections of human society, aggressiveness is praised as a virtue - or at least as a valuable asset - and it is constantly advertised in the motion pictures and on television. We need - more than anything else - to educate people to tolerance and gentility.*

Only a few days ago there was yet more news of a gang of youths in Melbourne beating up two lone people at separate locations in Melbourne late at night. Melbourne used to be considered a quiet, if not dull city, and now it is developing a history of crime reminiscent of Chicago.

The mass media, particularly the many movies that glorify crime and violence play a large role in desensitizing people to violence to the point at which is comes almost naturally to them.

The final insult is not only the violence, but to find oneself in a city half covered in graffiti painted by mindless louts who enjoy other irresponsible and dangerous practices such as throwing rocks and bottles at the windows of cars, trams and trains.

We need to draw a firm line quickly regarding mass media that encourages this sort of behaviour before life in this society becomes intolerable for decent people.

TV ADVERTISING

TV advertising has moved from the simple situation of a presenter reading a script while holding the product in question up in front of the camera to ads that have various styles such as:

- ➤ 'Basic' ads that mention the product and concentrate on telling you its name and where to get it. Sometimes these have no presenter and only text messages.
- ➤ Sophisticated ads that show the product in 'classy' surroundings.
- ➤ "Laid back' ads were the presenter extols the virtue of the product.
- ➤ Semi-humorous ads which sometimes use cartoon characters to present their message.
- ➤ Ads where the reader just about screams at you not to miss some bargain sale or to go to some cheap store.
- ➤ Ads targeting children which involve cuddly characters and fantasy scenes and the like.

More than other forms of advertising, TV advertising is sometimes very psychological. Many ads aimed at children, for example, are tested on young children who are asked whether they feel persuaded by them to pester their parents into buying the product.

Most important, however, is that ads only have to persuade a few children to try a product and they will spread the idea to their friends by the powerful pyramid effect of social learning which, unfortunately, is the main way in which children pick up bad habits like smoking and drugs.

MOVIES

An example of the Christian church using movies for brainwashing is a set of 5 movies of about 40 minutes duration and involving the following leading characters and languages:

1. Dini – Indonesian.
2. Khalil – Arabic.
3. Ali – Turkish.
4. Khosrow – Tarsi.
5. Mohammad – Hausa.

#3 is about a bossy, bad-tempered, alcoholic Muslim husband who beats his wife. He has a vision that leads him to Saudi Arabia and en route he has a vision of Jesus. Telling others it, his wife is doubtful, whilst his friends deride him. He hears the voice of Jesus again, however, and converts to Christianity, his wife doing the same, feeling it has saved them.

#5 is about a young African boy who while herding has a vision of Jesus, moving him to go to Saudi Arabia where he stays 18 months and learns Arabic. Returning home, his father pesters him about beginning to acquire wives but he has another vision, this of Jesus saving a man from attack by black-hooded men. He tells his father who sends him to a medicine man where he is given a potion without result. Another medicine man is tried before the boy has visions on six successive nights of Jesus defending him from the devil. A 7th dream promotes the Bible and the boy converts to Christianity. This upsets his father who calls him an "infidel" and the boy leaves home. Two years later, hearing his father to be ill, he returns to visit him, when his father forgives him, dying 3 hours later.

THE INTERNET

The Internet has provided a new form of mass media which combines all the other mass media. Thus the now ubiquitous PC is linked by modem to the Internet and thence to web sites that link to newspapers, radio and TV, as well as to countless other information and advertising sites.

Through e-mail the Internet also provides an important new means of communication for both social and business purposes.

For business it also provides an alternative medium for both marketing and sales, as well as for other transactions such as bank account transactions and bill payments.

For children seeking information for school projects, for example, the Internet is often useful.

The widespread use of the Internet to present University courses, on the other hand, is deplorable and debases these greatly. Such a practice also tends to encourage lightweight courses like the absurd postgraduate courses in Sexology and Puppetry introduced at two Australian 'latter-day' Universities.

In recent years increasing numbers of people are becoming addicted to various 'social sites' such as Facebook and spend up to hours a day sharing mindless and useless gossip on them.

Undoubtedly the worst result of the Internet is the many sites devoted to sexual matters. Some of these involve the sex chat lines and dating services advertised in newspapers and on TV. Others involve pornography, including illegal child pornography, yet another indication of an increasingly sick society perhaps.

CONCLUSION

The mass media play a great part in our lives. They 'condition' us to accept our culture and the attitudes of our government and society.

TV is perhaps the most potent of the mass media as it is the centrepiece of the modern home and often some of its bedrooms as well.

The Internet provides social, educational and business access via telephone links and also links to the other mass media.

TV programs and advertising, however, provide the most powerful means of brainwashing people politically and behaviourally, and advertising is the subject of the next chapter.

The major newspapers, however, have considerable political influence by way of frequent poll results and editorial comment, particularly in the weeks leading up to an election.

Chapter 14
ADVERTISING

The chief customers of the public house today are the elderly and middle-aged men. Unless you can attract the younger generation to take the place of the older men, there is no doubt that we shall have to face a steadily falling consumption ..... if we begin advertising in the press we shall see that the continuance of our advertising is contingent upon the fact that we get educational support as well in the same papers. In that way it is wonderful how you can educate public opinion, generally, without making it too obvious that there is a public campaign behind it all ...
Sir Edgar Saunders, Director of the Brewers' Society, Birmingham, 1930 (Sargent, 1979).

THE PURPOSE OF ADVERTISING

Nowadays, of course, there are massive media and advertising industries devoted to turning us into consumer zombies.

The main objectives of ads, in approximate order of priority, are to:

1. Make the brand name familiar.
2. To give the brand a distinct image.
3. Attribute at least one key attribute to that brand name.
4. Associate the product with certain usages.
5. To convince us that this brand is the best (for us).
6. To persuade us that we should buy the product.

To meet these objectives ads will involve: slogans, demonstrations, comparisons, testimonials, and repetition.

Comparisons, of course, are usually of price, but sometimes also some sort of semi-official rating, for example safety ratings for cars.

By way of style ad types include basic facts, 'mood', feel-good, social setting, slice-of-life, humour, fantasy, hard-sell, and anxiety/danger/risk or 'fear' ads.

An example of fear type ads are those for household insect sprays, and the TV program *More Hidden Killers Of The Victorian Home* reminds us that fear ads have been around for a long time, ads in the Victorian era selling such products as poisonous Borax (sodium borate) as a household cleanser, the "new science of germs and microbes" helping promote a fear of myriad household 'bugs'.

To make ads more appealing attractive female models, smooth talkers, or sports and movie stars are often used to promote products.

To give ads more authority statements by experts or organizations may be used to convince us of the merits of a product.

To make purchase more imperative ads will scream of huge price reductions for a limited time, huge bargains for as little as two days only, and buy on the never-never deals with no interest for a year or two.

In their efforts to get you in ads will go to ends which range from boring to extremely irritating, from dull and routine to the heights of excess and absurdity, from mere suggestion to downright pleading, and from slight desperation to screaming at us to buy the product.

More subtle are 'advertorials' of bought space in newspapers, conspicuous 'product placement' in movies, or internet sites. For maximum tedium there are half-hour infomercials on afternoon or late night TV which sometimes repeat night after night, week after week, and year after year. In these and most other types of ads there are often trial offers, bonus products for quick purchase etc.

In Equation 11.1 we equated aggregate demand and aggregate supply to obtain $MV = PQ$ where M is the amount of money in circulation, V is its velocity of circulation (in transactions per year), P is the price of goods in circulation, and Q is the quantity of goods in circulation per year.

Then if, for example, we increase Q we should advertise to ensure a corresponding increase in V or turnover. As the first author puts it, Mohr's First Law of Advertising is that we *'increase the velocity of bullshit in order to increase turnover.'*

As pointed out in Chapter 12, one way of maintaining higher levels of production is through planned obsolescence of which there are three types (Packard, 1963):

[1] Quality: the product wears out in some planned manner.
[2] Function: a new product performs the function better.
[3] Desirability: the product is 'restyled', making the old version seem obsolete.

In case [1] we would hardly advertise product deficiencies. On the contrary we would do everything we could to prevent bad publicity and would always advertise claiming quality and reliability or at least ignoring these points. Cases [2] and [3] would be advertised as 'new, improved' and 'the new - - - ."

THE PSYCHOLOGY OF ATTITUDES

Attitude can be defined as 'psychological *tendency* expressed by *evaluating* a particular entity with some degree of favour or disfavour.'

Figure 14.1 illustrates the three types of response involved in attitudinal psychology. These are:

1. *Cognitive response*. This response is that of recognition of, for example, a name, a picture or other stimulus.
2. *Affective response*. This is a hypothetical construct and a latent variable. Here the sympathetic nervous system responds to (1) with feelings or emotions.
3. *Behavioural response*. This is the outward expression of (2) and may be a positive, neutral or negative response of some degree or intensity involving some observable action.

In this context conservatism, environmentalism or racism are objects. Then when we label a person a conservative,

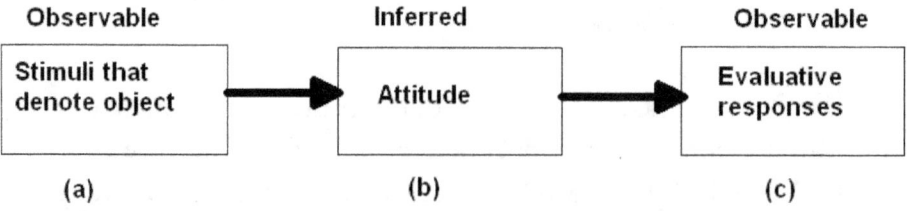

Figure 14.1. Psychological responses

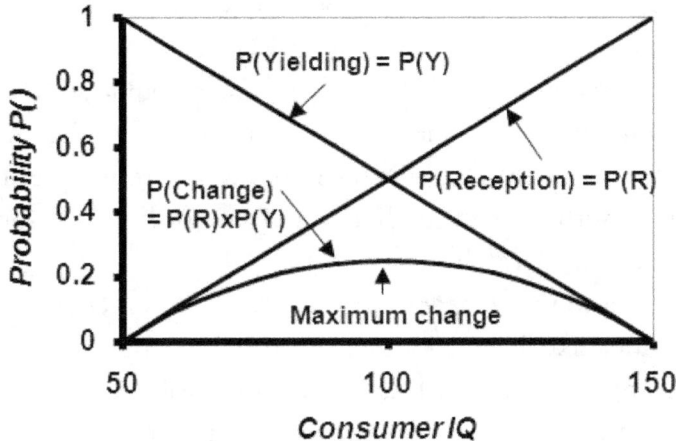

Figure 14.2. Probability of reception, yielding and attitude change.

environmentalist or racist we infer an attitudinal position. Such attitudes are evidenced and also developed by the 'CAB' mechanism illustrated in Figure 14.1.

Schemas are cognitive structures that represent a person's past experience in a stimulus domain by a higher order or abstract cognitive structure. Then attitude is a subset of such a schema.

Schemas have a selective effect on the remembering of information so that people have a better remembrance of stimuli that 'fit' their schemas and also for those that 'oppose.' This same selectivity applies to the 'output' of information as well as its input.

Figure 14.2 illustrates the reception-yielding model of attitude formation (Eagly and Chaiken, 1993). Here 'reception' refers to comprehending a 'message', for example an advertisement. This model postulates that the probability of attitude change is given by

$$P(C) = P(R) \times P(Y)$$

so that a maximum change is obtained where the reception and yielding curves intersect, as shown in Figure 14.2.

One application of this idea is to 'get them young' so that advertising companies target the young and naive before they have the maturity or 'consumer intelligence' to develop resistance. Indeed, the present authors hold the horizontal axis in Fig. 14.1 should be labeled Consumer Intelligence.

The quotation that opens this chapter is an excellent example. Once an idea like 'beer is for men' is buried in a boy's brain he may become a beer drinker for life, the habit occasionally reinforced by ads that make the habit look completely appropriate.

The basic mechanism of persuasion, therefore, is to 'get them young' (and naive or 'less intelligent consumers') as Figure 14.2 suggests. To do this ads need only persuade/brainwash some of the target audience and then imitative or 'social' learning ensures that many of the rest follow them.

Advertisements having achieved this, regular advertising reminds the audience of a product. Then in Figure 14.1 the 'C' response will be one of recognition of your brand, the 'A' response will be one of approval of it, and the 'B' response will be to make a mental note to buy it.

Learning curves were discussed in Chapter 10 and in advertising it is important to have sufficient repetitions of an ad to ensure adequate average learning by the audience. The forgetting curves of Figure 14.3 also have important application in developing long-term marketing plans. Here curves A and B are for two messages and curve B* is the result after the second message is repeated.

Then, when time has elapsed after an advertisement its 'residual' effect depends upon both the *primacy* (strength) of the ad compared to others and its *recency*.

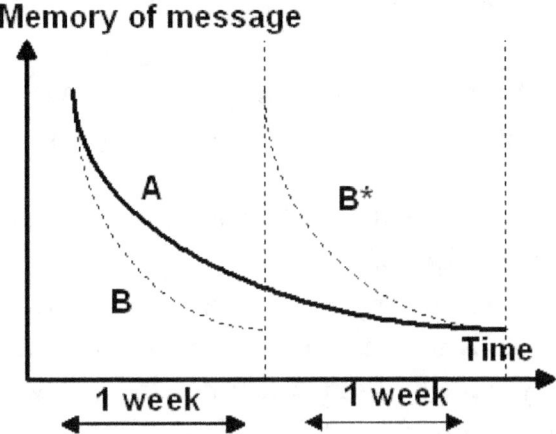

Figure 14.3. Forgetting curves.

In Figure 14.3, after two weeks ad B* has greater recency than ad A, but less primacy so that they have nearly equal effect.

Such repetition of ads will ensure long-term potentiation of the remembered message, an important objective (Vander et al., 1994). Correlation between retention and persuasion, however, is by no means guaranteed and ads can be tailored to these two ends.

TARGETING ADVERTISING

Maslow defined two kinds of needs (Lindzey at all, 1978):

(a) *Basic needs* such as hunger, thirst, sex and security.
(b) *Metaneeds* such as achievement, beauty, goodness, justice, order and unity.

Maslow defines achievement as a basic need but the present authors prefer to classify it as a 'higher' or more human metaneed.

First, we must meet our basic or 'animal' needs. That done we can turn our attention to the higher 'human' metaneeds and thence

Maslow's 'meaning of life' goal of 'self-actualization' as a human being.

These needs provide *primary goals* that may motivate us towards *secondary goals* such as money in order to achieve them.

Most of our basic needs are *intrinsic motivations* whereas most of our metaneeds are *learned goals.*

Advertising usually targets the metaneeds of your *ego*. A Coke ad, for example, is not designed to remind you that you may be thirsty. If so, you might rush to the fridge and grab whatever drink you can find to satisfy that thirst. No, a Coke ad makes it look 'cool' to drink Coke with your friends and being 'cool' is a meta-need! So next day a young boy will want to be 'cool' when hanging out with his friends so they will all drink Coke and act foolishly, just like the actors in the Coke ads

Here again we see the down side of advertising, namely that increasingly ambitious executives will stop at nothing to sell their product, even if it has to brainwash the young into acquiring both bad behaviour and bad teeth.

In marketing to children, of course, familiar cuddly looking cartoon figures are often displayed on packaging and used to speak the lines of TV ads. Here, however, ads usually target the *Id*, the basic 'animal' personality that has basic needs like hunger. Young children tend to eat in smaller doses and often so that almost any time they are awake is a good one to put a picture of confectionery in front of them.

One of the best examples of brainwashing, however, is the use of *consumer panels* of children in marketing research. The children are often asked what they will say and do to persuade parents to buy them the product.

Finally, the extent to which children are exposed to advertising is incredible:

— "it is estimated that children between two and 11 years old may see over 20,000 advertisements in a year," (O'Guinn et al., 2006).

Advertising, therefore, will brainwash someone in your family, even if it doesn't brainwash you!

In marketing to adults well known sporting identities are often used to market such things as golf clubs, household appliances and cars and houses. Indeed, this was the basis of Mark McCormack's very successful IMG (McCormack, 1986) and one of his earliest clients was Greg Norman who, marketed as 'The Shark', was made out to be a much better golfer than he was and made an awful lot of money from TV ads.

ADDICTION

There is no doubt that advertising has the effect of conditioning people. Just as Pavlov's dogs were conditioned to associate a bell with the appearance of food so that they then salivated when only given the stimulus of the bell, so too will a psychological 'trigger' be thrown in our minds when the 'CAB' responses to an ad are invoked.

In the same way advertising seeks to develop *habits*. Habits can be quickly formed and very hard to break. It only takes as little as one or two first exposures to learn something. Then only a few repetitions are needed for the memory to become *long-term potentiated* (Vander et al, 1994) and more easily recalled than most other memories in your brain.

In young children the result of confectionery advertising is often a virtual addiction to sugar. In teenagers this continues but junk food and Coke are added to their habits, soon followed by bourbon and Coke and then beer for the boys and perhaps some of the new vodka based mixed drinks for the girls.

Booze ads often *associate* booze with celebration so that at 'rave' parties for young people primeval music seems to go hand in hand with drugs and booze.

The psychology of this sort of behaviour is doubtless based on imitative learning from adults. In other words, as long as adults are stupid enough to drink booze children will too.

Since cigarettes are now discouraged in the media teenagers will smoke marijuana, arguing that it is not as harmful. This is not only an intoxicating drug but a hallucinogenic one as well. So, why not harder drugs like a little cocaine after that?

Then addiction quickly becomes likely. From booze to most other drugs, poisons have two problems:

(a) They don't really taste nice unless diluted enough by other things such as water and sugar in the case of booze.
(b) They alter the metabolic rate, resulting in changes in pulse rate and blood pressure, and contraction or dilation of blood vessels in the brain and elsewhere. Thus every fair sized dose of most drugs gives you withdrawal symptoms, whether you realize it or not. If you have an overdose you will realize it and you might want some 'hair of the dog' (that bit you) as alcoholics call a dose of booze early in the day to help overcome a hangover.

Celebration is not the only excuse for booze. Wine goes well with food, it is said, so that is another. The reality is that, because alcohol is a poison, wine will tend to eat at your stomach so it is best to line your stomach with a little food to ease the discomfort that you should be able to feel after a few glasses of wine.

This somewhat corrosive property of alcohol is the reason why it causes stomach ulcers and cancer of the oesophagus and stomach. It is also the reason why, as noted in Chapter 8, it was used to dissolve the connective tissue in the frontal lobes of the brain in the first lobotomy operations.

One way or the other, booze is inculcated as a daily habit, whether that be granny's tot of fortified wine, a bottle or two of wine with dinner, or a six pack while watching TV in the evening.

In other words *advertising* does reduce us to brainwashed zombies who will enjoy drinking poison if told to. We will leap about to primitive music like savages if told to. Many of us still smoke because ads used to tell us to.

All too many of us take drugs like marijuana, heroin and cocaine. All these addictions are practices that supposedly more civilized European explorers learnt from primitive societies and took back to Europe with them!

PUSH AND PULL MARKETING

Some marketing campaigns use *push strategies* which concentrate on the availability of products. In this case the ads are 'basic' and concentrate on telling you the product name and where to get it. Examples of such ads on TV are

- ➢ A presenter reads a script while holding the product in question up in front of the camera.
- ➢ Ads with only text messages and a voice-over.

- Semi-humorous ads which sometimes use cartoon characters to present their message.
- Ads targeting children which involve cuddly characters and fantasy scenes and the like.
- Ads for junk food which play on having a high 'reward/effort' ratio (Govoni et al., 1988). That 50 million people a day eat McDonald's stuff is testament enough to the success of their advertising.
- Ads where the reader just about screams at you not to miss some bargain sale or to go to some cheap store.

Advertisements for 'basic' food, junk food, confectionery, clothing and home appliances are usually of the 'push' type.

Marketing campaigns often use *pull strategies* which promote the product in order to attract buyers. In this case the ads concentrate on 'image' to attract the audience to the product and the product name is secondary and *associated* with the imagery. Examples of this sort of ad on TV are:

- Sophisticated ads that show the product in 'classy' surroundings with actors dressed stylishly.
- "Laid back' ads were the presenter extols the virtue of the product with, for example, an island resort as a backdrop.
- Ads that use glamorous people such as movie stars as actors.

This type of advertising is usually used for higher priced or more 'up market' products, including fashion clothing, cosmetics, expensive furniture, luxury cars and overseas holidays.

One of the most important 'levers' in advertising, undoubtedly, is *keeping up with the Jones's*. This is exploited heavily in marketing cars and new gadgets of which the mobile phone is the supreme example at present.

Another powerful inducement is selling on the 'never-never', for example with no repayments for a year.

UBIQUITOUS ADVERTISING

Today advertising is literally everywhere. On TV in Australia there used to be regulations limiting the amount of advertisements per hour to something bearable. Now there seem like 20 minutes or more of ads per hour at times. Worse still, owing to the increasing cost of TV advertising time a truly bewildering string of ads appears in each ad break, sometimes up to about a dozen.

It is almost as bad on radio where there are sometimes as many as half a dozen ads at once on the higher rating commercial stations.

Junk mail from supermarkets and other retail chains has reached epidemic proportions. Other 'direct marketing' is done by phone and is increasingly irritating, often involving requests to complete lengthy market research surveys over the phone.

In addition, free local papers almost totally full of advertisements are also stuffed into millions of letterboxes in major cities.

Trams, trains and buses carry plenty of ads, as do train stations and tram and bus stops.

Taxis and trucks all carry signage, as do many vehicles belonging to small businesses.

Shopping strips are becoming more and more cluttered with advertising signs above the shops, and sandwich boards and often products on the footpath.

More and more restaurants, coffee shops and juice bars have also spilled out onto footpaths, sometimes making little room for the pedestrians for which they were originally intended.

Shopping malls are filled with advertising and more and more stalls with spruikers have appeared in them.

Sporting grounds carry more and more advertising and sporting teams now carry prominent advertising on their clothing.

Casual clothing often comes complete with the brand name writ large upon it.

The Internet is full of advertising, of course, some of it of a lurid nature.

Then there is the despicable practice of placing confectionery and soft drinks near the checkouts at supermarkets, resulting in many a tantrum as young children taken shopping throw a tantrum to get another dose of perhaps the first 'drug' of addiction, sugar.

Perhaps the most predatory advertiser of all, Coca Cola, has its vending machines just about everywhere, including pubs and clubs, office buildings, stations and heaven knows where else (they are probably there too!).

USING RELIGION

In the West Christianity has been heavily exploited in marketing for example by

- ➢ The use of religious symbols such as stylized crosses in the jewelry business.
- ➢ The confectionery industry makes heavy use of Easter to sell chocolate. Bakeries join in by selling Easter buns and industries such as the entertainment and travel industries rely heavily on the Easter holiday period.
- ➢ Christmas, of course, is a bonanza for business and has become almost completely devoid of its original meaning.

As noted in Chapter 5, the image of Santa is actually from a 19th century cartoon of a rich robber baron with some of *his* toys which he certainly isn't going to give away (Solomon, 1992).
- ➢ Not too distantly related to this are Mother's Day and Father's Day which are also exploited by, and were probably created by, big business.

As noted in Chapters Five and Thirteen, religion also makes increasing use of TV and radio programs for promotion and in the US some religious sects have also spent large sums of money to employ advertising companies to run PR campaigns to promote themselves.

NEW TRENDS IN MARKETING

Some of the many new trends of late include:

1. Healthy foods, for example low fat products.
2. Recycling.
3. Pollution free and environmentally friendly products.
4. Diets and weight watching.
5. Alternative therapies. Of these the list grows daily:
    a. Aromatherapy.
    b. Herbal remedies.
    c. Acupuncture and Chinese medicine.
    d. Group therapy.
    e. Exercise therapy, for example Yoga and Pilates.
    f. Transcendental meditation.
    g. Reflexology - and so on.

In many large cities where house prices have tended to become unaffordable to new entrants to the market there is a growing 'live for today' approach to consumer spending and this is seen in:

1. The growing fast food industry, including take-away food and packaged 'heat only' meals sold in grocery stores.
2. Increasing diversity in consumption of alcohol.
3. Increasing use of drugs which may perhaps be encouraged by the legalization of marijuana.
4. Increasing use of leisure industries such as gambling.
5. Increasing use of restaurants by young childless workers (who may remain childless).
6. Greater spending by young and independent working women on cosmetics, clothes, jewelry and other beauty and fashion products including hair dressing and magazines.
7. Greater spending on magazines, videos, books, computer games, music and other home entertainment products.
8. Greater spending on cars, holidays and other major items by young childless couples or unattached persons.

In these and many other areas there seems to be a growing market which advertisers are busy exploiting. In some communities, however, one or two of the foregoing examples may be on the wane.

THE DISASTROUS SOCIOLOGICAL RESULTS

The extent to which advertising has reduced us to zombies strolling around in uncomfortable jeans and carrying a mobile phone in one hand and a bottle of drink in the other is mind boggling.

An article in *The Australian* newspaper on 23 May 2005 reported that psychologists had found that regular use of text messaging on mobile phones could reduce IQ by as much as 10 points, a staggering outcome.

More important, advertising corrupts young minds by showing young people behaving irresponsibly, for example a recent Pepsi Cola ad showing a few youths riding a large wheeled garbage container down a steep street and into a harbour.

In the early 1960s a US Department of Justice official expressed alarm at the "startling" pace at which youthful lawlessness was increasing and concluded that by 1962 a million American teenagers would be arrested each year.

The same official remarked (Packard, 1963):

> *We seem to have misplaced the sense of values which made this a great nation. Self-indulgence and the principle of pleasure before duty on a vast and growing scale have become a phenomenon of the adult world. These are warning symptoms of the decadence disease which has contributed to the decay of so many civilizations throughout history.*

The role that advertising has played in promoting decadent movies, music and behaviour has resulted in a more violent, lawless, indebted, miserable and brainwashed society.

Propaganda has always painted socialism as communism which permits little freedom. How free are we when we are all brainwashed to dress and behave in the same, often stupid way?

Advertising contributes heavily to the increasing debt levels carried by families in the West. Many people have half a dozen credit cards and get way above their heads in debt, often leading to family disunity and breakups.

THE DISASTROUS ENVIRONMENTAL RESULTS

Closely related to advertising is the slick packaging of many products, an example being the easy to use 'heat in the tray' packaging of frozen pizza and lasagna. The economic cost of such packaging is enormous and the environmental consequences drastic.

Another example of this are the thin plastic supermarket bags used in Australian supermarkets. Unbelievable numbers of these are used each year and many of them end up littering streets and parks and clogging creeks and storm water drainage systems.

Atmospheric pollution has reached serious levels in many large industrialized cities and global warming has already been significant not long after the term was first coined.

Parkinson's well known law *work expands so as to fill the time available for its completion* was mentioned in Chapter 10 where it is highly appropriate. The present authors prefer to generalize this to Mohr's Universal Law:

Junk fills the time and space available.

This covers a wide range of the problems of mankind including:

- Bureaucratic inefficiency, as in Parkinson's Law that work expands to fill the time available, when people are the junk.
- The Peter Principle problem of the most incompetent people being those that rise in hierarchies. Here those rising are the junk.
- The problems of pollution.
- The problems of resource depletion as a result of excessive consumption of 'junk products' which are unnecessary, extravagant and wasteful, and have planned obsolescence built into them.

Four wheel drives and other cars with massive engines are a good example. The Club or Rome Report (Meadows et al., 1974) pointed out that we were then running out of chromium, once so heavily used by ostentatious American cars. That we are now running out of oil promises to be a major catastrophe because we have built our major cities around the car.

All this has occurred because we have long been brainwashed into becoming mindless zombies consuming not for our own benefit, but for the benefit of insanely greedy and highly overpaid executives whose motivation is an even bigger multimillion dollar bonus.

Though the world was already becoming overpopulated by then, "adman-columnist" E.B. Weiss commented in the 1950s (Packard, 1963):

> *Ever since I've been regaled with the current multitude of wonderful forecasts of a population future sparked by a remarkable growth of our population I have wondered about the magical powers of a large population automatically to assure eternal prosperity - at successively higher peaks . . . The most populous regions of this mortal coil tend to be the most poverty-stricken.*

In other words, capitalist industry has been happy to brainwash us into mindless consumption and has even been happy to count on excessive population growth to help boost profits even further, all the while ignoring the finite nature of the world's resources and its finite capacity to absorb the waste products and pollution arising from extravagant consumption.

A reader's letter in *The Age* newspaper on Friday 29 July, 2016, sums up another key issue:

> *Congratulations to - - on realizing that selling off state assets leaves us, the public, out of pocket. Let's hope the scales will now fall from the eyes of other masters in relation to tax evasion dressed up as tax avoidance.*

Chapter 15
ECONOBABBLE

Economics is as much a study in fantasy and aspirations as in hard numbers - maybe more so.
    Theodore Roszak,
        The Making of a Counter Culture (1975).

The science [economics] hangs like a gathering fog in a valley, a fog which begins nowhere and goes nowhere, an incidental, unmeaning inconvenience to passers-by.
    H. G. Wells, A Modern Utopia (1905).

*If all economists were laid end to end,
they would not reach a conclusion.*
    George Bernard Shaw (attributed to).

FINANCIAL JARGON

To many of us the most unendurable thing on TV is the slot in the evening news where some person with their finger on the economic pulse mumbles about the share market trends of the day, the exchange rate, and prognosticates about whether the central bank will alter its interest rates. This sort of waffle goes on day and night all over the world. Here we shall refer to it as *econobabble*.

Not long after this segment, which seems highly appropriate, the 'weather man' gives you the weather forecast for the next few days. This is the main thing you watch the news for so, of course, they put it right at the very end so that you have to watch all the ads earlier in the news.

These days the weather forecasts are usually a lot more reliable than the econobabble.

As a brief introduction to financial jargon, however, one of the most important concepts is that of *compound interest*. A sum of money P (the principal) subjected to compound interest at an annual rate of i % has an accumulated value S after n years given by the formula

$$S = P[1 + (i/100)]^n \qquad (15.1)$$

Even more important is Mohr's Law of Money (Equation 12.4) as the growth ratio given by this is the fundamental principle of capitalism.

If you want to start a business and become a capitalist another simple but important concept is the *weighted average cost of capital* (WACC):

$$\text{WACC} = k_0 = k_e(E/V) + k_d(1 - t_c)(D/V) \qquad (15.2)$$

where k_e = WAC of equity, k_d = WAC of debt
E = monetary value of the company's equity
D = monetary value of the company's debt
$V = E + D$ = 'MV' of total capital
t_c = company tax rate

The *leverage* of a company is the ratio of D to the net worth of the company, whilst the OCS (optimal capital structure) is the optimum value of the ratio E/D.

GROSS NATIONAL PRODUCT (GNP)

GNP is one of the most widely publicized economic yardsticks and is defined as the sum of several terms, namely:

$$GNP = C + G + I_g + X - M \quad (15.3)$$

where

C = NP = private *consumption* and expenditures

G = government purchases of goods and services (not including transfer payments such as social security benefits)

I_g = gross domestic investment (plant and equipment, including inventories)

X = exports of goods and services

M = imports of goods and services

A net national product (NNP) can be calculated by adjusting I_g for depreciation but, because depreciation is difficult to estimate accurately, GNP is usually used.

Keynes proposed that if government spending (G) is increased there is a *multiplier effect* which results in a much larger increase in GNP.

This is illustrated in Figure 15.1. Here, increased government spending has resulted in an increase in demand which shifts us from point A to an equilibrium point E (hence we have shifted to another demand curve).

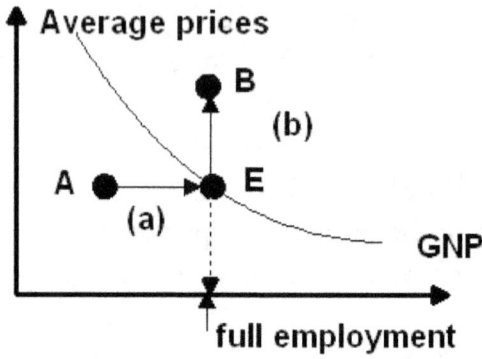

Figure 15.1. A Keynesian argument.

There may then, however, be a further increase in demand as a result of increased competition (by those now employed etc.). This will result in an increase in price and we move to point B in Figure 15.1. Hence inflation has resulted and moves to curb this will reduce employment, the by now all too familiar cycle.

To give a measure of step (a) in Figure 15.1 Keynes defined a *marginal propensity to consume* (MPC) and a *marginal propensity to save* (MPS) as proportions of a change in disposable income DI

$$\text{MPC} = \delta C/\delta DI, \quad \text{MPS} = \delta S/\delta DI \qquad (15.4)$$

and MPC is the slope of the consumption function whilst MPC + MPS = 1.

Then, supposing we have MPC = 0.8, an increase in government spending (δG) of \$M100 will, as recipients of spent money in turn spend 80% of it, result in a *multiplier effect* with the cumulative result:

$$\delta \text{GNP (\$M)} = 100 + 100(\text{MPC}) + 100(\text{MPC})^2 + 100(\text{MPC})^3$$
$$= 100/(1 - \text{MPC}) = 100/\text{MPS} = \$500\text{M}$$

a result comparable to that for bank lending and SRDs in Eqn 12.5.

The foregoing discussion of GNP considers only variation of G and its effect. To generalize how government *fiscal policy* affects the GNP we write the budget B in terms of revenue R and expenditure G as

$$B = R - G \qquad (15.5)$$

and if $R > G$ (surplus), for example as a result of higher taxes, then demand is reduced and prices fall.

If $R < G$ (deficit), on the other hand, the deficit spending may stimulate the economy in the short term at the expense of greater government debt.

If this increase of $G = \delta G = \$M100$ and the tax rate is $t = 25\%$ we amend the multiplier effect calculated above to

$$\delta GNP = \delta G / [MPS(1-t) + t] = \$M250 \qquad (15.6)$$

so that inclusion of tax (or an increase therein) reduces the effect on the economy (this phenomenon is called *fiscal drag*).

Then in formulating *fiscal policy* the aim should be to 'juggle' R and G in such a way as to control unemployment and then balance the budget (so that $R = G$) when that objective has been attained.

THE FREE MARKET OR MONETARY POLICY APPROACH

Milton Friedman and other economists favour the free market or *monetarist* economic philosophy (Wonnacott and Wonnacott, 1979) given by equation 15.7, i.e.:

$$MV \text{ (aggregate demand)} = PQ \text{ (aggregate supply)}$$

where
  M = the amount of money in circulation (per year)
  V is its velocity of circulation (in transactions per year)
  P = the price of goods in circulation
  Q = the quantity of goods in circulation (per year)

Here V is the only relatively stable quantity and is based on the fact that, when you buy a product, the money you pay for it might be passed on quite soon as wages for somebody in the company you bought the product from. Then that person spends his wages on food and other necessities, and so on. Typically V takes a value of around 4 in modern economies.

Monetarists argue that governments should increase M by between 2 and 4% each year to create a corresponding increase in Q and thence in GNP. This can be achieved simply by reducing interest rates.

This works because a reduction in interest rates increases the value of securities. This is because for a $100 bond with a yield of 8% the present value if it has a ten year term is given by

$$PV = 8/r + 8/r^2 + 8/r^3 + - - - - + (100 + 8)/r^{10}$$

where $r = 1 + i$ and i is the market interest rate. From this it is clear that the PV increases when the market rate decreases.

In addition, reducing interest rates reduces the fiscal drag effect in Equation 15.6.

The trouble with the monetarist approach is that it favours rampant capitalism and spares little thought for the workers (= slaves), the environment or anything else except profits and huge executive salaries.

TWO PARETO PROBLEMS

Two of the greatest problems Western economies face relate to Pareto's Law (Burch et al., 1983):

In most situations a relatively small percentage of certain objects contributes a relatively high percentage of output.

This is the basis of *contribution-by-value analysis* (also called ABC or Pareto analysis). For instance 15-30 percent of the population contributes 70-90 percent of the tax revenue, 20 percent of the employees in an office may do 80 percent of the work, or 20 percent of the items in inventory may account for 80 percent of the sales.

As an example of ABC analysis, the percentage of total dollar annual sales for each product are calculated and tabulated in descending order. Then the cumulative percentage contribution is added as a final column to show how much, say, the first 20% of products contributes.

The two great problems are:

[1] As a result of the Industrial Revolution, followed more recently by the Electronic Revolution (TV, PCs, mobile phones, the Internet etc.), an ever shrinking proportion of people *produce* anything tangible such as the three things essential for human life, that is food, clothing and shelter.

   The rest of us are involved in *service industries* that are, for the most part, redundant. The rest of us sit and watch, reminding me of a good line by the singer Kamahl about critics:

   > *They're like eunuchs, they like watching*
   > *but they can't do it.*

   Thus, as the world's population continues to grow alarmingly, still fewer and fewer of us do the important work of farming.

[2] As a result of rampant capitalism a small proportion of the population has a large share of its wealth. In some countries the richest 5% of people have a 90% share of the wealth.

This situation has become so bad that in the US one in six children live in poverty and in the UK the poor have a life expectancy 11 years less than that of the rich.

Here we shall term such problems *Pareto Problems*.

TURNING S&D AROUND

The cornerstone of modern economics is the law of supply and demand. Some economics textbooks are so filled with obtuse S&D diagrams that they literally drive you mad.

Figure 15.2 shows typical supply and demand curves for which it is frequently assumed that there is *perfect competition*, that is there are many buyers and sellers and none are able to influence the price individually. Then the result is called a *competitive market*.

Here the supply goes up as the price goes up because the supplier is more motivated to produce more goods. The S curve, therefore, is drawn from the point of view of the *supplier*.

The demand curve, on the other hand, goes down as the price goes down because with a greater quantity of goods available competition forces the price down (or conversely shortages result in increased prices). Hence the D curve is drawn from the point of view of the buyer.

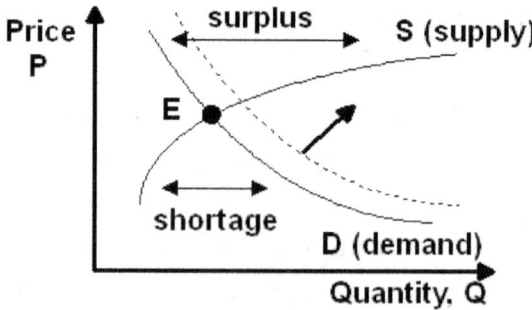

Figure 15.2. Traditional supply and demand curves.

The two curves intersect at point E, the equilibrium point at which supply equals demand.

That economists stick to the old fashioned S&D model of Figure 15.2 is a sure indication that they are behind the times. The model of Figure 15.2 applies well enough to agricultural or mineral products, for example, but not to heavily marketed products such Coke or McDonald's.

For these there is really no such thing as a shortage in supply, but, if there were to be such a shortage it would certainly reduce demand. No, these products have *created* a demand by using mass production to reduce costs and then advertising heavily.

The car industry, however, is perhaps the classic example. Australia, for example, is said to have begun to become 'motorized' in the mid 1950s. Before that relatively few people had cars and public transport was used to commute to work and school and holidays were taken by using buses, trains and, to a lesser extent, airplanes to get there.

Now, thanks to marketing, just about everybody has a car and, for example, dad parks his car all day at the station and takes the train to the city to work, and mum uses hers simply to go shopping and perhaps pick up young children from the nearest school.

It was in the mid 1950s, however, that the world's population needed to reach a plateau fairly quickly. Then we wouldn't have such sprawling megacities and we wouldn't all need cars and the world wouldn't be on the verge of rapidly running out of oil and badly depleting many other vital resources.

INVERSE LAW OF SUPPLY AND DEMAND

The cornerstone of modern economics is the law of supply and demand. In this the supply curve goes up as price increases,

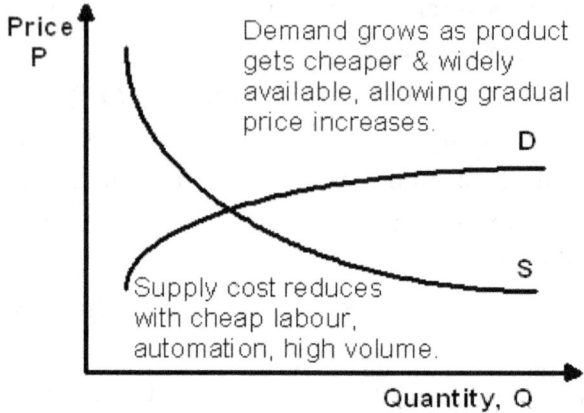

Figure 15.3. Inverse law of supply and demand, Mohr (2012, 2012b, 2014).

motivating greater production, and the demand curve goes down with increasing production, greater availability of goods decreasing their price. The two curves intersect at the equilibrium point at which supply equals demand.

The original 'D down' form applied OK in Adam Smith's day (1723 – 1790) but for today's global market S & D curves should often be the reverse, as shown in Figure 15.3, because:

(a) Economies of scale, use of casual labour, cheap labour in developing countries, etc. reduce cost.
(b) Mass marketing tends to sell as much as is produced.

The original 'D down' form still applies sometimes, for example in the case of food and commodities such as oil:

> The first law of economics is that when the price goes up, consumption goes down. This is a divine law. You cannot change it.

Sheikh Ahmed Yamani, Saudi Arabian Politician referring to OPEC's raising of oil prices in the early 1970s.

In modern global markets in which products are mass produced and heavily marketed the 'reversed' S&D model is that which applies and the massive growth in China's economy in recent decades is testament to this.

Some years ago the PC might have been a good example. The first microcomputers were tiny affairs suitable only for hobbyists but Clive Sinclair brought their price down to the point that they were affordable as toys for children. Then the first PCs suitable for business purposes, however, were quite expensive at first. Along came the IBM 'clone' from Asia, however, and that brought the price of PCs down to the affordable levels we still see today for 'bottom of the range' but extremely powerful PCs with dazzling clock speeds compared to those of yore.

THE LM AND IS CURVES

For decades central banks have counter-intuitively increased interest rates to, supposedly, control inflation, resulting in long periods of steadily increasing rates followed by a recession. Working with the simple equations of Jack Vernon's LM (liquid money supply) and IS (interest sensitive expenditure) curves it is not difficult to prove that, in fact, increasing interest rates increases inflation, as the 'man in the street' expects if you ask him (Vernon, 1980).

Indeed the first author e-mailed five pages on this matter to Australia's current Prime Minister few years ago, who acknowledged their receipt, but he assumes that little notice will be taken of them. As for the reader, the first author's modified/extended version of Vernon's LM/IS curve model in presented in the following section (Mohr, 2014).

MACROECONOMIC MODELLING

Many economists still mistakenly believe that increasing interest rates reduces inflation. Intuition suggests otherwise, as does Australia's economic history of the last 60 years, there having only been one instance of interest rates and inflation going in opposite directions, this being some time after the OPEC oil shocks of 1979/80 and the floating of the Australian dollar in 1983.

> The proof is found using the equations of Jack Vernon's *liquid money supply* (LMS) and *interest sensitive expenditure* curves (ISE) given in his book *Macroeconomics* (Vernon, 1980).

Very concisely, with the modification transfer payments $D = f(r)$, the proof is as follows:

Real money supply = MS = M/P
 = money demand = MD = $L + kQ - qr$

where P = price inflation = 1
M is non-inflation deflated money supply = 200
L is money demand constant = 50
Q is total output
r is the official interest rate
k is income responsiveness of money demand = 0.2
q is interest responsiveness of money demand = 1,000

giving

$$qr - kQ = L - M/P \qquad (15.8)$$

and this is the LMS curve, an 'up' supply curve with r the up/rate axis and Q the across/quantity axis.

For demand, we have expenditure

$$E = C + I + G$$

with C the consumption expenditure function $= a + bQ^* - sr$ where $a = 50$, $b = 0.8$, $s =$ interest responsiveness of $C = 1{,}000$ so that

$$C = 50 + 0.8Q^* - 1{,}000r$$

with

$$Q^* = Q(1 - t) - T + D$$

where T is the tax constant, t is the tax rate, D is the transfer payments, and I is the investment expenditure function

$$= I^* - ir = 200 - 1{,}000r$$

where i is interest responsiveness of I and $i = 1{,}000$ (early versions of the Fed-MIT model take s approx. $= i$) and G is equal to 230 (government spending) so that

$$E = E^* + b(1 - t)Q - (i + s)r$$

with

$$E^* = a - bT + bD + I^* + G$$

where $a = 50$, $b = 0.8$, $t = 0.25$, $T = 50$, $I^* = 200$, $G = 230$

Now let $D =$ transfer payments $= D^* + yU$ with

$$D^* = 25, y = 1{,}000$$

where $U =$ unemployment rate $= U^* + r/2$ with $U^* = 0.025$

so that $E^* = a - bT + bD^* + byU^* + byr/2 + I^* + G$
Then $E = Q$ for equilibrium gives

$$Q = a - bT + bD^* + byU^* + byr/2 + I^* + G + b(1 - t)Q - (i + s)r$$

or

$$(i + s - by/2)r + [1 - b(1 - t)]Q$$
$$= a - bT + bD^* + byU^* + I^* + G \qquad (15.9)$$

and this is the ISE curve, a 'down' demand curve.

Solving Equations (15.8) and (15.9) gives the equilibrium values of r and Q (and thence U).

With the values of constants stated above, we obtain

$$1{,}000r - 0.2Q = -150 \qquad (15.10a)$$
$$1{,}600r + 0.4Q = 480 \qquad (15.10b)$$

Adding twice the first to the second gives $r = 0.05$ and thence $Q = 1{,}000$ and $U = 0.05$.

With inflation $P = 1.1$, however, the solution is

$$r = 0.0601, \qquad Q = 959.6, \qquad \text{and } U = 0.0551.$$

Looking in reverse, this shows that increasing interest rates to 6% will cause 10% inflation, increase unemployment by 0.5%, and reduce total output by 4%.

To prove this beyond doubt, put $r = 0.0601$ in Equation 15.10b [not Equation 15.10a as this originally involved P which is now taken unknown], giving $Q = 959.6$ and put these values of r and Q (and $L = 50$, $M = 200$, $q = 1{,}000$, $k = 0.2$) in Equation 15.8, giving $P = 1.10$.

The bottom line is that increasing official interest rates increases inflation. This is because greater interest rates increase company debt repayments, leading to higher costs which are passed on to the consumer and the economy at large.

CHINA'S ECONOMIC BOOM

We believe that China has, at least in effect, reversed the Keynes multiplier effect. That is, they have allowed private capital from the major capitalist countries such as the US to stimulate their economy. The imported capital investment came from greedy American companies that set up in China to exploit their cheap labour and have helped kick-start China into an economic boom.

In addition, the Chinese government has supported over 20 major Chinese companies so that they could grow into major multinational operations, a practice more like the conventional Keynes effect.

The result has been that Chinese companies now dominate the global market for household electrical goods and have also became major players in the PC business and in the huge white goods business. In addition, cheap Chinese clothing and $2+ shop products are sold globally and priced so low that nobody else can compete. In addition Chinese government companies now own, for example, much of Australia's electricity network.

Some of us remember, however, that some Japanese products such as cars were viewed as being somewhat cheap and nasty in the mid 1960s. That certainly changed a great deal and their product quality in some areas is undoubtedly unsurpassable.

In the fullness of time the cheaper Chinese products will improve in quality and increase in price, further swelling their trade surplus with countries like the US.

The US is already seeing red (ink) about this and suggesting that China should devalue its currency which it pegs and does not float.

Pegging a currency, in fact, does have some advantages, for example that occasional adjustments, rather than constant daily fluctuations, tend to have more effect so that the government has much more control over its economy and importers and exporters have much greater certainty.

Australia floated its currency around 1970 but perhaps should not have:

> *If traded goods with prices determined exogenously on world markets constitute a large proportion of the economy, then exchange rate uncertainty translates into a high degree of uncertainty in the economy's overall price level. Such an economy may be too small and too open to have an independently floating currency.*
>
> Caves et al., *World Trade and Payments* (1990).

As for the econobabblers, they always sound like a record stuck in the same damaged groove when exchange rates alter significantly. If our currency goes down they say that it will be good for the economy because exports will be cheaper and will therefore increase in quantity. If it goes up they say that it will be good for the economy because exports will be dearer and earn us more money, neglecting to point out that the quantity of exports should be expected to fall.

In other words, they have no idea of what they are talking about.

CONCLUSIONS

One great mistake made by economists is that they don't see that S&D diagrams should have two alternative forms, depending upon whether:

(a) One is dealing with agricultural or mineral products prone to supply variations depending on such factors as the weather or discovery of new deposits.
(b) One is dealing with nonessential mass produced products for which large scale production reduces unit costs and for which the demand is stimulated by advertising.

Another is failing to see that the monetarist free market approach applied globally must eventually favour countries like China with stable governments, low labour costs and large populations.

Furthermore, in contrast to the laissez faire perfect competition notions of the monetarists, the Chinese government has very considerable influence over Chinese companies and this is having positive results.

In addition, China has not floated its currency, allowing even greater government control. Indeed, in 2016 Republican Presidential Nominee Donald Trump spent of lot of campaigning time raving about China, and in particular it's pegged exchange rate, threatening to impose 45% tariffs on Chinese imports to the USA to help rebuild US manufacturing.

Up until the last few years, during which China's economy has slowed considerably, the results have been spectacular with double digit growth rates reminiscent of those in the USSR in the 1960s and Germany in the 1930s. In July 2016, for example, China's English TV news service said that thousands of "new corporate entities" were registering themselves in the city of Chengoua because it was much cheaper to operate there than in China's largest cities such as Beijing. In the same program it was announced that China had unveiled "the world's largest amphibious aircraft", the AG 600, which could pick up 20 tons of water for firefighting in just 20 seconds, or pick up 30 or more people from the ocean very quickly. Such a plane, of course, would also have a few military applications.

The US, on the other hand, has rarely been in surplus over the last two or three decades and has reached its agreed limits of accumulated foreign debt.

The bottom line is: are all the ideas and econobabble of the economic experts and textbooks in the USA full of hot flammable air and ready to explode in their face sometime soon? It sure looks like it.

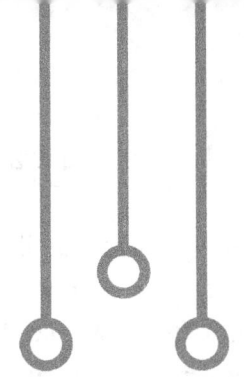

Chapter 16
SO HAVE YOU BEEN BRAINWASHED?

An asylum for the sane would be empty in America.
George Bernard Shaw, attributed.

Fools are in a terrible, overwhelming majority, all the wide world over.
Henrik Ibsen, *An Enemy of the People* (1882).

Few, if any, escape for long

Few of us get wise to the fact that we have been brainwashed almost from birth so that by the age of 20 or 30 or so we end up zombies more defined by the products and habits we have been brainwashed into than anything else. This is illustrated beautifully on the cover of a book on consumer behaviour (Solomon, 1992) which shows people in a city street dressed according to some product they indulge, for example a man 'dressed' in a Coke can.

If you, dear reader, have already realized what a brainwashed mess you have become then you are one of the few people coming to their senses. You might, for example, have given up smoking, then realizing what a sucker you were in the first place to fall for whatever bullshit that brainwashed you into taking up such a disgusting and unhealthy habit.

You may not be the typical brainwashed zombie with mobile in one hand, drink bottle or cigarette in the other, jeans, baseball hat and perhaps a 4WD if you are old enough and affluent enough to waste that much money on a heap of gas-guzzling metallic junk.

Chances are, however, that you still have other behaviours that are the result of brainwashing earlier in life and which you would be better off without.

HOW WE ARE BRAINWASHED

We are brought up and educated, of course, with a good deal of conditioning in which various kinds of rewards and punishments, most of them verbal, are dished out along the way.

As part of that education moral, religious, ethical and legal arguments will be brought to our notice to influence and control our behaviour.

On top of all that, of course, modern people spend a large part of their lives absorbing TV and other media bullshit half full of repetitive advertising and, consequently, they also spend a lot of time at sporting venues or in pubs and clubs where they are indulging some brand or other, whether it be a sporting team or a brand of beer.

At work, as at school, we are likely to be at the bottom end of a hierarchical system of 'top-down one-way' (TDOW) communication which treats us no better than slaves or lab rats.

The result is that our behaviour at times can often be likened to that of animals in conditioning experiments, for example:

(a) Rats in a Skinner box pushing a lever to receive food pellets [c.f. working in a production line to receive pay and thence food].
(b) Pigs using their snouts to push the right spot on a PC screen to receive a food reward [c.f. gambling machines].
(c) Rats in 'running wheels' etc. [c.f. humans with their myriad and usually ridiculous sports].
(d) Pavlov's dogs salivating at the sight of food [c.f. humans doing likewise over food or wine].

Humans at times, however, are far more ridiculous than animals could ever be, for example how we carry on and 'perv' over sex and now have our media littered with it. We have no doubt that a good deal of *social learning* that is very equatable with conditioning is associated with that sort of behaviour.

Social learning and *imitative learning* (IL) are much the same thing but we associate IL more with infants who at the outset imitate their parents with whom they have *imprinted*. People of all ages, however, imprint a group of friends or role models whose behaviours they imitate.

HOW BRAINWASHED A CONSUMER ARE YOU?

The simple test of Table 16.1 uses Likert scaling (much used in market research) to rate your consumption habits.

Give scores to each item (RH column) according to whether you consume/indulge the particular item to the following levels:

1 = Not at all or minimally
2 = To some extent/a little

Table 16.1. Survey of consumption habits.

#	Item	Score
1	Soft drinks, confectionery and snack 'foods'.	
2	Fast food	
3	Booze	
4	Smoking	
5	Drugs - illegal or unnecessary prescription drugs	
6	Jeans, baseball hat or other originally foreign clothes	
7	Cosmetics	
8	The fitness industry: gyms and fitness equipment	
9	Do you indulge in insane activities like skate boarding, roller blading, bowls or golf?	
10	How much attention do you pay to TV ads?	
11	Do you buy the latest pop music?	
12	Do you go to restaurants and pubs?	
13	Do you go to the movies?	
14	Do you gamble (pokies, horses etc.)?	
15	Do you pay to attend commercialized sporting events?	
16	How much do you use your mobile phone?	
17	Do you have a 4WD or other 'fashionable' car?	
18	Do you have domestic pets?	
19	Do you take holiday trips?	
20	Do you buy things just because they are 'on special' and supposedly a bargain?	
	Total	

3 = Moderately
4 = Quite a lot/a bit too much
5 = Much too much

If your total score (/100) is greater than 20 you are fairly badly brainwashed. If your total score exceeds 30 you are a hopeless case!

[The first author's score at an earlier age would have been about 20].

Of course countless other questions could have been included in Table 16.1, for example:

(a) Do you give regular allegiance to a particular political party?
(b) Do you 'consume' sex products, that is, prostitution, pornography, sex chat lines etc.?

DO YOU REALLY BELIEVE THE BULLSHIT?

The foregoing crude quantitative test is of consumption habits. At a more qualitative level the following subjects are areas in which your views may have resulted from brainwashing, that is, mere acceptance of the bullshit given on the topic in the media.

- ➢ Propaganda has always painted socialism as communism which permits little freedom. How free are we when we are all brainwashed to dress and behave in the same, often stupid way?
- ➢ How free are we in schools, Universities, workplaces and hospitals increasingly operated like assembly lines and in which our roles are reduced to those of mere automatons?
- ➢ How free are we when increasing numbers of us spend time in jail or psychiatric institutions, massive numbers of school children are doped to help them tolerate an educational

process that becomes more and more meaningless, massive numbers of us take to booze and other drugs, massive numbers of us commit suicide or simply drop out of society?

- ➢ How secure are we when 50% of marriages end in divorce, we have to work longer and longer hours, children are sent to long-day-care almost at birth and women have to work as well when once they didn't?
- ➢ How free are we when there is less and less job security and the idea of one career or occupation for life has vanished? Now you are expected to be prepared to change career three or more times which cannot be a reasonable or economically efficient way of life.
- ➢ Do you really believe in God or that Jesus Christ did the definitively impossible and rose from the dead? Do you really think it is right that religious sects throughout history have kept on killing each other, as they still are right now in many parts of the world?
- ➢ Do you really believe that Coke or booze, or whatever junk is pushed at you by advertising, is a smart and healthy thing to consume?
- ➢ Do you really believe locking infants up in day care is right?
- ➢ Do you really believe 12 years at school is necessary when Francis Bacon left Cambridge at age 14 and Michelangelo and da Vinci were apprenticed at that age?
- ➢ Do you believe that increasingly corporatized Universities should be able to con people with crap courses like postgraduate courses in Sexology and Puppetry?
- ➢ Do you really believe it is sensible that Australian Unis increased their output of PhDs by 85% between 1996 and 2006 (the increase in the USA was only 15% in that time)?

- Do you really believe the Westminster 'revolving door' two-party system is anything like halfway democratic?
- Do you really believe that 'she'll be right' and the pollies and other leaders who have always led us into wars or profited from them will fix everything when we have just about bred ourselves out of existence and ruined and depleted the planet beyond repair?

THE FIRST AUTHOR: A PATHETIC EXAMPLE

On the subject of being a brainwashed moron the first author writes from considerable personal experience.

Like all the other kids he knew he became a sugar addict early on and ate plenty of chocolate and other confectionery. We would gorge ourselves on lollies at Saturday afternoon matinees run for children and eat chocolate, ice cream, cakes and biscuits at every opportunity, slaking our thirst with soft drinks and milk shakes. At one early stage he would sometimes even stoop to eating the icing off cakes that his parents bought every week. Inevitably his teeth suffered as a result of his sugar habit and had lots of fillings by the time he was 20 and were half-full of fillings and somewhat precarious by his fifties.

And yes, he experimented with smoking from a fairly early age, progressing thus into a full-blown wreck:

- Smoking his mother's cigarette butts at around age 9.
- A couple of smoking sessions with fellow choir boys at around 11.
- Smoking with a couple of rat bags at school at age 13, eventually getting caught with cigars in his locker.
- In his teens trying a wide range of cigarettes, for example Sobranie, Galloise, Senoussi, Pall Mall, and Spring.

- Trying a pipe in his early twenties (still having cigarettes too).
- A medium to heavy smoker from age 18 to when he finally quit when nearly 49.

As you might expect he also had the occasional teenage experiment with booze, some of it pinched from his father's locked booze cupboard in his study/bedroom. With marriage he took up booze on a daily basis and eventually became a 'hardened' drinker, drowning his sorrows of lack of promotion, bullying both at home and work, and difficulties in publishing his vicarious and sometimes copious research and writing.

In other words, like most people, he did his best to develop atherosclerosis at an early age and succeeded, having his first heart symptoms at less than 30. These were initially very rare but, of course, become more serious and frequent in his fifties.

But wait, there's more. Like other kids he also listened to the latest pop music of his day on the radio and bought much of this crap on records (and later CDs) over the years, along with a smattering of mostly pretty 'common' classical music, most of it pompous crap.

This then fully brainwashed zombie used to, each day after work, spend time frustratedly wrestling with a record player trying to find just two consecutive tracks that appealed to him from a pile of 'one track records', at the same time, of course, smoking a cigarette and having a few drinks, typically beer or cheap cask wine.

Along with the 'CAB' process illustrated in Figure 14.1, you see, his BW and thus tortured mind felt only familiar with the 'hit tracks' which he therefore taped from all his records to make 'compilation tapes' that he could at least play continuously in a vain attempt to relax.

He never succeeded and it was only in his forties did he begin to listen only to a couple of classical music radio stations and collect some reasonably decent and relaxing classical music.

Later, he moved on to real 'musak' such as nature sounds + soft music and, eventually, had a small collection of quiet music that he could play without distraction even while working intensely.

His regret is, of course, that he did not find this sane approach to music and thus relaxing much earlier because for much of his life his miserable, lonely and boozy 'standup DJ habit' prevented him from thinking much or well, despite his best efforts, and thus did his life and career considerable harm.

On other follies, he recalls that the one and only new car he bought when newly married and with a little financial help from a relative suffered slight damage to the 'synchro' on one gear when driving it home from the showroom. It was a Mazda RX2 with a Wankel rotary engine, almost experimental still at that stage, and a hole wore in the engine casing after not much more than a year. With only one year warranties in those days that cost a lot to fix!

Though he did drink booze, generally he made his choices of this fairly economical, although he did often consume a bit more than he should have for much of his life, and, therefore, a lot more than he should have overall.

Once he had children restaurants were given up and he very rarely took holidays, let alone spent money traveling away during them. He rarely went to pubs, never gambled, rarely went to the movies, and never went to sporting events.

He rarely saw a doctor or dentist and always cut his own hair which, in fact, saved a good deal of time as well as money over the years.

As for clothes, he was generally economical, sensible and practical with these. It must be said, however, that a heavy smoker and drinker he couldn't afford anything else in the way of extravagances!

In his years of heavy smoking and moderately excessive drinking, needless to say, he had no need for confectionery or snacks such as biscuits and cake. When he gave up smoking and minimized my regular booze consumption, however, such snacks became an important substitute and, indeed, a necessary one to give him enough calories.

Married with two children he did have a dog, however, just to complete the typical moronic family picture. Needless to say the children had little or nothing to do with the dog and he was urged to buy it simply so 'the wife' could satisfy her urge to *imitate* her mother's dog habit.

He did, of course, watch TV for much of his life and, as had his father before him, often deplored the advertisements. Even when he had a remote control, however, he rarely muted the ads, eventually wishing there were some automatic means of doing so or even a foot operated switch for the purpose below my lounge chair.

The bottom line, however, is that his habit of crap music, cigarettes and beer combined into an absent-minded 'stand up DJ habit' stemmed from his impressionable 'teenage +' years. A solitary teenage sort of a habit (except perhaps for the beer) it was incompatible with married life and contributed to a marriage breakup and career collapse. The latter could be attributed to the fact that, outside working, he had no sensible quiet relaxation time in which to think about solving problems he might be having at work. In addition, he had a bullying, uncommunicative wife and no friends to talk to about any problems, an unhealthy situation.

That he was yet another brainwashed zombie, therefore, had life-ruining consequences, as is often, if not usually the case. He can only hope many a reader of this book, therefore, might be inspired to change their lives for the better and give up bad habits and make sure their decisions in life are not influenced by advertising or thoughtless copying of other suckers.

JUST WHAT THEN IS SENSIBLE?

If one wishes to avoid being a sucker for advertising and other bullshit one should do almost nothing. There are, however, a few necessities of life such as:

- **Food:** obviously one should try and develop a healthy diet which has minimal fat and sugar, plenty of complex carbohydrate, and sufficient protein, fibre and essential nutrients. To that end, therefore, junk food, fatty snack foods and confectionery should be largely avoided.
- **Clothing:** Neat, well fitting and practical clothing at modest prices should be sufficient for all but those with too much money. Other money spent on appearances should be minimal, for example women should not have to spend heaps on cosmetics and hairdressing.

In the old days, of course, women did their own hair. Now we have to have people do this, mow the lawn, wash the dog and, before long, wipe our bums. Now there's our business idea for the day:

JIM'S BUM WIPING SERVICE - WE COME TO YOU.
- **Shelter:** Modest, practical and not too cramped housing should be all that we need. Indeed, with our collapsing standards of living and everybody but the children needing to work at often menial jobs most young families can barely afford that or pay at least double or triple in the long run to a greedy bank.
- **A partner:** It is difficult to do or achieve much in life alone. A writer, for example, needs above all else a publisher, and preferably an agent also to get publishers interested in the first place.
- **A job:** As did the hunter-gatherers, society needs people to produce food, clothing, shelter and a myriad of other things, production of these involving countless 'service' occupations such as selling products. Whether one needs the money or not, however, some sort of occupation is necessary to pass the time so that, for example, geriatrics are given OT or *occupational therapy*.
- **Exercise:** Most of us have relatively sedentary occupations so that we need healthy exercise such as walking, running, calisthenics and weights training.
- **Relaxation and sleep:** Rest and sleep are, of course, absolutely necessary and for good health one must make sure of getting enough of both.
- **Pastimes and entertainment:** After the foregoing essential activities have been done one normally still has spare time each day as well as days off from work. To fill the gaps we need 'pastimes' which for most people include watching TV, listening to music, interacting with immediate family, or going out to dinner or the movies.

In most of the foregoing there is considerable scope for excess. In the last, for example, it is possible to spend a fortune on restaurants, pubs, gambling and going on holidays over a lifetime.

If we consider needless habits such as smoking, booze and expensive clothes and cosmetics, however, then even the average married couple can spend the price of a halfway decent house (two if they were still fairly priced!) on such habits over a lifetime.

CONCLUSIONS

Most of we ordinary peasants can greatly improve our lives by being careful and economical in our consumption practices and habits, in turn improving the prospects of the planet as a whole. Not least of these, of course, is making every effort not to have more than a couple of children, if that. In addition, we should not waste precious time and resources on keeping unhygienic household pets and it would be a great deal saner to instead spend a few dollars supporting a starving child in Africa, or better still, supporting population reduction programs in such countries.

We can also make a difference by actively supporting ethical and sustainable business practices, perhaps by joining organizations that push for sustainable practices and conservation.

Most of all, however, people should push for real democracy that might limit wasteful global marketing and reduce the greed and influence of ruthless transnational companies.

The bottom line, therefore, is that both at a personal and public level we should do what we can to reverse the power and influence of the 'brainwashers'.

Chapter 17
GLOBAL DISASTER

The human race will be the cancer of the planet.
Sir Julian Huxley,
British biologist (1887 - 1975), attributed.

...there were no more than twenty-six days ... in which there was no war somewhere in the world ... on any given day ... there is an average of twelve wars going on somewhere in the world.
Anthony Sampson, *The Arms Bazaar* (1978),
referring to the results of a study
of the years 1945 - 1978.

OVERPOPULATION

In this author's view the world's (human) population is about twice the level that can be sustainable with any reasonable standard of living for all. The prodigious effects of unchecked population increase can easily be demonstrated by simple calculations:

*In 1956 Professor W.A. Lewis calculated that if the
world population were to double every 25 years
(a rate of increase currently observable in some parts
of Africa and Asia), it would reach 173,500 thousand
million by the year 2330, at which time there would
be standing room only, since this is the number of
square yards on the land surface of the earth.*
    John Carey, *The Faber Book of Science* (1995),
                'The Menace of Population.'

Such calculations are easily made using Equation 12.4 in which putting $k = 0.028$ a little more than doubles population in 25 years. Currently k is more like 0.014, giving doubling in just under 50 years and this rate will give standing room only in about 735 years from now.

Cipolla (1974) shows that a graph of human population growth from the beginning of the Agricultural Revolution (12,000 BC) has a gently sloping line until the Industrial Revolution (1750 AD), at which point it 'takes off' vertically upwards to 2,485 million in 1950 AD.

He notes that a biologist likened this enormous human population explosion to that of a microbe population in a body suddenly afflicted with an infectious disease!

One reason for this great spurt in human population are advances in medical science such as the discovery of bacteria by Pasteur and Koch, the first use of antiseptics by Lister, and Fleming's discovery of penicillin.

Cipolla points out that what we need to aim for now is an improvement in the quality of the human species, not growth in its quantity. As he laments, however, our continuing predilection for war has the opposite result:

> *Instructing a savage in advanced techniques*
> *does not change him into a civilized person;*
> *it just makes him an efficient savage.*

Had the richer nations not indulged in the insanity of the Cold War NBC arms race after WWII the massive amounts of money wasted on stockpiling WMDs could have been spent on educating and improving the quality of life for the starving millions in the poorest parts of the world.

That, in turn, would have done a great deal to slow the alarming population growth.

Why? Because if you fill a house with, for example, a TV and a PC for each member of a family of four (if we want ZPG), there tends to be sufficient activity going on without the need to add further children or other distractions.

POLLUTION

Pollution is a much greater problem than most of us realize, for example (Wagner, 1978):

- The harmful effects of asbestos are now well known but still surface from time to time. Asbestos, however, is a good example of how long it takes for us to become aware of problem pollutants.
- Sulphur dioxide smogs caused by domestic and industrial coal burning were once common in the UK and other countries, sometimes causing heavy casualties and fatalities. Coal is still widely used for electrical power production in, for

example, the Australian state of Victoria which has large reserves of brown coal.
- Mercury compounds are used by more than 80 industries and are found in such products as plastics, electronics, and fungicides for agriculture. As a result disturbing levels of mercury in fish and birds eggs have been found.
- Lead was once added to paints and petrol and is still used in the ink used for the glossy colour pages of magazines. Observations in the Arctic, the Antarctic and world oceans indicate that lead is increasing in the environment. In the 1980s studies showed that children living close to city freeways had lower IQ.
- Cadmium is used in twice the quantities of mercury. Like lead and mercury it accumulates in the body. A limiting level of cadmium in food suggested by some experts would be exceeded by most oysters harvested in the US. Smokers accumulate significant levels of cadmium.
- Beryllium is used in the phosphor of fluorescent lights. It is highly toxic and has caused deaths of factory workers.
- The harmful global effects of DDT became evident over 20 years ago but remain an example of how *biocides* can cause serious environmental problems. DDT is one of a number of organochlorides, another being the polychlorinated biphenyls (PCBs) which cause suffocation and have also emerged as an environmental problem.

PCBs are also used in manufacturing electrical capacitors, insulating fluids, carbonless copy paper and many other products.

- Organophosphates are used as biocides and interfere with the action of nerves, quickly resulting in convulsions,

paralysis and death. Their use is now limited in most countries.
- Shortly after WWII herbicides called auxins which involve plant hormones were developed. The most famous of these was Agent Orange which caused massive defoliation in Vietnam but also stillbirths and deformities in children in Indochina.
- Antibiotics control various poultry and stock diseases but some people are allergic to them. The greater danger, however, is that of bacteria developing resistance to them, and this has already happened to the point that bacteria have evolved that are resistant to all man-made antibiotics.
- Hormones are given to animals to fatten them up. One of these, diethylstilbesterol (DES), has been found to cause cancer in humans.
- Vinyl chloride is used to make 'plastic' bottles and packaging. In the US the exposure limit for workers in 7500 plants using the substance in manufacturing was set at 1 ppm. Levels of 2 ppm have been found in the air above landfills in the US.
- Bis-chloromethyl ether (BCE) is widely used in the textile, chemical, and paper/wood industries and has been found to cause cancer in animals exposed to concentrations of BCE of as little as 0.1 ppm.
- Pollution by carcinogenic chlorinated hydrocarbons is caused by petrochemical industry wastes and by the use of chlorine to 'purify' some water supplies.
- Overexposure to some food additives such as antioxidants, acids, and emulsifiers can cause minor health problems.
- Food dyes used to make cherries red, oranges orange and butter yellow are a risk. Many dyes have been found to be carcinogenic.

There is much propaganda and misinformation too about nuclear power. According to the Club of Rome's report on man's environmental and resource depletion problems, projected annual release of nuclear wastes from the cooling towers of nuclear power plants in the US in the year 2000 was a massive 30 million Curies (Meadows et al., 1974). A Curie is the radioactive equivalent of one gram of radium and is such a large amount that environmental concentrations are usually measured in microcuries.

In other words, the long-term safety of nuclear power is very doubtful.

Depletion of the ozone layer as a result of burning oil and coal around the world has been responsible for significant global warming already.

Pollution problems are, of course, greatly exacerbated by our spiraling population, as well as by poorer parts of the world being modernized.

RESOURCE DEPLETION

The world's finite resources are being depleted at an alarming rate, for example:

- Thanks to largely unnecessarily widespread use of the car as a heavily marketed status symbol we have almost exhausted reserves of oil in only some 100 years.
- We have also largely used up coal and natural gas reserves.
- Several other minerals such as chromium are now in short supply and many others, such as gold, mercury, tin and zinc will be in short supply in the foreseeable future (Meadows et al., 1974).

- Up to two-thirds of the Australia's original tree cover has been removed and the situation is worse in some other countries (Bell and Hall, 1991).
- Up to 75% of Australia's rain forest has been lost to logging and other human activities (Bell and Hall, 1991).
- Fish stocks in several parts of the world have been seriously depleted.
- In Australia some 78 plant species have become extinct and many are threatened (Bell and Hall, 1999).
- In Australia 16 species of mammal are now extinct with 106 of the remaining 204 being threatened.
- The environmentalist David Suzuki predicts that in 200 years up to 80% of all animal and plant species will be extinct.
- Around 20% of all land is desert and each year some 6 million hectares of land is lost to desert.

The bottom line is that the human species has reached plague proportions and we are, so to speak, eating ourselves out of house and home and vandalizing that home in the process.

PRIVATIZATION AND GLOBALIZATION

For the last few decades the establishments of leading capitalist countries have been privatizing public utilities and globalizing the world's economy.

A long-term problem of this is that, many governments having crowed about having reduced government debt by selling off transport, water, power and gas industries, are faced with the serious future problem of never being able to reduce debt in this way again.

Under increasing pressure from the private sector, however, governments have consistently reduced company tax, having roughly halved it in Australia in the last three decades.

This means that more and more taxes, for example a GST in Australia about a decade ago, must be introduced to keep the budget manageable. The result is a continuing decline in *real* living standards for the people while the overpaid CEOs of big business laugh all the way to the bank.

A result of this lowering of real family income is that more and more women with young children have work and thus confine their children in long-day-care from the earliest of ages, an inhumane situation. In these children are treated rather like Krech's lab rats discussed in Chapter 21 (even complete with a tiny playground with comparable equipment). In other words, bringing up preschool children like lab rats or monkeys is becoming the norm and thence a big business.

After this children are forced to spend 12 years at school which, as discussed in Chapter 10, is far too long. Why so long? Because repeating the same old stuff from a book day after day is a cushy job and the teachers, like the medical profession, are pretty good at keeping up their numbers and their business.

Having finished school more and more children are obliged to pay ever higher fees to attend once nonexistent and unnecessary University courses that have literally reached the situation of having degrees in such things as bee-keeping, once an idea advanced as a joke about American Universities.

Then, chances are, they will find that, after working a couple of years for a multinational company, it will close and move its operations to another country where labour is cheaper.

MODERN SLAVERY

In Australia the 40 hour week was introduced almost a century ago and this is still commemorated by a public holiday called *Labour Day*. Now, however, people enslaved by increasingly greedy big businesses have to work longer and longer hours in ever poorer conditions.

There is less and less job security and greater use of casual labour without holiday or any other entitlements.

More and more people commute huge distances on clogged freeways, for which they pay a toll, to then work in soul destroying tower blocks like human filing cabinets in which the open office layout introduced by the Japanese is favoured. The purpose of this is to make sure supervisors can see everybody to make sure nobody takes more than a few seconds off the job.

Every effort must be made to improve the bottom line at all costs yet, if we were really concerned with efficiency, wouldn't we want to consider just how much value for money do highly paid people in higher management provide? Some of them make in the order of $500 a minute for sitting around a big table and making decisions that are, as often as not, poor ones. On the gigantic salaries of many CEOs, however, they can retire comfortably with a 'golden parachute', after a few years, even if the company crashes.

We can all understand the concept of a minimum wage, so why not a maximum one? Plato thought the ratio of these should not be more than about 5. A century ago some thought it should not be more than 20. Now it reaches a ratio of around 500 quite often.

In addition, surely it is more important that *people* are able to make a decent profit and save some of their earnings. Business, on the other hand, need not make huge profits. What counts from the community point of view is that local workplaces survive and continue to provide employment in the area at decent wages. Whether the business is profitable enough to expand to other areas and perhaps nationally, or even internationally, should not be quite as important.

Most absurd, however, is regression to Dickensian working conditions when the world is grossly overpopulated. Unemployment is unavoidable unless we create service industry jobs in which people are busy in such meaningless activities as shuffling paper.

Like Packard (1963), we recommend introduction of a four day week. This could involve 36 hours, rather than 40, only a 10% reduction. If in a family both husband and wife worked 8 days a week between them surely that should be sufficient, bearing in mind that not long ago women did not work at all but stayed home to look after home and family.

Packard also suggests that there should be less emphasis on more efficiency and a little more on quality of life.

As Keynes put it:

> *The moral problem of our age is concerned with the love of money.*
> John Maynard Keynes,
> *Essays in Persuasion* (1925).

From overpaid CEOs who enslave thousands to those of us brainwashed into spending our hard-earned money on often frivolous junk this statement certainly appears to be true.

SOCIOLOGICAL DEVOLUTION

In the Western world sociological devolution is taking place at an alarming rate. In the megacities built around grouped towers that are a shrine to global capitalism inner suburban areas of many cities have spiraling crime rates.

Much of these cities is covered in graffiti produced by bored youth, many of them addicted to drugs and living without hope.

Divorce rates are around 50% so that most children have direct or indirect contact with shattered families.

Unemployed men over 40 live without hope of ever getting a job again. Many have been retrenched by factories seeking to improve their bottom line with greater efficiency or by moving to a location where their operations will be cheaper.

In schools, the church, and homes, bullying and sexual abuse is rampant to the point that newspapers have articles about bullying in schools every week and public libraries often have at least a couple of dozen books on bullying on their shelves.

In the megacities house prices have escalated absurdly so that the young have little hope of getting into the house market.

In the US it is said that 1 in 6 children live in poverty. In the UK a BBC radio report on 29 April 2005 said that the gap between rich and poor in the UK had increased to what it was in Victorian times. As a result people living in such places as Glasgow had a life expectancy 11 years less than that of better-off people living in places like Dorset.

A LITTLE DIVINATION

So what is the future likely to hold for us? In another 50 years the human population, already being at least twice that which is sustainable, will have continued the 'almost vertical rise' compared to that before the industrial revolution and doubled again.

By that time:

- We will have run out of the earth's reserves of oil, coal, natural gas, chromium, mercury, gold, tin, zinc, aluminium etc.
- Stored waste from nuclear power plants will have rendered large areas of the world uninhabitable. Pollution of the air and waterways by nuclear power plants will be massive.

- Up to 99% of the world's original tree cover will have gone.
- All the world's rain forests will have long gone.
- Half of the arable land remaining will have been reduced to desert. As a result food and water will be in short supply almost everywhere.
- Around 80% of the species of animals, birds and other wildlife in the world will have become extinct or nearly so.
- The world's oceans will be so heavily polluted that most marine life will be extinct and safely edible fish stocks will be few and far between.
- The ozone layer will have become do depleted that humans in most parts of the world will have to dress like Arabs to prevent sunburn and melanoma. Blindness will be epidemic.
- Many bacteria will be resistant to antibiotics and human mortality rates will begin to revert to those before the time of Pasteur and Lister.
- Epidemics of new strains of influenza will appear and kill hundreds of millions of people.
- Viruses like Ebola and Marburg will have evolved to wipe out half the populations in countries in Africa and elsewhere and affected countries will have to be quarantined.
- Other viruses like Asian Bird Flu will have jumped to humans and will be decimating populations.
- Religious conflicts such as those between Islamic sects and Islam, Christianity and Hinduism will have killed millions of people.
- Political unrest and revolution as a result of unemployment and poverty will have occurred in many countries, including the US which is likely to have major southern states devolve from the union.

- Nuclear wars will have occurred in one or more regions of the world, for example between China and its allies and the British-American alliance (Clark, 1967). These will have rendered large parts of the world uninhabitable.
- Biochemical warfare with hybrid smallpox-Marburg type viruses will have been used extensively, killing billions.
- Since suicide bombings are now routine it is very likely that before long terrorists will infect themselves with deadly viruses such as smallpox and Marburg and promptly fly to their target countries while the disease they carry is still in the incubation period. The results are certain to be far more frightening than anything the human race has even dreamt of in its worst nightmares.

What will be left when the last three events occur? As the first author has written in the book *2045* (Mohr, 2014), small pockets of survivors in remote parts of the world will return to life like that after the Agricultural Revolution. Then, however, such permanent damage will have been done to the earth that their long-term survival is unlikely.

For example:

(a) There will no longer be enough plant life to provide oxygen at previous levels and ozone levels will be so depleted that growing plants for food will be difficult.
(b) Newly evolved deadly viruses, or viruses spread by biological warfare might be carried by birds or insects such as mosquitoes to the last remaining arable regions inhabited by these survivors and wipe them out.

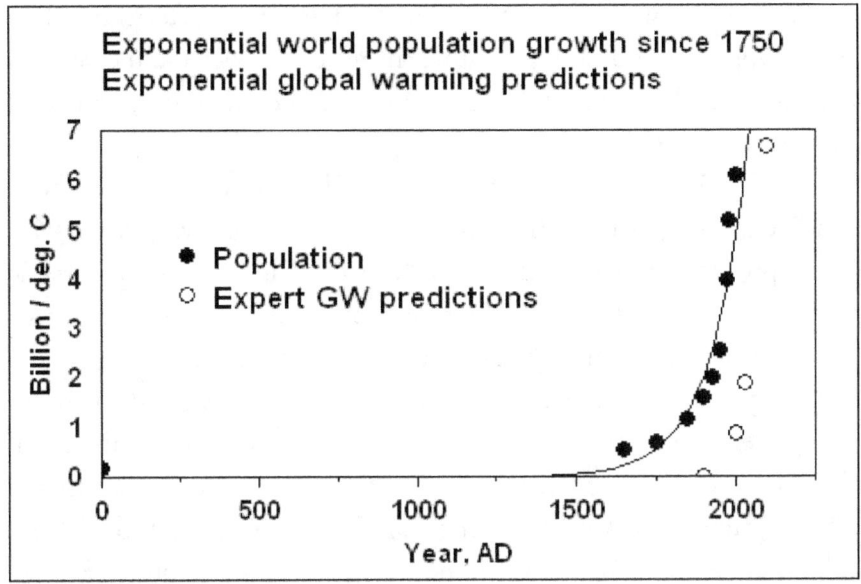

Figure 17.1. Predictions of global warming.

GLOBAL WARMING

Recent findings suggest that global warming is proceeding far more quickly than expected. According to the UN's Intergovernmental Panel on Climate Change (IPCC) the earth's temperature increased by up to 0.9°C during the 20th century. Colorado's National Centre for Atmospheric Research predicted a further rise of about 1°C by 2030 and the IPCC up to a whopping 5.8°C by 2100 and there are more pessimistic estimates.

These estimates fit closely (with $R^2 = 0.999$) to the exponential curve

$$T = 0.134 \exp(0.0197\, t) \qquad (17.1)$$

where T = temperature and t = years since 1900, giving the result shown in Figure 17.1.

This clearly shows how our population 'took off' after the industrial revolution and how global warming has now done likewise as a result of both the greater population and the increasing spread of industrialization.

If GW is indeed taking off exponentially then within a few thousand years the planet will become a lifeless dust bowl. Worse still, in all probability much, if not all, the GW to date is irreversible and, even worse still, it may be that the planet is already stuck in a 'one-way street' of rapidly accelerating GW no matter what we do.

In any case, it is perfectly obvious to all but the most purblind that governments and big biz are, as usual, just spouting bullshit on the issue and making token efforts, if that. This, after all, is normal politics, that is, for any problem give glib assurances that something is or will be done and set up some new committee to prognosticate interminably at high rates of pay over the matter and, eventually, do little or nothing beyond make some facile recommendations.

CONCLUSION

Many of us expect that the stresses of overpopulation and diminishing resources will lead to steady economic decline, in turn resulting in disputes, political unrest and instability, and as usual, human conflict in many parts of the world.

In other words, as usual we will behave just like lab rats when housed beyond a certain population density, we will start killing each other.

We, however, will be in an even worse situation, suffering not only increased overcrowding but also a worsening physical, economic and political environment.

The first author shows in his book *The Doomsday Calculation* that man will be extinct before the year 3000 as a result of resource depletion, loss of arable land, starvation, war and disease. Even with half the rate of global warming shown in Figure 17.1 our population will have halved by the year 3000.

A good example of how this might come about is the very new Zika virus that originated in South America and became particularly prevalent in Brazil. On 31st July, 2016, Australia's ABC News 24 radio station reported that four cases of Zika virus had been reported in Florida, and that these were the first cases of "local transmission" reported in the USA, it being thought that the transmission had been from Miami.

The bottom line is that the human race has been collectively stupid to behave like second or third rate animals and breed like vermin and ravage our planet so badly.

In Chapter 21 another disturbing consequence, that of *reverse evolution*, is discussed.

Chapter 18
ISLAMISM AND JIHAD

"The most convulsive conflict of the past century, and indeed the most convulsive conflict of the past millennium has undoubtedly been between Islam and Civilization; it has been between Islam and Freedom; it has between Islam and Order; it has been between Islam and Progress; it has been between Islam and Hope."
Forward by Dr George Grant to the book *Slavery, Terrorism and Islam* (Hammond, 2010).

INTRODUCTION

Islamic conflict has gone through three phases:

The first began when the prophet Muhammad and his followers fled from Mecca to Medina to escape persecution in 622. It then took only two years for them to convert the desert tribes to Islam, and then jihad against the Jews of Medina and the pagans of Mecca gained control of those cities. The next six decades saw the evil Muslim religion expand from Saudi Arabia into the other Arab lands of the Middle East.

The second lasted 1,000 years, during which Persia, North Africa, southern Spain, Eastern Europe, the Indian subcontinent, and east to Indonesia were conquered. The Holy Land was also successfully defended against the European crusaders of the Middle Ages. Those conquered had three choices, convert to Islam and be saved, pay a tax to the caliph, or be slaughtered. This period ended with defeat in Vienna in 1683.

From 1683 to 1945, the West counter-attacked and colonized Islamic areas and avenged the defeat of the crusades to the point at which Britain's Queen Victoria had more Muslim subjects than any other ruler in history in the Indian subcontinent, and in northern and eastern Africa.

Expansion of the West began with Diaz rounding the Cape of Hope to reach the Indian Ocean in 1488, and Columbus' discovery of the Americas. Thenceforth European colonization and development left the Arab world a backwater. The subsequent rise of the European nation-state system was also a blow to the Islam which sees itself as a global community.

The third phase of Islamic conflict began with the creation of Israel in 1948, conflict continuing between Israel and its neighbours, particularly Palestine, to this day.

The threat of Islam is now greater than ever because today Muslims are almost 20 per cent of the world's population, in part because of greater breeding rates.

Islam defines Jihad as (Massoulié, 2003):

Literally "Holy War for the benefit of God." The individual must first purify himself, and then those close to him, and then if, under threat, he must take a stand against the enemies of Islam. In the sixties, as a result of Nasser's persecutions, the Muslim brother, Sayyid Qotb, radicalized this idea to "unholy" governments.

A PRIMITIVE RELIGION

Muhammad's first marriage lasted 25 years, but after the death of his first wife he married at least another 15 wives, many of whom were widows or divorcees. One of his wives, Ayesha, was only six years old when she was given in marriage to him, and nine years old when he consummated the marriage, according to the Hadith.

In AD628 Mary The Copt, a Christian slave, was given to Muhammad by the governor of Egypt. When he married his daughter-in-law, Zainab, he claimed that Allah had instructed him to do so.

Muhammad died in 632 and the four Caliphas who followed the 'apostolic' tradition of Muhammad were Abu Bakr (d. 634), Umar (d. 633), Uthman (d. 656), and Ali who was Muhammad's cousin and son-in-law.

After the Battle of the Camel, in which 10,000 Muslims were killed, the governor of Syria, Mu'awiya, accused Ali of complicity in the murder of Uthman and engaged in battle but without a decisive result.

Soon after this Ali was assassinated and his eldest son Hassan was seen as rightful heir, but Mu'awiya opposed his succession and he fled, leaving Mu'awiya to rule the whole Islamic empire.

Then Ali's other son, Al-Hussein, was murdered on the orders of Calipha Yazid in October AD 680, his head being sent to Yazid in Damascus. This began the split between Sunnis and Shi'ites, the latter regarding Ali's sons as the only legitimate line of succession (Hammond, 2010).

For many years, if not decades, the Middle East has been in turmoil, and at present terrorism is rife in almost every country. Terrorism was discussed at modest length in Chapter 6 where it is seen that today most terrorism is Islamic in origin.

This is in part because much of the Koran is vengeful in nature and from its outset Islam was spread by violence, beginning with Muhammad's attack on Medina in 627AD, and then conquest of Mecca in 630AD (Mohr & Fear, 2015).

Islam is a primitive religion, disparaging those who are not 'true believers' as infidels, often savagely attacking them, at the same time feuding incessantly about its own sectarian differences, particularly those of the Sunni and Shiite sects.

One person who observed this was Sir Vidia Naipaul who visited the four Islamic societies of Iran, Pakistan, Malaysia, and Indonesia (Watson, 2001). He found Iran confused and angry: "the confusion of the people of high mediaeval culture awakening to oil and money, a sense of power and violation, and a knowledge of a great new encircling civilization. . . That civilization couldn't be mastered. It was to be rejected; at the same time it was to be depended upon."

Pakistan he found a fragmented country, economically stagnant, "its gifted people close to hysteria." He said the failure of Pakistan as a society "led back again and again to the assertion of the faith." As with Iran there was an emotional rejection of the West, especially its attitudes towards women. He found no industry, no science, the universities stifled by fundamentalism which "provides an intellectual thermostat set low."

The Malays he found had an "inability to compete" with the Chinese, who made up half its population and dominated the country economically.

Naipaul described the Islam of Indonesia as "stupefaction"; community life was breaking down, and the faith was the inevitable response.

He said that in all four places Islam drew its strength from a focus on the past that prevented development and kept it lagging behind the West. The "rage and anarchy" induced by this kept them locked in the faith.

INCITIVE PASSAGES IN THE KORAN

Of these there are literally hundreds in this evil book, just a couple of examples being (Dawood, 2006):

(a) 6.111 says that unbelievers are ignorant.
(b) 7.176 compares unbelievers to "panting dogs" with regard to their idiocy and worthlessness.
(c) 7.179 says unbelievers are like "cattle", but worse.
(d) 8:30. *And remember how the unbelievers plotted against you, seeking to take you captive or to have you slain or banished. They schemed – and God also schemed. God is the most adroit of schemers.*
(e) 9.28 says that unbelievers are unclean.
(f) 9.5. *When the sacred months are over kill the idolaters wherever you find them. Arrest them, besiege them, and lie in ambush everywhere for them. If they repent and take to prayer and render the alms levy, allow them to go their way; God is forgiving and compassionate.*

Similarly, verse 47.1 of the Sura is:

When you meet the unbelievers on the battlefield strike off their heads and, when you have laid them low, bind *your captives firmly. Then grant them their freedom or take ransom from them, until War shall lay down her burdens.*

No wonder then, that Hindu philosopher Vivekananda said:

Now the Muslims are the crudest in this respect, and the most sectarian. Their watch-word is: there is one God (Allah), and Mohammed is His Prophet. Everything beyond that not only is bad, but must be destroyed forthwith, at a moment's notice, every man or woman who does not exactly believe in that must be killed; everything that does not belong to this worship must be immediately broken; every book that teaches anything else must be burnt. From the Pacific to the Atlantic, for five hundred years blood ran all over the world. That is Mohammedanism.

Dayanand Saraswati concluded that the concept of Islam is highly offensive, and doubted that there is any connection between Islam and God.

ISLAMIC SLAVERY

The practice of slavery has existed for much of human history, and particularly in Rome and the Roman Empire where it lasted for several hundred years.

European involvement in the Trans-Atlantic slave trade to the Americas lasted three centuries, whereas Arab involvement in the slave trade has lasted fourteen centuries and continues in the Muslim world (Hammond, 2010).

In the American slave trade two out of every three slaves shipped across the Atlantic were men and the mortality rate was 10%. In the Islamic Trans Sahara and East African slave trade to the

Arab world, two out of three slaves were women and the mortality rate was between 80 and 90%.

According to Hammond (2010): "While most of the slaves shipped across the Atlantic were for agricultural work, most of the slaves destined for the Muslim Middle East were for sexual exploitation as concubines, in harems, and for military service.

"While many children were born to slaves in the Americas, and millions of their descendants are citizens in Brazil and the USA to this day, very few descendants of the slaves that ended up in the Middle East survived."

While most of the slaves who went to the Americas married and had families, most of the male slaves destined for the Middle East were castrated, and most of the children born to the women were killed at birth.

About 11 million Africans were transported across the Atlantic, 95% going to South and Central America, mainly to Portuguese, Spanish and French possessions, and only 5% went to the United States.

At least 28 million Africans were enslaved in the Muslim Middle East. According to Hammond (2010):

> . . . it is believed that the death toll from 14 centuries of Muslim slave raids into Africa could have been over 112 million. When added to the number of those sold in the slave markets, the total number of African victims of the Trans Saharan and East African slave trade could be significantly higher than 140 million people.

That slavery still exists in the Muslim world is yet another indication of its backwardness, treatment of women in Islam as second rate citizens, if not sexual and domestic slaves, another.

ISLAMIC BRUTALITY AND POLYGAMY

As for sheer brutality, when a fire was reported at a girls school in Mecca, Muslim police forced the girls back into the burning building because in their haste to escape many had not put on their obligatory head coverings (Newsweek, 22/7/2002).

In Pakistan, Zahida Perveen, a 29 year-old mother of three, was disfigured when her husband attacked her after accusing her of being unfaithful and bringing shame to the family. He cut off her ears, tongue and nose, as well as gouged out her eyes.

Divorce is simple in Muslim communities because a husband can end a marriage simply by saying to his wife *"I divorce you"* three times.

Iben Saud of Saudi Arabia reported having had over two hundred wives, but claimed that he had never had more than four at one time, and had thus not sinned in this respect.

Kamarudin Mohammad, a 72 year-old Malaysian policeman who had just had his 52nd wedding said: "I am not a playboy. He also claimed to have never had more than four wives at a time, his marriages having lasted on average 193 days each.

"THE GREATEST CONFLICT"

In the Forward to the book *Slavery, Terrorism and Islam* (Hammond, 2010), Dr George Grant writes:

> *"The greatest conflict of the past century has not been between Communism and Democracy. . . . It has not been between Socialism and Capitalism."*
> *"The most convulsive conflict of the past century, and indeed the most convulsive conflict of the past millennium has undoubtedly been between Islam and*

Civilization; it has been between Islam and Freedom; it has between Islam and Order; it has been between Islam and Progress; it has been between Islam and Hope."

Indeed, Islamic conquest and slaughter goes back to Muhammad's early conquests so that: *"By the 10th Century, Muslims had annihilated 50% of all the Christians in the world of that time. Today, repression of Christian lands continues"* (Hammond, 2010).

ISLAMIC INTENTIONS

At a conference in Mecca in 1974 the World Islamic Organization adopted the following programme:

1. Muslim organizations should set up centres to resist Christian missionary activities.
2. Islamic radio and TV stations should be established.
3. All Christian activities, no matter the secular expression, should be stopped.
4. Christian hospitals, orphanages, schools and universities should be taken over.
5. Muslim organizations should set up Intelligence Centres about Christian activities.
6. All Christian literature should be banned in Muslim countries.

Muhammad declared Jihad (religious fighting) to be the second most important activity in Islam:

Allah's apostle was asked, 'What is the best deed?'
He replied, 'To believe in Allah and his Apostle.'

> *The questioner then asked,*
> *'What is the next (in goodness)?'*
> *He replied, 'To participate in Jihad in Allah's cause.'*
> The Hadith, Al Bukhari, Vol. 1, no. 25.

According to Hammond (2010):

> *Muslims in fact divide the world into two sectors: Dar-al-Islam (the House of Islam) and Dar-al-Harb (the House of War). The only countries considered to be at peace are those where Islamic law (the sharia) is enforced. Islam does not recognize the right of any other religion or worldview to exist.*

Writing in *The Weekend Australian* of October 10-11, 2015, Anthony Klan reported that:

> *For the highly vocal Hizb ut-Tahrir Australia, the local arm of the global movement with as many as one million members, abolishing Australia's democracy, ideology and way of life is its purpose.*

He suggested that this group should be banned in Australia, as it is "in several Middle Eastern countries."

Regarding the general issue of Islamic jihad, he wrote:

> *Recruiters portray such jihad as part of a distorted sense of religious obligation and social media is awash with religious references to the fighting [in Syria and Iraq].*

THE SIX PILLARS OF ISLAM

These are:

1. *Shahada*, the open **confession** of faith.
2. *Salah*, the five daily **prayers**.
3. *Sawn*, fasting during the month of **Ramadan** during which Muslims can only eat from sunset to sunrise.
4. *Zakat*, the giving of **alms**.
5. *Hajj*, the **Pilgrimage** to Mecca at least once in a lifetime, given one has the means for it.
6. *Jihad*, Holy **War**.

Jihad has no 'official' status as the sixth pillar, but in the Twelver Shi'a Islam, it is one of the ten Practices of the Religion.

FORMS OF ISLAMIC JIHAD

According to Hammond (2010), Islamic scholars identify many forms that Jihad can take:

1. The Jihad of Words, ravings aimed at inspiring Muslims with a sense of their own superiority whilst mocking and cursing the opposition.
2. The Jihad of Deception. When Muslims are small in number they follow the example of Muhammad's 83 followers who fled from persecution in Mecca to Abysinnia where they sought protection when the Meccans demanded their return as slaves by pointing out the Koran's references to the life of Jesus that corresponded to those in the Bible.
3. The Jihad of the Sword. Rejecting Islam equates to attacking it and therefore inviting Jihad so that any war against non-Muslims can be condoned as 'defensive'.

4. The Jihad of Taxation, an extortionist tax for non-Muslims.
5. The Jihad of Slavery. According to the sharia, Muslims are allowed to own and sell slaves and in Sudan the Islamic government uses slavery to encourage Arab northerners to attack Christians in the South.
6. The Jihad of sharia Law. The testimony of non-Muslims is not valid against a Muslim, and the death penalty is applied to those who renounce Islam and convert to another religion.
7. The Jihad of Polygamy. When many of his men were killed by Meccans in AD625 at the battle of Uhud, Muhammad allowed them to take up to 4 wives. This same policy now allows Muslims to increase in number twice as fast as other religions.
8. The Jihad of the Spirits. According to the Quran Muslims are not only humans, but spirits who fight for the spread of Islam both in life and after death.

He concludes:

We need to have the courage and integrity to describe an intolerant religion of violence and oppression as it is. No Muslim has the freedom to change or leave his religion. The huge block of over one billion Muslims presents the greatest political and military threat to the free world and the greatest missionary challenge to the Christian Church. Muslim states are the most severe persecutors of Christians, and Muslim terrorist groups are the most vicious hijackers, kidnappers, bombers and assassins. Islam is a challenge we cannot ignore.

How we choose to respond, in prayer, publication, projects and persistent vigilance will determine much of the course of history in the 21st Century.

ISLAMIC PREACHING OF VIOLENCE AND JIHAD

You must wage jihad for it is the monasticism of believers.
Reported as spoken by Muhammad
by Abu Dharr al-Ghifari,
quoted in *The Complete Forty Hadith*
(Muhyid-Din al-Nawawi, 13 century), 12th Hadith

The Quran preaches supremacy, hatred, hostility and violence:

Verse 7.176 compares unbelievers to "panting dogs" with regard to their idiocy and worthlessness.

Verse 7.179 says they are like "cattle" but worse.

Verse 9.28 says the unbelievers are unclean.

Verse 6.111 says they are ignorant.

In 400 verses the Quran describes the torment that Allah has prepared for the people of other religions or no religion, for example saying:

But for those who disbelieve, garments of fire will be cut out for them; boiling fluid will be poured down on their heads, Whereby that which is in their bellies, and their skins too, will be melted; And for them are hooked rods of iron. Whenever, in their anguish, they would go forth from thence they are driven back therein and (it is said unto them): Taste the doom of burning (22:19-22).

In more than 100 places the Quran orders jihad against unbelievers:

Listen not to the unbelievers, but strive (Jihad) against them with the utmost strenuousness (25.52).

Those with "diseased hearts" – which include Christians and Jews according to 5.52 – are to be *seized wherever found and slain with a (fierce) slaughter* (33:60-62).

Remember thy Lord inspired the angels (with the message): "I am with you: give firmness to the Believers: I will instill terror into the hearts of the Unbelievers: smite ye above their necks and smite all their finger-tips off them (8.12-13). When you meet the unbelievers in the battlefield strike off their head and, when you have laid them low, bind your captives firmly. Then grant them their freedom, or take ransom from them, until War shall lay down her burdens (Sura 47:1).

Qur'an 9:5, known as the "verse of the sword", declares:

Fight and slay the pagans wherever you find them, and seize them, beleaguer them, and lie in wait for them in every stratagem.

The Qur'an promises those who commit to Jihad in the name of Allah rewards such as eternal life:

3:169. And reckon not those who are killed in Allah's way as dead: nay, they are alive (and) are provided sustenance from their Lord [meaning they are enjoying the 72 virgins in heaven].
24.055. Allah has promised to those of you who believe and do good that He will most certainly make them rulers in the earth [as a reward for going on Jihad – see K 024:053].

ISLAM ON THE OFFENSIVE

Harris (2007) points out that in the West we are largely accustomed to relative continuity of government:

So long as the various nations of the world went about their ordinary business, selecting their leadership in the same old corrupt or not so corrupt ways, it was quite easy to predict what figures would play a role on the world stage. Like the revolving door of leadership during the various parliamentary crises of the French Third Republic, new governments might be formed, but those that formed them were always the same old familiar faces. Similarly, in the United States, no one expects either the republicans or the democrats to pick a candidate for the next election whose name is not already a household word. The deck may be reshuffled, but it still contains the same old cards.

He then points out that this sort of 'relative continuity' does not exist in the Muslim world, so that it is difficult to predict who will be ruling Iraq, Iran, or Pakistan in a few years time, and that the leadership of Muslims nations is sometimes given to "wild cards" who were hitherto unknown to all but a few supporters.

This often makes it difficult for the West to know which side it should back in Middle East conflicts. In addition, it poses the problem of dealing with men who have risen the hard way, men of the people who are 'rabble rousers' or 'demagogues'.

Such leaders are unpredictable, leaving the West constantly guessing what their next move might be:

Herein lies the danger of the Western crisis of leadership: As our current crisis drifts aimlessly toward a world historical catastrophe in which policy is no longer an option and our leadership is forced simply to react to the events initiated by others, the people will become increasingly cynical and angry - - - as the system seems more and more inept, the search for radical alternatives will intensify (Harris, 2007).

In this way the pressures of widespread Islamic conflict, much of it directed against the West and thus involving Western military responses, may ultimately have a negative effect on both sides leading back towards the 'law of the jungle' and thence increasing conflict so that, what might already be termed World War 3, escalates with the widespread use of nuclear and biochemical weapons.

ISLAMISM

Islam is a very strict religion involving dress codes, countless prayers, and jihad against infidels, encouraging the most rabid Muslims sometimes, as the ongoing history of sectarian conflict continues in the Muslim world between Sunnis and Shiites, particularly in Iraq.

In the context of terrorism, Emerick (2011) states: *"Islam is misused as much as any other faith."* At present, however, rampant Islamists have undertaken terrorism to an extent unparalleled in history.

Islamists are those who derive an uncompromising interpretation from Islamic scripture. The central aim of Islamism is creation of a pan-Islamic caliphate that transcends national boundaries, an aim requiring elimination of the non-Muslim world (the West). The origins of Islamism go back to the Muslim Brotherhood founded by Hassan al Banna in Egypt in 1928. The movement rapidly spread, having 500,000 supporters and an armed wing in the 1940s that carried out many bombings and killings. It was officially banned after failing to assassinate President Nasser but still remains active in Egyptian politics on an unofficial basis.

The capitulation of Arab troops during the six-day war in 1967 brought an Islamist reaction, and in the 1970s and 1980s Islamists took part in the battle against the Soviet Union in Afghanistan, and in the Lebanese civil war.

According to Clare Lopez:

> *Given the long history of Muslim brotherhood activity in this country (the U.S.), its declared objective to "destroy the Western civilization from within", and the extensive evidence of successful influence operations at the highest levels of the U.S. government, it is urgent that we recognize this clear and present danger that threatens not only our Republic but the values of Western civilization (www.gatestoneInstitute.org/3672/muslim-brotherhood-us-government).*

INCREASING ISLAMIC JIHAD

Before the crusades began, prominent Islamic scholar Abu Ala Al-Mawardi produced a formal blueprint for Islamic government reiterating division of the world into the House of Islam, where sharia law is enforced, and the House of War – the rest of the world with which Islam is in a permanent state of war.

He made it clear that Jihad was an obligation for all Muslims who could use tactical cease fires, but could never abandon Jihad until all unbelievers had been subjugated (Hammond, 2010).

When the Muslim Brotherhood was founded in 1928 five tenets were laid down, the fifth being (Massoulié, 2003):

> I believe that the Muslim has the right to bring Islam to life
> by the renaissance of its various peoples, and that the
> banner of Islam should cover mankind, and that each
> Muslim should educate the world in Muslim principles.
> And I promise to fight to achieve this aim as long as
> I live, and to sacrifice everything I have to this end.

Serge Tritkovic in *The Sword of the Prophet* observes that:
> ... the massacres perpetrated by Muslims in India are
> unparalleled in history, bigger in sheer numbers than
> the holocaust, or the massacre of the Armenians by
> the Turks; more extensive even than the slaughter of
> the South American native populations by invading
> Spanish and Portuguese. They are insufficiently known in
> the outside world, however ... Ghandi and Nehru went
> around encrusting even thicker coats of whitewash
> so that they could pretend a façade of Hindu/Muslim
> unity against British colonial rule. After Independence,
> Marxist Indian writers, blinded by their distorting
> ideology, repeated the big lie about the Muslim
> record. Militant Islam sees India as 'unfinished business'
> and it remains high on the agenda of oil rich Muslim
> countries such as Saudi Arabia, which are spending
> millions every year trying to convert Hindus to Islam.

At the end of a long and distinguished career Orientalist William Muir (1819-1905) declared:

> ... the sword of Muhammad and the Quran are
> the most fatal enemies of civilization, liberty,

and truth which the world has yet known ... an unmitigated disaster parading as God's will . . .

Hammond (2010) concludes:
Islam cannot survive freedom. The Quran cannot survive intense scrutiny and critical investigation. In this technological age, Islam's days are numbered. Although they can hijack Western technology to use against the West, the foundations of Islam are rotten to the core and cannot stand.

Hammond hopes that Islam can be subdued by Christian prayer and missionary work, but this view is naively optimistic.

In his book *The Legacy of Jihad*, Boston physician Andrew Bostom wishes that his children and grandchildren may "thrive in a world where the devastating institution of *jihad* has been acknowledged, renounced, dismantled, and relegated to the dustbin of history by Muslims themselves."

Chillingly, Harris (2007) concludes:

Islamic jihad has demonstrated an astonishing adaptability to different historical and material conditions – and in the post-9/11 epoch, there is no reason to believe the spirit of jihad cannot be adapted to challenges of modernity.

In the West we assume that democracy is the answer to problems posed by fanaticism but Harris (2007) points out that in the Muslim world the most tolerant people are ruling elite and the rich, "whilst the religious class and the bulk of the population have been precisely those who are most fanatically opposed to Western ways - - thus the spread of democracy in Muslim countries will end by empowering those who are most opposed to the very modernization that the West wishes to bring about in Islamic culture."

ISLAMIC TERRORISM

Islamists such as Osama Bin Laden were incensed by non-Muslim troops being based in Saudi Arabia during the First Gulf War of 1990-1991, believing it had become a puppet of the West.

Revolution in Iran in 1978 and the rise of Islamic fundamentalism saw terrorism spread globally thanks to new groups such as al-Qa'ida and Islamic State, notable examples over the last couple of decades including:

- The 1976 hijacking of an Air France airplane at Entebbe by the Black September Group (an offshoot of the PLO).
- The 1980 attack on a synagogue in the Rue de Copernic in Paris.
- The 1981 assassination of the French ambassador in Lebanon.
- The 1982 assassination of the Israeli diplomat Yacob Barsimentov by the Lebanese Revolutionary Army.
- The 1982 attack on the Goldenberg Restaurant in the Rue des Rosiers in Paris by Abu Nidal (an offshoot of the PLO).
- The 1983 attack on Orly by the Secret Army for the Liberation of Armenia (SAALA).
- The 1983 suicide truck bombing of the American HQ in Lebanon, killing 241 marines, and on the French HQ, killing 58 paratroopers.
- The 1985 hijacking of the Italian ship the Achille Lauro by the PLF (Palestine Liberation Front).
- The 1985 simultaneous hijacking of El Al Airline counters in Vienna and Rome (Abu Nidal).

- The 1986 wave of public explosions in public places in Paris (5 in September alone) by the CSAPP (Committee for the Support of Arab Political Prisoners).
- In 1988 a bomb destroyed a Pan American Flight over Lockerbie, Scotland, killing all 259 people on board and 11 on the ground. Subsequently two Libyan agents were charged with the crime and one of them convicted.
- The 1989 mid-air explosion of a UTA plane, killing 171.
- Fundamentalist terrorism directed against the socialist government of Algeria led to virtual civil war in the 1990s.
- Bombing of New York's World Trade Centre in 1993.*
- Bombing of US embassies in Kenya and Tanzania in 1998 with the loss of 224 lives.*
- Bombing of the USS Cole in 2000.*
- Attacks on the US by three hijacked planes on September 11, 2001 which cost almost 3,000 lives.*
- A car bomb attack in Bali on a bar popular with Westerners that killed almost 200 people in 2002.
- The Nov. 2003 Istanbul truck bomb attacks.*
- Chechen 'hostaging' of 800 people in a Moscow theatre. Russian troops gassed the building, resulting in 200 deaths.
- The 2004 Khobar massacre.*
- Attacks on trains and buses in Spain and England in 2004 and 2005.*
- June 2008 car bombing of Danish embassy in Pakistan.*
- Sept. 2008 truck bombing of Marriot Hotel in Pakistan.*
- The 2009 Khost CIA bombing killed 8 agents.*
- 2003-present: many bombings in Iraq.*
- April 2015: The Somalia-based terrorist group Al Shabaab captured and killed 140 Kenyan University students, separating Christians to do so.

➢ 2010-present: much of Iraq and Syria overtaken by Islamic State (IS) with many atrocities (public beheadings etc.), high casualty rates, abductions of large numbers of women, with millions displaces from their homes.

* = known or believed to be due to al-Qa'ida.

Besides the globally active al-Qa'ida, there are many other terrorist organizations around the world besides those mentioned above, most of them Muslim, including:

➢ Gaza and the West Bank: Hamas and the PLO.
➢ Israel: Kahane Chai (Kach).
➢ Lebanon: Hezbollah.
➢ Iraq: QJBR (al-Qa'ida in Iraq).
➢ Afghanistan: the Taliban
➢ Turkey: Revolutionary People's Liberation Party/Front.
➢ Iraq, Syria and Libya: Islamic State (IS or ISIL, ISIS).
➢ Bangladesh: Harkat-ul-Jihad al-Islami (HUJI-B)
➢ Sri Lanka: Liberation Tigers of Tamil Eelam (LTTE).
➢ India: Indian Mujahideen (IM).
➢ Japan: Aum Shinrikyo.
➢ Pakistan: Harakat ul-Mujahadin (HUM).
➢ South-East Asia: al-Jama'a al-Islamiya (JI).
➢ Uzbekistan: Islamic Jihad Union (IJU).
➢ Somalia: Al-Shabaab
➢ Uganda: Lord's Resistance Army.
➢ UK & Ireland: Continuity IRA (CIRA), Real IRA (RIRA).
➢ Greece: Revolutionary Organization 11 November.
➢ Spain: Euskadi Ta Askatasuna (ETA).
➢ Colombia: FARC & the National Liberation Army (ELN).
➢ Peru: Shining Path (SL).

AL-QA'IDA

Osama Bin Laden, of course, had been on the side of the Americans in helping the Taliban fight the occupying Russian forces in Afghanistan in the 1980s (Nojumi, 2002).

In the 1990s, enraged at the presence of US troops in Saudi Arabia during the Persian Gulf War, he and his associates in al-Qa'ida turned their attention to the Americans with the bombing of several US embassies in the Middle East and Africa, culminating in the spectacular plane attacks of September 11, 2001.

An article in *The Australian* newspaper on 3 November 2004 reported that Bin Laden had vowed in one of his regularly released videotapes to send the US broke. He claimed that every dollar spent by al-Qa'ida on terrorist strikes had cost the US $1 million in economic damage. He estimated the US deficit at more than $US 1 trillion.

Al-Qa'ida's attacks often involve simultaneous suicide attacks on neighbouring targets. Its aim is removal of all foreign influences in Muslim countries and creation of a world-wide Islamic caliphate. As Salafist jihadists they oppose man-made laws yet ignore any religious scripture which might forbid the murder of civilians and bloody conflict.

Al-Qa'ida is intolerant of non-Sunnis and regards liberal Muslims as heretics and has carried out numerous sectarian attacks, for example the Sadr City bombings and the April 2007 Baghdad bombings, and such activities continue to this day.

Al-Qa'ida operates through unregulated banks and the 9/11 Commission report estimated that it needed $30M/year for its operations which include military training, finance, operations management, and a media division.

AL-JAMA'A AL-ISLAMIYA

Established circa 1969, this militant Islamist terrorist organization is dedicated to establishing an Islamic caliphate in Southeast Asia. JI has cells in Thailand, Singapore, Malaysia, the Phillipines, Irian Jaya and Australia, and has connections with al-Qa'ida and the Moro Islamic Liberation Front.

JI was responsible for the 2000 bombing of the Jakarta Stock Exchange, the 2002 Bali bombing, the 2003 JW Marriott hotel bombing in Jakarta, the 2004 Australian embassy bombing in Jakarta, the 2005 Bali bombing, and the 2009 JW Marriott and Ritz-Carlton hotel bombings in Jakarta. JI was also responsible for dozens of bombings in the southern Philippines, usually with the help of the Abu Sayyaf Group (ASG).

Several JI leaders have been captured in the last decade.

AL-SHABAAB

Al Shabaab (Harakat al-Shabaab al-Mujahideen, HSM), is a jihadist terrorist group based in Somalia. In 2012, it pledged allegiance to the militant Islamist organization Al-Qaeda but some of the group's leaders quarreled with Al-Qaeda over the union, and quickly lost ground.

Al-Shabaab's troop strength was estimated at 7,000 to 9,000 militants in 2014. As of 2015, the group has retreated from the major cities, controlling a few rural areas.

Al-Shabaab is an off-shoot of the Islamic Courts Union (ICU), which splintered into several smaller factions after its defeat in 2006 by Somalia's Transitional Federal Government (TFG) and the TFG's Ethiopian military allies. The group describes itself as waging jihad against "enemies of Islam", and is engaged in combat against the Federal Government of Somalia and the African Union Mission to Somalia (AMISOM).

Al-Shabaab has been designated as a terrorist organization by Australia, Canada, the United Arab Emirates, the United Kingdom and the United States. As of June 2012, the US State Department has open bounties on several of the group's senior commanders.

In early August 2011, the Transitional Federal Government's troops and their AMISOM allies managed to capture all of Mogadishu from the Al-Shabaab militants.

An ideological rift within the group's leadership also emerged, and several of the organization's senior commanders were assassinated. Due to its Wahhabi roots, Al Shabaab is hostile to Sufi traditions, and has often clashed with the militant Sufi group Ahlu Sunna Waliama'a. The group has also been suspected of having links with Al-Qaeda in Islamic Maghreb and Boko Haram.

In August 2014, the Somali government-led Operation Indian Ocean was launched to remove remaining insurgent-held pockets in the countryside. On 1 September 2014, a US drone strike carried out as part of the broader mission killed Al-Shabaab's leader and optimistic political analysts suggested that the insurgent commander's death might lead to Al-Shabaab's fragmentation and eventual dissolution.

BOKO HARAM

Boko Haram, meaning "Western education is forbidden", is a jihadist group based in north-east Nigeria but also active in Chad, Niger and Cameroon. Estimates of the group's membership vary from 7,000 to 10,000 fighters.

The group initially had links to al-Qaeda, but in 2014 it expressed support for the Islamic State of Iraq and the Levant before pledging formal allegiance to it in March 2015.

After its founding in 2002, Boko Haram's increasing radicalization led to a violent uprising in July 2009 in which its leader was executed. Its unexpected resurgence, following a mass prison break in September 2010, was accompanied by increasingly sophisticated attacks, initially against soft targets, and progressing in 2011 to include suicide bombings of police buildings and the United Nations office in Abuja.

The government's establishment of a state of emergency at the beginning of 2012, extended in the following year to cover the entire northeast of Nigeria, resulted in a marked increase in both security force abuses and militant attacks. Boko Haram killed more than 13,000 civilians between 2009 and 2015, including around 10,000 in 2014, in attacks occurring mainly in northeast Nigeria.

More than 1.5 million people have been displaced in the violence. Corruption in the security services, and human rights abuses committed by them, have hindered efforts to counter the unrest.

Since 2009 Boko Haram have abducted more than 500 men, women and children, including the kidnapping of 276 schoolgirls from Chibok in April 2014.

650,000 people had fled the conflict zone by August 2014, an increase of 200,000 since May, and by the end of the year 1.5 million had fled.

The Nigerian military initially proved ineffective in countering the insurgency, hampered by an entrenched culture of official corruption. Since mid-2014, the militants have been in control of swathes of territory in and around their home state of Borno, estimated at 50,000 square kilometres (20,000 sq mi) in January 2015, but have not captured the capital of Borno state, where the group was originally based.

As a result of joint military operations by the Nigerian, Chadian and Cameroonian armies, local vigilante groups, local hunters and local fishermen, Boko Haram lost its capital Gwoza and most of its occupied territories but it still controls southern parts of Borno State.

THE TALIBAN

This fundamentalist Islamic political movement spread into Afghanistan where it formed government in 1996 but gained diplomatic recognition only from Pakistan, Saudi Arabia and the United Arab Emirates.

The Taliban strictly interpret sharia law, limiting the rights of women. The top leadership group is the Quetta Shura based since circa 2001 in the city of Quetta in the Balochistan province of Pakistan.

Members of Pakistan's Inter-Services Intelligence (ISI) are believed to have attended meetings of the Quetta Shurah and supported the Taliban. In 2009 the Pakistani government acknowledged the existence of Quetta Shurah for the first time and since that time several of its members have been detained at various locations in Pakistan.

ISLAMIC STATE

Originally an offshoot of al-Qa'ida, the Sunni terrorist organization Islamic State (IS), also known as Islamic State in Levant (ISIL), consider Shiites to be infidels. IS have been the major revolutionary terrorist group in recent years, having overtaken much of Iraq and Syria.

In Iraq, IS are said to have murdered 1,500 Yazidis in a single bloody day, killing some 5,000 overall.

IS has committed countless atrocities, beheading and burning people alive, and making propaganda videos of such actions. Such propaganda has succeeded in recruiting young Muslim men and women globally, the women being used for suicide bombings or as wives and household and sexual slaves.

Despite increased efforts to turn the tide of Islamic terrorism, including Russian bombing raids in Syria, and US drone attacks in Iraq and elsewhere, IS continues to control large areas of Iraq, Syria and Libya.

FUNDAMENTALISTS AND TERRORISTS

The term fundamentalism is used to describe conservative trends in various religious denominations, notably Islam, Judaism, and Hinduism. Fundamentalists oppose governments they consider too liberal, or try to win political office in order to represent fundamentalist views. In Israel, for example, the Likud party has a strong power base amongst Jewish fundamentalists who believe the Jewish scriptures justify Israel's possession of land claimed by the Palestinians.

Fundamentalist and radical leaders are, of course, at pains to differentiate themselves from mainstream society. Those who do not follow their extreme dictates they denigrate, often with long speeches that seem nonsensical to all but their 'disciples' who, all too often, are used to carry out acts of terrorism aimed at eventually empowering the leaders politically by weakening any political opposition.

All too many Muslim fundamentalists, however, hold impractically extreme views not in keeping with the modern technological world. Terrorism is to be abhorred at all times but yet Islamic terrorism continues around the world to the point at which most non-Muslims regard Muslims as primitive, unpleasant, and dangerous.

In non-Muslin countries, many journalists and politicians have linked Islamic fundamentalism to violence and terrorism. In fact, Islam preaches tolerance, but also requires its followers to protest against what they see as political and moral abuses of their societies. All too often such protest has been of the violent kind and there is all too little complaint from other Muslim leaders or the general Muslim community.

ISLAM VS THE WEST

Islam has a long history of conflict with the USA and the first countries to declare war on the newly formed United States were the Muslim Barbary States of North Africa.

Morocco seized the U.S. merchant brig Betsey off the coast of Spain in 1784, and subsequently several other U.S. ships were seized. That same year, Algeria declared war on the U.S., the first country to do so, and the first Barbary War began in 1801 during the presidency of Thomas Jefferson.

In recent decades the U.S. has been involved in several major conflicts trying to deal with Islamic terrorism, including those in Afghanistan, Iraq and Syria.

The 9/11 attacks, of course, did much to encourage further U.S. efforts at combating Islamic terrorism and it is generally believed that the Saudi Royal Family provided material and financial support to the hijackers.

According to Clare Lopez:

Given the long history of Muslim brotherhood activity in this country [the USA], its declared objective to "destroy the Western civilization from within," and the extensive evidence of successful influence operations at the highest

levels of the U.S. government, it is urgent that we recognize this clear and present danger that threatens not only our Republic but the values of Western civilization.
She writes that the motto of the Muslim brotherhood is:
Allah is our objective. The Prophet is our leader. The Qur'an is our law. Jihad is our way. Dying in the way of Allah is our highest aspiration.
(www.gatestoneInstitute.org/3672/muslim-brotherhood-us-government).

CONCLUSIONS

Winston Churchill in his 1899 book *The River War* said:

How dreadful are the curses which Mohammedanism lays on its votaries! Besides the fanatical frenzy, which is as dangerous in a man as hydrophobia in a dog, there is a fearful fatalistic apathy. - - - No stronger retrograde force exists in the world. Far from being moribund, Mohammedanism is a militant and proselytizing faith. It has already spread throughout Central Africa, raising fearless warriors at every step, and were it not that Christianity is sheltered in the strong arms of science, the science against which it had vainly struggled, the civilization of Europe might fall, as fell the civilization of ancient Rome.

Islamic terrorism remains a major and costly problem in the world today. In the countries from which it originates it is bad for business, especially tourism. Elsewhere it considerably increases government military and police expenditures, also increasing costs in many industries such as the airline industry.

Worldwide there were 11,604 terrorist attacks in 2010, 5% more than the year before. There are still hundreds of people active in al-Qa'ida and it still exerts much influence, particularly in Afghanistan, Iraq, Pakistan, and Yemen.

A former leader of the CIA bin Laden team during the 1990s said in 2011 that, far from winning the war against terrorism, the West was losing and did not understand the conflict (article in *The Times* by Tom Coghlan in May 2011).

He concluded:

> *It is support for Israel, support for the Saudi police state, it's our presence in the Arab peninsula, its support for the Russians in the Islamic Caucasus. There is no more effective recruiter for al-Qa'ida than the status quo of American foreign policy.*

The first three points are those which Bin Laden made when he openly declared war on the US in 1998.

That there has been no resolution of the 'Palestine question' after so long is shameful and firm UN resolutions are needed to force an ever-intransigent Israel to more equally share the area that was Palestine for most of the last two thousand years and right up to 1948. If Israel chose to ignore such resolutions then the West should withdraw all support for Israel, no matter what the consequences.

Conversely, since Korea was divided in 1945 it has remained a problem and, perhaps, the country should be reunited in some way.

On terrorism, civil war etc., the bottom line on such problems is that they are often caused by the stirrings of a few radical outcastes with nothing better to do, Bin Laden perhaps having been an example. That they sometimes have such influence on the gullible, in turn resulting in enormous loss of life, is tragic and the human race has to wise up to the propaganda and lies it has been fed from pulpits, lecterns, soap boxes, and by the media for millennia.

A recent example of this was the bombing of the 2013 Boston marathon by two young Muslim men who had been influenced by the ravings of radical Muslim clerics, little Hitlers that this world needs to rid itself of as soon as possible. As it is, however, is it likely that the Muslim religion will come to be regarded as somewhat evil for the rest of human history in the same way as the Nazis will be.

In the recent book *Inside IS – Ten Days In The Islamic State* German journalist Jürgen Todenhöfer, who had spent 10 days embedded with IS in Iraq and Syria, said that the West is "drastically underestimating the power of IS" who he called "a nuclear tsunami preparing the largest religious cleansing in history" with plans to kill "several hundred million people."

"They now control land greater in size than the United Kingdom and are supported by an almost ecstatic enthusiasm the like of which I've never encountered before in a war zone."

In late September 2015 the Jakarta chief of police was reported as saying that Australia was an obvious target for Islamic extremists: "But you are accommodating asylum-seekers, including those coming from the conflict areas. The main ones today are from the Muslim world: Afghanistan, Pakistan, Iraq. They are seeking asylum but … they still have this emotional connection with the Muslim world."

At the end of September 2015, Russian President Vladimir Putin called for "genuinely broad alliances against terrorism, just like the one against Hitler."

He said: "Similar to the anti-Hitler coalition, it could unite a broad range of forces that are willing to resolutely resist those who just like the Nazis sow evil and hatred of human kind."

Recently, an old colleague of the first author's replied to an email attaching the file of this book saying:

> *The Islam mystery to me is that the original leader was by all accounts such a violent fellow, yet the religion is supposed to spout peace and goodwill to all.*

The second half surely has Christianity in mind with its messages of tolerance and sacrifice for others etcetera, in stark contrast to the very frequent advocation of jihad in the Qu'ran.

The bottom line is that strong measures must be taken by several nations, particularly the US and Russia and their allies, to reduce the level of Islamic conflict substantially and, hopefully, largely eliminate it eventually.

There should be major revision in shariah law and Islamic thinking to reduce their intolerance and violence. In particular, a revised edition of the Quran in which references to such nefarious activities as jihad are removed is badly needed.

Democratic government should be introduced throughout the Middle-East, along with formation of independent nations for such disaffected groups as the Kurds and Palestinians. Initially, elections in such new nations should be supervised internationally to ensure that they are democratic.

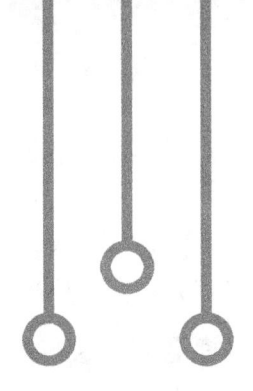

Chapter 19
THE BIOCHEMICAL THREAT

In late May 2015, there were reports that ISIS was recruiting top scientists to work on producing advanced biochemical weapons.

Media reports in 2015.

BIOLOGICAL WARFARE

Biological warfare (BW) dates back to Roman times when dead soldiers were thrown into the water supplies of cities under attack.

During air raids in the 1930s the Japanese dropped porcelain canisters of fleas infected with plague on the Chinese. These and other primitive biological weapons killed thousands in rural areas of Manchuria (Alibek, 2000).

During WW2 the Russians dropped tularemia on the stalled German Panzer divisions freezing on the outskirts of Stalingrad (Alibek, 2000).

It is well known that Sadam Hussein used chemical weapons on the Kurds in Northern Iraq in the late 1980s, and other countries

Table 19.1. Soviet & US peak BW agent production levels in metric tons per year (Miller et al., 2001).

Agent	USA	Soviet U
staphylococcal enterotoxin B	1.9	0
tularemia	1.6	1,500
Q fever	1.1	0
anthrax	0.9	4,500
Venezuelan equine encephalitis	0.8	150
botulinum	0.2	0
bubonic plague	0	1,500
smallpox	0	100
glanders	0	2,000
Marburg	0	250

in the Middle East, including Israel, have engaged in biological weapons (BW) research.

As shown in Table 6.2 the USSR had an enormous BW research program with some 50 research centres and storage facilities (Alibek, 2000). Table 19.1 shows the extensive BW programs of the USSR and US at their peak, whilst Table 19.2 shows further biological warfare agents produced by the USSR.

After WW2 the US also implemented a large BW research program, though not nearly as extensive as that of the USSR (see Tables 19.1 and 19.2). The US program was based mainly at one facility, Fort Detrick in Maryland.

In this massive arsenal the haemorrhagic filoviruses Ebola and Marburg are the most frightening because they are highly contagious and liquefy the body's organs.

Table 19.2. Other Russian BW agents (Alibek, 2000).

Argentinian haemorrhagic fever (Jinin)
Bolivian haemorrhagic fever (Machupo)
brucellosis
dengue fever
Ebola virus
epidemic typhus
Lassa fever
Russian spring-summer encephalitis

At the main Russian BW research facility Vektor a scientist, Ustinov, was accidentally infected with Marburg virus. It took 15 days to kill him, developing into a new, more virulent strain that was called Marburg Variant U and weaponized for delivery by Soviet rockets.

To date there have been no large scale BW attacks but in December 1943 news arrived in London that Germany intended to use a pilotless plane or rocket called the V-1 to deliver biological weapons. US intelligence learnt that they intended to use botulinum and the US had already developed an antidote to botulinum. By the summer of 1944 they had manufactured 4,000 gallons of this antidote, enough to immunize 700,000 troops (Regis, 1999).

In the spring of 1944 a worried Winston Churchill asked the US to provide him with 500,000 anthrax bombs. Churchill wrote in a memorandum, *"We should regard it as a first instalment."*

The Americans set up for production, aiming to produce a further 500,000 anthrax bombs for their own use. The task was never completed owing to the first atomic bomb test in July 1945, and then its use on Hiroshima and Nagasaki in August, ending the war a month later.

That Germany, the US and UK were preparing for massive BW warfare towards the end of WW2 suggests that there is a serious risk of BW warfare on a large scale at some time in the future.

In March 2013 the Syrian government, which has not joined a convention banning the use of chemical weapons, claimed that rebel forces had used chemical weapons in a rocket attack, a claim refuted by the rebels. Since then, both sides have continued to accuse the other of using chemical weapons.

CONCLUSIONS

Enormous nuclear and biological arsenals having been established, all history suggests that they are likely to be used eventually.

The 1972 the Biological and Toxic Weapons Convention bans the development, production and deployment of biological weapons. In contravention of this the Soviet Union is believed to have continued anthrax research which resulted in an anthrax outbreak at Sverdlovsk (now Yekaterinburg) in 1979 which killed 64 people.

Shortly after the 9/11 attacks on New York there were a series of anthrax mailings. The first victim was Robert Stevens, a photo editor at a Florida newspaper, who was hospitalized on 2 October 2001, and died three days later. The perpetrator was never found and since then much more money has been spent on precautions against bio-terrorism (Suter, 2008).

After Iraq's use of chemical weapons in 1990 an international treaty banning chemical warfare was established, but this binds governments and not 'non-state' organizations such as terrorist groups (Suter, 2008). As for the 2001 invasion of Iraq because of WMDs and purported mobile biochemical labs, in fact these might have been trucks carrying the BCW stuff and perhaps able to launch missiles carrying it. With the US+ invasion forthcoming, of course, these vehicles would have been taken across the border.

In March 2013 the Syrian government claimed that rebel forces had carried out a rocket attack using chemical weapons, a claim which the rebels denied, saying that they did not have rockets. As usual, who did what is hard to know. The rebels have had support from the US, which might have included short range rockets, whilst until now the Syrian government has not joined a UN convention banning the use of chemical weapons.

In late May 2015, there were reports that IS was recruiting top scientists to work on producing advanced biochemical weapons. As Table 19.1 suggests, this is a frightening prospect. Worse still, IS is also trying to collect radioactive material, perhaps to 'crop-dust' New York and London from helicopters.

Chapter 20
WORLD WAR 3

We cannot let terrorist and rogue nations hold this nation hostile or hold our allies hostile.
　　　　　　　　　George W. Bush, speaking in Des Moines, Iowa, 21 Aug. 2001.

Britain must, and I am sure will, stand shoulder to shoulder with the United States of America and peaceful nations across the world in deploying every possible resource to bring to justice the people responsible and make sure terrorism never prevails.
　　　　　　　　　Tony Blair, statement, 11 Sep. 2001.

Every nation, in every region, now has a decision to make. Either you are with us, or you are with the terrorists. From this day forward, any nation that continues to harbor or support terrorism will be regarded by the United States as a hostile regime.
　　　　　　　　　George W. Bush, address to a joint session of Congress, 20 Sep. 2001.

INTRODUCTION

Most of this chapter is borrowed from the chapter 'Recent Acts of Terrorism' in *World War 3: How and When Will It End?* (Mohr, Fear & Sinclair, 2015). In this the authors suggest that perhaps the first seed of WW3, that is, the current global scourge of Islamic terrorism, was the creation of the state of Israel in 1948 in the UN-mandated British protectorate of Palestine. Another such seed, of course, was the division of India to create the Muslim country of Pakistan to house much of the Muslim population of India, the motivation being to try and reduce Muslim-Hindu conflict. This 'state creation' was also a disaster, however, and conflict between migrating Muslims and Hindus is said to have killed some 1 million people, though perhaps the real death toll was much higher.

Since that time, dozens of Islamic terrorist organizations have been founded in many countries, the most notable of these of late being al-Qa'ida and Islamic State (IS). The latter, in particular, relies on brainwashing young Muslim men via preachers and other local Muslim leaders around the world, and via the Internet. An example of the latter is the notorious Australian ISIS propaganda pusher Neil Prakash who the *Herald-Sun* reported on on 27/6/06 remained at large in Syria.

THE MUNICH MASSACRE

On the eighth day of the 1972 Munich Olympics the Palestinian 'Black September' terrorist group killed two Israeli athletes and took nine others hostage. They demanded the release of 232 Palestinians held in Israeli prisons, two local terrorists held in Germany, as well as their own safe passage out of Europe.

When brief negotiations stalled the terrorists took their hostages to the military airport in Munich by helicopter for a flight back to the Middle East. German sharpshooters opened fire and the terrorists fired back, blowing up the helicopter and killing all nine hostages, along with one German police officer and five terrorists. Three terrorists were captured.

On 29 October a Lufthansa jet was hijacked by Arab terrorists demanding release of the three captured terrorists and the Germans agreed.

Israel responded with an air strike, using 75 aircraft to attack guerrilla targets in Lebanon and killing 66 with hundreds wounded. Then Mossad, Israel's foreign intelligence agency, created independent assassination teams to kill every Palestinian involved in the Munich massacre.

About 35 targets were selected, including the three terrorists released by West Germany. The first person killed was a cousin of Yasser Arafat who was an organizer of PLO terrorism in Europe. The next was the coordinator of the Munich operation.

In one incident the target was killed, but also a KGB agent who blocked the exit of the assassination team. In 1974 a freelance assassin seduced one of the Israeli assassins and killed him, but the Israeli's found and disposed of her.

When a person in Norway was killed because he looked like the target six Israeli's were captured and imprisoned for two years.

Of the three surviving terrorists directly involved in the Munich massacre, two were assassinated and the other died of natural causes.

The last person on the hit list was killed in a booby-trapped car in Beirut in 1979.

Each assassination had cost an average of US$350,000, one of the "most cost-effective – and least publicized operations every conducted by Israel" ((Suter, 2008).

THE SYMBIONESE LIBERATION ARMY (SLA)

The Symbionese Liberation Army, a terrorist organization, was formed in the USA in 1973 but only operated for a few years. Some SLA members were killed by police and others were arrested and jailed.

The SLA came to wide attention by planting bombs under police cars and its motto was:

> *Death to the fascist insect that preys upon the life of people.*

In 1973 they killed Marcus Foster, and educator who headed the Oakland, California, school system. Two SLA members were arrested and convicted for the murder.

In 1974 the SLA kidnapped 19 year-old Patty Hearst, whose grandfather was the famous publishing magnate Randolph Hearst and one of America's richest men.

The SLA forced the Hearst family to give two million dollars for food for the poor, but refused to release Patty.

Two months after the kidnapping the SLA robbed a bank and hidden cameras caught the robbery on camera, showing Patty Hearst carrying an automatic rifle.

Newspapers published this picture and the SLA responded with a videotape in which Patty said she had joined the SLA, and that her new name was Tania.

The police located the SLA hideout where Patty was being held and raided it. There was a shootout in which six SLA members were killed and the house was burned to the ground.

Patty Hearst was captured a year and a half later. At her trial she claimed she had been tortured and brainwashed, and forced to join the group. She was found guilty and sentenced to seven years for armed robbery, but was in jail for less than two years after President Jimmy Carter shortened her sentence. Many years later President Bill Clinton pardoned her.

During another SLA bank robbery in 1975 a customer was shot dead. She had four children and had been at the bank to deposit collection money from her church.

One SLA member, Kathleen Soliah, escaped capture by changing her name to Sarah Jane Olsen. Under this name she married and had a family, and seemed to have left the past behind.

Her past caught up with her in 1999 when she was arrested and accused of planting bombs under police cars. She pleaded guilty to the charge and was sentenced to 20 years to life in prison (Weil, 2004).

THE UNABOMBER

On 26 May 1978 a package was found in the parking lot of the University of Illinois in Chicago. It had been posted from another university near Chicago and was sent back and exploded when opened, injuring one person.

Several more such bombs were posted over the next 17 years, killing three people and injuring 23 others.

In 1979 another bomb exploded at Northwestern University. Like the first it was made from scraps of metal, wood, and lamp cord and the unknown perpetrator was called the "Junkyard Bomber". Later a pattern emerged in which many of the victims were university professors, airline executives, or people involved in the computer industry.

In December 1985 a bomb hidden inside a paper bag killed the owner of a computer store. In 1987 a woman who worked in a computer store saw a man put a bag under the wheel of her car and it exploded and injured another person who worked at the shop when they tried to open it.

From this episode, however, the police had a picture of the culprit which the newspapers published, but without result because he had been wearing a hood and sunglasses.

In 1995 the Unabomber offered to stop his attacks if the newspapers published a statement he had written. They agreed and the statement was published in September 1995. In its several pages it said that modern technology was destroying the human race.

David Kaczynski, the Unabomber's brother, read the statement and it reminded him of his brother 'Ted', and he told the FBI this.

On 3 April 1996, Theodore John Kaczynski, who had come to be known as the "Unabomber", was arrested in a hideout in the mountains of Montana. He was 53, a former maths professor at a Californian university, and police found a diary he had kept of his bombings.

The Unabomber pleaded guilty and was sentenced to four life terms plus 30 years in the 'Supermax' prison near Colorado Springs (Weil, 2013).

In summary his bombings were:

1. Universities: 1978, 1979, 1981, 1982, 1982, 1985, 1985
2. University staff: 1993, 1993
3. Airplanes and airline executives: 1979, 1980, 1985
4. Computer stores: 1985, 1987
5. Advertising & forestry assoc. executives: 1994, 1995

MEDITERRANEAN HIJACK

On 7 October 1985 hundreds of passengers on the cruise ship *Achille Lauro* were taken hostage by four members of the

Palestine Liberation Front (PLF). They demanded the release of 50 Palestinians held by Israel.

The hostage crisis lasted for two days, during which the terrorists shot a wheelchair bound 69 year-old American because he was Jewish, throwing his body into the sea.

Egypt intervened and offered the terrorists safe harbour if they freed their hostages. The terrorists agreed and boarded an Egyptian jet but American Navy fighter planes surrounded it and forced it to land on the island of Sicily where the terrorists were arrested.

When Italy released one of the hijackers on parole in 1991 the family of the murdered American protested.

Other PLF members involved in the hijack are still at large, but in 2003 US troops captured the leader of the hijacking, Abu Abbas, in Baghdad.

PLANE BOMBINGS

On 21 September 1988 a Pan Am Boeing 747 blew up over the Scottish village of Lockerbie killing 270 people, including 11 on the ground. An April 1990 British investigators announced finding an electronic component linking two Libyan agents to the explosion. The UN imposed sanctions on Libya to force it to hand over the two agents for international trial.

In March 1989 Libyan agents blew up a French UTA plane over Niger, killing 170 people, including the wife of the US ambassador to Chad.

BOMBING OF JEWISH CULTURAL CENTRE

In 1994 a suicide bombing of the Jewish cultural centre in Buenos Aires killed 85 people and wounded 300. Investigators concluded that the attack had been carried out by Hezbollah on orders from

Tehran. Only two years earlier the Israeli embassy in Buenos Aires was bombed, killing 29 people and wounding 200.

THE OKLAHOMA CITY BOMBING

The 1995 Oklahoma City bombing, in which 168 people were killed, was the most spectacular act of terrorism on US soil before the September 11 attacks. It was in revenge for the mass deaths in 1993 of members of the Branch Davidian movement at Waco after a 51-day siege by federal agents.

The FBI charged Timothy McVeigh and Terry Nichols with the bombing but only McVeigh was convicted and executed on 11 June 2001. McVeigh's chief defence counselor, however, found that McVeigh and Nichols had had contacts with Aryan Nation, other people with neo-Nazi sympathies and, most interesting of all, Nicholls had been to the Philippines several times where he had been in contact with Ramzi Yousef, who in turn had had contact with al-Qa'ida and Osama Bin Laden.

Ramzi Yousef was responsible for the 1993 bombing of the World Trade Centre, and for the plot to destroy Philippines Airlines Flight 434 in 1994 (Jones & Israel, 1998).

Such groups as Aryan Nation, if their rhetoric is to be believed, may pose a serious threat to the US in future:

We must in one voice, cry out that we will not tolerate their stinking, murdering, lying, corrupt government.

Louis Beam, speech at the 'Rocky Mountain Rendezvous' (1992), a meeting of several far-right groups.

I suspect Americans will begin engaging in terrorism on a scale the world has never known.
William Pearce, author of *The Turner Diaries* (1978) and leader of the National Alliance, a US neo-Nazi group.

THE 9/11 WORLD TRADE CENTRE ATTACKS

On 11 September 2001 the most spectacular terrorist attack in history took place. It had been planned by al-Qa'ida, which opposes non-Islamic governments, then led by the notorious Osama Bin Laden. Al-Qa'ida had also bombed the World Trade Center in 1993, killing six and injuring more than a 1,000.

Terrorists hijacked four passenger planes and crashed two of them into the upper levels of the Twin Towers of the World Trade Center in New York City. As Bin Laden would have expected, having had a knowledge of structural engineering, the floors impacted fell, the resulting dynamic load on the floors below quickly bringing those crashing down also, both buildings quickly collapsing into a pile of smoking rubble within a couple of minutes.

The third jet crashed into the Pentagon building, and the fourth into a field near Pittsburgh after the passengers prevented it reaching another target building. All those on board the four planes were killed.

About 50,000 people worked in the World Trade Center, and almost 3,000 people were killed at the site on that fateful day, a hundred of them fire fighters and police.

About 23,000 people work at the Pentagon, and 120 people in it were killed.

After the twin towers were destroyed all New York City's airports were closed, and then all US flights were cancelled, those in the air over the US having to land at the nearest airport, those from other countries being redirected to Canada.

From that fateful day the USA's 'War on Terror' began in earnest.

Soon after the September 11 attacks numerous anthrax letters were posted around the country, resulting in the closure of public buildings for long periods. To this day it is now known who perpetrated these acts.

THE MOSCOW THEATRE SIEGE

On 23 October 2002, 40 to 50 armed Chechens, who claimed allegiance to the Islamist militant separatist movement in Chechnya, raided a Moscow theatre and took 850 hostages, demanding withdrawal of Russian forces from Chechnya and an end to the Second Chechen War.

The terrorists also had bombs that, if detonated, could have brought down the ceiling and caused in excess of 80 percent casualties. After a two-and-a-half day siege and the execution of two female hostages, Russian security units pumped a chemical agent into the building's ventilation system and raided it.

All 40 of the attackers were killed, along with 130 hostages, but there were no casualties among the security units. The use of the gas was widely condemned as heavy-handed, but the American and British governments deemed Russia's actions justifiable.

Physicians in Moscow condemned the refusal to disclose the identity of the gas that prevented them from saving more lives. Some reports said the drug naloxone was successfully used to save some hostages.

THE MADRID SUBWAY BOMBINGS

Since the 9/11 attacks in the US, many European cities had been on high alert for terrorist attacks.

Three days before a Spanish election, on 11 March 2004 suicide bombers detonated ten bombs on four commuter trains in Madrid. Seven of the explosions were in or close to Madrid's main station, the Atocha station, the other three exploding near Atocha.

The first three bombs exploded just after 7:30 AM inside Atocha station, severely damaging several carriages and killing at least 34 people, wounding dozens of others.

At the same time four more bombs exploded on a second train, killing 59 people and wounding many others.

Three more bombs exploded on two trains en route to Madrid, killing at least 85 and wounding many others.

Later police found three more unexploded bombs at Atocha station, two of them in backpacks.

A cell phone was found in one of these backpacks, leading to the arrest of several men, one of whom had ties to al-Qa'ida. Then, when police were closing on a suspect apartment a bomb exploded in it, killing the occupants.

Spanish authorities searched worldwide for other suspects and in October 2007 Spain's National Court convicted 21 men of the Madrid bombings, finding another seven not guilty (Weil, 2013).

The Madrid subway attacks were the worst terrorist attack in Spain's history.

THE LONDON UNDERGROUND BOMBINGS

On 7 July 2005 at about 8:50 AM bombs planted by terrorists exploded in three trains shortly after they had left King's Cross under-ground station.

A train which had been waiting in the tunnel 100 yards away from Aldgate Street was severely damaged and eight people killed.

A second bomb exploded in a train between King's Cross and Russel Square stations, killing 27 people.

The third bomb exploded in a train arriving at Edgeware Road, blowing holes in several nearby trains and killing 7 people.

Almost an hour after the last Underground explosion a bomb exploded on the upper deck of a Number 30 double-decker bus as it stopped at the junction of Upper Woburn Place and Tavistock Square. The roof of the bus was ripped off and fourteen people killed.

The fourth bomb had also been intended for an Underground train but the bomber, 18 year-old Hasid Hussain, was turned back from the Underground because the Northern Line station was closed.

The four bombings killed 56 people, including the four bombers, and injured 700 others, some very seriously. Al-Qa'ida claimed responsibility (Weil, 2013).

AUSTRALIAN PLOT

In 2005 police Operation Pendennis raided two terrorist cells in Melbourne and Sydney inspired by Melbourne man Abdul Nacer Benbrika. It was believed that the Sydney cell was close to launching a major attack.

Eighteen men were prosecuted and sentenced, one for 28 years. Most, however, have been released, some of them then going overseas to fight with IS, others radicalizing young men in Australia who left to fight with IS.

THE 2011 OSLO BOMBING

In 2011, 32 year-old Anders Behring Breivik, a body-builder and committed Christian, posted messages on the Internet saying he wanted to keep Muslims out of Norway.

At around 3:30 PM on 22 July 2011 a huge blast shook the centre of Oslo, severely damaging the offices of Norway's Prime

Minister and other government buildings. Eight people were killed and dozens injured.

Breivik had planted the bomb, then driving to catch a ferry to the island of Utoya disguised as a policeman and carrying a fake police ID card, a pistol, and an automatic rifle.

On Utoya, Norway's Labor Party was holding a summer camp for hundreds of young people, most of them less than 20 years old.

On arriving, Breivik told people to go to the main building on the island to watch news of the Oslo bombing. Then he put on earplugs and rushed in and began shooting people. Many ran out of the building but Breivik pursued them to the water's edge and into caves and shot them, one person drowning while trying to escape, other being shot while trying to swim to safety.

When police arrived an hour after the shooting had begun Breivik was still shooting. When the police found him he surrendered and was later convicted and jailed.

Eight people died in the Oslo bombing, and more than 200 were injured. The death toll at Utoya was 69, with more than 100 injured. The attacks were the worst massacre in Norway's modern history (Weil, 2013).

KENYAN SHOPPING CENTRE ATTACK

In 2013 the Al Shabab terrorist group attacked the crowded Westgate shopping centre in Kenya, inflicting many casualties.

NIGERIA

According to Amnesty International, Boko Haram kidnapped 2000 women in Nigeria in the period January 2014 to March 2015.

In April 2014 Boko Haram abducted 219 Nigerian schoolgirls from Chibok, in the north-eastern state of Borno. It was believed that they had been split into three or four groups and held at different Boko Haram camps.

In May 2014 Boko Haram released a video message showing 100 of the girls in Muslim dress and reciting verses of the Koran. The message said that the women had been converted to Islam and been "married off".

Women who have escaped from Boko Haram have told of being kept in overcrowded prisons, being forced to cook and clean, and being forced to marry Islamist fighters.

According to the Melbourne Herald-Sun newspaper (15/4/2015): "One human rights advocate who interviewed more than 80 abducted women and girls after their escape said that in 23 cases they had been raped either before arrival at camps or after forced marriage."

In May 2015 Boko Haram were reported to have fired rockets into a Nigerian city, the Nigerian army returning fire.

MH370

On 8 March 2014 Malaysian Airlines flight MH370 disappeared en route from Kuala Lumpur to China with 227 passengers on board. Despite extensive searches, it was not until 16 months later that parts of the plane were found on Reunion Island near Madagascar.

Such a location suggests that the plane might have been highjacked by Islamic terrorists (as in the 9/11 attacks) and then flown to a remote location and ditched. No other sensible explanation is plausible as pilot error could not take a plane so far off course.

SYDNEY ATTACK

In December 2014 a self-styled Muslim preacher held about 20 people hostages in a Sydney café for several hours. When police heard shots they stormed the café and killed him, hitting him with several bullets to do so, but two hostages were also killed during the siege and several others injured.

THE CHARLIE HEBDOE SIEGE

In 2006 riots broke out in various parts of the Muslim world about cartoons published in an obscure periodical in Denmark. According to Harris (2007): "What to liberal Westerners appeared to be a harmless cartoon led to outbreaks of lethal violence in Afghanistan and Nigeria, where Muslims seized and murdered Christians in the streets."

On the morning of 7 January 2015 two masked brothers, Said and Cherif Kouachie, armed with Kalashnikovs and a rocket-launcher, invaded the offices of the French satirical magazine *Charlie Hebdoe* because it had published cartoons mocking the prophet Muhammad. Eleven people were killed and eleven injured in the offices by the Muslim fanatics, and after leaving they killed a police officer.

The gunmen identified themselves as belonging to the Yemen branch of al-Qa'ida. Several related attacks followed in the Île-de-France region in which five more people were killed and another eleven wounded.

France raised its alert to its highest level and deployed soldiers in Île-de-France and Picardy. When the brothers took hostages at a signage company in Dammartin-en-Goële on 9 January they were shot dead when they emerged from the building firing.

On 11 January, about 2 million people, including more than 40 world leaders, met in Paris for a rally of national unity, and 3.7 million people joined demonstrations across France. The phrase *Je suis Charlie* was a common slogan of support at the rallies and in social media. The remaining staff of *Charlie Hebdo* continued publication, the following issue's print run being 7.95 million copies in six languages, in contrast to the typical print run of 60,000 in only French.

Harris (2007) argues that, in contrast to Islamic fundamentalists, Christian fundamentalists are not fanatics, an example being peaceful protests when copies of the Ten Commandments were removed from a court house in Alabama in which: "None lifted a finger to stop the process - - no one was killed; no one received a scratch."

MYANMAR REFUGEE CRISIS

In the first half of 2015 yet another refugee crisis began when members of the Muslim minority in Myanmar fled, claiming persecution by the Buddhist majority, many of them on boats run by people smugglers. Many of the boats, as usual, were old and leaky, and many people died on them as they floated aimlessly in the sea after being refused entry by various countries, before a few countries agreed to intervene and save them.

On one boat survivors reported that Muslims threw many Christians overboard, so that other passengers had to form a human shield to protect a few remaining Christians still on board from the same fate.

SAUDI ARABIA ATTACKED

In early April 2015 Somalia-based terrorist group Al Shabaab captured and killed 140 Kenyan University students, first separating out Christian students to be killed.

CHRISTIANS DROWNED BY MUSLIMS

On 18 April 2015, Melbourne's *Herald-Sun* newspaper reported that Muslims on a boat full of Libyan asylum seekers off the coast of Africa threw 12 Christians overboard. It was reported that survivors, when picked up by Italian police, told a "dreadful" story of "forcefully resisting attempts to drown them, forming a veritable human chain in some cases".

MELBOURNE PLOTS

On 18 April 2015 police arrested five young men over an alleged plot to kill police officers with knives and swords during Melbourne's centenary Anzac Day celebrations.

Melbourne police had been alerted by police in England who had discovered suspicious communications between a 14 year-old from the north-western city of Blackburn and the Melbourne men. In one of these he had urged the Melbourne teenagers to carry out a knife, car or gun attack, suggesting they run over a policeman and then decapitate him.

More than 200 officers conducted seven raids at 3:30 AM, finding knives, swords and IS material. Two men were kept in custody, one being charged with preparations for, or planning, terrorist raids. Two others were charged later.

One of those arrested told police that a school friend of his had recently been killed fighting in Iraq or Syria.

It is believed that one motive of the would-be terrorists was to avenge the death of Numan Haider, a Muslim man who had been shot and killed by police after he attacked and stabbed two of them on 23/9/2014. Two of the group had been to Haider's funeral, whilst the two leaders of the group had frequented a controversial Islamic group run by a "firebrand" Islamic cleric.

Haider had attended lectures by this cleric at the Al-Furqan Information Centre in Melbourne where the cleric, Harun

Mehicevic, had in 2012 told his followers not to take the oath of citizenship pledging allegiance to an 'unbeliever' government. He is reported to have ended each lecture by saying that Allah would help the mujahideen (holy warriors) build an Islamic State for Muslims.

A senior IS recruiter from Melbourne who went overseas to fight with IS had ties to the Al-Furqan centre and was alleged to have communicated with the men accused of the 2015 Anzac Day terror plot in Melbourne.

THE UKRAINE

In recent years there has been conflict between Russian-supported rebel forces and government forces in the region containing important port cities such as Odessa and Berdyansk. Currently there is, supposedly, a ceasefire, but conflict continues with considerable intensity.

Trade sanctions against Russia for supporting the rebel forces in Ukraine were put in place but had little effect, and it is still quite likely that a separate Russian-speaking province in the north of the Ukraine might eventually achieve independence.

ISLAMIC STATE TERROR

In June 2014, the group then known as Islamic State in Iraq and Levant (ISIS) attacked the city of Mosul, population 1.8 million, in northern Iraq. Confronted by as few as 800 militants, about 30,000 Iraqi soldiers fled, leaving behind US armoured vehicles and weapons.

At the end of June 2014, ISIS renamed itself Islamic State and formally declared the establishment of a "caliphate", demanding allegiance from Muslims worldwide.

In August 2014, IS attacked the semi-autonomous Kurdistan region, forcing the inferior Kurdish forces to flee, leaving IS free to kill many men and boys, and rape and enslave many women and girls.

Early in 2015, IS captured the key city of Tikrit, a major embarrassment to the Iraqi government and the US.

In May 2015, Islamic State terrorists herded an audience into an ancient Roman amphitheatre in Syria and publicly shot 20 captives in front of them.

IS having overrun much of Iraq and Syria, it is now believed to control 90% of the oil fields in Syria, using mobile refineries to produce petrol which is smuggled into Iran and other countries to make at least US$2M per day to finance its widespread terrorist activities.

APRIL 2015

In April 2015, Iraqi government forces retook Tikrit after a month-long offensive.

The following short article comes from Melbourne's Herald-Sun newspaper on 15 April, 2015:

> *IRAQ has exhumed the remains of 164 military cadets massacred by Islamic State terrorists and dumped in mass graves in Tikrit, the Human Rights Ministry has said.*
> *The remains were discovered at ex-president Saddam Hussein's palace compound.*
> *They are among an estimated 1700 victims from a military academy tricked by IS gunmen into boarding buses last year then all shot.*

MAY 2015

In late May 2015, there were reports that ISIS was recruiting top scientists to work on producing advanced biochemical weapons. As Table 26.1 suggests, this is a frightening prospect.

Most disturbing of all, reports that ISIS has also begun collecting radioactive material from hospitals to make 'dirty bombs' have caused concern. Such reports occurred a few years ago, then the concern being al-Qa'ida, but ISIS, of course, is hardly unconnected in thinking and operations from 'AQ.'

JUNE 2015

On 8 June 2015 a BBC interviewer on the 'Hard Talk' program was bemoaning the fact that relative peace was still not forthcoming in Nigeria after many years, and the hostilities of Boko Haram which had resulted in the death of 50,000 people and displaced half a million.

On Wednesday 10 June, 2015, Melbourne's *Herald-Sun* newspaper carried a report from Syria headed "Virgins sold cheap" which began:

> Teenage girls abducted by Islamic State fighters are being sold in slave markets "for as little as a packet of cigarettes", says the UN envoy on sexual violence.

The article ended with:

> A recent UN report said close to 25,000 foreign fighters from over 100 countries were involved in conflicts, with the largest influx into Syria and Iraq. Ms Bangura [the envoy] said the abuse of women and girls was "medieval", because IS wanted to "build a society that reflects the 13th century."

That same paper on (14/6/15) had an article beginning:

TURKEY TERRORIST LINK PROBE.

THE Turkish government will investigate a terrorist recruitment network with an Australian extremist at its head.

On Saturday 20 June, 2015 an article in Melbourne's *Herald-Sun* newspaper began:

JIHADI TEACHER

> A NOTORIOUS jihadi in Syria has boasted of helping
> a young Melbourne extremist make a bomb.
> The Herald Sun has obtained transcripts of encrypted
> messages in which hacker and bomb-maker
> Junaid Hussain – acknowledged as one of Islamic
> State's most dangerous operatives – claims that
> he "mentored" a young Australian to develop a
> deadly weapon from easily accessible materials.

The young Australian was caught before he could blow up people at Australia's annual Anzac Day commemoration ceremony in Melbourne – a typical "we're tougher than you" etcetera act of Muslim terrorism.

On Saturday June 27, 2015 an article in the *Herald-Sun* was headed:

WORLD TERROR STRIKES
19 die in Tunisia: 13 killed in Kuwait: French beheading

In the same edition, another article told of a border city in Syria being brutally attacked by ISIS, and of the Turkish President being accused of "allowing" ISIS forces to cross the border.

On June 29, 2015, page 7 of *The Australian* newspaper carried an article which began:

"UK's worst terror toll in a decade
SOUSSE: [in Tunisia] Britain has endured its blackest day at the hands of Islamist-inspired terrorism in a decade, with at least 15 Britons – including three members of the same family – among the dozens killed in the Tunisian carnage."

JULY 2015

The *Herald-Sun*, Thursday July 2, 2015 carried four articles involving ISIS in some way:

(a) The ISIS-linked terrorist who killed 38 people on a Tunisian beach a few days earlier was said by a hotel worker to be "laughing and smiling as he massacred his 38 victims with an AK-47 assault rifle." Fellow university students said that he disguised his fanaticism by "indulging in drinking and sex".

(b) The second article said:
A FRENCH prosecutor has confirmed that the man who beheaded his boss and tried to blow up a gas factory had a "terrorist motive" and links to Islamic State in Syria.

(c) The third article said:
ABOUT 1200 prisoners, including al-Qaeda suspects and convicted murderers, escaped from a prison in south-western Yemen after Shi'ite rebels let them out.

(d) The fourth article was headed:
'(IS) BEHEADING PEOPLE, KILLING CHILDREN, RAPING AND BEATING WOMEN, IT REALLY GOT TO HIM IN THE END'

and reported that an Australian man had gone to fight with the Kurdish YPG, known as the People's Defence Unit, because he was disillusioned with the brutality of ISIS, but was killed by a land mine laid by Islamic jihadist forces.

In early July 2015 it was reported that Syrian rebels led by the al-Nusra front had successfully begun an offensive against the northern city of Aleppo.

On July 2, 2015, it was reported that Islamic State had released a video showing them executing 25 captured Syrian soldiers.

On July 8, 2015, it was reported that attacks by Boko Haram militants seeking to overtake Nigeria had killed 300 people in a week.

On July 21, 2015, it was reported that rebel bombing in of a major city in Yemen had killed 57. The next day it was reported that shelling near the same city had killed almost 100.

AUGUST 2015

In early August 2015 jihadists associated with Islamic State carried out a suicide bombing of a mosque inside a police compound in Saudi Arabia, killing at least 15 people.

In early August reports surfaced that British jihadis planned to blow up the Queen during 70th anniversary of VJ Day celebrations.

In mid-August it was reported that Australia was considering joining the US in bombing strikes on IS targets in Syria, an activity it was already undertaking in Iraq. By mid-September 2015 Australian planes had begun this campaign.

On August 15 it was reported that a truck bomb had killed 67 and wounded 150 at a market in a Shi'ite neighbourhood in Baghdad. Such bombings continue in Iraq on an almost daily basis.

On August 20 the Australian government reported that, over a period of about 10 months, 336 potential jihadists had been prevented from leaving the country for hotspots such as Iraq and Syria. In two linked groups of 2 and 5 men each was carrying $10,000 in cash.

On 21/8/2015 the *Herald-Sun* reported that the archaeologist in charge of the ancient ruins of Palmyra in Syria had been beheaded by Islamic State militants and his body hung in the main square. Subsequently, IS then set about destroying ancient temples and monuments in the city.

In the *Weekend Australian* of August 22-23 it was reported that Israel blamed Iran for firing four rockets into the Upper Galilee and Golan Heights territories, the latter having been partly seized from Syria during the 1967 war, also blaming Iran for periodic fire into the Golan. In response Israel launched artillery and air strikes against 14 Syrian military posts.

On August 23 it was reported that a heavily armed Moroccan had opened fire on a train travelling from Amsterdam to Paris, wounding two and injuring three before being overcome by passengers, two of whom were members of US military forces.

SEPTEMBER 2015

Early in September 2015 a UNICEF report said that more than 13 million children were being denied education because of Middle East conflicts, UNICEF having documented 214 attacks on schools in Syria, Iraq, Libya, Sudan, Yemen, and the Palestinian territories during 2014.

On the 1st of September Melbourne's *Herald-Sun* newspaper reported that the Islamic group Boko Haram had killed 68 villagers in northeast Nigeria, bringing the death toll of their six-year uprising to nearly 20,000.

On the 2nd an IS suicide bomber killed 28 people at a Shi'ite mosque in the Yemeni capital of Sana'a. IS, which considers Shi'ites to be heretics, had claimed similar bombings of other Shi'ite mosques in the city.

On the 9th the *Herald-Sun* reported that Germany's foreign intelligence agency had "information that IS used mustard gas in northern Iraq." There have also been reports of IS using mustard gas in Syria, probably using stockpiles hidden by the Assad regime.

In mid-September fears of civil war in Turkey were reported as Government forces continued major operations against militants of the Kurdistan Workers' Party (PKK) and thousands of demonstrators took to the streets to protest against many bloody PKK attacks.

On the 20th a series of bomb blasts at a mosque in north-eastern Nigeria attributed to Boko Haram killed at least 117 people. Many such attacks had occurred since a new President had come to power late in May, vowing to crush the insurgency.

Throughout the month the refugee crisis in Europe deepened with more than a million refugees expected to have arrived by the end of 2015. By the middle of the month Hungary and neighbouring countries had begun closing off their borders to prevent migrant access, prompting urgent talks to set migrant quotas for all EU countries.

Towards the end of the month it was reported that after over four years of conflict in Syria 250,000 people had been killed and that 12 million Syrians were in need of assistance, nearly half of them children.

It was also reported that US intelligence estimated that nearly 30,000 foreign fighters, perhaps 250 of the American, had gone to Iraq and Syria, many of them to joining Islamic State.

On the 29th of September the Taliban captured the city of Kunduz in northern Afghanistan, the first time the insurgents had captured a major urban area since the 2001 US-led invasion of the country. More than 600 prisoners, including 140 Taliban, were released from the city's jail.

OCTOBER 2015

In early October 2015 Russia began air strikes against IS and also rebel forces opposing the Assad government. The US, which had supported the anti-Assad rebels, protested but Australia's foreign minister, Julie Bishop, was cautiously supportive of Russia's efforts, saying that "all transition options" should be considered, and that, in the short term at least, Assad and Iran should perhaps play a role in any peace process in Syria.

The *Weekend Australian* of October 3-4 reported that Iran believed that the US-led air campaign against IS had failed, and that:

> The original Obama idea of training rebel forces who would simultaneously fight both Assad and Islamic State turns out to have been a strategic fantasy.

Foreign editor Greg Sheridan wrote:

> The Russian moves transform strategic calculations in Syria and have left Washington completely flat-footed and almost irrelevant. The Russians now control the narrative. Obama has become that most grotesque of strategic players – an impotent enemy and a dangerous friend.

Reports of civilian casualties from the first Russian air strikes soon emerged, but these were followed by reports of an American air strike on a hospital in the embattled city of Kunduz in Afghanistan. The hospital, run by Medicine sans Frontiers, reported many casualties and patients were burnt alive in their beds, also disputing US claims that insurgents were hiding in the hospital.

The final death toll was 22, including several medical staff, and the US military subsequently apologized for this "tragic event."

On Friday October 3rd a 14-year old Muslim boy fatally shot a police worker in the back of the head at point-blank range outside a Sydney police station, before being killed by police. Only the day before the shooting his sister had left Australia for the Middle East.

In response to the shooting police raided four homes, two of them linked to convicted criminals, and arrested two young men, one a 16-year old who had been to school with the shooter and who had previously been charged with waving an IS flag at a nun and threatening to kill Christians.

On October 16 it was reported that police had charged a 22-year old man with supplying the gun used in the killing, and also an 18-year old man with giving it to the killer at a nearby mosque shortly before the killing.

In early October 2015, it was reported that ISIS groups were forming in Australian jails, and that there were at least 30 members of an ISIS gang in Goulbourne jail in NSW, forcing management to reserve a section of the prison for Muslims after threats were made to behead prison staff.

By early October 2015, Islamic State group forces had advanced to the outskirts of Aleppo, Syria's second city, killing one of the senior commanders of Iran's Revolutionary Guards.

In early October it was reported that IS was recruiting heavily in Indonesia where the government reported circa 1000 Indonesians to be fighting for IS and its allies in Iraq and Syria. It was also reported that Islamic State's 20 mosques in Indonesia were regularly collecting money to support IS, whilst many schools encouraged extremism, some giving classes in bomb-making. In mid-October it was reported that two churches in Indonesia had been attacked and destroyed.

By mid-October several Israelis and Palestinians had been killed by renewed urban conflict in the region, and talk of a third intifada having begun, a Hamas spokesman said: "The intifada is intensifying."

On Friday 16th of October, Palestinians torched a sacred Jewish site in the West Bank, Palestinians having earlier called for a "Friday of revolution" against Israel after it was announced that men less than 40 years of age would be barred from the main weekly prayers at the "flashpoint" Al-Aqsa mosque.

On the same day President Obama announced that a planned withdrawal of nearly all of US forces [about 10,000] serving in Afghanistan was to be deferred until 2017.

Also on that same day, it was reported that 300 Cuban troops were to being sent to Syria to man Russian tanks fighting Islamic State.

The Weekend Australian of October 17-18 (2015) reported that, as the result of a request by France, Australia was "likely" to send a naval frigate to the Persian Gulf to "help in the fight against Islamic State."

It also reported that the organization funding a mosque planned for the Victorian city of Bendigo, the Australian Islamic Mission, "has received financial support from an organization accused of channeling support funds to terrorists." That organization, Human Appeal International Australia, was reported to be one of 36 organizations banned by the Israeli government since 2008 because it "channeled funds to Hamas," in particular to hospitals in the Gaza strip run by Hamas, one such hospital being reported by *The Washington Post* as housing Hamas' headquarters.

In the same edition a reader's letter read:

> *Christianity is radical in that it stresses peace and forbearance in a world of violence. This is diametrically opposite to violence and forcible conversion. If we deradicalise Islam, and therefore remove its central inspiration, it will no longer be Islam, but a Christianized version. It is obvious to all scholars of religion that this is never going to occur. It is a pipedream of poorly informed postmodernist secularists who have no beliefs.*

NOVEMBER 2015

Conflict between Israelis and Palestinians having continued throughout October, in early November there seemed no end in sight to what had been termed by some Palestinians a third intifada, despite rallies by thousands of Israelis calling for Israeli-Palestinian peace talks.

Throughout October Russia stepped up its air strikes against ISIS and other rebels in Syria, on October 30 being reported to have flown 71 sorties and struck 118 terrorist targets in 24 hours.

On November 1, the US announced that it was going to deploy up to 50 special operations soldiers to assist Kurdish and Arab forces in northern Syria.

Conflict continued in Nigeria, mosques in two north-eastern towns having been bombed in late October.

Throughout October the flood of mostly Muslim refugees from Syria, Iraq and Northern Africa continued, despite attempts in some European countries to close their borders or redirect refugees elsewhere. By November the situation had reached crisis point, encouraging greater international efforts to combat Islamic terrorism that had caused the flood of refugees.

On Friday 13th terrorist attacks occurred at 6 sites in Paris, killing 129 people, and wounding some 350 more, about 100 of them critically. Seven attackers were killed, six of them killing themselves with suicide bomb vests, the other being shot by police. At one of the sites, a popular concert venue, the attackers opened fire on the crowd at random with automatic rifles, killing nearly 100 people.

A US terrorism expert now working at Royal Melbourne Institute of Technology said that the attacks were a "game changer", saying that ISIS now had "franchises" in several countries. On Melbourne radio a caller blamed the Muslim religion, and the acronym ISIS bears witness to that view.

JUNE 2016

In the *Herald-Sun* of 27/6/16, columnist Andrew Bolt wrote regarding how we are strongly discouraged from criticizing other religions such as the evil Muslim one at a time at which people around the world feel threatened by it. He said:

How insulted do you feel by those multiplying laws which now treat you as some vicious moron who cannot be trusted to read and speak as you think best, restricting your freedom to criticize any other faith or culture but your own?

On June 28 eight suicide bombers attacked a Lebanese Christian village, killing 5 and wounding dozens more in, "the latest violent spillover of the five-year-old Syrian war into Lebanon" (Herald-Sun, 29/6/2016).

Only the next day, three suicide bombers attacked Turkey's Ataturk airport, using guns and bombs to kill circa 40 people and wounding over one hundred.

Conflict between Australian nationalist and Muslim-sympathetic "anti-racism" groups occurred several times in 2015 and 16, for example:

(a) The burning down of a Church in a Victorian provincial town that was being used as a mosque in 2016.
(b) Clashes between protesting nationalist and anti-racism activists in Melbourne on Sunday 27 June, 2016, in which Melbourne's Herald-Sun newspaper reported that "Masked thugs burn Aussie flag", resulting in many readers' letters protesting this act, most attributing it to Muslim-sympathetic men. Many of those involved in the violence that ensued were wearing masks, resulting in suggestion that this be made illegal.

Indeed, a bottom line here is that the burka should be banned, as it is in France, and a new edition of the Qu'ran with less reference to jihad etcetera is badly needed. Until such measures can be achieved, it might eventually be necessary to create prison camps similar to those used by the Nazis in WW2 to house Muslims in some countries – and if that seems absurd note that Australia's offshore detention centres are, in effect, concentration camps in which people are held for years on end, 2000 'incident reports' on these vindicating many mistreatment claims by refuges held in these centre.

JULY 2016

On 1/7/16 Melbourne's *Herald-Sun* newspaper reported:

> *A teenager who pleaded guilty to terrorism offences for plotting to kill police on Anzac day left his parents a suicide note. Australian Federal Police allege Sevdet Besim planned to run down a police officer with a car, beheading him or her, and use the officer's gun to shoot others. - - Federal police found a "martyrdom note" to his parents.*

On 4/7/16 an ISIS attack in a Shiite district of Baghdad killed more than 200 people and injured hundreds more. The attack came a week after Iraqi forces recaptured Fallujah, 50km west of Baghdad from IS, leaving Mosul as the only Iraqi city under jihadist control. No doubt this attack, the worst in Iraq for 10 years, was carried out by ISIS members who had fled Fallujah before it was completely overtaken.

According to SBS1 TV news at 7.30 PM AEST on 6/7/2016 the death toll from this attack had risen to more than 250. A couple of days later the death toll had risen to 292.

A day later there were 3 suicide bomb attacks in Saudi Arabia:

1. Three attackers killed several people outside a mosque in Medina in which the prophet Muhammad is said to be buried.
2. A single attacker outside the US embassy in Jedda who killed only himself but injured many others.
3. A single attacker outside a Shiite mosque in Katif who again killed only himself but injured many others.

On the very same day there were terrorist attacks in Turkey and Bangladesh. The latter involved 7 "militants" and killed 22 people in a bakery popular with foreigners in Dhaka. It was reported that the terrorists separated Muslims from non-Muslims by asking them to recite a passage from the Koran.

This attack was reportedly carried out by supposedly well-off young Bangladeshi men who had been to private schools and fee-paying Universities. IS claimed responsibility for the attacks but the government insisted that the attackers were members of JMB, Jamaat-ul-Mujahadeen Bangladesh, which claims to represent IS but has no proven links to it.

On the same day there was also conflict between two rebels groups in central Africa, one being the UPC, yet another Muslim terrorist organization.

On 6/7/2016 the *Herald-Sun* newspaper reported that:

1. *A man acquitted in Australia's biggest terror trial has been interviewed by police investigating the murder of a woman whose battered body was found dumped in Melbourne's north.*

   The woman had been the wife of this Lebanese Muslim, Bassam Raad, and her body was found in car park opposite the home of "the jailed terror mastermind and co-accused, Abdul Nacer Benrika last month."

   On July 7 Raad appeared at the Melbourne Magistrate's court to be charged with murder, as well as three counts of intentionally causing serious injury to his children.

2. A woman's body was found in a Kew flat behind a kebab shop which had been closed for weeks. The owner, presumably a Muslim, was believed be overseas, no doubt fighting for IS just as the father and sons of an unpleasant Muslim

man whose home is in the same street as that of the first author are likely to be, their home having been left vacant for several months.
3. A Syrian national who had been freed by the US from Guantanamo to resettle in Uruguay had gone missing. He had been said to have gone to Brazil but Uruguayan authorities denied this. No doubt, like many others, he had gone to fight with IS during the month of holy month of Ramadan, during which Islamic terror groups such as IS, al-Qa'ida and al-Shabaab usually increase their attacks.
4. *Deadly attacks from terrorists pledging allegiance to Islamic State have taken place in countries as disparate as Bangladesh, the US, Jordan, Iraq, France, Turkey, Yemen, the Philippines, Lebanon and Saudi Arabia.*

    In late May Islamic State spokesman Abu Muhammed al-Adani called upon the group's followers to "make it (Ramadan), with God's permission a month of pain for infidels everywhere."
5. It was reported that a former activist and Islamist rejected that views of some that terrorism has no religion, saying:

    The fact is, claiming that IS has nothing to do with Islam is as unhelpful and ignorant as saying IS 'is' Islam per se.

    It's blindingly obvious they have something to do with Islam and everyone's laughing at us for trying to deny this.

BASTILLE DAY ATTACK

On 14th July 2016 France suffered yet another terrorist attack during Bastille Day celebrations. In this attack, for which IS later claimed responsibility, a large truck mowed down and killed 80 people and injured many others on a major promenade before the driver was killed by police gunfire. Such attacks will ensure that

Europe makes every effort to send the millions of Muslim migrants that have recently arrived there from jihad-ridden regions in the Middle East and North Africa back to where they came from.

YET MORE TERRORISM IN JULY 2016

With significant numbers of IS terrorists leaving areas of Iraq and Syria being retaken by the US + Russia etc. coalition, these insane sub humans had moved into Europe amidst the millions of "refugees" that had fled the Middle East and northern Africa in recent last years. Once based in Europe they would, of course, soon have made contact on the IS grapevine with other terrorists and have organized more killings, for example only:

1. On July 22 an 18-year old "German-Iranian" shot and killed 9 or more people in Munich, injuring more than 20 others, then moving to a rooftop car park and shooting himself after a standoff with police of a few hours. According to Deutsche Welle English News, Police said that he "was most likely acting alone" and perhaps had mental "problems", but this was only some 24 hours into the investigation, if that, and it is still quite likely that he had been influenced directly or indirectly by IS or its propaganda.
2. This was just a couple of days after an Afghan refugee had injured several people severely with a knife elsewhere in Germany before being shot dead by police.
3. According to France 24 English News, the very next day 3 IS suicide bombers killed over 80 and injured more than another 200 ethnic minority Hazeras while they were conducting a protest march in Kabul. One suicide vest failed to detonate or the death toll would have been higher.

Not surprisingly, NHK news reported that there was a growing distrust of refugees in Germany, where more a million more of whom had ended up there in only about a year, this because, of course, of several recent attacks, including those noted above.

Also on 22 July, 2016, several soldiers were missing after government forces had been ambushed in Nigeria by Boko Haram.

That same day, it was announced that the search for missing Malaysian airline flight MH370 would be discontinued at the end of 2016, having continued for almost 2 years. Around the same time, however, reports appeared saying Malaysian police had found evidence of what appeared to be a practice flight using a flight simulator by the captain of the aircraft a couple of days before MH370's final departure, and that it took approximately the same course that MH370 must have taken for the several pieces of debris that had been beached in various places to have appeared when and where they did. This suggested that the flight might indeed have been deliberately downed by the pilot, perhaps at the insistence of an armed terrorist, the sort of scenario the authors envisaged in the recent book *World War 3* (Mohr, Fear & Sinclair, 2015):

> On 8 March 2014 Malaysian Airlines flight MH370 disappeared en route from Kuala Lumpur to China with 227 passengers on board. Despite extensive searches, it was not until 16 months later that parts of the plane were found on Reunion Island near Madagascar. Such a location suggests that the plane might have been high-jacked by Islamic terrorists (as in the 9/11 attacks) and then flown to a remote location and ditched. No other sensible explanation is plausible as pilot error could not take a plane so far off course.

On 25/7/16 SBS1 TV's 6.30 PM news reported that "convicted terrorists [in Australia] might never be released if there is no evidence that they can be rehabilitated" if proposed new legislation were to be adopted.

The next day the *Herald Sun* reported that the government had adopted this new legislation and it's editorial began with:

> *The Turnbull Government's move to strengthen counter-terrorism laws in the wake of murderous attacks in Australia and overseas is likely to meet with strong community approval.*

On 25/7/16 SBS1 TV's 6.30 PM news reported that "Germany is on edge" after yet another terrorist attack, this time outside a wine bar during a music festival in a town near Nürenburg. One person had been killed and several others injured, three of these seriously. The villain this time was a 20-year old Syrian asylum seeker using a suicide backpack.

It was later reported that he had been denied asylum in Germany. Still later, it was reported by the *Herald Sun* that: *A man killed in an explosion near a music festival in southern Germany was the likely attacker.*

The same program also reported the "breaking news" of a shooting outside a nightclub in the US where young students were having a party. Two were killed and 14 injured, one of the two shooters had been arrested whilst the other was still on the run. The report then continued, saying Afghanistan was preparing to mount greater resistance to the growing ISIS threat there, as evidenced by the recent attack in Kabul mentioned above.

On 25/7/16 ABC1 TV's 7.30 Report told of an Australian Muslim preacher who had gone to Syria to "take up al-Qa'ida" membership and that he was soon elevated to a senior position in AQ so that he began to aim to bring Islamic State to the forefront with the help of the Al Nusra front. His public raves against the West included such statements as we in the West are "animals". It was also reported that Australia's foreign minister, Julie Bishop, believed that this evil man's efforts had "facilitated – terrorist acts".

The same program also reported that there were waiting times of up to 16 hours at the French side of the road/tunnel crossing from Dover thanks to heightened French security in the wake of the recent attack in Nice, and others in the months before that.

On 25/7/16 ABC TV's Q&A program reported that 30% of young Muslim men think that suicide bombing is justified, concluding that Sonya Kruger had been overzealously criticized for her recent advocation of banning of Muslim immigration.

On 26/7 Al Jazeera Newshour reported that Steven O'Brien, the UN's chief of it's Humanitarian Council, had said that there "cannot be a resolution of the conflict in Syria by means of armed conflict", reminding of awful sexual crimes against children and atrocious/"shameful" conditions in Aleppo because of the current bombardment of the town by coalition forces seeking to retake it from IS.

On 26/7/2016 the *Herald Sun* reported: *TWO people are dead and more than a dozen others injured after a mass shooting in a Florida nightclub last night.* This event may have been a copycat slaughter similar to an attack on a gay bar in the US a few days earlier.

On 27/7/16 the same newspaper reported that a priests throat had been cut by two men in front of terrified parishioners in his church in France. A shootout with police followed, and the two bearded attackers were shot dead. It transpired that one of the attackers, Adel Kermiche, was awaiting trial on terrorism charges, whilst DNA tests were required to try and determine the identity of the other attacker because his face had been hit by a number of police bullets. Worse still, several people who knew Kermiche had alerted authorities to his radicalism in an attempt to stop him from going to Syria to fight for Islamic State.

On 28/7/16 ABC News 24's 6.30 AM news reported that Pope Francis had declared that the world was at war – not over religion, but over politics, resources, territory etc. The authors, declared WW3 in 2014 while working on their book *World War 3*, whilst the present book emphasizes that religions are, and always have been, used as an excuse in bullshitting and brainwashing people into doing as corrupt leaders such as Hitler of Osama Bin Laden want in order to increase their power, wealth, egos etcetera.

On July 29, 2016, Melbourne's *The Age* newspaper reported that: *"We are worried there may be attacks that get through." Sir Bernard Hogan-Howe literally knocks on wood before saying the UK has not had any terror attacks recently. He admits frankly that one is "likely".*

That same day that newspaper reported:

> *At least 67 people have been killed and 185 wounded in an attack on a Kurdish-controlled town in north-eastern Syria that has been claimed by Islamic State. Rescue teams in the town of Qamishli are still searching for victims under the rubble of the buildings brought down in the attack, medical sources said.*

On July 30, ABC News 24 reported that a PhD student a Melbourne's Monash University had joined the radical Islamist

Al-Nusra Front and radicalized two men in Sydney, arguing for a "caliphate in Singapore". Subsequently he, himself, went to Singapore, arousing suspicions and anxiety because it was "not clear why he returned to Singapore".

A few hours later the same radio station told of the bombing by the pro-government coalition of a maternity hospital in northwest Syria, the only such hospital in a radius of circa 100 km, killing 2 people. One of those killed was a terrorist leader who was the target of the attack. In preceding months there had been many other such bombings in Syria seeking to kill terrorist leaders or IS troops.

On July 30, 2016, *The Weekend Australian* reported that:

> On the evening of September 16, 2014, police intercepted a phone call from Syria to Sydney that would transform the war against Islamic State in Australia.

The call was from a senior IS operative and recruiter to the younger brother of suspected extremist Mohamed Ali Baryalei and it said: *What guys need to do is just pick any random unbeliever. When finished, put the flag of the state in the background and film it and send it off ... Backpacker, tourist, American, French, or British even better.*

The article went on to discuss Australian Government actions to increase efforts to combat IS since that time, concluding: *By last September ... the AFP – an organization traditionally focused on organized crime – was devoting almost two-thirds of its resources to fighting Islamic State and ASIS was now all but based in the Middle East.*

That same edition reported that the Al-Nusra terrorist organization had 'cut its ties' with al-Qa'ida and would operate under the name "Levant Conquest Front", and that this new group would "have no links to any outside group".

On July 31 the *Herald Sun* reported:

A MELBOURNE-based university tutor, who also worked as a marketing manager at a Muslim community cooperative, has been jailed in Singapore for allegedly using Facebook to spread ideology linked to terrorism.

Singapore authorities said that in Melbourne he had established contact with a local Islamist preacher and joined the extremist Hizb ut Tahrir group.

AUGUST 2016

On August 1, the *Herald Sun* reported the arrest of a terror suspect after his return from Syria. The Australian man was a convert to Islam who had been a regular attendee at the Hume Islamic Youth Centre in Melbourne, yet his wife claimed that in Syria he had only been taking injured people to hospital, clearly unlikely to be true given his background.

A column by Laura McNally in the same edition discusses 7 arguments given to defend Islam, the first two being:

Argument 1: Islam has nothing to do with terrorism.

This kind of denial relies on the public ignoring all data on terror: the imams who preach hate, the statistics showing significant portions of Islamic nations support terrorism and the list of registered terrorist groups, the vast majority of which are Islamic. Instead, this argument relies on theologians who insist that on some intellectual or spiritual level, their interpretation of Islam reflects peace. Certainly, that may well be their interpretation. But unfortunately, this is not the reality for all followers.

Argument 2: Christianity is just as bad; it also has a history of violence.

On this point she says that this argument is simply dodging the issue, conceding that, like all religions, Christianity has undeniable failings. She then notes that Christianity is mostly practiced where church and state have been separated, saying that concentrating only on, for example, a few sometimes violent minor splinter groups in the USA, is just dodging the issue at hand, that is, the ever increasing global spate of Islamic terrorism and jihad in the world today.

The next day a reader's letter applauded this article:

> Great piece by Laura McNally, not afraid to write about the facts behind terrorism.

The same edition reported yet another arrest of a man planning a terrorist attack, this time in Belgium.

On August 4 the crash landing of an Emirates Boeing 777 whose landing gear had failed to lower at Dubai International Airport was reported. There were 300 passengers and crew on board but only 13 passengers suffered "minor injuries". A fire erupted in one wing, perhaps because of a ruptured fuel line and one firefighter was killed fighting the blaze.

A former Emirates captain described the incident as "a mystery", saying that normally landing would not be attempted if anything was known to be wrong, and that the control tower always informs the pilot if the landing gear is not down.

As with Malaysian airlines flight MH370, which was flown thousands of miles off course and deliberately ditched in the ocean by a Muslim pilot in March 2014, this Emirates crash also seems likely to have been an act of terrorism. As one reader's letter to the *Herald Sun* said on August 5, *You just don't forget to put the landing gear down,* another saying: *Highly unlikely the pilot "forgot" to lower the landing gear as why would he declare an emergency before landing? The plane's computers and sensors would know it is on final approach with flaps lowered and close to the ground with no gear down so there would be alarms going off in the cockpit.*

On August 5 it was reported that:

[1] A new leader of the Boko Haram Islamist extremists in Nigeria had appeared.
[2] Melbourne police had made arrests for armed robberies by a gang organized by "Middle Eastern crime outfits".
[3] US efforts to combat IS in Libya were to be increased.
[4] A man in the World Vision office in Jerusalem had stolen $56M and given it to Hamas, causing Australia to suspend aid to World Vision.
[6] There had been yet more Taliban attacks on tourists in Afghanistan.
[7] In London a Muslim man of "Somali origin" with a knife had attacked and injured several people, severely injuring an Israeli woman and killing a US woman. The August 10 edition of the *International Express* reported that Islamic State had trumpeted the attack as a *bloodbath in the centre of Christendom.*

On August 6 it was reported that Australia's Prime Minister had said that Australians fighting with IS faced "almost certain" death because: *ISIL has not yet been defeated in Syria and Iraq but it is being rolled back. We have not just halted ISIL's momentum, it has been turned back.*

That same day it was also reported that an Egyptian airstrike in the Sinai Peninsula had killed an important IS leader and his aides, along with dozens of other jihadists.

On August 6 Greg Sheridan, foreign editor of *The Weekend Australian* wrote:

> There is one minority group that is more persecuted than any other in the world, persecuted more frequently, more widely, and with more intensity. There is indeed in one substantial region an explicit campaign of genocide being carried out against this group.
> Yet you will hardly ever hear about it in the Western media. The minority group in question is Christians. A terrible process of ethnic cleansing of Christians from the Middle East is strongly in train. Although especially acute in Syria and Iraq, this reflects, and is a kind of grim culmination of, dynamics at work for decades, indeed for centuries.

In the same edition the third of a four-part article *War on Islamic State* concluded:

> But when the tide finally appeared to be turning in the war against Islamic State, a terrorist nightmare unfolded in Europe.

On August 8 (2016) it was announced that Victoria's government was considering "strict new security provisions" including airport-style screening of attendees for Melbourne's motor racing Grand Prix event at Albert Park. A departmental report said: *Australia is currently at a high level of alert in which the threat of terrorist attack is considered probable.*

That same day the *Herald Sun* reported that it's own investigation had found that:

> *Asylum seekers have sold their kidneys so they can pay people smugglers - - terror group Islamic State is organizing for Syrian refugees to sell their organs to get their family passage to Europe.*

Also on August 8, it was reported that in Belgium two women police had been wounded by a machete-wielding man shouting "Allahu Akhbar" before he was shot by a third officer, later dying from his wounds. Belgium was already on high alert after IS-organized suicide bombings had killed 32 people in Brussels on 22nd March.

On August 9 it was reported that:

[1] In Quetta in Pakistan a suicide bomber had killed 70 people and wounded another more than 100 in an attack on mourners at the funeral of a lawyer who had been assassinated earlier in the day. The attack echoed one in January which killed 15 outside a polio eradication centre, the Pakistani Taliban and a group linked to IS both claiming responsibility.
[2] That armed men had kidnapped an American professor and an Australian academic who worked at the American University of Afghanistan in Kabul.
[3] Syrian rebels were planning to recapture all of Aleppo, having begun to surround the city. A spokesman for the Syrian Observatory for Human rights said that this was one of the

most significant setbacks for government forces since conflict began in Syria in March 2011.

On August 10, Rita Panahi reported in the *Herald-Sun* that:

> Islamic schools are growing at a frantic pace, up to nine times faster than other schools, with the number of students jumping by close to 100 per cent since 2009. - - - At Taqwa college principal Omar Hallak also caused a stir by saying that Islamic State was not created by Muslims but was instead an Israeli and US conspiracy to control oil in the Middle East.

The front page article in the *International Express* of August 10, 2016 was:

EU'S MIGRANT CRISIS IS COLLOSAL
British borders face threat from terrorists and smuggling gangs.
   A FLOOD of migrants into the EU is leaving Britain open to terrorist attacks and people smugglers, MPs have warned.

> The article said that 227,316 migrants had arrived in Europe in the first 6 months of 2016, more than 1.2 million asylum applications having been made in EU nations in 2015. It concluded: *The EU external border must improve security, including deploying specialist equipment to fingerprint and check everyone against security databases. This is not happening. Terrorists do not see borders as barriers to their barbarism.*

Four page 4 articles of the same newspaper said that:

[1] According to a former head of the UK Border agency: *Britain is home to at least a million illegal migrants who may never be found. - - There are thought to be as many as 20,000 migrants camped along the northern French coast waiting for a chance to reach Britain.*
[2] *A LANDMARK ruling which let four Syrian refugees living in the Jungle camp in Calais come to Britain has been overturned.*
[3] There were heavily armed "elite" police patrolling London to counter any "Paris-style attack by Islamic State terrorists."
[4] A British army base had been put on full alert fearing a "second plot to kidnap a serviceman."

A page 6 article said that 8 British tourists had been "caught up" in a Taliban ambush in western Afghanistan, and that the UK Foreign Office was "urgently seeking further information about the incident."

A page 21 article said that attacks by "jihadist thugs" throughout Europe were tending to become simpler lone-wolf attacks, two recent attacks in France having used a lorry to kill many people and knives to kill a French priest.

A page 23 article said that
"airport queues and terrorism alerts mean that the lure of a holiday abroad is not what it was. - - Airport security and the fear of being blown up mid-air has removed every last hint of glamour from flying. Islamist terror – made worse by open borders and collapsing economies

– means that even when you get there you're still not safe, as many hundreds of travelers have discovered to their cost in Tunisia, Nice and Paris, to Turkey and the Sinai."

On August 11 Australia's SBS TV news reported an "entire province" in Afghanistan was in danger of failing into Taliban hands", and that government troops were being moved to try and prevent this.

On August 11 two bomb blasts outside a bar in a seaside resort in northern Thailand were reported. The first went off at 10PM, the second, which was hidden in a pot plant, a few minutes later, killing one person and injuring at 23 others, 11 of them foreigners. Later, three other related bomb attacks in the area were reported, killing three more people and injuring dozens. It was suspected that separatist Muslim insurgents from the country's south were responsible, another bomb attack having occurred earlier in the day at a southern resort.

On August 12 it was reported that a "counter-terrorism sting" in Sydney saw two Muslim men who ran an agency for 600 home-based childcare businesses charged with fraud for scamming the childcare benefits scheme, from which they had received $27M since 2012. The scam involved using fake names and addresses for children and childcare centres. Worse still, accusations surfaced that much as $20M of this money had been channeled to support IS.

On August 12 and 13 it was reported that there new anti-terror measures were to be announced in Germany, including a ban on the burka and a proposal to strip jihadist fighters of their German nationality, and on August 19 Germany's interior minister spoke in support of a "partial" ban on the burka in public places.

On August 13 the *Weekend Australian* reported that:

[1] Six long-range bombers based in Russia had struck several IS targets in "the group's de facto capital of Raqqa".
[2] Residents of the besieged city of Aleppo had reported a chlorine gas attack and the Syrian government denied responsibility for it.
[3] Having played a key role in preventing government forces and their allies overtaking Aleppo, the al-Nusra front, al-Qa'ida's "local spin-off" renamed the Syrian Conquest Front, could become the major player amongst the Sunni rebels seeking to oust President Bashar Assad.
[4] According to the Wall Street Journal, *Pakistan's response to a suicide bombing that killed dozens this week reflects an unwillingness to alter policies that enable jihadist groups to operate there, according to critics of Islamabad's approach on terrorism.*
[5] FBI information helped Canadian police identify a "balaclava-wearing would-be suicide bomber on the verge of committing a suicide attack". They shot at him in riding in a taxi and he detonated his explosive device, killing both himself and the taxi driver.

On August 14, 2016, it was reported:

[1] US-backed forces had gained control of the northern Syrian city of Manbij, freeing 2000 civilians who had been held as hostages by IS. The last IS fighters to leave the city took hostages with them but freed them once they were 'in the clear'.
[2] The mayor of the French resort city of Cannes had banned women from wearing full-body, head-covering swimming

suits on public beaches. The next day a riot began because two people photographed Muslim women wearing these 'burkinis' and in following days three other French resorts banned the burkini.

[3] There were 60 million refugees, asylum seekers and displaced people in the world, the most since WW2, whilst 600 million people live in conflict-affected countries.

On August 15 it was reported that:

[1] Two men wearing religious clothing had been shot outside a mosque in the New York borough of Queens.

[2] Boko Haram had released a video showing circa 50 of 218 Nigerian schoolgirls still missing after being kidnapped in April 2014. They were all shrouded in Islamic dress with a masked man carrying an assault rifle in front of them, the video demanding the release of imprisoned Boko Haram fighters in exchange for the girls.

On August 16 it was reported that a man of Somalian origin was likely to be deported from Australia, having been found guilty of planning to go to Syria to engage in hostile activities.

On August 17 Turkish Government claims that an Australian charity was part of the global Fethullah Gulen terrorist organization surfaced.

On August 18 it was reported that a London jury had found a "hate preacher" guilty of violating the Terrorism Act for influencing up to 100 people in Britain, Australia and elsewhere to support Islamic State. The Muslim man had said that he wished to see the IS flag flying above Downing Street and Buckingham Palace converted to a mosque.

CONCLUSION

World War 3, as we call it, and now the Pope agrees, has been going on too long – and it is far more serious and nasty than most realize. Just two of many possible examples are:

[1] From day 1 almost, the first author felt sure that Malaysian Airlines flight MH370 was deliberately downed as an act of Islamist terrorism and jihad in March 2014. Finally, in July 2016 it had become clear that this was indeed the case, and that the pilot himself was the villain, having used a home flight simulator just a couple of days before the actual flight to plot and simulate the very wayward flight path needed to ditch the plane in the Southern Pacific Ocean thousands of miles from its scheduled and intended destination.

[2] The first author has for several years felt sure that the summer rash of deliberately lit bush fires in Australia and the USA are acts of Islamist jihad, that is, a form of *infrastructure warfare*, and, indeed, in some cases in Australia, at least, this has been proved to be the case.

Perhaps a letter by 'Jason' printed in Melbourne's Herald-Sun newspaper on 5/7/2016 sums up the jihad problem well, saying that action is needed to deal with it, just as action is also needed cut back Australia's growing deficit:

> During 2015 alone there were 2865 Islamic attacks in 53 countries – 27,626 were killed and 26,149 injured. By all means just ignore it and it will go away. Like the spending problems.

Another reader's letter to the same newspaper on 28/7/16 said: *SO UNESCO declares Islam as the "most peaceful religion of the world".*

> *Who made that decision? Is UNESCO a Muslim-dominated organization? Where were the (unreported) terrorist attacks, massacres, etc, committed by Bahais, Buddhists, Christians, Hindus, Jews, Sikhs, Rastafarians, Zoroastrians, or others in this century? Thousands have been listed involving "the religion of peace". I'm really scared now. Probably won't go to church next Sunday.*

A reader's letter in *The Age* on 29/7/2016 says:

> *Major French media outlets are to no longer print the names and photos of terrorists and terror suspects, thereby denying them posthumous glorification in the case of death or notoriety in the case of living. This will deny them a platform to promote their ideals of hate. All Western media should follow suit.*

In Australia, *The Weekend Australian* reported on 30/7/2016 that: *Australia's foreign espionage agency [ASIS] has stripped officers from across its Southeast Asian and central Asian station, sending spies to the Middle East in an urgent bid to meet the growing threat posed by Islamic State.*

On 4 August 2016 the *Herald-Sun* reported that Syrian rebels had "accused government forces of toxic gas attacks on civilians" in Aleppo. The government denied this, blaming the rebels for these attacks, and the present authors are inclined to agree with the latter opinion.

On the same day it was reported that a "high level assessment" ranked Australia as third most likely to be victim of a "crowd sourced" terrorism attack, after the US and France.

On August 18 it was reported that Russia forces had increased their efforts at helping government forces retake the besieged Syrian city of Aleppo after they had suffered recent setbacks. On August 19, in response to UN calls for it, Russia agreed in principle to a short ceasefire in Aleppo to allow access for desperately needed humanitarian aid.

On August 20 a column in the *Weekend Australian* said:

We now know political correctness doesn't just place worrying limits on how freely we discuss Islamist extremist terrorism – it also dangerously inhibits our ability to fight it.

The bottom line is really that, the madness of Islamist terrorism and jihad having gone on for some 1500 years in the name of the satanic Muslim religion, non-Muslims are losing patience, so how much longer should we as a community tolerate it?

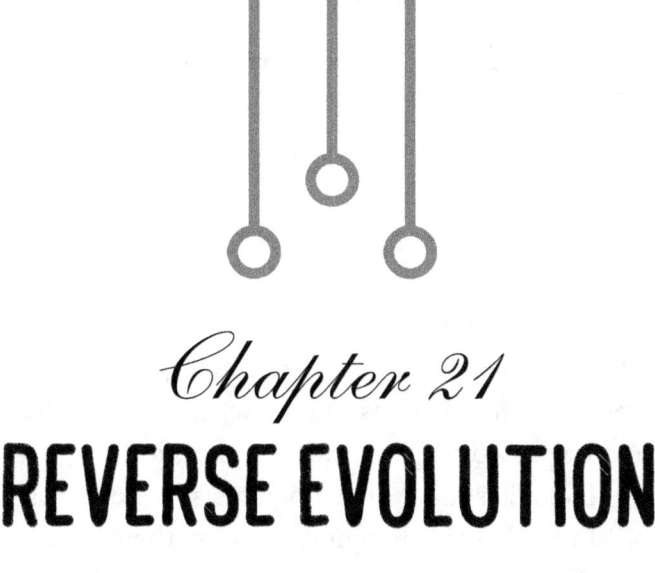

Chapter 21
REVERSE EVOLUTION

We must, however, acknowledge, as it seems to me, that man with all his noble qualities . . . still bears in his bodily frame the indelible stamp of his lowly origin.
Charles Darwin,
The Descent of Man (1871), ch. 23.

REVERSE EVOLUTION IN MANKIND?

Chapter One discussed brainwashing or *coercive persuasion* and gave a brief account of the evolution of mankind and its leadership.

Following chapters discussed how we are brainwashed by unscrupulous or incompetent leaders in every walk of life.

Chapter 17 discussed the disastrous global consequences that now threaten the survival of many species, including man.

Chapters 18 and 19 discuss Islamism and the now global scourge of jihad afflicting the world today.

The present chapter discusses a consequence of man's excessive breeding, that of *reverse evolution*, the following two sections discussing experiments with rats showing that:

(a) 'Enriched' environment improves their brain size and intelligence.
(b) Learning in rats changes their RNA.

Case (a) involves the *nurture* component of intelligence and case (b) the *nature* or genetic component of intelligence.

Findings (a) + (b) demonstrate how greater intelligence can develop and be passed on genetically in a species.

Leading biologists and anthropologists believe that we are evolving 100 times faster than our hunter gatherer ancestors were (Callaghan, 2008), but is this rapid evolution for the better or for the worse?

The thesis of this chapter is that our increasingly overpopulated, capitalist and greedy consumer societies have become unethical and are beginning to regress, resulting in lower physical and psychological standards, in turn resulting in reduced intelligence and *reverse evolution*.

THE EFFECT OF ENVIRONMENT

Modern man is distinguished from other creatures by having a larger cerebral cortex, the centre for our thinking and language. This larger cortex must have evolved by the adaptive processes inherent in Darwin's theory of natural selection.

Clues to just how this occurred were given by the work of social psychologist David Krech and his group at UC Berkeley (Packard, 1978).

In this they provided a group of rats with an "enriched environment" of large cages with various things rats enjoy such as slides, wheels and the like. Then a maze with a sugar reward at the end was added. This had a dark and a lighted alley and the rats soon learnt which led to the sugar.

Then the maze lighting was reversed regularly so that the rats had to relearn the 'sugar route'.

A second control group of rats lived normally and a third group was kept in a deprived dark and noiseless area.

After 90 days it was found that the 'enriched' rats had developed thicker cerebral cortexes!

This was perhaps the first evidence that the brain is modified by experience. The enrichment conditions caused the following changes (Atrens and Curthoys, 1982):

[1] The size of the cerebral cortex was increased.
[2] The size of the cortical neurons increased.
[3] The size and number of synaptic contacts increased.
[4] The quantity of acetylcholinesterase, the compound responsible for breakdown of the neurotransmitter acetylcholine, increased.

Therefore, the rats which had experienced environmental enrichment were apparently anatomically and biochemically superior to those which had endured a deprived environment.

This result provided laboratory evidence that environmental enrichment could physically and chemically alter the brain. This ability of neural tissue to change because of its activation is called *plasticity*.

It seems likely, therefore, that as early man discovered fire, began to make tools and advanced in many other ways his brain gradually evolved into that of *homo sapiens sapiens* or modern man.

BIOCHEMICAL LEARNING AND EVOLUTION

Two further research results indicative of the biochemical nature of learning processes have been obtained:

(a) The work by George Ungar's group (Ungar et al., 1972) in which peptides in rats conditioned to shun darkness were isolated. These peptides seemed able to transfer the conditioning to other rats. [Peptides are small organic molecules that link hundreds or even thousands of amino acid molecules together to form polypeptides].
(b) Changes in RNA in rats given a learning task found by Hyden's group in Sweden (Rosenfeld, 1972).

Hyden's group also found an increase in a brain-specific protein S-100 in rats trained to use their non-preferred paw. They then found that an antiserum to S-100 stopped this learning.

Subsequently much further work has been done to investigate the effects of inhibition of protein and RNA synthesis by antibiotics upon memory. One finding was that drugs that interfere with the uptake of amino acids by cells can selectively interfere with memory retrieval or formation.

Proteins are naturally occurring polypeptides.

Genes are nucleoproteins formed by combination of polypeptide and DNA (deoxyribonucleic acid) chains.

The process of cell reproduction or *mitosis* occurs when the two strands of the DNA double helix separate and manufacture protein and a new 'opposite' strand to form a new cell.

This process is assisted by RNA (ribonucleic acid).

If learning changes RNA then perhaps a process like the cell mutation that causes cancer (Weinberg, 1999) might also be responsible for human evolution, both physically (Selmes, 1974) and mentally (Darwin, 1999).

Cell mutation is the result of a DNA copying error. This may just be a statistical fluke, having a probability of one in a million or less.

A ground breaking case study of the mutation process was the *ras* oncogene found in a smoker with bladder cancer (Weinberg, 1999).

After 30 years of smoking, some of the many highly toxic carcinogens he had inhaled had not been detoxified in his liver and had passed into his urine.

The ras oncogene is 5000 DNA bases long but one base was incorrect where a sequence that should have been GCC GGC GGT was instead GCC GTC GGT with just one base incorrect, a T appearing instead of a G in the middle of this mutated 'string'.

The incorrect gene then governed the growth of this cell and its descendants, resulting in a cancer tumour years later.

It might be possible that, over time, gradual development of language 'enriched' our mental environment and produced lasting changes in human RNA and thence DNA that resulted in the evolution of our larger cerebral cortexes.

That we have a comparatively large brain size, therefore, might indeed be the evolutionary result of sometimes vicarious thinking over millennia, as often assumed.

MAN'S DETERIORATING ENVIRONMENT

If some of Krech's rats got smarter because of an 'enriched' environment then it would appear that in the more affluent West we are now going through the opposite process as our living standards decline.

Now more and more of us live in bloated and crowded megacities where even houses in the outer suburbs are becoming unaffordable and they also involve the downside of large numbers of hours spent commuting on crowded freeways or increasingly strained and packed public transport systems.

To cut commuting times many live in high rise apartment buildings that can only be likened to filing cabinets for forgotten and soulless people that have once again reverted to being troglodytes.

At the same time big business has bought out so many farms that many rural communities and towns have shrunk to a less than viable size.

Back in the 'big smoke' big business grows still further while job conditions and security have decreased drastically, for example most retail businesses now working seven days a week, often with extended hours, and often without compensating employees for these ludicrously unnecessary 'rat race' hours.

To make matters worse, these slaves are brainwashed zombies hooked on increasingly junky, if not frivolous, products.

In other words, most have become like Krech's deprived rats and, just as our lives become duller, so too do we and our children. When we start to talk about economics, however, the picture becomes even bleaker.

ECONOMIC INFLUENCES

According to Lynn and Vanhaven (2002), the world average IQ is 90, understandable bearing in mind that IQ tests originated in more advanced Europe and the USA. Only one in five countries have average IQ near the British average of 100, half have IQ < 90, and Africa rates bottom with average IQ of only 70.

They find that the GDP of nations correlates halfway well (to 0.7) with national IQ, the next most important factor being whether the country has a socialist or market economy, the third most important factor being it's natural resources.

They argue that more progressive and freer countries have greater inventiveness or IQ, in turn improving GDP, pointing to Japan's progress in the 20th century and China's current progress as examples.

In other words, some countries in Asia have undergone industrial revolution somewhat later than those in Europe and North America.

In the once most affluent countries, however, things are now doing downhill.

Thanks to wrongful marketing practices, government taxes and childishly crude economic modeling and management house prices in many countries have grown absurdly high.

At the same time governments in the more affluent countries have run up increasing national debts while their politicians electioneer with bullshit that we've never had it so good and that they have a budget surplus, that is, they have increased national debt only marginally less than their deliberately high forecast figure.

Meanwhile big biz continues to go offshore to use cheap labour so that, for example, most of our clothes and household goods now come from China or thereabouts.

Ourselves, we have increasing job insecurity and are expected to be prepared to retrain two or three times in our life, this despite being expected to study for increasingly long periods before beginning work in the first place. To add insult to injury more and more of the courses of study are ridiculous, ranging from postgraduate courses in sexology and puppetry to MBAs that are largely, if not totally, high school level.

Young students today, therefore, run up increasingly large higher education debts, study longer and thus spend less time in the work force, and yet face retraining further down the track along with ludicrous house prices. The result is that they can't afford to get married, let alone have children or buy a house, and are worse off than primitive man was!

LOWER STANDARDS

Standards are falling more generally than just economically, however. Big biz is increasingly unethical with tunnel vision for the bottom line so that CEOs make absurd amounts for sitting on their backsides and coming up with lousy ideas while the increasingly insecure workers suffer increasingly and are little better off than Roman slaves were.

Correspondingly, therefore, these modern slaves live increasingly miserable lives of brainwashed consumerism to the limited extent they can afford it. The result can only be a decline in intelligence.

To make matters worse, according to the Peter Principle that 'the sour cream rises' in human hierarchies, the rich brainwashers are even more stupid in most respects except for the something akin to animal cunning and viciousness with which they accumulate money for their own frivolous amusement.

Meanwhile, we see a 'reverse Keynes δG effect' of massive injection of capital by transnational companies setting up in China and India to find cheap labour [the original 'Keynes δG effect' was the notion that increasing government spending G has a snowball effect that increases GNP].

Now, therefore, the economies of these countries are growing rapidly and their peoples, at least to some extent, now see themselves as the smart ones.

In India, for example, their education sector has been turning out engineers in droves for decades. As noted in Chapter 10, however, in the West we have dumbed the education system down to the point at which:

(1) Teachers are sometimes not allowed to fail students.
(2) Up to half of primary students in the USA are given drugs for the recently 'invented' (by nut cases in the 'psycho' professions) ADHD.
(3) Almost from infancy children are locked up in long day care instead of being given the sort of specialist attention that, as noted in Chapter 10, would increase their intelligence.
(4) Apprenticeship to be a hairdresser takes up to 6 years.
(5) School remains an excessively drawn out 12 years.
(6) A high proportion of courses at so-called Universities are quite simply ridiculous, for example courses in sexology and puppetry, whilst others like MBAs are so low-level and commonplace that they are almost worthless like the latter-day institutions that run them simply because they are popular and therefore good money spinners.
(7) Only 40% of US school students score at the level that 80% of students in some other countries achieve (Sykes, 1995). A similar decline has occurred in Australia and like countries.

Speaking of education, however, where else but the USA could it happen? That is, there are more people in jail that at University. This in the 'land of the free' and all that bullshit.

This dumbing down has extended throughout our society. Long ago noted psychologist Hans Eysenck aroused public condemnation for saying the black people were less intelligent though in Africa to this day that does prove to be the case.

Recently a (male) president of Harvard University was heavily criticized for saying that women had somewhat different abilities to men.

The bottom line now, therefore, is that we must all be equally stupid and nobody is allowed to be otherwise.

BRAINWASHED ZOMBIES

It is pitiful to see how many of us are brainwashed into carrying a drink bottle or cigarette in one hand and a mobile phone in the other, wearing stiff denim jeans and choking ourselves with ties that derive from the scarves that Roman soldiers carried to bind sword wounds.

We morons must also have the latest fashion in cars, houses and other possessions. Never mind that the cars are often gas guzzling 4WDs with aircon and the houses 'McMansions' way beyond the needs of shrinking modern families and which consume massive amounts of energy, much of it for air conditioning that is usually unnecessary.

Then there are the lifetime habits, or should we say addictions, like smoking and booze, the quotation opening Chapter 14 being an excellent example of how the beer barons bring such public addictions about.

The startling reality is that a great many of the things we do we don't really like anyway. Few, for example, like smoking or beer at first try but like fools we persist and condition ourselves and especially our brains to bear each new and ludicrous habit.

The same goes for dry white wines such as Chardonnay which tend to eat away at the oesophagus and stomach like acid, a reminder that alcohol tends to cause cancer all the way through the digestive path.

As for food, the list of ludicrous and downright nasty things we eat and claim to enjoy is endless, including tripe, offal, frog's legs, snails and so forth.

Often, of course, we acquire such ridiculous habits by imitative learning, that so many of us must have dogs as pets being an excellent example, this simple being a comparatively modern 'fashion' that caught on and is copied by one generation after another.

Usually, however, we are encouraged a good deal, if not a lot, by the skillful brainwashing of attention demanding and repetitive advertising. Arguably, in fact, the way in which humans are affected by advertising is directly comparable to lab experiments on conditioning of animals.

No better example can be found in the mindless poker machines that seem to hypnotize countless people for hours and hours on end. Such suckers are very comparable to rats in a Skinner box except that they seem dumber than the rats because, far from being rewarded, they are punished by being 'milked' of a great deal of money.

As for mass BW, the bullshit about Saddam Hussein having 'WMDs' that the US administration used to justify their invasion of Iraq is one of the better BW examples in history. Like Vietnam, Iraq has been a disaster for the US army as is sadly highlighted by the statistic that at present 17 US war veterans commit suicide a day, this toll each year far exceeding the total toll of US soldiers in the mistaken Iraq campaign over five years.

EVER WORSENING DIET

Nowhere is evidence of our reverse evolution greater than in our deteriorating diet. Now, more and more of the global population fill up on fast junk food, salty and fatty snacks such as potato crisps, biscuits, cake, sugary soft-drinks and, of course, the demon booze.

Indeed the medical profession in the West at large considers the modern diet problem as something of a crisis because obesity has reached epidemic proportions as a result of excessive consumption of fatty and sugary foods.

Still probably a billion or so of us smoke, which we like to consider part of the 'total diet' because we believe substituting food for cigarettes, and especially chewing gum, is helpful in quitting smoking. Indeed the first author found this approach helpful in finally quitting.

Then, of course, there is the growing problem of drugs in society. As a result we have to have regular drug testing in sport and elsewhere, we would suggest in parliament judging by the raving performances one sees there which, everybody knows, may well be fuelled by generous doses of booze with lunch and long dinners in favourite restaurants.

Just a couple of days ago we saw an elderly man on crutches who had lost the lower third of his right leg. Interested in atherosclerosis, which we have researched a good deal, we asked him what had caused his loss of much of a lower limb. He told us that the cause had been a twenty-something male drunk driver, a hoon who had had a blood alcohol reading in excess of 0.20 and was also loaded up with illicit drugs.

Having moved to one of Melbourne's much cheaper, less affluent, Western suburbs from a suburb on its Mornington Peninsula of late, the first author noticed that more people smoke and/or are obese. This, he believes, relates to the Reception-Yielding model of Fig. 14.2. That is, as he prefers to term it, people here have lower 'consumer IQ.'

Himself, the first author's diet has often tended to be below healthy par, even thinking it a joke in his Auckland days. In childhood his friends and he indulged as much as they could afford from their 'pocket money' on lollies, chocolate and cakes, washing them down with soft-drink or 'milk-shakes' or 'malted milks' which Milk Bars did a good trade in the 1950s and 1960s, in those days always using full cream milk. Now we know, of course, that it is wiser to drink low fat or skim milk to help avoid excessive consumption of saturated fat, a key villain in atherosclerosis.

The first author's well meaning parents gave him plenty of food but breakfast eggs and bacon were cooked with fat laden and carcinogenic re-used dripping. They bought plenty of cake at the local Herbert Adams shop and tons of (full cream) milk was consumed. At dinner or Sunday lunch (a roast) he well recalls being exhorted to eat the fat on the meat, another no-no given our dietary science knowledge of today.

Then, of course, he was fool enough to take up smoking for keeps from age 15, eventually becoming a very heavy smoker.

His disastrous marriage made his diet hit rock bottom on a permanent basis. A wife who produced food with stubbornly bad grace in sluggardly and slack manner gave him what he thought of as his (one plate) dog's dinner each night, in his Auckland days one of two braised steak and rice dishes that he had heard of, but not tried, in his undergraduate days. These were cooked terribly and unappetizingly to say the least.

He drank gallons of coffee at work (2 or 3 litres) and gallons of tea at home, each mug had with a cigarette or two. If awoken at night by his wife's terrible snoring he'd make yet another pot of tea, drinking 2 or 3 mugs of it, each with a cigarette, before trying to get back to sleep.

He doesn't remember what he ate for breakfast at any stage of the marriage except the very beginning when, one day at least, he remembers being given some cereal with bad grace. He does remember always having a pot of tea for breakfast, always with about 3 'fags', of course.

For lunch in his Auckland days he would just get a single sandwich or local crumbed sausage on a stick oddity, and wash this down with 2 mugs of coffee, one taken back to his office to keep working (he often worked through lunch times during my all too short University career).

Finally, unable to afford wine, like the local men he had 3 'long neck' bottles of low quality local beer to drown his bullied at home and work sorrows.

MONKEY BUSINESS

Much of our so-called education of young children should be called monkey business because they are encouraged to act like monkeys on climbing frames and in often senseless ball games, some of which, like football, are positively dangerous and reduce some players to paraplegics.

Then there are the ludicrous crazes we fall for. When the first author was a child there was a mindless yo-yo craze. More recent were skateboard and roller blades crazes.

As for dangerous activities, roller blades and skate boards are bad enough but those concrete slopes built for kids to do bike tricks on are highly insane.

The list of insane human activities here is endless, including sky diving, climbing up vertical rock faces, skiing, and so on.

As for racing, it seems that we will race just about anything that can be made to move ranging from dogs to camels.

Most of these activities have become spectator sports, some of them viewed by massive audiences brainwashed by hype and heavy media publicity into taking childish games played by overpaid adults seriously.

The complete insanity of this is that worrying oneself greatly over who wins a silly ball game is supposed to be recreational, that is, entertaining and relaxing. That riots often occur both off and on the field, however, are anything but relaxing.

Worrying too are the increasingly animalistic celebrations that accompany scoring and victory in most sports.

In addition, that many people enjoy watching brutal sports such as boxing and kick boxing doesn't say much good about the human race and only suggests that it is somewhat sick.

When you think about it, in fact, most of our ridiculous sport and recreational activities make us look like Krech's 'environment enriched' rats on their running wheels and slides.

The bottom line is that, as they used to say, *small things amuse small minds*, in other words we sure as hell are not getting any smarter.

SOCIOLOGICAL DEVOLUTION

Not only is our environment in polluted and unsightly megacities unpleasant, but as noted in Chapter 17, our societies are becoming meaner, nastier and more violent at an alarming rate. Violence is on the increase everywhere to the point that many older people and women don't feel safe on the streets at night and, of course, there is no shortage of street crime during the day as well.

Experiments with rats show that when they are housed beyond a certain population density they begin to fight each other. Evidently humans do the same and we are now accustomed to associating crime and violence with big cities like Chicago and New York.

Increasing numbers of us are addicted to booze, illegal so-called 'party drugs,' as well as prescription drugs like valium for anxiety, Ritalin for ADHD, and lithium for bipolar disorder (formerly called manic depression).

With divorce rates around 50% we are living less safely in this respect at least than our Neanderthal ancestors did. Childhood is miserable enough at times under the best of circumstances and family breakups often make it much more so for far too many children.

Women loose tolerance of the fact that men, especially when younger, can drink far more booze than they. They also fear violence from men though are more often than not at least, the instigators by way of a foul, hysterical, bossy, and bullying tongue. Try that on the footy field and, predictably, you can 'get an opponent in' so that they take a shot at you and risk being 'rubbed out' for a few weeks by the umpires.

In marriage, as well as in courtship, there is little or no meaningful communication. If you eavesdrop on a couple that has been married for a decade or two, you will find the dialogue at all times entirely trivial, for example "do we need milk?," in modern times this being said as often as not over a mobile phone while one partner is in the supermarket.

To complicate matters further, in the fast declining West women are taking over to some extent. Only about 100 years ago women were not to be seen in Cambridge. Now far more women than men go to University in Australia.

Women also have a lower unemployment rate, already having the advantage that, merely by lying on their backs and having children they have a job for life as motherhood was certainly construed to be in the '[good] old days.'

One billion Muslims are more old-fashioned and tolerate the man being the boss still and, indeed, with the West in decay, it may well be that they have same sort of potentially winning advantage in this regard.

The ghastly music that young and not so young listen to and gyrate all night too mindlessly boozed and/or drugged in discos is another indicator of social decay. The manic pop groups of today dress and sing atrociously and leap about like primitive loonies.

The bottom line is that you can see the writing on the walls, that is, the graffiti that covers much of our miserable megacities, a sure sign that we are regressing back to grunting cave men once again.

SEXUAL PROLIFERATION AND DEVIANCE

Amongst the most disturbing indications of the corruption and decadence in our society are the all too frequent reports of sexual abuse of children by priests, teachers and others. It seems therefore that even the once most trusted people in our society can't be trusted any longer.

Sex, of course, is ubiquitous in our increasingly depraved society. Brothels were once illegal back street affairs. Now they and all manner of sexual products are widely advertised on late night TV, a pathetic attempt to shield children from it, and also in free local newspapers which children of all ages collect from the letterbox after coming home from school.

A fundamental change is that homosexuality is on the increase. Once a trait one had to keep secret it is now rampantly displayed at gay Mardi Gras festivals, at gay bars in major cities, and in late night TV ads for homosexual dating services.

Some claim that homosexuality is inherited and a study of 113 people in 33 families in which at least two brothers were homosexual found a genetic marker on the X-chromosome (Xq28) that had a very high correlation with sexual orientation (Galton, 2001).

Genes may play a minor 'predisposory' role but, largely, homosexuality is a learnt behaviour. Typically, for example, the normal heterosexual male has one or two homosexual experiences in adolescence (Robertson, 1981), and no doubt the same applies to women.

Those who become homosexuals, therefore, presumably do so as a result of imitative learning at an early age. There are, no doubt, also psychological factors involved, for example a lack of confidence in approaching the opposite sex coupled with the fact that there are earlier homosexual experiences to draw upon as an alternative behaviour model.

If alcoholism is to be regarded as a psychiatric illness, as it often is (Davies, 1971), then in my view homosexuality is even more obviously a treatable psychiatric condition as well.

That said, most of our heterosexual behaviours are also learnt ones, many of them hardly natural or healthy. A seemingly innocent example might be what was called 'French kissing' in my youth, that is what can be described as 'tongue kissing', a truly revolting and very unhealthy practice like many other modern sexual practices.

The bottom line on sex, though, might well be that if we were aiming to get any smarter and wiser then abstinence might be the wiser course, especially as a sound exercise regime is clearly a healthier option. Obviously, however, quite the opposite is happening, all part of our *reverse evolution*.

DECLINE AND FALL OF EMPIRES

Modern civilization is based on our learning from the Greek, Roman and also Middle Eastern civilizations of 2-5 thousand years ago.

From these civilizations we learnt sophisticated art, music, architecture, mathematics and philosophy.

These civilizations became great empires but declined and fell ultimately, suggesting that, in the long run at least, the basic need of humans to live on a more 'local' basis is paramount. That is, our priority is, and should be the wellbeing of ourselves, our family, and our immediate community, not grand visions of empire achieved by violent war, or grand visions of a global economy motivated by greed.

Thus, in the last few hundred years, the British, Dutch, French, Germans, Portuguese, Spanish and Turks have built empires and then lost them.

The British Empire dominated much of the world but finally collapsed after WWII, in part because of the massive debts, much of them to the USA, incurred by that war. As a result, in the words of Dwight Eisenhower: "This conjunction of an immense military establishment and a large arms industry is new in the American experience."

As always, the devastatingly accurate Peter Principle applies, and corruption and stupidity cause society at large to lose out, an example being that between 1978 and 1998 the US Air Force requested only 5 C-130 transport aircraft but funding for 256 was approved. An example of why came later when the four biggest arms manufacturers gave more than $11M in campaign donations for the 2000 election.

Then, in 2002, the proposed increase in the US military budget was $48B, more than the entire UK budget, bringing the US total budget to $396B, more than the combined total of the next 15 big military spenders, including Russia and China.

Long before that, however, the US had 'liberalized' its economy, cutting the top tax rate from 70% to 50%, and eventually to 28% and reducing controls on banks.

The result? During Reagan's 8-year Presidential tenure the total deficit grew from $900B to $3,000B (note that $1B = 10^9$) and in the 1980s more than 650 Savings & Loan companies collapsed as a result of widespread fraud.

During that period the average American's leisure time per week was reduced to 16.6 hours from the 26.2 it had been in 1973 while, of course, the rich got richer than ever as a result of increasing slavery.

Since then, of course, we have seen the spectacular demise of Enron and the 2008 GFC in which major US banks collapsed and others, along with GM and Chrysler, had to be bailed out at great expense, along with increased government expenditure to prop up the economy, further drowning the US in debt.

Yet another example of economic mismanagement, banks have been getting into trouble in the USA and Europe, in particular, because statutory reserve deposit (SRD) and liquidity guarantee ratios have been reduced to ridiculously low values, as little as 2%. Traditionally the very basis of the banking system was SRD circa 10% (it was 7% in Australia in 1985).

In 2011 the US raised its debt limit yet again, after a long drawn-out battle in congress, and it looks certain that the days of the US being the "world's only superpower" are numbered.

To add insult to injury, the last century having been referred to by some as "The American Century," we are now hearing this new century being referred to as "The Asian Century."

With Europe now in economic crisis as well, a total reversal of fortunes seems to be happening on a grand scale as China, India and other countries undergo their own, belated, industrial revolutions which, given their massive populations, are bound to have still further transformative effects on the world economy at the expense of the USA and Europe.

Globally, however, the problems of overpopulation, resource depletion, global warming, and desertification are likely to limit the prospects of future prosperity for all but the richest people in the world.

If the world's population reaches 10 or even 12 billion by the middle of the century, however, it seems certain that the long-term prospects for the human race are poor, this the subject of the recent book *The Doomsday Calculation* (Mohr, 2012b).

CULTURAL CRAP

Even the most intelligent of us, however, are likely to pick up a few mindless habits. Most of the intelligentsia laugh at modern pop music which certainly is crap, but many of them get dressed up as though they were going to a funeral to go to the opera, which is equally farcical. Opera singing at the best of times is somewhat ridiculous, involving both fat men and fat ladies making a ludicrous and comical racket. In the pop sphere 'rock' concerts and so-called 'musicals' are equally absurd.

Any form of dancing is animal stuff but ballet, with loonies in tights and ladies in very short skirts, is simply for closet perverts.

Even grandiose symphonies perhaps make little sense if one considers that music really should be for relaxation and thus should only require few instruments and fairly quiet scores.

The intelligentsia, however, is more concerned about snob value than intelligent culture so they still like stage plays. Whether Shakespearean or modern, plays are rather childish to say the least.

Many people regard choosing wine as an exercise in intelligence and 'wank' themselves into old age over the virtue of this or that 'red'. This too is pretty mindless stuff when, truth be told, most wines are really not as nice as some modern fruit juice mixtures and just an acquired taste.

When it comes to snob value, of course, flash cars and big houses are key items but these are expensive and not necessarily affordable to the intelligentsia, some of whom are happier to 'slum it' and, indeed, look like down and outs. This only indicates how stupid they really are, however, another symptom of our *reverse evolution*.

FALLING IQ

Vernon (1960) and Lynn and Vanhaven (2002) point out that we have dysgenic fertility trends so that the least intelligent people have the most children. Burt (1957) found that average IQ in the UK had dropped by 1.5% between the years 1920 and 1950 for this reason and he predicted a further 2.5% drop by the year 2000.

Vernon (1960) also points out that a Royal Commission on Mental Deficiency in the UK discovered a "big increase" in the numbers of defectives between the years 1907 and 1929.

It has also been suggested that IQ in the USA is in decline (Fancher, 1985), some claiming that the rate of decrease is 1 point per generation.

Remarkably, Internet search for 'declining human intelligence' yields over 3 million results, for example:

(a) Norwegian conscripts were found to have scored lower in IQ numerical subtests after the mid 1990s.
(b) Danish men assessed for military service in 2003/4 dropped in IQ by almost two points compared to those in 1998 (Teasdale and Owen, 2005, 2008).

The picture is far worse from a global point of view. As noted earlier, average IQ in Africa is only 70 and, of course, it is in such places that population has exploded in the last century while population growth in more advanced countries has ground to a halt.

The bottom line, therefore, is that, on average, the human race has become a good deal dumber simply as a result of demographic reasons. Considering that even the most intelligent of us in the most advanced countries, however, have been also reduced to brainwashed idiots in part, at least, the overall situation is grim to say the least.

The implications of declining average intelligence are far reaching. It has been shown, for example, that a drop of just 3 points in average IQ results in increasing numbers of:

(a) Men in jail - 13%.
(b) High school dropouts (permanent) - 15%.
(c) Women chronically dependent on welfare - 15%.

No doubt declining IQs have also produced even more 'low IQ/ high cunning' people trying to brainwash the rest of us into 'believe anything/buy anything' consumer oblivion.

INTERBREEDING AMONGST MUSLIMS

An article posted recently by Cairns News entitled *Muslims suffer insanity, low IQ, recessive disorders from 1400 years of inbreeding* said that "the massive inbreeding in Muslim culture may well have done virtually irreversible damage to the Muslim gene pool, including extensive damage to its intelligence, sanity, and health."

According to Danish psychologist Nikilai Sennels, close to half of all Muslims in the world are inbred, and in Pakistan the numbers approach 70%, whilst they are 67% in Saudi Arabia, 64% in Jordan and Kuwait, 63% in Sudan, 60% in Iraq, and 54% in the United Arab Emirates and Qatar. As a result British Pakistani families are 13 times more likely to have children with recessive genetic disorders.

According to Sennels, research shows that children of consanguineous marriages lose 10-16 points off their IQ and that social abilities develop much slower in inbred babies. The risk of having an IQ lower than 70, the official demarcation for being classified as "retarded", increases by an astonishing 400% among children of cousin marriages. He concluded: *There is no doubt that the wide spread tradition of first cousin marriages among Muslims has harmed the gene pool of Muslims.*

The article concluded:

> Bottom line: Islam is not simply a benign and morally equivalent alternative to the Judeo-Christian tradition. As Sennels points out, the first and biggest victims are Muslims. Simple Judeo-Christian compassion for Muslims and a common-sense desire to protect Western civilization from the ravages of Islam dictate a vigorous opposition to the spread of this dark and dangerous ideology.

These stark realities must be taken into account when we establish public policies dealing with immigration from Muslim countries and the building of Mosques.

PHYSICALLY PAST OPTIMUM

Let's face it, take our clothes off and have a look at homo sapiens sapiens. We look damn stupid, like an evolutionary mistake or Martians on this damned planet: like we don't belong.

We are, in fact, less evolved physically than chimpanzees.

Quite simply, we are pathetic, for example:

- Male baldness appears to be on the increase.
- In contrast, we have hair too long in places and have to cut and shave our hair off frequently, a ridiculous situation.
- Somewhat anachronistically we have evolved with men designed for hunter-gathering and women for child bearing.
- Since that time mankind got smaller, the average European male being only 165 cm tall in Shakespeare's time. Thanks to improved diet our height has returned to that of the hunter gatherers (178 cm average for men) but we have lost a good deal of muscle tissue (Callaghan, 2008), no doubt why it has been found that Negroes have a genetic factor that makes them better sprinters.
- The disturbing obesity epidemic sweeping more affluent countries where, of course, people are most brainwashed by advertising. The result has been that, although not a great deal taller, women weigh on average 20% more than they did in 1926 (Callaghan, 2008).
- Poor diet caused generations of us immense amounts of tooth decay and type II diabetes is now 5 times more prevalent.

- We seem increasingly susceptible to new viruses like HIV and VRE which already pose a very serious threat.
- The incidence of most types of cancer has increased dramatically, often as a result of defective genes (Weinberg, 1999).
- Even amongst children blood pressures are significantly higher.
- A French TV documentary *Men in Danger* (Cuthbertson, 2008) notes that pollution is causing significant changes in humans:
  (a) Decreased testosterone levels in men.
  (b) Greater prevalence of genital abnormalities in males at birth.
  (c) Male sperm counts decreased by 50% in Copenhagen in the last 50 years and by 40% in the last 20 years only in Paris.
  (d) A huge 150% increase in breast cancer in women since 1960.
- Our eyes evolved for far field vision but thanks to man's invention of writing and then TV and the PC we are 3 times more likely to be short-sighted, a telling example of how our evolution is unable to keep pace with our rapidly changing environment.

The inescapable conclusion, however, is that we are becoming a genetic joke physically, part of an overall *reverse evolution* process.

DETERIORATING GENE POOL

In *The Descent of Man* Charles Darwin cited the work of his cousin Francis Galton more than ten times. Galton did much important scientific work, including proposing and defining the term *eugenics*, on which subject Darwin wrote:

> *We civilized men, on the other hand, do our utmost to check the process of elimination; we build asylums for the imbecile, the maimed, and the sick; we institute poor-laws; and our medical men exert their utmost skill to save the life of every one to the last moment. Thus the weak members of civilized societies propagate their kind.*

Carlo Cipolla (1974) pointed out that our population growth graph went almost vertical with the coming of the industrial revolution and implored that what we needed was 'quality not quantity,' a phrase the first author recalls his fifth grade teacher Miss Bachelard repeating often.

As Lynn and Vanhaven (2002) point out, however, we have dysgenic fertility trends so that the least intelligent people have the most children.

As part of that the none-too-intelligent but overpaid greedy executives whose businesses brainwash us to buy their often shoddy products can indeed afford to have children and buy them the right qualifications to carry on the family line in a capitalist fashion.

In contrast, many of the brightest children who struggle to come top at school will end up as scientists and engineers and the like, make relatively little money and struggle to afford a house and children, avoid divorce and stay sane enslaved as underpaid back room boys.

In addition, modern medical science is able to keep alive people with serious genetic disorders and there is concern in some quarters that this will lead to a deterioration of the human gene pool:

> *Many people are born each year with genetic defects that in the past would have hampered their reproductive potential. Now, medical treatment enables them to*

survive, reproduce, and pass on the defective genes. Followers of this view, such as the Nobel Prize winning geneticist H.J. Mueller, see this tampering with selection as a black cloud hanging over our future. Someday, Mueller says, all people will be born with one major genetic problem or another: diabetes, PKU, hemophilia.

M.L. Weiss, A.E. Mann,
Human Biology and Behaviour (1978).

The bottom line once again, therefore, is that we are into reverse evolution both mentally and physically, in part because eugenics became a dirty word because of ill-conceived attempts at reducing 'bad breeding,' for example:

(a) From 1907, 27 US states passed sterilization laws to prevent such people as epileptics, the feeble-minded, habitual criminals, and 'moral perverts' from having children. In most states these laws were not enforced but in California 10,000 people were sterilized by 1935.

(b) Other countries including Denmark, Germany, Norway, Sweden and Switzerland passed similar laws, in Sweden 60,000 young women being sterilized between 1935 and 1976.

(c) Eugenics was supposedly the justification for the massive extermination programs of the scientists and geneticists of the Third Reich, leading to the stigma attached to the word.

In the economically decaying West, having spent the best part of a century fighting socialism, we have now have gone too far in our quest for equality, insisting that regardless of sex, race or any other factor, we are all equal.

We have dumbed down our education systems, our political systems, and our 'consumer zombie' society in general in which we now breed 'willy-nilly,' perhaps with a quick copulatory act between yet another raft of mindless TV ads.

As our society regresses it is now, once again in history, more and more a fight for survival in an increasingly fierce economic rat race whilst the planet's resources and its environment gradually diminish in quantity and quality.

The first author's father, despite having had 3 children (he was the third!), believed in ZPG (zero population growth), quite correctly at that time.

Since then China has had its one-child policy which we might call NPG, and has become the world's second largest and strongest economy.

The first author, told by a woman he had made pregnant that the child would be "mildly retarded", consulted some experts who inferred that 'mildly' was really quite serious. He then persuaded the woman to have an abortion though 5 months pregnant. She did, about which he has no conscience.

David Galton concludes that:

> *Society as a whole should embrace the new* [eugenics] *technology and the opportunities if offers less timorously, or even with some measure of enthusiasm* (Galton, 2001).

ANIMAL FARM

Most, if not all, the terrorism, revolutions and wars in history have been about a "fair go" because it isn't really sane, for example, that just Buckingham Palace alone should have 650 rooms!

No doubt that sort of anomaly, along with hard times, helped inspire the French and Russian revolutions.

Few countries, if any, are still governed by monarchies and most have so-called democracy. These are not truly democratic, however, and are in fact corrupt capitalist oligarchies in which a few rich families, powerful bureaucrats and business leaders are able to make most of the input into the important decisions at all levels of government.

All too often our leaders fit the Peter Principle well, that is, they are incompetent. This is borne out by the results as we are always lurching from one disaster to another and constantly fed a load of bullshit saying we've never had it so good.

Lynn and Vanhaven note that in the richest nations the correlation of IQ with earnings is only 0.35. This is a low figure bearing in mind that high earnings should enhance performance. Indeed, if we do bear this in mind, then the real correlation would be a negative one showing that the fattest capitalist pigs have more animal cunning and greed and less intelligence.

George Orwell was a socialist, of course, and we think of capitalist pigs when we think of his *Animal Farm* and wish that we had *real democracy*, a topic we return to in the next and last 'solutions' chapter.

On being bossed around, it should be noted that it is not usually the truly superior person that runs the show. An example is how a baby's cry can automatically start lactation in its mother. This, of course, is just a survival mechanism, but it is also an exemplar of how rich bosses live off enslaved workers and it is not hard, of course, to relate their frequent whinges to those of infants, after all that is what they are paid megabucks to do, along with produce shit products which they hire expert brainwashers usually called advertising agencies to addict you to.

The bottom line is, therefore, that our leaders are usually greedy unethical pigs of pretty average intelligence, if that, thus being an important cog in the machinery of our *reverse evolution*.

CONCLUSION

A 'Cambridge man' like the first author, Ian Morris, author of the book *Why the West Rules - For Now*, opines that people everywhere are essentially clever chimps.

We guess is that the human race past its peak around the 1960s. WWII was long over and there was relative peace in the world, we had TV, tape recorders and transistor radios, and the first PCs were just a few years away. Then the world's human population was perhaps already about double that for comfort if everybody was to have a good standard of living that might be sustainable for the long term. Now it has more than doubled again to a clearly unsustainable level.

Overpopulation, overconsumption, pollution, global warming, resource depletion and land degradation are such serious problems that the survival of many species, including ours, is threatened.

Everywhere you look real standards are declining though we are usually told the opposite while incompetent and overpaid CEO's are simply looting the planet while they still can.

The heading for an article posted on the Internet is

> *Beware of Corporate Media Brainwashing.*
> *Through Corporate Media Brainwashing,*
> *the World's Elite Disguises Their New World*
> *Order Plan as it Dumbs America Down.*

The article is, in fact, a gripe about banks in the wake of the sub-prime lending crisis in the US, but it can be viewed as a reminder of what brainwashed consumer and believe any bullshit zombies we are.

19th century French lunatic asylums used to make money by having inmates perform for the public once a week. In Australia in recent years the treasurer has said year that his deliberately pessimistic national budget was in surplus but not reminded us that each time the national debt was continuing to rise.

This is the typical econobabble of economists and business leaders, stuff that would have been suitable in the public performances in 19th century French 'funny farms'.

Yet we brainwashed zombies accept such crap. No wonder that we are in *reverse evolution* and, as we slowly grow less intelligent we are, of course, blissfully unaware of it and too busy trying to survive the 'rat race' to care even if we were.

Finally, a good and sometimes humourous example of consumer zombies can be found in the movie *Dawn of The Dead* with many scenes of hoards of zombies creeping around a huge shopping centre. In this story, however, the zombies are not looking to buy anything, they are simply looking for a meal of human flesh from a 'non-zombie', who even if just bitten will ere long become a zombie too. This 'contagion' aspect of the story reminds one of the importance of imitative learning in the very young and social learning in teenagers and adults.

As for BW zombies – what better example than Muslim terrorists? In July 2016 the Australian media began to talk of "terror health checks", that is, checking suspected Muslim activists for mental health problems. As noted earlier in this chapter, thanks to centuries of interbreeding, most Muslims are 'retards' to a considerable degree, whilst anyone following this savage, vile and primitive religion in this day and age should be certified in some way, if not several, e.g. as somewhat insane, at risk of radicalization, and thus perhaps a terrorist risk etcetera. Then, for treatment of their mental health the only sensible course would be to give them radical prefrontal lobotomies using the simple 'drilling holes from the side' method of Freeman and Watts discussed in Chapter 8.

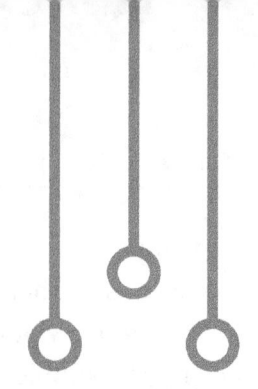

Chapter 22
SOME SOLUTIONS

*All inequality that has no special utility
to justify it is injustice.*
Jeremy Bentham, British jurist and
philosopher (1748 - 1832).
Writings (W Stark ed.), 1952.

*Oil, despite its far reaching importance,
is a transient phenomenon, whose finite
life span will end, sooner or later.*
Sheikh Ahmed Yamani, referring to
OPEC raising of oil prices, quoted in *Arabia:
The Islamic World Review* (October 1981).

*We must try to find ways to starve the terrorist and the
hijacker of the oxygen of publicity on which they depend.*
Margaret Thatcher, Speech to
American Bar Association,
15 July 1985, London (*The Times*, 16 July 1985).

WHAT CAN WE DO TO AVOID THE COMING HORRORS?

The first two quotations above remind us that action is needed to deal with problems such as population explosion, resource depletion and pollution discussed in Chapter 17. The third reminds us that the grim global situation is largely the result of the greed of a few powerful and wealthy people.

Some of the things we that might help ameliorate our already catastrophic situation are:

- Make the 4 day working week the standard.
- Allow families with a single breadwinner to split their income before tax with their spouse to help reduce the need for women with children of preschool age, if not any age, to work.
- To help reduce our excessive population women should be encouraged to consider having only one child by being reminded that it has often been found that only children tend to have higher IQs and do better academically (Vernon, 1960).
- Improve our education system by cutting school back to 10 years and using on the job training as we used to do for nursing and many other occupations. The remaining sensible University courses would be more responsibly run by separate professional colleges.
- Encourage a return to small 'local' businesses and reverse the trend to globalization and industries run by heartless and overpaid executives who are nothing more than little Hitlers.
- Reduce the hierarchical nature of our society so that young people in their 20s and 30s and at their productive and imaginative peak are not lived off by these little Hitlers. In other

words, create a *fairer society*, the topic of the next section of this chapter.
- Raise minimum wages and put a ceiling on executive salaries. Remove *all* executive perks and bonuses.
- Decentralize industry so that vast countries like Australia do not have nearly all their population crammed into huge megacities more like large scale ant hills than anything sane people should want to live in. To encourage this, rail networks should be extended and precious oil used to run these in remote areas, not absurdly wasteful cars with huge engines used as shopping buggies.
- Encourage a return back to farming by family concerns and not big business to help revitalize decaying rural communities.
- Government bodies should be established to see to it that people are not brainwashed into buying unnecessary and wasteful products like junk food, four-wheel drive city cars and swimming pools. A society in which we are brainwashed into becoming zombies that wear uncomfortable jeans and carry a mobile phone in one hand and a bottle of drink in the other is not really free, quite the opposite.

Examples of actions taken on advertising include:

(a) Restriction of and compulsory warnings on tobacco products in most countries.
(b) At one time, at least, TV commercials in Italy were limited to 10 showings a year with no two showings closer than 10 days apart (Cateora, 1996).
   - Increase efforts at developing sustainable energy sources such as wind, solar and tidal.

The Brainwashed | 445

- Legislate against planned obsolescence in cars, electrical, building and other products.
- Increase efforts at introducing electric cars, especially small personal transport vehicles that might be a restyled form of Clive Sinclair's £400 (1975) tricycle using nickel cadmium batteries.
- Create a society in which housing stock is affordable to those beginning careers and family. This could be done by appropriate legislation setting land values at prescribed rather than market values.
- Return to government economic management that protects those governed by the use of fixed currency rates and at least modest tariffs in places like Australia.
- Introduce *real democracy* allowing everybody to vote on major issues. This could easily be accomplished using the Internet and polling stations like bank ATMs in all shopping centres. Voting could also be accessible free of charge via all public telephones.

Parliament should be composed of *independent* members of the various electoral regions and collusion by them should be illegal.

- The UN should be provided with a large and sophisticated army to help maintain peace and combat terrorism.
- Religions and sects responsible, directly or indirectly, for terrorism and war should be outlawed and their religious sites and offices around the world should be closed down by the UN.
- A UN funded organization should be established to educate people around the world that God does not exist

so that people cannot be duped by self-serving religions and sects.
- ➢ Ban nuclear and biochemical weapons. Ban land mines.
- ➢ Take steps to ban war and limit all weapons.
- ➢ Develop a fairer society, the need for which is illustrated by a simple Finite Element Method (FEM) network example in the next section.

A FAIRER SOCIETY

Figure 22.1 shows a small hierarchical network which we shall model using the simple BASIC program given in Chapter Three. At node 1 we have the pyramid building and lunatic 'boss' and a current 'load' of 100 is input. This is done by inserting the BASIC statement

$$V(1) = 100$$

between the 13th and 14th lines of the program.

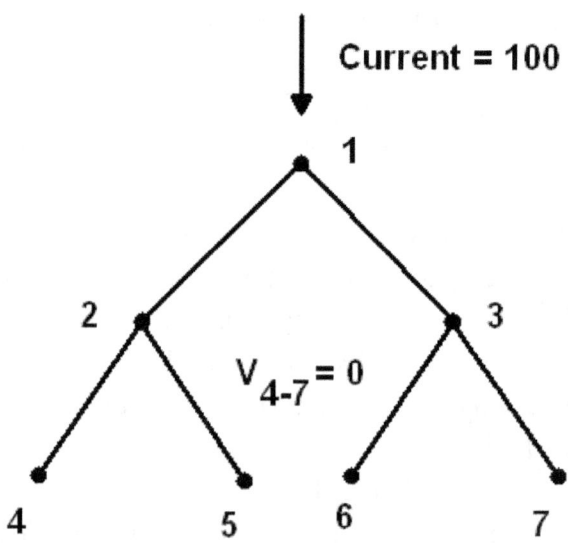

Figure 22.1. Hierarchical network.

Then zero datum voltage is specified at nodes 4-7 and unit resistance is given to all 6 elements so that the entire data for the program is:

DATA 7,6,4
DATA 1,2,1, 1,3,1, 2,4,1, 2,5,1, 3,6,1, 3,7,1
DATA 4,0, 5,0, 6,0, 7,0

The program results will be:
Voltage 75 at node 1, 25 at nodes 2 &3, and zero at nodes 4 to 7. Currents 50 in the top two elements and 25 in the rest.

This illustrates what the econobabble calls 'the trickledown effect', that is, the boss of this very small hierarchy has 3 times the voltage (or power, money and status) as his subordinates (the front line managers) one rung below. The workers at the bottom have no status at all.

If we add a further bottom row of 8 nodes in Figure 22.1 then now the 'voltage hierarchy' is 87.5, 37.5, 12.5, 0 so that the boss now does 7 times as well as the 'front line managers' on the row above the bottom row.

Then if we add a further fifth row of 16 nodes the voltage hierarchy is 93.75, 43.75, 18.75, 6.25, 0 and the boss does 15 times as well as the front line managers and infinitely better than the workers at the bottom!

If Mohr's exponential law of money (Equation 12.4) is the fundamental principle of capitalism then the latter 'voltage hierarchy' is that of modern management, leading to Mohr's Law of Hierarchies:

> **In hierarchical organizations the amount of real material-producing work people do is inversely proportional to their rank or level in the organization.**

> **The amount of compensation they receive, however, is proportional to their level, sometimes to an exponential degree.**

This, of course, is not fair at all.

To add insult to the injury of poverty the worker-slaves endure 'top-down one-way' (TDOW) communication as they did all through their long years at school, in other words, they are treated like shit.

It is not always this way, however, as shown by the counter example of modern movie and sports stars, in those businesses the people who do the actual work! The trouble is that they are doing what is at school called play, not work, so that they make zillions more than the poor peasants who work on farms, in factories or on building sites to produce what is essential to human life is not fair at all either.

So those posters that were so common in the USSR decades ago which pictured the workers as heroic perhaps made some sense. Then, of course, the hammer and sickle on their flag was also symbolic of the importance of the workers.

So the bottom line is that we have to create fairer societies which have *real democracy*. In these greed, hunger and famine, war and other evils will not accepted by the people. In the next and last section is an opinion on this from a dying but wise old man.

REAL DEMOCRACY

The first author used to talk to a famous Greek engineer, John Argyris, in Stuttgart who had done much to pioneer a major field he had spent most of his adult life working in. This went on happily for 10 years and Argyris was always very complimentary about the first author's abilities and work and very modest about his own, for example saying one night:

> "I have no great intelligence, I have imagination."

He used to go to his University office every week day until he was almost 90 years old. Then his health took a turn for the worse which he had foreseen a couple of years earlier when going off to have his second cataract operation. He said: *"You are now number one."* He could still read the writing on the wall! The last time he got to the phone the first author could hear a noise that may have been a walking frame. Clearly the end was nigh: when you are no longer ambulatory and are 90 the prognosis is poor.

The first author asked him two questions:

(a) *"Is the problem of the human race anthropology?"*
(b) *"Are real democracy and socialism the same?"*

Two quick and identical answers as always from a quick mind: **"Of course!"**
In other words:

(a) The chief apes, whether of religion, politics or business, that have led us to the brink of extinction have a lot to answer for.
(b) Don't be brainwashed by bullshit about products of any kind, including religion, politics or whatsoever. We are all animals with a halfway well developed cerebral cortex and yet are so stupid that we continually make a mess of nearly everything, including ourselves.

We are slow learners, however, and have a very hard time learning to walk, let alone talk sense. We can't be born knowing the answers or being wise to the wiles of unscrupulous old men and women trying to push their products at us.

We need new, more responsible forms of government that don't build up industrial-military states and kowtow to big business but represent *our interests*. All of us should have a *direct* and democratic voice in major decisions at all levels of government and, for that matter, in the running of the organizations that we work for if we are not self-employed.

In other words we should have *freedom*. Specifically, we should have freedom of:

- **Speech:** we should be allowed to express our views.
- **Opinion:** we should be allowed to democratically express our opinion on *all* major issues.
- **Association:** we should be able to meet with and talk to whoever we choose.
- **Education:** we should have more educational paths, some of them with faster pacing and shortcuts for example.
- **Careers:** we should have a society in which children develop a vocational idea relatively early in life, rather than a lottery process based on a few marks 'either way' in just one set of exams.
- **Employment:** we need a return to the 'a career for life' approach so that people in the work force are committed to and good at what they do.
- **Choice:** industry should make a reasonable effort to provide us with responsible and genuinely innovative and beneficial products which do not have obsolescence built into them.
- **Power:** we should have a truly democratic system in which all eligible voters are able to vote on all major issues.

> - - and so on, but with some restrictions, of course, and this is always a difficult question. Most obviously these would preclude violations of common law.

As Martin Luther King put it during his famous 'I have a dream' speech:"**Let freedom reign !! "**

That sounds fine to us. Just so long as the bullshit of the brain washers does not rain down upon us quite so heavily, whether that be via advertising, the lectern or the pulpit, and that we can make some progress towards *real democracy* so that the wishes of the people can be heard, not the BS artists.

DON'T BECOME A CONSUMER ZOMBIE

Those of us who cannot accept that we are in reverse evolution and getting even more stupid should at least realize that we are animals after all and were never all that clever to begin with.

An article in *The Australian* on December 5, 2007, was nicely headed:

Chimps make monkeys of humans

and went on to say that Japanese researchers had found that, overall, chimpanzees outscored humans on two tests of short-term memory. The tests involved quickly remembering and reproducing a sequence of 5 or 9 numbers on a PC touch screen, the chimps having been taught the order of the Arabic numerals 1 to 9.

Today, indeed, the human race spends an inordinate amount of its time in front of TV screens, PC screens, mobile phone screens, movie screens and so on, thus having been reduced to little better than lab rats constantly brainwashed by the often ridiculous bullshit produced by advertising weirdos.

The ratbags in big biz who have us brainwashed with ads are also those almost entirely responsible for looting the planet and then making it a polluted rubbish dump. For them the exploding population has been a huge bonus but it is already proving to be a terminal disaster in the making for mankind.

Politicians have said and done little or nothing on the population issue over decades and have for the most part been very slow on the uptake concerning pollution, resource depletion and GW, preferring to kowtow to big biz instead, as usual.

On the issue of unnecessary consumption, the first author's late father's dictum

"It's not a bargain/cheap if you don't need it"

applies awfully well to 'junk products' like fast foods, confectionery, booze, cigarettes and overseas holidays. *To add insult to injury, advertising is a large chunk of the cost of most 'junk products.'*

In other words we need to 'get wise' and realize that the bullshit and brainwashing we are subjected to so constantly is, as the rat race intensifies, more and more a form of bullying and something that we should do our utmost to resist.

We must also realize that to be truly free we must be cautious about imitative and social learning which mostly involves *copying* others.

In summary, we need both personally and collectively to:

- Largely ignore advertising, only taking notice of the rare ad that may promote something we actually do need at a good price.
- Ignore other bullshit from business, political and religious organizations, only taking notice if, after careful analysis

and thought, we can judge that a particular message is worth taking some notice of.
- Push for consumer education programs relatively early on in schools, including in these cautions about avoiding thoughtless imitative and social learning.
- Push for decent products rather than junk, for example healthy food, affordable not 'showy' housing, and sensible, economical cars more like Clive Sinclair's 1975 C5, a new supposedly US$2000+ petrol engine car released in India a couple of years ago perhaps being an example and prompting people interviewed in the street on TV to say:

"Now I can afford a car."

- Push for reversal of the growth of wasteful and greedy trends of globalization in business.
- Push for reductions in pollution, including greenhouse gasses.
- Push for reduced consumption of fast disappearing fossil fuel resources such as oil.
- Push for conservation of other precious resources, particularly water, farming land, forests and natural habitats for threatened wild life species.
- Push for plans to reduce our population to levels at which a reasonable standard of living is sustainable for all.

PREVENT THE SPREAD OF ISLAMISM AND JIHAD

From witch doctors onward through history, most religious leaders have been evil. Their greed for gain of status, influence, power and wealth has always led to conflicts, terrorism and war.

There is no better example than Muhammad. This exceedingly evil man, having been thrown out of Medina, sought revenge by gathering disciples on the pretext of his claims of having heard the word of God in the desert. These lies were evil, and his ideas and aims were evil, and Vladimir Putin's comparison of the current world situation with WW2, and Islamists with the Nazis, is entirely justified, and of course, the present authors term this present period *World War 3* (Mohr, Fear & Sinclair, 2015). Indeed, Muhammad was far more evil than Hitler as for circa 1500 years his satanic doctrines have led to slaughter on a massive scale, beginning with his taking of Medina, and then Mecca, and then the spread of the Satanic Religion throughout much of the world.

Note, however, that leaders of many religions have been evil, and those of the Catholic and other Christian sects, so many of whom have been found guilty of sexual abuse of the young, are of course evil, as were the many Muslim leaders who had harems of dozens, if not hundreds, and in a few cases thousands of wives and/or concubines. And, of course, the Christian Church had its reformation which cost many thousands of lives.

But the scale of slaughter, persecution and church-burning by Muslims over the centuries defies belief, as does the absurd 'voice from God' lie that started their Satanic Religion. For that reason, every effort should be made to reverse the current spread of this evil epidemic,

Clearly those influenced by such evil ideas are victims of the 'devil-like' leaders/preachers of the BS of their Satanic Religion. Clearly, therefore, these leaders should, like witches in the middle ages, be burnt at the stake or treated in some comparable fashion to prevent further spread or 'infection' of their evil ideas. Clearly too, those Muslims seen to prove the greatest threat to society should be locked up in places like Guantanamo Bay, whilst those posing lesser threat should also be jailed for an appropriate period.

The bottom line is, however, that the closest thing to the devil thus far in history, was Muhammad himself, so if his followers give you the 'creeps', as they most certainly do the first author, then that perhaps is appropriate.

Indeed, the first author gives a good example in the evil and self-confessed "Islamist" Fayez Horrible in the Preface of this book. His public ravings and writings motivate Muslims to do minor things like the Lindt Café siege and also start up some of the summer bush fires that plague both Australia and the USA in summer. If the intelligence services ignore him as a threat and don't put him under surveillance &/or lock him up they will look very bad indeed in the press if he is connected to terrorist events within the next few years

SOME SOLUTIONS

A 2004 academic analysis of consumption concluded: "It is trickling into all aspects of being an individual. It is – for good or bad – the foundation of human existence" (*The Australian*, 3rd Aug. 2005).

Indeed, pretentious persuasion by bullshit artists has been at the core of the ongoing disaster of human history. Now the resulting combination of excessive population and excessive per capita consumption is inevitably leading us towards catastrophe and we consumer zombies, like the earth itself, are deteriorating along the way.

The bottom line, therefore, is that we should:

(1) Largely ignore the bullshit and brainwashing efforts of business, political and other organizations seeking only to improve their situation and, in most cases, make our situation and that of the planet worse.

(2) Insist on eliminating corruption and greed in our societies as far as possible. To that end we should ensure, for example:
 (a) Rational limits on executive salaries.
 (b) Profit proportional company tax.

(3) Campaign to replace the outdated and farcical Westminster 'revolving door' two party system with *real democracy* in which electorates are represented by truly independent people not influenced by big business or any other section of the community.

An example might be Iceland which, mired in government debt to the unprecedented extent of 10 times GDP, has established a "Constitutional Assembly" of people in Reykjavik as well as a social network Internet site on which the public can make suggestions for reform. The result has already been 300 amendments to the constitution.

(4) Insist on sensible economic management, for example:
 (a) The inverse law of supply and demand and the LM and IS curves noted in Chapter 15 should be understood to avoid the cycles of boom and bust caused by incorrect fiscal fiddling.
 (b) A least limited tariffs should be the norm to protect local industries and jobs.

(5) Greater efforts must be made to solve the many problems such as overpopulation, resource depletion and pollution that threaten both our quality of life and survival.

(6) Be more careful in choosing who runs what.

Noting that circa 50% of personality may be genetic (Galton, 2001), the first author's first law, 'Mohr's

Morphology,' postulates three personality types based on a scale of aggressiveness:

(a) Placid (the meek).
(b) Neutral (the OK guys).
(c) Aggressive/assertive (the bossy types).

The meek do not inherit the earth, as The Bible has it, for the bossy little Hitler types usually end up as boss!

These bossy types typically have 'type A' behaviour associated with stress. Research has found that, contrary to popular belief enshrined in such terms as "executive stress," being boss involves less work stress and thus it is the slaves, of course, that really are stressed, and perhaps never much more so than in today's high-paced consumer society.

Human history might not have been so catastrophic, in fact, had quieter, less aggressive, more intelligent, more honest, and harder working people been leading us.

(7) We must solve the global 'Muslim conflicts' problem almost invariably instigated by Islamic terrorists, an exception being the TAMIL Tigers of Sri Lanka who effect ethnic cleansing of Sinhalese and Muslim inhabitants from areas under their control. Indeed, increasingly commentators now refer to global Islamic terrorism and the fight against it as 'World War 3.'

ENDING WORLD WAR 3

Ending global Islamic terrorism will be difficult and may take many more years. Some solutions were proposed in the book *World War 3, When & How Will It End?* (Mohr, Fear & Sinclair, 2015), those proposals including many of the 'solutions' discussed in the present chapter such as 'real democracy'.

The August 10, 2016, edition of *The International Express* said that, according to the Metropolitan Police Commissioner, another terrorist attack in the UK was certain to occur before long, the page 12 editorial comment saying that:

Protecting borders must be a Government priority.

Melbourne's Herald-Sun newspaper reported on 5/7/2016 that: *Would be terrorists are being caught up in airport stings as they try to join extremist groups overseas.*

Security agencies secretly cancel the passports of would-be foreign fighters, allowing them to go to airports where they are intercepted, questioned and have their electronic devices scanned for information.

The article said that 170 passports had been cancelled since June 2014, and that since then 500 people had been taken off planes by security officers of the Border Force.

The same newspaper reported on 3/8/2016 that a new counter-terrorism intelligence service was to be established to provide ASIO with an early warning system for possible terrorists trying to leave or enter the country.

On August 13 it was reported that Australia's intake of Syrian refugees had been slowed by increased security checks.

Elected to Australia's senate after a federal election on 2/7/2016, well-known anti-immigration personality Pauline Hanson called for an end to Muslim immigration and a ban on new mosques, also saying:

> *You can't deny the fact that in these mosques they have been known to preach hate towards us. It's not me, it's our society that are on the streets against the building of mosques.*

About Islam she said:

> *We're talking about a political ideology.
> They would say it is a religion. I know
> and they say it's a religion of peace.
> We know that's not true either.*

Another senator-elect, Derren Hinch objected to Hanson's suggestion that CCTV cameras be placed in all mosques, saying that they should therefore also be placed in Catholic churches to catch paedophiles. However, about Australia's Racial Discrimination Act which forbids anything which is "reasonably likely ... to offend, insult, humiliate or intimidate another person or group of people" because of their "race, colour or national or ethnic origin," Hinch said:

> *I'm offended and insulted that they say I can't
> say anything that will offend or insult.*

Here he was in agreement with Hanson who had said:

> *We are entitled to freedom of speech and
> freedom of expression, saying that the laws were
> stifling people's right to have an opinion.*

A reader agreed with this in the Herald-Sun of 4/8/16:

> *Free speech is only free until you
> offend someone, or a group.*

A reader of the Weekend Australian also agreed on 6/8/16:

> *She [Hanson] is in direct touch with the
> concerns and fears of ordinary people, who
> are all too often ignored by our superiors.*

In conclusion, as noted at the end of Chapter 18:

> *There should be major revision in shariah law and Islamic thinking to reduce their intolerance and violence. In particular, a revised edition of the Qur'an in which references to such nefarious activities as jihad are removed is badly needed. Democratic government should be introduced throughout the Middle-East, along with formation of independent nations for such disaffected groups as the Kurds and Palestinians. Initially, elections in such new nations should be supervised internationally to ensure that they are democratic.*

More important right now, perhaps, Muslims leaders and preachers should be encouraged, if not required, to speak out at every possible opportunity against Muslim violence and terrorism, wherever it may occur. To monitor this, therefore, Pauline Hanson's suggestion of CCTV cameras in mosques might make sense. After all, there are 2 million CCTV cameras in London, nearly all of these in public places such as streets, parks and the lobbies of large buildings.

A letter published by the Herald-Sun on 8/7/2016 read:

> *Haven't radical Islamists killed us infidels with planes, pressure cooker bombs, suitcase bombs, improvised explosive devices, knives, pistols, rifles, grenades, truck bombs, suicide vests, stones, rockets, and even chucked us off tall buildings? Isn't the ideology the problem, and not the weapon of choice?*

A column by Rita Panahi in the same newspaper on 13/7/2016 said:

> *you cannot blame the continual fighting and sectarian violence on Western imperialism, the Iraq war or the state of Israel. The truth is that Islam desperately needs some reformation. Railing against the West for its racism, decadence and immorality will not bring peace to the Middle East or other regions torn apart by sectarian violence.*

Whilst IS has lost ground of late, the Taliban now controls more territory than at any time since before the invasion of Afghanistan, so an end to 'WW3' is not yet in sight. The authors hope, however, that some of the ideas in the present book, and also in their previous book *World War 3*, will point in the right direction, perhaps the most urgent of these being that a new, 'friendlier' edition of the Koran is badly needed.

Without this, young Muslims will continue to find encouragement in the Koran's many incitements to jihad and join such evil organizations as IS and al-Qa'ida, or commit 'lone wolf' or small-group attacks in such countries as Australia. If such attacks continue, calls for banning of Muslim immigration, and even banning of mosques and the religion itself, will grow louder around the world.

Indeed, circa 18/7/2016, TV host Sonya Kruger echoed Pauline Hanson's call to end Muslim migration to Australia, saying:

> *I want to feel safe. There is a correlation between the number of people who are Muslim in a country and the number of terrorist attacks,* adding: *You're not allowed to talk about it.*

Andrew Bolt wrote in the *Herald-Sun* of 15/8/16 about the need to at least 'free up' Australia's Racial Discrimination Act, saying: *At last Australians are finally refusing to be treated like scum, too stupid and vicious to be free to speak,* and noted that 600,000 had voted for Pauline Hanson's One Nation Party at the federal elections of the previous month.

On a historical note, *The Weekend Australian* on 30/7/216 printed a recent article from *The Times* about the upcoming centenary of the *Balfour Declaration* [which was briefly discussed in the last section of ch. 6] which said:

> The Balfour Declaration set the scene for a century of conflict but it also contains within it the germ of a two-state solution.

We, as noted more than once earlier, see the final outcome of that declaration, namely the creation of the state of Israel in the UN-mandated British Protectorate of 'Palestine' in 1948 as the main seed of WW3, i.e., the seemingly endless spate of Islamist jihad and terrorism that has plagued the Middle East and more recently the world since that time.

We do, however, agree that it was meant, of course, to be a 'two-state solution', one which failed because of high levels of Israeli-Palestinian conflict, for example the 5 day war of 1967 which saw Israel claim control of a great deal more territory which it retains control of to this day.

If Israel can belatedly be persuaded to hand back those regions 'stolen' from the Palestinians in 1967, however, that would go a long way towards restoring peace in that region, and it can only be hoped that some of the many territorial disputes elsewhere in the conflict-ridden Middle East will also be settled peacefully in the not too distant future.

Helpful too, one hopes, are plans by the US and Russia to increase investment in new hi-tech military equipment to help combat hostile nations and terrorists.

During August 2016 media commentators concluded that:

[1] After 5 years of civil war in Syria between Sunni rebels, IS, the government, and US & Russian forces, there is no end in sight to the slaughter and mass emigration.
[2] Aleppo could be termed the "Syrian Stalingrad".
[3] Terrorist attacks on the West have "steadily" increased over the last 15 years and more than "half-measures" are needed to deal with the ongoing jihad of IS etcetera.

On the latter point we can't agree more that even stronger attacks on IS are needed, along with restriction of Muslim migration and religious practice in the West.

THE END

BIBLIOGRAPHY

Aarons M, Loftus B, *The Secret War Against the Jews*, Mandarin Press, Melbourne (1999).
Adams, J, *The Next World War*, Simon & Schuster, New York (1998).
Adamson I, Kennedy R, *Sinclair and the 'Sunrise' Technology*, Penguin, Harmondsworth (1986).
Alder B, Fernbach S, Rotenberg M, *Methods in Computational Physics*, Academic Press, New York (1963).
Alexander W, *Future War*, Thomas Dunne Books, New York (1999).
Alibek, K, *Biohazard*, Arrow, London (2000).
Argyris JH, *Energy Theorems and Structural Analysis*, Butterworth, London (1960, reprinted from *Aircraft Engineering* 1954 - 55).
Atkinson RC, Shiffrin RM, Human memory: A proposed system and its control processes. RW Spence, JT Spence (eds), *The Psychology of Learning and Motivation, Vol. 2*, Academic Press, New York (1968).
Atrens D, Curthoys I, *The Neurosciences and Behaviour: An Introduction*, 2nd edn, Academic Press, Sydney (1982).
Baker DB, *Power Quotes*, The Business Library/Information Australia, Melbourne (1992).
Batra R, *Surviving the Great Depression of 1990*, Bantam/Schartz, Sydney (1988).
Bell R, Hall, R, *Impacts: Contemporary Issues & Global Problems*, The Jacaranda Press, Milton QLD (1991).
Bethe HA, *The Road from Los Alamos*, Touchstone Books, New York NY (1991).

Black E, *IBM and the Holocaust*, Little Brown, London (2001).
Blondel J, *Voters, Parties, and Leaders*, Penguin, Harmondsworth (1963).
Brook-Shepherd G, *Iron Maze, The Western Secret Services and the Bolsheviks*, Pan, London (1998).
Broom L, Jones FL, McDonnell P, Williams T, *The Inheritance of Inequality*, Routledge & Kegan Paul, London (1980).
Buchanan JM, Tullock G, *The Calculus of Consent*, The University of Michigan Press, Ann Arbor (1974).
Buchdahl Tintner, Tanya, *Out Of Time: The Vexed Life Of Georg Tintner*, University of Western Australia Press, Perth (2011).
Burch JG, Strater FR, Grudnitski, *Information Theory and Practice*, 3rd edn, Wiley, New York (1983).
Burt C, The distribution of intelligence, *British Journal of Psychology* 48 (161-174) 1957.
Callaghan G, Taller, Wider, *The Weekend Australian Magazine*, April 5-6, 2008, pp 13-17.
Cateora, PR, *International Marketing*, 9th edn, Irwin, Chicago (1996).
Carey J (ed.), *The Faber Book of Science*, Faber and Faber, London (1995).
Carter P, *Material Thinking*, Melbourne University Press, Melbourne (2004).
Caves RE, Frankel JA, Jones RW, *World Trade and Payments: An Introduction*, Scott Foresman/Little Brown, Glenview IL (1990).
Chambers Dictionary of World History, Chambers Harrap, Edinburgh, 1993.
Churchill WS, *My Early Life, A Roving Commission*, Fontana, London (1959).
Churchill WS, *Churchill in His Own Words*, Capricorn Books, New York (1966).
Cipolla, CM, *The Economic History of World Population*, 6th edn, Penguin, London (1974).
Clark G, *In Fear of China*, Lansdowne Press, Melbourne (1967).
Collins AM, Quillian MR, Retrieval time from semantic memory, *Journal of Verbal Learning and Verbal Behaviour* 8 (1969) 240-247.

Cooke JP, Zimmer J, *The Cardiovascular Cure*, Broadway Books, New York (2002).

Cornwell J, *Hitler's Scientists, Science, War and the Devil's Pact*, Viking, London (2003).

Cowie HR, Collins MB, Ryan DB, *Imperialism, Racism and Re-Assessments*, Nelson, Melbourne (1994).

Crough G, Wheelwright T, Wilshire T (eds), *Australia and World Capitalism*, Penguin (1980).

Cuthbertson I, article on TV documentary program 'Men in Danger', *The Weekend Australian*, Review p 28, March 29, 2008.

Darwin, Charles, *The Expression of the Emotions in Man and Animals*, Harper Collins (Fontana), London (1999).

Davies B, *An Introduction to Clinical Psychiatry*, Melbourne University Press, Melbourne (1971).

Davis JW, *An Introduction to Public Administration*, The Free Press, New York (1974).

Dawood NF (translator), *The Koran*, 50th anniversary edition, Penguin, London (2006).

Dees M, *Gathering Storm, America's Militia Threat*, Harper Perennial, New York (1996).

Delgado JMR, *Physical Control of the Mind: Towards a Psychocivilized Society*, Colophon Books (Harper & Row), New York (1971).

Doyle D, *Inside Espionage, A Memoir of True Men and Traitors*, St Ermin's Press, London (2000).

Eagly AH, Chaiken S, *The Psychology of Attitudes*, Harcourt Brace Jovanovich, Orlando FL (1993).

Eddington AS, *The Mathematical Theory of Relativity*, Cambridge University Press, Cambridge (1924).

Egerton Eastwick RW (ed.), *The Oracle Encyclopaedia*, George Newnes, London (1896).

Einstein A, *The Meaning of Relativity*, Methuen, London (1922).

Emerick Y, *The Complete Idiot's Guide to Islam*, 3rd edn, Alpha/Penguin, New York (2011).

Famighetti R (ed.), *The World Almanac and Book of Facts*, World Almanac Books, Mahwah NJ (1998).
Fancher RE, *The intelligence men: Makers of the IQ Controversy*, WW Norton, New York (1985).
Forbes HD, *Ethnic Conflict: Commerce, Culture, and the Contact Hypothesis*, Yale University Press, New Haven (1997).
Foss, DJ, Hakes, DT, *Psycholinguistics, An Introduction to the Psychology of Language*, Prentice-Hall, Englewood-Cliffs NJ (1978).
Gaines M, *Atomic Energy*, Grosset & Dunlap, New York (1970).
Galton D, *In Our Own Image, Eugenics and the Genetic Modification of People*, Little Brown & Co, London (2001).
Gardner L, *Bloodline of the Holy Grail, The Hidden Lineage of Jesus Revealed*, Penguin, London (2001).
Goodwin S, *Hubble's Universe, A New Picture of Space*, Constable, London (1996).
Govoni N, Eng R, Morton G, *Promotional Management: Issues and Perspectives*, Prentice-Hall, Englewood Cliffs NJ (1988).
Hall, T, *White Collar Crime in Australia*, Harper & Row, Sydney (1979).
Hammond P, *Slavery, Terrorism and Islam*, Frontline Fellowship, Cape Town (2010).
Harris L, *The Suicide of Reason, Radical Islam's Threat to the Enlightenment*, Basic Books, New York (2007).
Hersha C, Hersha L, Griffis D, *Secret Weapons, Two Sisters' Terrifying Story of Sex, Spies and Sabotage*, New Horizon Press, Far Hills NJ (2001).
Holland Jack, *Hope Against History, The Course of Conflict in Northern Ireland*, Hodder & Stoughton, London (1999).
Hollingsworth M, Fielding N, *Defending the Realm, MI5 and the Shayler Affair*, André Deutsch, London (1999).
Hughes-Wilson J, *Military Intelligence Blunders*, Carroll & Graf, New York (1999).
Insight vol. 7, part 91, Marshall Cavendish, London (1982).
Jay P, *The Crisis of Western Political Economy*, The Australian Broadcasting Commission, Sydney (1981).

Jencks C, Smith M, Acland H, Bane MJ, Cohen D, Gintis H, Heyns B, Michelson S, *Inequality: A Reassessment of the Effect of Family and Schooling in America*, Penguin, Harmondsworth (1975).

Jones S, Israel P, *Others Unknown: The Oklahoma City Bombing Case and Conspiracy*, Public Affairs, New York (1998).

Kirk RE, *Statistical Issues, A Reader for the Behavioural Sciences*, Brooks/Cole, Monterey CA (1972).

Kissinger H, *Years of Renewal*, Simon & Schuster, New York (1999).

Kluckhohn C, 'As an anthropologist views it', in *Sex Habits of American Men*, Albert Deutch (ed.), Prentice-Hall, New York (1948).

Knightley P, *Philby, KGB Masterspy*. Andre Deutsch, London (1988).

Lifton RJ, *Destroying the World to Save It: Aum Shinrikyo, Apocalyptic Violence, and the New Global Terrorism*, Metropolitan Books, New York (1999).

Likert R, *New Patterns of Management*, McGraw-Hill, New York (1961).

Lindzey G, Hall CS, Thompson RF, *Psychology*, 2nd edn, Worth, New York (1978).

Lynne R, Vanhanen T, *IQ and The Wealth of Nations*, Praeger, Westport CT (2002).

Mackenzie KR, *The English Parliament*, Penguin, Harmondsworth (1950).

Marx K, *Capital*, Dent & Sons, London (1933, first published 1867).

Marx K, The eighteenth brumaire of Loius Napoleon, in *Selected Works*, vol. 1, Progress Publishers, Moscow (1969, originally published in 1852).

Massoulié F, *Middle East Conflicts*, Interlink Books, New York (2003).

Maxwell N, Yahuda M, Wheelwright T, Jayawardena C, The Chinese model: politics in command, in *Political Economy of Development*, Australian Broadcasting Commission, Sydney (1977).

McCormack MH, *What They Don't Teach You at Harvard Business School*, Fontana/Collins, London (1986).

McGuire WJ, A syllogistic analysis of cognitive relationships, in *Attitude Organization And Change*, CI Hovland and MJ Rosenberg (eds.), Yale University Press, New Haven (1960).

Meadows DH, Meadows DL, Randers J, Behrens WW, *The Limits to Growth*, Pan, London (1974).

Miller J, Engelbert S, Broad W, *Germs, The Ultimate Weapon*, Simon & Schuster, New York (2001).

Mohr GA, *The Finite Element Method for Solids, Fluids, and Optimization*, Oxford University Press, Oxford (1992).

Mohr GA, Flow ratio design of primal and dual network models of distribution, *Australian and New Zealand Journal of Industrial and Applied Mathematics* 45 (2004) 573-583.

Mohr GA, Finite element modeling and optimization of traffic flow networks, *Transportmetrica* 2 (2005) 151-159.

Mohr GA, *The Pretentious Persuaders*, Horizon, Sydney (2012).

Mohr GA, *The Doomsday Calculation*, Xlibris, Sydney (2012b).

Mohr GA, *2045, A Small Town Survives Global Nuclear Holocaust*, Xlibris, Bloomington, IN (2014).

Mohr GA, *Elementary Thinking*, Xlibris, Sydney (2014).

Mohr GA, Richard Sinclair & Edwin Fear, *The Evolving Universe: Relativity, Redshift, and Life From Space*, Xlibris, Sydney (2014).

Mohr GA, Fear E, *World Religions, The History, Issues & Truth*, Xlibris, Sydney (2015).

Mohr GA, Edwin Fear & Richard Sinclair, *World War 3: When and How Will It End?*, Inspiring Publishers (2015).

Morgan CT, King RA, Robinson NM, *Introduction to Psychology*, 6th edn, McGraw-Hill, Tokyo (1979).

Newcomb TM, Persistance and regression of changed attitudes, *Journal of Sociological Issues* 19 (1963) 3-14.

Niblett WR (ed.), *Higher Education: Demand and Response*, Tavistock Publications, London (1969).

Nicholas M, *The World's Greatest Cranks and Crackpots*, Exeter Books, New York (1984).

Nojumi N, *The Rise of the Taliban in Afghanistan*, Palgrave, New York (2002).

Odle F, *The Picture Story of British Inventions*, World Distributors, Manchester (1966).

O'Guinn TC, Allen CT, Semenik RJ, *Advertising and Integrated Brand Promotion*. Thomson South-Western, Mason OH 2006.
Oppenheimer JR, *Science and the Common Understanding*, Oxford University Press, London (1954).
Packard V, *The Status Seekers*, Pelican, Harmondsworth, London (1961).
Packard V, *The Waste Makers*, Pelican, Harmondsworth, London (1963).
Packard V, *The People Shapers*, Nelson, Melbourne (1978).
Parkinson CN, *The Law*, Schwartz, Melbourne (1980).
Peter LJ, Hull R, *The Peter Principle*, Souvenir Press, London (1969).
Philby R, Lyubimov M, Peake H, *The Private Life of Kim Philby*, Fromm International, New York (2000).
Pringle P, Spigelman J, *The Nuclear Barons*, Holt, Rinehart and Winston, New York (1981).
Przemieniecki JS, *Theory of Matrix Structural Analysis*, McGraw-Hill, New York (1968).
Regis, *The Biology of Doom, The History of America's Secret Germ Warfare Project*, Henry Holt, New York (1999).
Richardson M, *The Penguin Book of Firsts*, Penguin, Melbourne 1997.
Ripps LJ, Schoben EJ, Smith EE, Semantic distance and the verification of semantic relations, *Journal of Verbal Learning and Verbal Behaviour* 12 (1973) 203-210.
Robertson I, *Sociology*, 2nd edn, Worth, New York (1981).
Robertson TS, *Consumer Behaviour*, Scott Foresman, Glenview IL (1970).
Rosenfeld A, *The Second Genesis: The Coming Control of Life*, Pyramid Communications, New York (1972).
Sampson A, *The Arms Bazaar*, Coronet Books, London (1977).
Sargent M, *Drinking and Alcoholism in Australia: A Power Relations Theory*, Longman Cheshire, Melbourne (1979).
Sauerbruch F, *A Surgeon's Life*, André Deutsch, London (1953).
Schmidt-Nielsen K, *Animal Physiology: Adaptation and Environment*, 2nd edn, Cambridge University Press, Cambridge (1979),
Self P, *Administrative Theories and Policies*, 2nd edn, George Allen & Unwin, London (1977).

Selmes C (ed.), *New Movements in the Study and Teaching of Biology*, Temple Smith, London (1974).
Silber L, Little A, *Yugoslavia: Death of a Nation*, TV Books, New York (1995).
Smith A, *Paper Money*, Summit Books, New York (1981).
Snow RL, *Terrorists Amongst Us, The Militia Threat*, Perseus Publishing, Cambridge MA (1999).
Solomon MR, *Consumer Behaviour: Buying, Having and Being*, Allyn and Bacon, Boston (1992).
Southwell RV, *Relaxation Methods in Theoretical Physics*, Oxford University Press, Oxford (1946).
Sternberg S, High speed scanning in human memory, *Science* 153 (1966) 652-654.
Swainson B (ed), *Encarta Book of Quotations*, Pan Macmillan, Sydney (2000).
Sweezy PM, *The Theory of Capitalist Development*, Dennis Dobson, London (1946).
Sykes CJ, *Dumbing Down Our Kids: Why American Children Feel Good About Themselves But Can't Read, Write or Add*, St Martin's Griffin, New York (1995).
Taylor FW, *Principles of Scientific Management*, Harper, New York (1911).
Teasdale T, Owen D, A long-term rise and recent decline in intelligence test performance: The Flynn Effect in reverse, *Personality and Individual Differences* 39(4), 837 - 843 (2005).
Teasdale T, Owen D, Secular declines in cognitive test scores: A reversal of the Flynn Effect, *Intelligence* 36(2), 121-126 (2008).
Townsend P (ed.), *The Concept of Poverty*, Heinemann, London (1970).
Turner MJ, Clough RW, Martin HC, Topp LJ, Stiffness and deflection analysis in complex structures, *J. Aero. Sci.* 23 (1956) 805-823.
Ungar G, Desidero DM, Parr W, Isolation, identification and synthesis of a specific behaviour inducing brain peptide, *Nature* 238 (1972) 198-202.
Vander AJ, Sherman JH, Luciano DS, *Human Physiology*, 6th edn, McGraw-Hill, New York (1994).

van Lawick-Goodall, Jane, *In the Shadow of Man*, Houghton Mifflin, Boston (1971).
Vernon, Jack, *Macroeconomics* (2nd end), The Dryden Press, Hinsdale IL (1980).
Vernon PE, *Intelligence and Attainment Tests*, University of London Press, London (1960).
Wagner RH, *Environment and Man*, 3rd edn, W.W. Norton, New York (1978)
Watson P, *The Modern Mind, An Intellectual History of the 20th Century*, Harper Collins, New York (2001).
Weinberg R, *One Renegade Cell*, Phoenix, London (1999).
Weiss ML, Mann AE, *Human Biology and Behaviour, An Anthropological Perspective*, 2nd edn, Little Brown, Boston MA (1978).
Wells HG, Huxley J, Wells GP, *The Science of Life* vol. 1, The Amalgamated Press, London (circa 1930).
Wheen F, *Karl Marx*, Fourth Estate, London (1999).
White M, *Rivals, Conflict as the Fuel of Science*, Vintage, London (2002).
Wolfe L, Brainwashing: How the British Use The Media For Mass Psychological Warfare Brainwashing. Posted on the Internet and originally printed in *The American Almanac*, May 5, 1997.
Wolfe L, Americans Target Of Largest Media Brainwashing Campaign In History. Posted on the Internet and originally in *Executive Intelligence Review*, 16/10/01.
Wonnacott P, Wonnacott R, *Economics*, McGraw-Hill, New York (1979).
Wright R, *Sacred Rage: The Wrath of Militant Islam*, Touchstone, New York (1985).
Youngson RM, Schott I, *Medical Blunders*, Robinson, London (1996).
Yuan SW, *Foundations of Fluid Mechanics*, Prentice-Hall, Englewood Cliffs NJ (1967).

www.ingramcontent.com/pod-product-compliance
Lightning Source LLC
Chambersburg PA
CBHW071328080526
44587CB00017B/2768